THE PRINCETON REVIEW

THE
COMPLETE BOOK
OF CATHOLIC
COLLEGES

1998 EDITION

THE PRINCETON REVIEW

THE
COMPLETE BOOK
OF CATHOLIC
COLLEGES

1998 EDITION

BY ED CUSTARD and DAN SARACENO

Random House, Inc.
New York 1997
http://www.randomhouse.com

Princeton Review Publishing, L.L.C.
2315 Broadway
New York, NY 10024
e-mail: info@review.com

ISSN 1093-9857
ISBN 0-679-77889-6

Editor: Amy Zavatto
Production Editor: James Petrozzello
Production Manager: Mike Faivre
Designer: Meher Khambata
Illustrator: John Bergdahl

Manufactured in the United States of America on partially recycled paper.

9 8 7 6 5 4 3 2 1

1998 Edition

FOREWORD

Welcome to *The Complete Book of Catholic Colleges*, the only comprehensive guide to Catholic colleges and universities. We've included reviews of nearly 200 colleges—that's every Catholic college in the United States and Puerto Rico (with the exception of seminaries).

The impetus to develop and publish this guide comes from many sources. Religion has enjoyed a renaissance among Americans over the past several years, and students are no exception. In the individually-focused, time-starved, value-numbed world that we live in today, many view organized religion as an oasis, a place to revitalize critical energies of faith, compassion, and concern for others. It's only logical that this would also manifest itself on college campuses—historical centers for the acquisition of knowledge and values within the larger context of developing potential and contributing to society. Though church and state are constitutionally separated, church and classroom often join in an effective synergy of faith and learning.

Catholic education, long the brunt of jokes about nuns and rulers, shines under closer, more serious scrutiny. More than one study has shown that Catholic elementary and secondary schools produce strong, competitive results, often at a lower cost or more efficiently than other schools, both public and private. Catholic schools successful track-records and cost-efficiency have even resulted in their being considered a source of relief for overcrowded New York City public schools. At the college level, recent national movements promoting volunteerism and community service among our young people simply reflect time-honored tradition on our country's Catholic campuses. In addition to demonstrating a wide variety of strengths in other academic disciplines, Catholic colleges are leading producers of teachers, doctors, nurses, and others in helping professions. A brief pass through this guide will confirm that many of the nation's finest colleges and universities are Catholic institutions.

You're about to make one of the biggest decisions of your life. Never trust any one source too much–even us. This book contains a lot of useful general information, statistics, and deadlines. There are also some great general tips on conducting a college search, and lots of charts and lists to help you sort through the colleges included. As is the case with any college guide, it shouldn't be the only tool that you use to make a decision about where to attend. This book is only the beginning. There's a lot more to choosing a college. Until you've thoroughly explored a variety of educational options on your own, it's all just guessing. This is no time to rely on hunches or sentiment.

College will consume four years of your life, and can cost up to $150,000 of your folks' savings or your future earnings. It's not only good financial sense to make an informed decision, it's good common sense. College is an opportunity for personal growth that won't likely present itself in the same way ever again. There's nothing that compares to the experience—most grads will never forget their college years. We wish the same for you, and hope that the *The Complete Book of Catholic Colleges* is helpful in your search for the right place.

Edward Custard and Dan Saraceno

May 1997

ACKNOWLEDGMENTS

Many thanks to the countless individuals on Catholic college campuses throughout the United States, as well as Newman Center chaplains, directors, advisors, and student officers whose input helped immensely in the creation of this guide. We could not have done it without you.

Ed would like to thank his former colleagues and students at Ladycliff College, especially Sr. Eileen Mary Halloran, who hired him for his first paid position in college admissions. Bruce Hunter provided invaluable assistance in the form of a rare copy of *The Student Guide to Catholic Colleges and Universities*, by John R. Crocker, S.J. Crocker's ambitious work, now out of print, was a wonderful resource for historical perspective on the involvement of the Catholic Church in U.S. higher education.

Dan owes a deep debt of gratitude and love to his parents—Mike and Antonetta Saraceno. To his brother Dario and his sister Diana, and her husband André. Thanks to Craig Farewell and Joanne Dyroff for their support and assistance. To Brother Hilary Rodgers, O.F.M. Cap. for his insight and involvement in Dan's Catholic experience. To his colleague Leo Flynn, and former bosses Father Thomas Acker, S.J. and Father Charles Currie, S.J. (Yes, there *is* a difference between Catholic and Jesuit.) Special thanks to Dr. John Maguire and Linda Cox Maguire for making impossible goals become reality. And, to his daughter Nichole—may your college experience produce the foundation to a wonderful life. *Sempre avanti.*

Dr. Monika K. Hellwig, executive director of the Association of Catholic Colleges and Universities, referred us to Fr. Charles Hagan of the United States Catholic Conference Department of Education. We thank Fr. Hagan for his helpful discussion of campus ministry, and for lending an ear regarding many of the early questions we had in undertaking this project.

Many of our friends and colleagues at Princeton Review Publishing were instrumental to the realization of this guide; Amy Zavatto (Editor par excellence), Jeannie Yoon and Christine Chung in the database department, and Editor-in-Chief Evan Schnittman all deserve praise and thanks beyond the space allotted here. Zack Brown provided instrumental assistance in the creation and development of the Catholic colleges data tables.

Meher Khambata has no peer in desktop publishing; it is through the efforts of Meher and her staff that *The Complete Book of Catholic Colleges* looks so good. Special thanks to John Bergdahl for a great job on the icons, and Mike Faivre and James Petrozzello for keeping things humming along.

Many others who we haven't named contributed to the successful outcome of this project; to all of you, we offer our heartfelt thanks.

CONTENTS

HOW THIS BOOK IS ORGANIZED

Each of the colleges and universities listed in this book has its own one-page entry, provided that the necessary data required to create every individual category within an entry was reported. We've created half-page narrative entries on those colleges for which reported data was not sufficient to complete all elements on a full page. To make it easier to find information about the schools of your choice, we've used the same format for every college. Look at the sample page below:

Each entry has several major components. First, at the very top of the spread you will see the college's address, telephone and fax numbers for the admissions office, the telephone number for the financial aid office, and the college's web site and/or E-mail address. Second, there is a series of icons that describe each college's enrollment, environment, cost, admissions selectivity, level of intercollegiate athletic competition, and, where applicable, inclusion in our *Best 311 Colleges* guide. (These icons are described in detail in the section that follows entitled "The *The Complete Book of Catholic Colleges* Icon System.") Third is the main body text, lead by a paragraph that provides a broad overview of the college and followed by two sections, headed Admissions and Financial Aid. Each college entry is rounded out by a section at the bottom of the page with categories headed Student Body, Academics, Admissions, Freshman Profile, and Financial Facts. Here's what each part contains:

The Statistical Categories

The bottom section of each entry contains various statistics culled either from our own research or from questionnaires sent to the colleges by College Counsel, a major college research and database publishing organization. Keep in mind that not every category will appear for every college, since in some cases the information is not reported (indicated by "NR") or not applicable.

Here is what each heading tells you:

■ Student body

From *total undergrad enrollment* through # *countries represented*

The demographic breakdown of the undergraduate student body, including the total number of undergraduates who attend the college, the percent of students who are Catholic, percent male and female, percent from out-of-state, percent who live on-campus, percent who are transfers, percent from Catholic high schools and public high schools, the racial/ethnic composition of the college, and, finally, the number of countries represented in the student body.

Academics

■ Calendar

The college's academic schedule. A "semester" system has two long terms, usually starting in September and January. A "trimester" system has three terms, usually one before Christmas and two after. A "quarter" system has four terms, which go by very quickly: the entire term, including exams, usually lasts only nine or ten weeks. A "4-1-4" calendar is similar to a semester schedule, but with a month-long term in between the fall and spring terms. In cases where a college's academic calendar doesn't match any of these traditional systems we note that by indicating "other." For colleges that have "other" listed as their calendar we suggest a call to the admissions office for details.

■ Student/faculty ratio

The ratio of full-time faculty members to undergraduates.

■ FT faculty

The total number of full-time instructional faculty at the college

■ % faculty from religious order

The percentage of the college's faculty who are members of a Catholic religious order or congregation.

■ Most popular majors

The three most popular majors at the school.

■ 4 yr. grad rate

The percentage of freshmen who graduate in four years.

Admissions

■ Admissions process is need blind (noted within Admissions text)

Indicates that the college does not consider a candidate's ability to pay its cost when evaluating applications. The absence of this statement in a particular college's entry cannot be taken to indicate that the opposite is true—in such cases, students are encouraged to contact the admissions office for clarification of the college's policy. If your research indicates that the admissions process is "need aware," "need conscious," or "need sensitive," ability to pay may be a factor in your candidacy.

Admissions rating

How competitive admission is at the college, on a scale of 60 to 100. This rating is determined by several factors, including the class rank of entering freshmen, test score averages, percentage of applicants accepted, and the percentage of acceptees who enroll. By incorporating all these factors, our competitiveness rating adjusts for "self-selecting" applicant pools. Boston College, for example, has a very high competitiveness rating, even though it admits a large proportion of its applicants. BC's applicant pool is "self-selecting;" nearly all the college's applicants are exceptional students.

Regular admission deadline

The date by which all materials must be postmarked (we'd suggest "received in the admissions office") in order to be considered for regular admission for the fall term.

Regular admission notification

The date by which you can expect a decision on your application under the regular admission plan.

Early decision/action deadline

The deadline for submission of application materials under early decision or early action plans. Students whose first-choice college offers early decision can apply early through this process. Candidates make a commitment to attend the college if admitted; in return, the college renders an early decision, usually in December or January. If accepted, the applicant doesn't have to spend the time and money to apply elsewhere. In most cases, students may apply for early decision to only one college, and must forgo applying elsewhere unless denied admission to that college. Early action is similar to early decision, but less binding; applicants need not commit to attending the college, and in some cases may apply early action to more than one college. The college, in turn, may choose not to render an absolute decision, and instead defer the applicant to the regular admissions cycle. Each college's guidelines are a little different, and some offer more than one early decision cycle; it's a good idea to call and get full details if you plan to pursue one of these options.

Early decision/action admission notification

The date by which you can expect a decision on your application under early decision or early action admission plans.

of applicants

The total number of students who applied for fall admission

■ % of applicants accepted

The percentage of applicants to which the college offered admission.

■ % acceptees attending

The percentage of those who were accepted who eventually enrolled.

Freshman Profile

Range verbal SAT (avg.), Range math SAT (avg.), Range composite ACT (avg.)

The average or range of test scores for entering freshmen. SAT scores in this book are all "recentered" scores. When specific averages were not available, we report scores using ranges provided by each college for the middle 50 percent of those freshmen who submitted scores. Don't be discouraged from applying to the college of your choice even if your combined SAT scores are 80 or even 120 points below the average, because you may still have a chance of getting in. Remember that many colleges emphasize other aspects of your application (e.g., your grades, how good a match you make) more heavily than test scores.

■ Minimum TOEFL

The minimum test score necessary for entering freshmen who are required to take the TOEFL (Test of English as a Foreign Language). Most colleges will require all international students who are non-native English speakers to take the TOEFL in order to be considered for admission.

■ Graduated top 10%, top 25%, top 50% of class

Of those students for whom class rank was reported, the percentage of entering freshman who ranked in the top tenth, quarter, and half of their high school classes.

■ Average HS GPA or avg.

We report this on a scale of 1–4 (occasionally colleges report averages on a 100 scale, in which case we report those figures). This is one of the key factors in college admissions. Be sure to keep your GPA as high as possible straight through until graduation from high school.

Financial Facts

■ Tuition

The tuition for a full-time student at the college.

■ Room & board

Estimated room and board costs.

■ Estimated book expense

Estimated annual cost of necessary textbooks.

■ % aid is need-based

According to the school's financial aid department, the percentage of all financial aid awarded that is based strictly on demonstrated financial need.

■ % frosh receiving aid

According to the college's financial aid department, the percentage of all freshmen who received some form of aid.

■ % undergrads receiving aid

According to the college's financial aid department, the percentage of all undergrads who receive some form of financial aid.

■ % frosh rec. grant (avg.)

The percentage of freshmen who received grants or scholarships, and the average grant or scholarship value.

■ % frosh rec. loan (avg.)

The percentage of freshmen who received loans, and the average amount of loan.

PART ONE
IN THE BEGINNING...

CHAPTER 1
GOING CATHOLIC

SOME FAIRLY USEFUL BACKGROUND
ABOUT CATHOLIC COLLEGES

Once upon a time there was this guy. He was a carpenter, and he...well, never mind. That wouldn't exactly be the quick route to learning about Catholic colleges. They've got a long history, and it would take far too much space in this book to cover all that ground. Suffice it to say that the world's very first universities were Catholic, and they were a lot different from the colleges and universities that we know and love today.

They didn't have football teams, for one. (Okay, so they were European. They didn't have soccer teams either.) It was centuries ago. Cars didn't exist, so parking posed little or no problem. Since everyone studied the same curriculum, there were no long lines for registration. And they were all tuition-free.

As the Catholic Church expanded around the globe, so did Catholic higher education. Today one can find Catholic colleges and universities all over the world. But nowhere are there more Catholic colleges and universities than here in the U.S. It's not surprising when you consider some basic facts: There are nearly sixty million Catholics in the United States. That's almost a quarter of the entire population of the country. Fourteen percent of all private secondary schools are Catholic, and they account for almost 55 percent of the total national enrollment in private secondary schools. Nearly 600,000 students are enrolled at U.S. Catholic colleges and universities. And UCLA's annual freshman survey of about 500 colleges this year revealed that 29 percent of new, first-time-in-college students are Catholic.

Not that Catholic higher education exists solely for the purpose of educating Catholics. To do so would be to drift from the very meaning of the word:

> **cath•o•lic** (kåth´e-lîk, kàth´lîk) adj. **1.** Of broad or liberal scope; comprehensive: *"The 100-odd pages of formulas and constants are surely the most catholic to be found"* (Scientific American). **2.** Including or concerning all humankind; universal: *"what was of catholic rather than national interest"* (J.A. Froude). **3. Catholic.** *Abbr.* **C. a.** Of or involving the Roman Catholic Church. **b.** Of or relating to the universal Christian church. **c.** Of or relating to the ancient undivided Christian church. **d.** Of or relating to those churches that have claimed to be representatives of the ancient undivided church.

(American Heritage Dictionary of the English Language, Third Edition)

Though you may not already be aware of it, as you browse through this guide you'll come to realize that many non-Catholics attend Catholic colleges and universities. They do so for a variety of reasons, among them academic, social, personal, and spiritual. Yes, even spiritual. For not only in its churches but on its campuses too, the Catholic Church strives to offer opportunities to all seekers. When it comes to higher education, Catholics spell universal with a capital U. They're not just educators and students. They're missionaries, community activists, business leaders, environmentalists, catalysts for social change. And some of them can hit three-pointers at will from NBA distance.

Perhaps these ambitious goals are best described by J.H. Newman in his essay "The Aim of a Catholic University":

> Some persons will say that I am thinking of confining, distorting, and stunting the growth of the intellect by ecclesiastical supervision. I have no such thought. Nor have I any thought of a compromise, as if religion must give up something, and science something. I wish the intellect to range with the utmost freedom, and religion to enjoy an equal freedom; but what I am stipulating for is that they should be found in one and the same place, and exemplified in the same person...I wish the same spots and the same individuals to be at once oracles of philosophy and shrines of devotion...I want the intellectual layman to be religious, and the devout ecclesiastic to be intellectual.

SO, WHY CHOOSE A CATHOLIC COLLEGE?

The primary reasons aren't really any different from the reasons why students choose to attend *any* college—academic, financial, social, and personal. Let's look at each of these categories individually, as they apply both to your college search in general, and to Catholic colleges.

Academics

There are two basic considerations here—developing your mind and developing career potential. Never before have career options played a larger part in students' decisions regarding what college they attend. But intellectualism and financial security need not be mutually exclusive. We're hardly the first to tout the virtues of an education in the liberal arts, but we're the only ones who can do so in this guide. So here goes: Liberal arts majors—English, history, and sociology—go a long way toward developing and enhancing communications skills and critical thinking abilities through lots of research, reading, in-class discussions, and presentations. Name a job that doesn't require you to think and communicate. Before we rest our case, also note that liberal arts programs have proven to be terrific preparation for graduate and professional school. The colleges that are the leading producers of graduates who continue on for Ph.D.s are small liberal arts colleges.

Though there are liberal arts graduates working in every imaginable job and profession, some students nonetheless feel much more comfortable pursuing a course of study that provides knowledge of a more directly practical nature—majors like business administration, accounting, journalism, physical therapy, and engineering. Such programs can provide a more expedient career path to follow, but the narrow focus of such choices makes it especially important to make a sound decision concerning your direction right from the start. Research shows that *nearly 75 percent of all students change their majors at least once by the end of their freshman year of college.* If you choose a specific career orientation for your academic program, be sure to choose wisely. Make your decision based on sound research of the possibilities; be sure to consult your counselor, teachers, family friends, and business acquaintances, and reference sources like the *Wall Street Journal* for good information on career trends and growth.

Regardless of the direction you choose—the liberal arts, or a specific vocation or career focus—there's a Catholic college that can serve you well. Taken as a whole, they are themselves catholic—universal—in nature, offering the widest range of intellectual inquiry. Throughout this guide you'll encounter colleges with academic specialties in business, teacher education, the arts, engineering, and nearly every other field you can imagine. For at Catholic colleges it's not so much *what* is offered but *how*:

> In a word, being both a university and Catholic, it must be both a community of scholars representing various branches of human knowledge and an academic institution in which Catholicism is vitally present and operative.
>
> *Apostolic Constitution On Catholic Universities (Ex Corde Ecclesiae)*
> *Pope John Paul II 8/15/90*

In practice, this can translate into anything and everything, from religion courses and community service as universal degree requirements to faculty hiring practices that emphasize belief in, and practical classroom application of, Catholic doctrine. If these considerations are important to you (they probably should be to some extent), be sure to read each college's viewbook and catalog carefully—virtually all of them will address issues of how the Catholic faith manifests itself on campus, academically, and otherwise.

Financial

Most students who are planning to attend college must consider the cost. The price tag for higher education continues to increase at a rate above inflation and there is, unfortunately, no end in sight. If there's a silver lining to this cloud, it's that few students actually pay a college's full cost as listed in admissions literature. Financial aid helps to make things manageable through a combination of scholarships, grants, loans, and work. At Catholic colleges, it's an essential part of their mission to help those students who need it:

The Christian spirit of service to others for the promotion of social justice is of particular importance for each Catholic university, to be shared by its teachers and developed in its students...Every Catholic university feels responsible to contribute concretely to the progress of the society within which it works: For example, it will be capable for ways to make university education accessible to all those who are able to benefit from it, especially the poor or members of minority groups who customarily have been deprived of it.

Apostolic Constitution On Catholic Universities (Ex Corde Ecclesiae)
Pope John Paul II 8/15/90

Virtually every college offers some form of financial aid; at the very least the federal forms of aid like Stafford loans, the College Work-Study Program, and Pell grants. Most offer their own scholarships and grants as well. If you're a Catholic student considering a Catholic college, the possibilities could be even better. Many Catholic colleges offer some scholarships and grants specifically for students who are Catholic and/or who are graduates of Catholic secondary schools. Be sure to ask the admissions office about such opportunities at Catholic colleges if you fit this general profile. If you attend a Catholic secondary school, you should also ask your counselor about any scholarship programs at your school that are intended for students who go on to attend a Catholic college.

Social/Personal

Most college guides spend loads of time focusing on the academic aspects of college life. There's some measure of appropriateness to this, since getting an education is the main reason students go to college. But the education you'll get in college isn't limited to the classroom. Many students experience even more significant learning and growth outside the classroom than within the hallowed halls of academe. Be sure to spend just as much time considering what type of community you'd like to be a part of as you do thinking about the academic department in which you want to study. Once you arrive on campus you'll be thankful that you did.

There are many types of academic communities from which to choose. Community is a fairly broad term when applied to colleges. Academic communities range from small to large. They're in urban settings and on rural campuses. Some have students from all over the world, while some draw students only from within their immediate vicinity. The community is the personality of a college.

There are several elements that work together to make Catholic college communities distinctly Catholic. Perhaps the most obvious of these elements is a large population of students who are Catholic. On its own this does not a Catholic college make—when measured simply through numbers of enrolled students by faith, New York University is one of the largest Catholic colleges in the U.S. Yet no one would mistake it for Catholic. Though a similar measure, the percentage of a college's students who are graduates of Catholic high schools might be somewhat more significant. These students have already had considerable exposure to Church philosophies and teachings prior to their arrival on campus, and have chosen to continue their education in the Catholic tradition.

Another "people" element is the faculty and administration. Catholic colleges aren't simply good choices for students, they're attractive to professors and administrators too. While no Catholic college explicitly requires prospective faculty or administrators to be members of the Catholic faith, it is understood that those personnel who are not Catholic nonetheless enthusiastically support the intertwined missions of higher learning and faith. Many among the staff are Catholic priests and nuns, some of who serve as presidents, deans, and directors of departments and administrative offices. It is these individuals in particular who serve as bridges between the intellectual and spiritual realms on Catholic campuses. Some have very specific roles in this regard—campus ministers, for example.

Few faculty or administrative positions carry as wide-ranging a set of responsibilities as those of the campus ministry. They offer Mass, hear confessions, lead discussion groups, sponsor potlucks, intervene in crises of varying degrees, and have been known to hoist a few cold frosty ones too. As a result of their active involvement in the daily lives of the student body, campus ministers do more to provide a Catholic atmosphere than almost anyone else on campus.

The ability to attend Mass and confess on campus are important elements of community life for many Catholic students. While campus ministers enable students to pursue their faith on a human level, chapels and other religious facilities encourage this practice. These and other symbolic structures create physical environments that confirm the presence of Catholic tradition. Few Catholic college campuses are without a statue—or five—honoring Christ, the Blessed Virgin, St. Francis, or any of a number of other figures from Catholic history.

On a pragmatic note of a nonpastoral nature, residence life is another realm in which Catholicism can make its presence felt. Since each college functions independently of others—even those run by the same order—there are a wide range of dormitory policies in effect at Catholic colleges. Most are no different than those in effect at any other American college, while some are significantly more strict. You'll likely find available as housing options single-sex halls, floors, or entire dormitories with limited visitation hours for members of the opposite sex—just like you will at "State." You may also find strict bans on premarital sex, and severe consequences for violating such policies— including the possibility of expulsion. Just as individuals range from liberal to conservative in their interpretations of Church doctrine, so do Catholic campuses. If you plan to live on campus, be sure to consider how your attitude compares with the college's point of view.

Beyond the Church's direct influence on campus ministry and residence life, extracurriculars are an important part of the Catholic emphasis on mind, body, and spirit. Students on these campuses tend to be enthusiastic participants in the full range of activities common to today's colleges and universities, from academically-oriented discussion groups to theater and dance. Volunteerism and community service is prevalent in and out of the classroom on both organized and individual levels. Newspapers and radio stations on Catholic campuses include some of the very best in the nation. But in no other extracurricular activity are Catholic colleges as nationally prominent as they are in sports—so much so that we've covered the subject in a separate section.

Ultimately, what it's all about is having the best experience possible. Although no college is well-suited to everyone, there is a college that's best for you. Perhaps it's within the covers of this guide.

CHAPTER 2
CATHOLIC
COLLEGE SPORTS

Let's cut right to the chase. Notre Dame. Our Lady, source of more sports legends than we care to talk about. Knute Rockne. The Four Horsemen. George Gip. Joe Montana. Touchdown Jesus. No discussion of Catholic college sports could begin with anyone but the Fighting Irish.

The Irish's strong suit is football. Their initial taste of fame came in 1913 against Army, when they threw the first forward pass in the history of the game and revolutionized its future. It's been one wild ride since then. Perhaps the most legendary tale in sports is Knute Rockne's 1928 locker-room speech exhorting the Irish to "win one for the Gipper," hospitalized teammate George Gip—later played by Ronald Reagan in the movie version. Win they did, and they've kept on winning for sixty years. Notre Dame's all-time winning percentage is the highest in NCAA Division I-A; it is one of six I-A schools with over 700 victories. The Irish have won eight national championships, and no other college in the nation has had more players win the Heisman Trophy, the award for the outstanding college football player of the year. The NFL's ranks are chock-full of Notre Dame alums; five of them have been the number one pick in the NFL draft.

Touchdown Jesus, by the way, refers to the large stained-glass window depicting Jesus that graces Notre Dame's famous golden dome chapel which overlooks one end-zone in the football stadium. With his outstretched arms, Christ appears to be signaling yet another Irish touchdown.

It doesn't stop with football. During the 1970's the Fighting Irish showed their basketball muscle. Under the coaching of Digger Phelps, they regularly contended for the national championship. The men's cross-country team has also won a national title. And Notre Dame's women are talented athletes as well—women's swimming, diving, tennis, and basketball teams are all current powers in NCAA Division I competition. Since over 80 percent of all students at ND lettered in at least one sport in high school, even intramural sports are taken super-seriously—at last count, intramural basketball had more than 350 teams.

The only other Catholic college to field a Division I-A football team, Boston College, is one of fewer than 60 schools to have notched more than 500 victories. But its claim to fame focuses on just one–one of the most memorable victories in college football history. In a 1984 contest now referred to as the *Hail Mary* game, Doug Flutie hurled a 48-yard touchdown pass to Gerard Phelan at the final gun to give BC a stunning 47-45 victory over national power Miami in their home stadium, the Orange Bowl. Flutie became a Heisman Trophy winner later that year.

In addition to BC, two other Jesuit colleges have made their marks in college football. Though the *Seven Blocks of Granite* and Fordham's days as a football power have long since passed, its all-time gridiron victories total places them as one of the top twenty colleges in Division I overall and fifth in their current Division, I-AA. Holy Cross, their Division I-AA catholic companion, ranks ninth in all-time victories among that group.

Speaking of victories, we'd be remiss in any discussion of Catholic college football if we didn't mention St. John's University in Minnesota. An NCAA Division III team, they last suffered a losing season in 1967. St. John's has won three national championships and lost in the semifinals four additional times. With over 327 wins under his belt, coach John Gagliardi is number two on the NCAA all-time coaching victories list, after Alabama's Bear Bryant.

You're probably wondering why, after all this hype about Catholic colleges as sports powers, we've only mentioned five of them as noteworthy so far. Patience is a virtue; have some. We're ready to discuss basketball.

There is no other sport that Catholic colleges have dominated to the degree that they have dominated basketball. And they've done so across nearly the entire history of the game. Before the Final Four really mattered, the National Invitational Tournament was the premier test of the best college teams in the country. The NIT began in 1938; since then catholic colleges have won 19 of the 59 tournaments. St. John's (NY), DePaul, Saint Louis, San Francisco, LaSalle, Seton Hall, Holy Cross, Duquesne, Xavier, Providence, Dayton, Marquette, and Saint Bonaventure have all won NIT championships. Many other catholic colleges have also appeared in the tournament, among them Notre Dame, Manhattan, Fordham, Canisius, Niagara, and Boston College.

Many of these teams have also made strong showings in NCAA tournament play. Prior to the development of *March Madness* and the Final Four, the NCAA Division I basketball championship was a relatively low-key affair for all but the students and fans of the few teams involved. Even then Catholic colleges drew attention. In literally every decade since the first championship game, Catholic schools have reached the finals. In 1943, Georgetown was the first to play in the final, but they lost to Wyoming. Early national champions include Holy Cross (the first Catholic champ), LaSalle, San Francisco (led by all-time NBA great Bill Russell), Seattle (with another NBA great, Elgin Baylor), and Loyola (Chicago), who played in the first televised championship game. In the mid-1970s the Marquette Warriors appeared in the final game twice, winning on their second attempt.

Despite this long record of championship victories, there were more milestones to reach for Catholic college basketball. In the early 1980s Georgetown, led by Patrick Ewing, made it to the championship game in three of four consecutive years. Although they would win only one of these contests, their popularity grew nationwide. Their relentless pace eventually placed coach John Thompson among the ten winningest Division I basketball coaches of all time. (He joined Catholic university colleague Jim Phelan of Mount Saint Mary's of Maryland, who quietly ranks third in all-time victories after Adolph Rupp of Kentucky and Dean Smith of North Carolina.) During this run, the Hoyas played a part in what many feel was the greatest championship game in the history of college basketball.

In 1985 Villanova made its second appearance in the NCAA title game, facing Big East rival Georgetown. Because of the rivalry and Villanova's *cinderella* status as major underdogs, the event drew a television audience of 19.8 million, and 21 million listeners tuned in to the NCAA Radio Network, an all-time record radio audience for any sports event. The Wildcats relied on an NCAA championship record field-goal percentage and tenacious defense, refusing to relinquish a slim lead, and they won the game 66-64. As CBS television signed off from the game, viewers were left with a shot of the Wildcat celebration, punctuated by players' shouts of "Villanova national champs, who would have thought it?" It was truly Catholic basketball's finest hour.

Far from underdogs, Villanova's runners have been at the forefront of their sport for years. While the men's cross-country team has won four Division I titles, the women's team won six in a row from 1989 to 1994, four more than any other college in Division I. Villanova track and field teams remain powers today.

Perhaps the most consistent championship-caliber team from any Catholic college is the men's soccer team at Saint Louis University. The Billikens (Visit SLU's web site for the answer to the question "What's a Billiken?" at http://www.slu.edu) have made a record number of appearances in the Division I championship game, winning the title nine times. Another perennial soccer power is the University of San Francisco. In the late 1970s the Dons made it to the championship final in five of six years, winning four. The fifth was one of the biggest upsets in Division I history, a loss to tiny Hartwick College, the smallest school in Division I. The Dons eventually reached the finals two more times, winning their fifth NCAA title in the process.

Many other Catholic colleges exhibit considerable prowess on the athletic field; you'll find more about their sports achievements within the individual college entries in this guide. It may seem that we've devoted a huge amount of space to sports—we have. Successful college athletic teams not only provide physical outlets for the athletes who participate on them, but act as catalysts for vibrant student life on campus by generating community spirit. And don't forget that winning teams can attract lots of money to their campuses, in the form of ticket sales, parking fees, stadium and arena concessions, sales of team apparel, television and radio broadcasts, and championship tournament revenues—not to mention increased alumni giving. Whether you play sports, watch them, or ignore them, the success of the teams at the college you attend can improve your experience there.

CHAPTER 3
CATHOLIC
RELIGIOUS ORDERS

If you've read this far, you're probably considering the notion of attending a Catholic college pretty seriously. Given that, it's important for you to know a bit about the people who founded and/or run the colleges that you're considering. They'll play a big part in the next four years of your life.

Most Catholic colleges in the U.S. were founded by members of distinct religious organizations within the structure of the mother Church. These groups, more commonly known as communities, congregations, societies, and orders, all have long histories and traditions, and well-developed tenets. You may have already experienced the teachings of nuns, priests, sisters, or brothers in primary or secondary school.

Each institution's personality and aims depend in large part on the leadership and representation of its parent community. Putting philosophy into practice, the affiliated nuns and priests—and the laypeople who work with them among the faculties and administrations on the campuses in this guide—help to determine the atmosphere and direction for the colleges and universities they run. As a result, even relatively young Catholic colleges have long-standing community traditions and rich religious histories.

Most of these groups date back centuries, and have spent much of their time in the business of education. Their educational philosophies and approaches have undergone more field-testing and fine-tuning than McDonald's latest breakfast sandwich. Not to mention the wheel.

Coincidentally, both religious orders and colleges express their institutional philosophies through mission statements. Every college *must* have one in order to be accredited. Most put them in their catalogs, somewhere near the front. You'll know one when you see one. Written in passionate "academese," these statements generally discuss founding principles and purposes, and articulate approaches for the practical implementation of these convictions. Today, secular college mission statements have largely become pieces of idealistic nostalgia that must be revisited once every ten years solely for the purpose of reaffirming accreditation. The same cannot be said of those for Catholic colleges. There's one significant difference.

Mission statements for Catholic colleges also embrace the mission statements of their parent Catholic community. Far from token gestures, mission statements for Catholic communities include principles for day-to-day living that members of the community have made a vow to follow. These guidelines serve as the moral foundations of the colleges founded by their respective communities. To varying degrees, depending on the college, they manifest themselves throughout all aspects of campus life. The diversity of founding communities and philosophies that govern Catholic colleges in large part explains the wide-ranging variety of their personalities and offerings.

We've compiled some general background on the ten religious orders (listed below by their founding dates) that are responsible for the vast majority of Catholic colleges in the U.S. Several other orders also run a college or two; you'll find them listed in the entry of each college that they operate and as part of the index called "Colleges By Order" in the back of the guide. Twelve Catholic colleges in the U.S. are *diocesan*, run under the auspices of the local archdiocese in their respective cities. They are not affiliated with any specific religious order.

Benedictines (O.S.B.). Known as the "monk par excellence," Saint Benedict of Nursia (480–547) founded the Benedictine Order near Naples in 529. Western Europe's first organized monks, the Benedictines were founded to preserve monastic traditions dating from the third century. Commonly known as the "Black Monks" (a reference to their black robes), the Benedictines were the first librarians of the Church. Their early work centered around scriptoriums, precursors to today's libraries, where monks developed languages, and archived important works of the day.

Franciscans (O.F.M., O.F.M. Conv., and T.O.R.). No saint has had greater impact on non-Catholics than Francis of Assisi (1182–1226), whose life and work personified the "universal" definition of Catholicism. Saint Francis founded the Order of Friars Minor in 1209. More commonly known as Franciscans, the Friars Minor are "the people's preachers." The men and women of this order take three vows: poverty, chastity, and obedience. In the order's early years there was little interest in scholarly pursuits; the focus was instead on the needs of the poor and humble acts of charity. Today Franciscans administer several colleges and are among the leaders in Catholic higher education.

Dominicans (O.P.). Despite the fact that there are lots of Dominicans found in sunny climes near the beach, "O.P." is not an ecclesiastical plug for sportswear by Ocean Pacific. It stands for Order of Preachers. Founded by Saint Dominic (1170–1221) in southern France around the year 1216, the Dominican Order developed and authored preaching aids (pamphlets) for other priests to use in putting together their sermons. It was rumored that their powerful homilies were so moving that worshipers would immediately seek to confess their sins. They are tremendous teachers. Saint Thomas Aquinas, the patron saint of both universities and students, was a Dominican. (You might want to keep him in mind during exam week.) Both men and women belong to the Dominican Order. Most affiliated colleges are run by Dominican Sisters.

Jesuits (S.J.). Also known as the Society of Jesus, the Jesuits were founded in 1540 by Saint Ignatius Loyola (1491–1556) in northern Spain. As a soldier bedridden while recovering from a war injury, Ignatius became convinced, through readings of the New Testament, that his calling was to be a great confessor for the ruling class of Europe, and a servant of the pope. His motto was "the more universal the good, the more divine." Throughout history the Jesuits have been catalysts for social change and justice. Though Ignatius's original plans never included education, today there are many Jesuit schools throughout the world (including twenty-eight colleges and universities in the United States alone).

De LaSalle Christian Brothers (C.F.C.). Founded in 1684 by Saint John Baptist de LaSalle (1651–1719) in Rheims, France. The Christian Brothers' primary purpose is to serve the educational needs of society, particularly among the poor. Pope Leo XIII hailed Saint John de LaSalle upon his canonization as the "patron of teachers." While the men of the congregation are called Christian Brothers, institutions run by the community are referred to as LaSallian.

Sisters of Saint Joseph (C.S.J.). Founded in the early 1800s in France by the Venerable Anne-Marie Javouhey (1779–1851). Initially focused on alleviating the suffering borne by those who had endured the French Revolution, the Sisters of Saint Joseph later expanded their reach into missionary work on the African continent. Today various congregations of the Sisters administer several U.S. colleges.

American Sisters of Charity (B.V.M.). Founded by Saint Elizabeth Seton (1774–1821, America's first saint) in Emmitsburg, Maryland, in 1812. From the beginning the Sisters of Charity have devoted themselves to the education and health-care needs of society, especially as related to women, children, and the poor. The Sisters run eight U.S. colleges.

Sisters of Mercy (R.S.M.). The Sisters of Mercy began in Dublin in 1831, founded by Mother Catherine McAuley. Their mission focused on the education of poor women, social work, caring for the sick, and acts of mercy. The Sisters came to the United States in the 1840s and now run thirteen colleges in the U.S.

The Congregation of the Holy Cross (C.S.C). Founded by Fr. Basil Anthony Moreau (1799–1873) in 1840. Established on the principle that "we will not educate the mind at the expense of the heart." This principle remains key to the educational mission of the Holy Cross Fathers. The Congregation operates seven four-year institutions of higher learning but, curiously enough, not the College of the Holy Cross. It's Jesuit.

Sisters of Notre Dame (S.N.D.). Saint Julie Billiart (1751–1816) founded the Sisters of Notre Dame in Amiens, France in 1804. The community was dedicated from its beginning to the salvation of poor children, making its lifework the education of girls and the training of religious teachers. Seven colleges in the U.S. are run by the Sisters of Notre Dame.

CHAPTER 4
CONDUCTING A COLLEGE SEARCH

A FEW GOOD TIPS ON CONDUCTING A COLLEGE SEARCH

Now that you've gotten an introduction to some of the basics about Catholic colleges, we thought we'd use a few pages to give you some tips for your college search—especially on how to get the most out of this book and what to do once you've made your choices and are ready to apply. Since the most important thing for you to do now is to get started on your search, we'll start right off by revealing the secret to getting admitted to the college of your choice.

It's almost never the focus of talk about college admission in the media, and parents and students discuss the subject all the time without even realizing that it's the crucial element to getting admitted. We're talking about matchmaking—finding colleges that have the educational and social environment you're looking for, where you are well-suited academically and have something that the college is looking for in return. You have a lot more control over where you'll wind up going to college than you might think.

Matchmaking is a two-step process. To be most effective, you should begin with a thorough self-examination, or *personal inventory*. Your personal inventory is best structured in the form of a spreadsheet or chart, so that when you begin to consider your options you can use it to check off those colleges that satisfy the various needs or wants you've identified. In this way, the best of your college choices will gradually begin to identify themselves.

Divide it into two sections. One section should be biographical, including your high school course selection, GPA, SAT or ACT scores, rank in class, and personal information like extracurricular activities (especially those you plan on continuing in college). This will help you to assess how you stack up against each college's admissions standards and student body.

The second section is a list of the characteristics you need or want in the college you'll choose to attend. This list should include anything and everything that you consider to be important, such as location, size of the student body, availability of scholarships, dormitory options, clubs, and activities—whatever has some kind of significance to you. This part of your inventory should be ever-changing as you become more and more aware of what is truly important for you to find in the college of your choice.

Armed with your personal inventory, you can begin to take advantage of the many resources available to help you narrow your choices for where to apply. There are five sources for information and advice that have become standard for most college-bound students.

1. College Admissions Viewbooks, Videos, Brochures, and Catalogs

If you are a junior or senior in high school, you know more about the kinds of information these materials should include than the people who are responsible for designing and writing them. No college that spends half a million dollars on glossy literature is going to be objective about its content. In the best of this material, you can probably get a decent idea of the academic offerings on the campus and the basic admissions requirements. In all of it, you will never see any but the best- looking students and the most appealing architecture on campus, nor will you hear about the years of tuition increases above the rate of inflation. Look this stuff over, but don't make any decisions based solely on what you read or see.

2. Your Friends

No one knows colleges and universities better than the students who currently attend them. Seek out any and all of your friends, sons and daughters of family friends, and recent graduates of your high school who attend college, especially those who attend colleges that you are considering. Talk to them when they come home. Arrange to stay with them when you visit their colleges. Pick their brains for everything you can get. It doesn't get any more direct and honest than this.

3. Books and College Guides

There are two types of books that can be helpful in your search: Those that discuss specific aspects of going to college, and college guides. In the first category, naturally we like our own *Paying for College. Choosing A College*, by Thomas Sowell, is out of print but well worth seeking out; many of the most significant points Sowell makes about how to evaluate colleges can't be found in any other work. On the side of college guides, our *Best 311 Colleges* is not only a personal favorite, but the best-seller among all qualitative college guides. In addition to the *Best 311*, look at *The Fiske Guide to Colleges* or the *Yale Daily News' Insiders Guide to the Colleges* for good second opinions. As for comprehensive guides–those that emphasize data over narrative content, *The Complete Book of Colleges* can help you cut to the chase more quickly than any other guide. There's a smaller version of one of its best tools, the "Admissions Wizard," included in this guide.

4. Computers

There's a lot of help out there in the world of software and cyberspace. The section in this book entitled "College Admission Goes Electronic" will give you full details on ways that you can turn the Internet into an enormous college database and how to apply for admission electronically. Our site on the World Wide Web will provide you with access to all of the information that we have on colleges and testing and direct links to hundreds of colleges. And our *College Advisor* software is an award-winning CD-ROM that will help you narrow your list of colleges right on your computer.

Alternatives to our site include the Guidance Information System (GIS), found in many guidance or college counseling offices as well as in some public libraries. Regardless of the medium you choose to conduct your search—books, software, the Internet, personal visits and interviews, or better yet, some combination of all of the above—once you have your hands on this information, be sure to look it over carefully and share it with your college counselor.

5. Your Counselor

Once you've developed some ideas about your personal inventory and college options, schedule a meeting with your counselor. The more research you've done before you get together, the more help you're likely to get. Good advice comes out of thoughtful discussion, not from the expectation that your counselor will do your work. When it comes time to file applications, look over the materials and requirements together, and allow plenty of time to put forth your best.

Using College Information in the *The Complete Book of Catholic Colleges* and Elsewhere

Throughout the course of your college search, you'll confront an amazing array of statistics and other data related to every college you consider. In order for all of this information to be helpful, you need to have some sense of how to interpret it. We've included a detailed key to the college entries in this book in the section entitled "How This Book Works." Almost all the statistics we've compiled are self-explanatory, but there are a few that you'll encounter in the course of your search that will be more useful with some elaboration.

Don't use student/teacher ratio to assess average class size; they are not interchangeable terms. At almost every college, the average class size is larger than its student/teacher ratio. At many big universities, it is considerably larger. What is useful about the ratio is that it can give you an idea of how accessible your professors will be outside of the classroom. Once you are in college, you'll realize just how important this is.

In the same way, the percentage of faculty who hold doctorates is useful information. When you're paying thousands of dollars in tuition each year, there's something comforting about knowing that your professors have a considerably broader and deeper grasp of what you're studying than you do. In contrast, teaching assistants (TAs) are just one or two steps ahead of you.

Another interesting group of statistics are those that deal with the percentage of students who go on to graduate or professional school. Never allow yourself to be overly impressed by such statistics unless you've taken the time to ponder their meaning and visited the college in question. High percentages almost always mean one of two things: that the college is an intellectual enclave, which inspires students onward to further their education, or that it is a preprofessional bastion of aggressive careerists. There isn't anything inherently wrong with either one, but neither has universal appeal to prospective students. Colleges that are exceptions to this rule are rare and precious.

The most misleading figures of all provided to prospective students are those for medical school acceptance rates. Virtually every college in the country can boast of high acceptance rates to medical school for its graduates; premed programs are designed to weed out those who will not be strong candidates before they even get to apply! If you're thinking about medical school, also ask colleges about how many of their students apply to medical school each year.

One final piece of advice about statistics relates to the college's own acceptance rate. Simply knowing the percentage of applicants who are admitted each year is helpful, but it is even more helpful if you know how many applied as well. When you compare these figures to the freshman profile, you have the most accurate picture of just how tough it is to get in. An 80-percent acceptance rate doesn't mean there's an open door if you don't match up well to the academic achievements of the college's typical freshman.

A few final thoughts about your college search and the admissions process. Once you've narrowed down your options and decided where to apply, don't waste any time requesting application materials and getting to work. The admissions process is stressful enough without putting extra pressure on yourself by waiting until the last minute. The first thing you should do when you receive the necessary forms is to go over them with your college counselor. Immediately remove the recommendation forms (if they are required) and give them to the teacher(s) and counselor who will be completing them for you. They'll have a better opportunity to write a thorough and supportive recommendation if you give them more than the night before they are due in the mail to complete them. This is also the time to make your request for official transcripts. Again, it takes time to do these things. Plan ahead.

As for completing the applications, organize yourself and all the materials. Keep everything in folders and accessible in case you need to speak with an admissions officer over the telephone. When essays and information on your extracurricular activities are required, do some outlining and rough drafts before you commit yourself to the actual forms. It's not a bad idea to ask colleges for two applications. It's amazing what damage your little brother or a flying cup of coffee can do.

Speaking of damage, paying for college requires some of your attention too. We don't have nearly the space or time to go into such a complicated and stressful subject here, but it's also important that you get to work on your financial circumstances right away. We mentioned earlier that our own *Paying for College* is a good source of information. As a comforting thought, keep in mind that while college is costly, few pay the "sticker price" and millions of students are currently attending. Regardless, you have to have your finances in order before you can attend or get the best financial aid possible.

Last but not least, *DON'T TAKE IT EASY DURING YOUR SENIOR YEAR!* Colleges routinely request midyear grades, and they expect you to continue taking challenging academic courses and keep your grades up throughout your high school career. Doing so takes you one step closer to getting good news. Hopefully, so will your experience with *The Complete Book of Catholic Colleges*. On behalf of The Princeton Review, have a good time, and good luck. We'll see you on campus!

CHAPTER 5
COLLEGE ADMISSION GOES ELECTRONIC

College admission has finally moved onto the "information superhighway." Among the first organizations on the Internet, not surprisingly, many colleges have lots of useful information online. Checking out a school's web site can be a great way to gather more information. Once you're on the Internet, you can reach colleges directly (we've listed each college's Internet address at the top right of its entry), or through The Princeton Review Online, one of the best places to start your search.

Looking For Colleges Online

The Princeton Review offers a variety of services to help you gather information about colleges and learn more about the college admissions process.

Find-O-Rama—Our college search engine is the most sophisticated college search tool available on the Internet. To use Find-O-Rama, select the things that are important to you in choosing a college—everything from average SAT scores to our quality of life rating. The results of a Find-O-Rama search are a list of the schools that match your needs, along with links to the colleges' Web sites.

College Admissions Discussion—share your college admissions experiences and get expert advice from Princeton Review moderators. It's the most popular college admissions discussion area anywhere on the Net.

Counselor-O-Matic—Get a general sense of the level of schools to which you should consider applying. You start by completing an admissions profile. From this profile we create three custom lists of schools based on your overall rating: Safety schools, ballpark schools, and reach schools.

Remind-O-Rama—The college admissions process is filled with dates and deadlines. Remind-O-Rama can help you keep on top of all of this by sending you E-mail reminders for everything from application deadlines at the colleges to which you are applying to the last day to buy tickets for the Junior Prom.

To reach The Princeton Review on the World Wide Web, use the following address: www.review.com

Applying to College Via Electronic Application

Once you've gathered all the information that you need about colleges and universities and have decided where to apply, you may not need to leave your computer keyboard. Just a handful of years ago, electronic applications were never going to happen. Today, colleges are scrambling to make electronic versions of their applications available.

The colleges and universities that currently accept electronic applications are identified in our write-ups by the icon you see at right. You can get many of them directly from the colleges through the mail or by downloading them off the school's Internet site.

One especially good package is called Apply!, and is available for both Macintosh and Windows platforms. Through Apply! you have access to electronic applications from hundreds of colleges and universities. The software produces an exact duplicate of each college's application, complete with logos and graphics. Once you've received your Apply! software, you simply fill out the application(s) onscreen, print, and submit directly to the college or university admissions office(s). Apply! software is available on CD-ROM only, and is free of charge. To order Apply! visit their web site at www.weapply.com, E-mail them at info@weapply.com, call (203) 740-3504, or write them at Apply Technology, PO Box 8406, New Milford, Connecticut 06776-9848.

Another package is the Common Application, an electronic version of the notorious paper forms that purport to be a quick and easy way to apply to several colleges with one application. We aren't big fans of the paper version and can't endorse the electronic one either—unlike Apply!, the application is generic, and stands out like a sore thumb in a stack of the college's own forms. If colleges really wanted you to use the common application, they wouldn't bother printing their own. (A few, including Harvard, don't use any other app.) Unless it is the college's primary application, the message you send when you use the common app. is that this school is not your first choice; this is all the reason that we need to advise against using it when the college prints its own app.

None of the few other electronic application packages that are currently available excite us either. College Link is a package that has gotten some attention, but it includes one major flaw—you've got to send your completed disk back to the source, where the applications are then printed and returned to you to sign and then send on to the admissions office. This is a needless step that delays the submission of your application. Some colleges have already put their application forms online, allowing you to fill them out and submit them via the Internet, but this is probably two or three years off for most admissions offices.

A final note of advice: No matter what form of electronic application you choose, if you go the electronic route you must still contact the admissions office for an application packet. You're taking a risk if you don't. This is the only way that you can be sure to have all the information and materials that you need to put together the strongest candidacy possible. Despite the increasing online presence of colleges and the convenience of the electronic medium, "snail mail" remains an integral part of the process.

PART TWO

AND THEN THERE WERE SCHOOLS

CHAPTER 6
THE ADMISSIONS WIZARD

WHAT'S THE ADMISSIONS WIZARD?

The Complete Book of Catholic Colleges contains a lot of useful information about each of the colleges included, but you may be wondering how to begin using it. As much as we hate to admit it, you're probably not going to read through all 193 entries. So we've swallowed our pride and put together the following index to help you identify colleges that might be interesting to you.

To use it, you first have to answer a few questions about your college preferences in the boxes to the right. Feel free to blow off a category you don't care about (put an * instead of a letter or number).

Selectivity

Every college listed in *The Complete Book of Catholic Colleges* has an admissions selectivity rating between 60 and 100. This is *not* a measurement of the academic quality of the college, but simply an indication of how tough it is to get admitted.

M If you're an *A*-student taking tough courses with SAT scores over 1300 (or ACT over 30) and a solid extracurricular record, you have a good shot at colleges with a selectivity rating of 90 or higher—the "mega-selective" colleges.

H You're in the top 20% of your high school class, and scored above 1100 on the SAT. And you're looking for a highly selective school.

S You're a pretty good student (probably in the top half of your class) looking for a selective college whose students also did well in school.

N You're not looking for a selective college.

* You don't care how many people got turned away so that you could attend a particular college.

Region

1 New England. (Everywhere from Maine through Connecticut.)

2 Middle States. (New York to Washington, D.C., including Pennsylvania.)

3 Midwest. (Ohio north to the Dakotas and west to Kansas.)

4 South. (Virginia south to Puerto Rico and west to Louisiana.)

5 Southwest. (Texas, New Mexico.)

6 West. (Colorado, Montana, and west, including Hawaii.)

* Anyplace that's not home.

Cost

m Tuition is under $10,000 per year. (Remember: room, board, books, and other expenses will add another $5,000 to $10,000 for each category here.

e Tuition is between $10,000 and $15,000.

v You're willing to pay (or borrow) tuition of over $15,000 per year.

* That's my folks' problem.

Size

1 You want a college with 5,000 or more undergraduates. Not a bad idea; larger colleges can generally provide more resources and satisfy more varied interests.

2 You want a college with 2,000 to 5,000 undergrads. Some students feel this offers a nice balance between the personal attention a small college can give and the resources of a large college.

3 You want a college with fewer than 2,000 undergrads. These colleges generally provide the most personal attention; you'll rarely feel like a number here.

* We recommend you keep an open mind on size—visit colleges of all sizes before you narrow your choice here.

Environment

R Rural colleges provide plenty of fresh air, lots of space, and a more "laid-back" atmosphere.

S Suburban colleges are often in small towns within an hour or two of a good-sized city, and always close to a mall.

U Urban colleges provide the widest variety of off-campus activities, like museums, restaurants, and clubs.

* This is important to some people, but again, you should look at colleges of all settings before deciding—what's on the campus is often more important than what's next door.

Put your letters and numbers together to form your *search string*. It should look something like this: H6e*S (that would be a highly selective college in the west that is expensive, and in a suburban setting).

Now simply scan the (long) list that follows, and note the colleges whose code is similar to your search string. If your search string is S2*2U, for example, you might put a check mark next to a college whose code is S2v3S, but not check off a college whose code is N4e2R. When in doubt, check it off—this will give you the widest variety of options. If you need more space for your list of target colleges and Wizard-related calculations, use the notes pages in the back of the guide. You're using this book to start your search, not to make any final decisions about where you should spend your next four or five years.

Enjoy your search!

M1v2U	College of the Holy Cross	92
M1v1S	Boston College	54
M2v1U	Georgetown University	87
M3v1S	University of Notre Dame	141
H1e3S	Saint Michael's College	182
H1e2U	Assumption College	47
H2e3S	College Misericordia	67
H2e3S	Rosemont College	152
H2e2U	Marist College	114
H2e2U	Saint Joseph's University	172
H2e2U	University of Scranton	198
H2v2U	Loyola College (MD)	106
H2v2U	The Catholic University of America	62
H2v3S	Villanova University	210
H3m3R	Mount Marty College	125
H3e2S	John Carroll University	98
H3e2S	Saint Norbert College	183
H4m3U	Our Lady of Holy Cross College	143
H5m3U	University of Saint Thomas (TX)	188
H6m3U	University of Great Falls	90
H6e2U	Seattle University	199
S1e3S	Merrimack College	123
S1e3U	Saint Anselm College	155
S1e3~	Saint Joseph's College (ME)	171
S1m2S	Stonehill College	206
S1m~U	Albertus Magnus College	216*
S1v2S	Fairfield University	81
S1v2U	Providence College	146

S2m3U	D'Youville College	69
S2m2S	Saint Thomas Aquinas College	189
S2e3R	Saint Vincent College	191
S2e3S	Caldwell College	56
S2e3S	College of Saint Elizabeth	160
S2e3S	Marywood College	121
S2e3S	Saint John Fisher College	165
S2e3S	LeMoyne College	102
S2e3S	Nazareth College of Rochester	133
S2e3S	Chestnut Hill College	64
S2e3S	Gwynedd-Mercy College	91
S2e3~	Saint Francis College (PA)	163
S2m1~	Trinity College (DC)	208
S2e2S	Mercyhurst College	122
S2e2S	Siena College	202
S2e2S	Seton Hall University	200
S2e2S	Niagara University	136
S2e2U	College of Notre Dame of Maryland	140
S2e2U	Gannon University	86
S2e2U	LaSalle University	101
S2e2U	Manhattan College	111
S2e2U	The College of Saint Rose	185
S2e2U	Canisius College	58
S2e2U	King's College (PA)	99
S2e1U	Duquesne University	78
S2v2U	Fordham University	84
S3m3S	Fontbonne College	83
S3m3U	Marygrove College	117
S3m3U	Saint Francis College (IN)	161
S3m3U	Saint Mary College	176
S3m3U	University of Mary	116
S3m3U	Siena Heights College	203
S3e1U	Walsh University	212
S3m2S	Cardinal Stritch College	59
S3m2U	Alverno College	44
S3e~U	Edgewood College	219*
S3e3R	Saint John's University (MN)	166

S3e3R	Benedictine College	52
S3e3S	Benedictine University	53
S3e3S	College of Saint Benedict	156
S3e3S	College of Saint Scholastica	186
S3e3S	College of Mount Saint Joseph	128
S3e3S	College of Saint Francis	164
S3e3S	Dominican University	77
S3e3U	Clarke College	66
S3e3U	Franciscan University of Steubenville	85
S3e3U	Quincy University	147
S3e3U	Loras College	104
S3e3U	Saint Ambrose University	154
S3e3U	Saint Mary's University of Minnesota	179
S3e3~	Saint Mary's College (IN)	178
S3e2U	Rockhurst College	151
S3e2U	The College of Saint Catherine	158
S3e2U	University of Detroit Mercy	74
S3e2U	Xavier University (OH)	214
S3e2U	Creighton University	68
S3e2~	University of Saint Thomas (MN)	187
S3e1S	University of Dayton	72
S3e1U	DePaul University	73
S3e1U	Marquette University	115
S3e1U	Saint Louis University	174
S3e1U	Loyola University of Chicago	109
S3m~U	Briar Cliff College	218*
S3m~U	Mount Mary College	221*
S3m~U	Avila College	216*
S4e2U	Xavier University of Louisiana	215
S4e~U	Brescia College	217*
S4m1S	Thomas More College	207
S4m1S	Wheeling Jesuit University	213
S4m1U	Spring Hill College	205
S4e3U	Christian Brothers University	65
S4e1U	Bellarmine College	50
S4e2U	Loyola University New Orleans	108
S5m2U	Our Lady of the Lake University	144

S5m~U	Saint Mary's University	180
S5e3S	University of Dallas	71
S5e3U	College of Santa Fe	197
S6m3U	Carroll College (MT)	61
S6e3U	Mount Saint Mary's College (CA)	130
S6e3U	Regis University	149
S6e2U	University of San Francisco	195
S6e2U	University of San Diego	194
S6e2U	Gonzaga University	89
S6e2U	University of Portland	145
S6v2S	Saint Mary's College (CA)	177
S6v2S	Loyola Marymount University	107
S6v2U	Santa Clara University	196
N1e~R	College of Saint Joseph in Vermont	223*
N1e1R	Anna Maria College	45
N1e3S	Elms College	79
N1e3S	Regis College	148
N1e3S	Rivier College	150
N1e3S	Saint Joseph College	168
N1e3U	Emmanuel College (MA)	80
N1e3U	Salve Regina University	193
N1m1U	Trinity College of Vermont	209
N1e2S	Sacred Heart University	153
N1e~U	Notre Dame College	138
N2m3S	Felician College	82
N2m3S	Molloy College	124
N2e1S	Daemen College	70
N2m3S	Dominican College of Blauvelt	75
N2m3U	Mount Saint Mary College	129
N2m2U	Saint Francis College (NY)	162
N2m2U	Saint Joseph's College (Brooklyn)	169
N2m~S	LaRoche College	100
N2e3R	Mount Saint Mary's College (MD)	131
N2e3R	Saint Bonaventure University	157
N2e3S	Alvernia College	43
N2e3S	Cabrini College	55
N2e3S	Georgian Court College	88

N2e3S	Immaculata College	95
N2e3S	Neumann College	134
N2e3S	Marymount College	118
N2e3S	Seton Hill College	201
N2e3U	College of Mount Saint Vincent	132
N2e3U	Marymount Manhattan College	119
N2e3U	College of New Rochelle	135
N2e2S	Iona College	97
N2e2U	Carlow College	60
N2e2U	Holy Family College	93
N2e2U	Saint Peter's College	184
N2e1R	Saint John's University (NY)	167
N2e~R	Allentown College of Saint Francis de Sales	42
N3m3S	Calumet College of Saint Joseph	57
N3e1U	Viterbo College	211
N3m3U	Ohio Dominican College	142
N3m2S	Madonna University	110
N3e~U	Kansas Newman College	219*
N3m~U	Lourdes College	105
N3e~U	Silver Lake College	224*
N3e3R	Saint Joseph's College (IN)	170
N3e1S	Barat College	48
N3e3U	College of Saint Mary	181
N3e3S	Marian College of Fond Du Lac	113
N3e3U	Marian College	112
N3e3U	Mount Mercy College	126
N3e1U	Aquinas College	46
N3e2S	Lewis University	103
N3e2U	Saint Xavier University	192
N3m~R	Saint Mary-of-the-Woods College	224*
N3m~S	Ursuline College	225*
N3m~S	Notre Dame College of Ohio	139
N3e~U	Mount Saint Clare College	127
N4m3R	Saint Leo College	173
N4m3S	Belmont Abbey College	51
N4m~U	Spalding University	204
N4e3U	Saint Thomas University	190

N4e2U	Marymount University	120
N4e3S	Barry University	49
N5e2U	Incarnate Word College	96
N5e2U	Saint Edward's University	159
N6e3S	Chaminade University of Honolulu	63
N6e3S	College of Notre Dame (CA)	137
N6e3S	Saint Martin's College	175
N6e3U	Holy Names College	94
N6e3U	Dominican College of San Rafael	76
~2~~~	Mount Aloysius College	220*
~3e~S	Saint Mary's College (MI)	223*
~3~~~	Presentation College	222*
~4~~~	Bayamon Central University	217*
~4~~~	Christendom College	218*
~4~~~	Pontifical Catholic University	221*
~4~~~	University of the Sacred Heart	222*
~6e~U	Marylhurst College	220*

CHAPTER 7
COLLEGE PROFILES

This chapter includes information on all U.S. Catholic colleges, including those in the Commonwealth of Puerto Rico. (Institutions that function solely as seminaries are not a part of our listings.) Each of the colleges and universities in the guide has its own entry, of which there are two types. The first part of the chapter includes detailed one-page profiles on each of the colleges, provided that the necessary data required to create every individual section within an entry was supplied to us. The last portion of the chapter (starting on page 216) consists of half-page profiles on those colleges for which data was not available to produce all of the elements of a full-page entry.

ALLENTOWN COLLEGE OF SAINT FRANCIS DE SALES

2755 Station Avenue, Center Valley, PA 18034 • Admissions: 610-282-4443 • Fax: 610-282-2254
• Financial Aid: Call-Admissions • E-mail: ajs2@emailallencol.edu • Web Site: allencol.edu/~admiss

Allentown College was founded in 1964 by the Oblates of Saint Francis de Sales (Salesians) and is located on a 300-acre campus in Lehigh Valley in eastern Pennsylvania, near Allentown and Bethlehem. The vast majority of the college's students hail from within a 100-mile radius, and lean to the conservative side politically. Academic offerings range from the liberal arts to business, theater arts, the health sciences, and theology. Popular majors include theater, business, and nursing, although Allentown has recently added programs in environmental sciences and environmental studies. The college's Labuda Center for the Performing Arts is the home of the Pennsylvania Shakespeare Festival, Pennsylvania's official Shakespeare Festival.

ADMISSIONS
Special Requirements: TOEFL is required of all international students.

FINANCIAL AID
Students should submit: FAFSA (due February 15), the school's own financial aid form (due February 15), state aid form (due February 15), a copy of parents' most recent income tax filing (due February 15). The Princeton Review suggests that all financial aid forms be submitted as soon as possible after January 1. *The following grants/scholarships are offered:* Pell, SEOG, academic merit, the school's own scholarships, the school's own grants, state grants, private scholarships, private grants, ROTC, foreign aid. *Students borrow from the following loan programs:* Stafford, unsubsidized Stafford, Perkins, PLUS, the school's own loan fund, supplemental loans, state loans, private loans. College Work-Study Program is available.

STUDENT BODY
% from out of state	24
% live on campus	80
% African American	3
% Asian	1
% Caucasian	93
% Hispanic	3
% international	1

ACADEMICS
Calendar	semester
Student/teacher ratio	23:1
FT faculty	93
% graduate in 4 yrs.	64

ADMISSIONS
Admissions Rating	69
# of applicants	1,111
% of applicants accepted	81
% of acceptees attending	34

Deadlines
Regular admission	8/1

FRESHMAN PROFILE
Average verbal SAT	505
Average math SAT	477
Minimum TOEFL	550
Graduated top 10% of class	10
Graduated top 25% of class	37
Graduated top 50% of class	59

FINANCIAL FACTS
Tuition	$10,990
Room & board	$5,260
Estimated book expense	$500
% frosh receiving aid	67
% undergrads receiving aid	85
% frosh w/ grant	70
Avg. grant	$3,000
% frosh w/ loan	90
Avg. loan	$2,128

ALVERNIA COLLEGE

400 St. Bernardine Street, Reading, PA 19607 • Admissions: 610-796-8220 • Fax: 610-796-8336
• Financial Aid: 610-796-8215

Originally founded as a teachers' seminary by the Bernardine Sisters of Saint Francis, Alvernia became a liberal arts college in 1958. The College's 85-acre campus, complete with its own Lourdes Grotto and shrines, is located about an hour from Philadelphia. Academic offerings cover more than three dozen majors; among the most popular are business, education, and criminal justice. Clubs and activities cover a full range, from standard offerings like the newspaper, debate, and theater to community volunteer groups focused on assisting the homeless. Athletics, especially basketball, are popular. Both the men's and women's basketball teams are highly ranked in NCAA Division III competition. A variety of special scholarships are available, including those for academic talent, leadership, minority status, children of alumni, and Catholic students.

ADMISSIONS

The admissions committee considers (in descending order of importance): HS record, test scores, recommendations. *Also considered (in descending order of importance):* extracurriculars, personality, special talents. Either the SAT or ACT is required; SAT is preferred. An interview is required. *High school units required/recommended:* 16 total units are required; 4 English required, 2 math required, 2 science required, 2 foreign language required, 2 social studies required. Minimum composite SAT I score of 900 and minimum 2.0 GPA required. *Special Requirements:* TOEFL is required of all international students. PSB or NLN tests required of nursing program applicants.

FINANCIAL AID

Students should submit: FAFSA. The Princeton Review suggests that all financial aid forms be submitted as soon as possible after January 1. *The following grants/scholarships are offered:* state scholarships. *Students borrow from the following loan programs:* Stafford, PLUS. College Work-Study Program is available. Institutional employment is available. The off-campus job outlook is excellent.

STUDENT BODY		ACADEMICS		Deadlines		FINANCIAL FACTS	
Total undergrad enrollment	1,265	Calendar	semester	Regular admission	rolling	Tuition	$10,250
% male/female	39/61	Student/teacher ratio	9:1	Regular notification	rolling	Room & board	$4,600
% from out of state	20	FT faculty	134			Estimated book expense	$650
% transfers	40	% faculty from religious order	15	**FRESHMAN PROFILE**		% frosh receiving aid	80
% from catholic high school	25			Average verbal SAT	430	% undergrads receiving aid	85
% live on campus	30	**Most Popular Majors**		Average math SAT	410		
% African American	4	business		Average ACT	18		
% Caucasian	95	education		Minimum TOEFL	550		
% Hispanic	1	criminal justice		Graduated top 10% of class	10		
# of countries represented	5			Graduated top 25% of class	30		
		ADMISSIONS		Graduated top 50% of class	75		
		Admissions Rating	60				
		% of acceptees attending	27				

ALVERNO COLLEGE

3401 South 39th Street, P.O. Box 343922, Milwaukee, WI 53234 • *Admissions: 414-382-6000* • *Fax: 414-382-6354*
• *Financial Aid: 414-382-6046* • *E-mail: alvadmsh@execpc.com* • *Web Site: www.alverno.edu*

Alverno College was founded by the Sisters of Saint Francis in 1887 as a school for young women studying to become teachers. Still single-sex, the college is on a 52-acre campus in Milwaukee. More than half the women attending Alverno come from greater Milwaukee; most others hail from northern Illinois, Wisconsin, and other midwestern states. The college offers more than two dozen majors in a wide variety of academic disciplines. Among the most popular are business management, professional communication, nursing, education, and psychology. Cross-registration is also possible at the Milwaukee Institute of Art and Design and at Marquette University. While dormitory housing is available, most students at Alverno commute. Students who wish to be considered for the college's broad range of institutional scholarships must participate in Scholarship Opportunity Day, an on-campus review program that includes writing, interviews, and group-discussion sessions on a variety of issues related to scholarship worthiness.

ADMISSIONS

The admissions committee considers (in descending order of importance): HS record, test scores, class rank. Either the SAT or ACT is required; ACT is preferred. An interview is recommended. Admissions process is need-blind. *High school units required/recommended:* 17 total units are required; 4 English recommended, 3 math recommended, 3 science recommended, 2 foreign language recommended, 4 social studies recommended, 3 history recommended. Minimum composite ACT score of 19, rank in top half of secondary school class, and minimum 2.5 GPA recommended. *Special Requirements:* Biology and chemistry required of music therapy program applicants. Biology, chemistry, and algebra required of nursing program applicants. Biology, chemistry, algebra, and geometry recommended of nuclear medicine technology program applicants. Audition (or tape) and music theory exam required of music program applicants.

FINANCIAL AID

Students should submit: FAFSA (due March 15), the school's own financial aid form (due March 15), a copy of parents' most recent income tax filing (due March 15). The Princeton Review suggests that all financial aid forms be submitted as soon as possible after January 1. *The following grants/scholarships are offered:* state scholarships. *Students borrow from the following loan programs:* Stafford, PLUS. College Work-Study Program is available. Institutional employment is available. The off-campus job outlook is good.

STUDENT BODY		ACADEMICS		Deadlines		FINANCIAL FACTS	
Total undergrad enrollment	2,163	Calendar	semester	Regular admission	8/1	Tuition	$9,288
% male/female	0/100	Student/teacher ratio	11:1	Regular notification	rolling	Room & board	$3,890
% from out of state	3	FT faculty	197			Estimated book expense	$550
% transfers	49	% graduate in 4 yrs.	54	**FRESHMAN PROFILE**		% frosh receiving aid	75
% from catholic high school	27			Range ACT	20-28	% undergrads receiving aid	63
% live on campus	11	**Most Popular Majors**		Average ACT	20	% frosh w/ grant	45
% African American	15	business/management		Minimum TOEFL	500	Avg. grant	NR
% Asian	2	professional communication		Graduated top 10% of class	7	% frosh w/ loan	62
% Caucasian	74	nursing		Graduated top 25% of class	36	Avg. loan	$2,965
% Hispanic	5			Graduated top 50% of class	98		
% Native American	1	**ADMISSIONS**					
% international	1	Admissions Rating	72				
# of countries represented	5	# of applicants	760				
		% of applicants accepted	68				
		% of acceptees attending	42				

ANNA MARIA COLLEGE

Sunset Lane, Paxton, MA 01612 • Admissions: 508-849-3360 • Fax: 508-849-3362
• Financial Aid: 508-849-3366 • E-mail: admission@anna-maria.edu • Web Site: www.anna-maria.edu

Anna Maria College was founded in 1946 by the Sisters of Saint Anne, and became coed in 1973. Its suburban campus covers 180 acres. Worcester, the second largest city in New England, is eight miles away, while Boston and Providence are each about an hour's drive. The college offers twenty-five majors, most of which are decidedly career oriented. Other options run the gamut, ranging from gerontology to fire science-fire fighting. Those who seek additional academic offerings need not look far: Anna Maria is also a member of the Worcester Consortium, a group of ten local colleges that allows its students cross-registration privileges and the opportunity to participate in clubs and activities available on other local campuses.

ADMISSIONS

The admissions committee considers (in descending order of importance): HS record, class rank, test scores, recommendations, essay. *Also considered (in descending order of importance):* extracurriculars, personality, special talents. Either the SAT or ACT is required; SAT is preferred. An interview is recommended. Admissions process is need-blind. *High school units required/recommended:* 16 total units are required; 4 English required, 2 math required, 2 science required, 2 foreign language recommended, 2 social studies required, 2 history required. Minimum combined SAT I score of 850, rank in top half of secondary school class, and minimum 2.50 GPA recommended. *Special Requirements:* A portfolio is required for art program applicants. An audition is required for music program applicants. An RN is required for nursing program applicants.

FINANCIAL AID

Students should submit: FAFSA (due March 1), CSS Profile, the school's own financial aid form (due March 1), a copy of parents' most recent income tax filing (due March 1). The Princeton Review suggests that all financial aid forms be submitted as soon as possible after January 1. *The following grants/scholarships are offered:* Pell, SEOG, the school's own scholarships, the school's own grants, state scholarships, state grants, private scholarships, private grants, foreign aid. *Students borrow from the following loan programs:* Stafford, unsubsidized Stafford, Perkins, PLUS, the school's own loan fund, supplemental loans, private loans. Applicants will be notified of awards beginning April 1. College Work-Study Program is available. Institutional employment is available. The off-campus job outlook is good.

STUDENT BODY		ACADEMICS		Deadlines		FINANCIAL FACTS	
Total undergrad enrollment	866	Calendar	semester	Regular admission	rolling	Tuition	$11,230
% male/female	39/61	Student/teacher ratio	23:1	Regular notification	rolling	Room & board	$5,030
% from out of state	6	FT faculty	84			Estimated book expense	$500
% transfers	28	% faculty from religious order	0	**FRESHMAN PROFILE**		% frosh receiving aid	73
% live on campus	52			Average verbal SAT	480	% undergrads receiving aid	71
% African American	3	**Most Popular Majors**		Average math SAT	458		
% Asian	1	education		Minimum TOEFL	500		
% Caucasian	92	criminal justice		Average HS GPA or Avg	3.2		
% Hispanic	5	business administration		Graduated top 10% of class	4		
% international	3			Graduated top 25% of class	28		
# of countries represented	6	**ADMISSIONS**		Graduated top 50% of class	61		
		Admissions Rating	66				
		# of applicants	444				
		% of applicants accepted	84				
		% of acceptees attending	29				

AQUINAS COLLEGE

1607 Robinson Road SE, Grand Rapids, MI 49506 • *Admissions: 616-732-4460* • *Fax: 616-732-4431*
• *Financial Aid: 616-459-8281, ext. 5129* • *E-mail: admissions@aquinas.edu* • *Web Site: www.aquinas.edu*

Founded in 1922 by the Dominicans, in 1931 Aquinas College became the first Catholic college in the United States to go coeducational. The college's 107-acre Grand Rapids campus is located 140 miles from Detroit. Forty majors are offered in total; among the most popular programs at Aquinas are business administration, social science, and education. Despite this seemingly well-grounded approach, much of the physical campus seems to actually focus skyward. The Foster Planet Walk uses the system of campus trails and roadways to carry visitors 93 million miles through space via bronze models of the planets. The college's Baldwin Observatory, located atop the Albertus Hall Science Building, houses 16-inch Meade and 8-inch Celestron telescopes to support a variety of undergraduate astronomy courses and other educational activities.

ADMISSIONS
The admissions committee considers (in descending order of importance): HS record, test scores, recommendations, class rank, essay. *Also considered (in descending order of importance):* extracurriculars, personality, special talents, geographical distribution. Either the SAT or ACT is required; ACT is preferred. An interview is recommended. Admissions process is need-blind. *High school units required/recommended:* 15 total units are required; 4 English required, 3 math required, 3 science required, 4 social studies required. Rank in top half of secondary school class and minimum 2.5 GPA required. *Special Requirements:* TOEFL is required of all international students.

FINANCIAL AID
Students should submit: FAFSA (due February 15), a copy of parents' most recent income tax filing (due April 1). The Princeton Review suggests that all financial aid forms be submitted as soon as possible after January 1. *The following grants/scholarships are offered:* Pell, SEOG, academic merit, athletic, state scholarships, state grants, private scholarships, private grants. *Students borrow from the following loan programs:* Stafford, unsubsidized Stafford, Perkins, PLUS, supplemental loans, private loans. Applicants will be notified of awards beginning March 15. College Work-Study Program is available. Institutional employment is available. The off-campus job outlook is excellent.

STUDENT BODY		ACADEMICS				FINANCIAL FACTS	
Total undergrad enrollment	1,825	Calendar	semester	% of applicants accepted	92	Tuition	$12,534
% male/female	36/64	Student/teacher ratio	13:1	% of acceptees attending	40	Room & board	$4,198
% from out of state	4	FT faculty	177	**Deadlines**		Estimated book expense	$380
% transfers	26	% faculty from religious order	50	Regular admission	rolling	% frosh receiving aid	91
% from catholic high school	18	% graduate in 4 yrs.	50	Regular notification	rolling	% undergrads receiving aid	87
% live on campus	44			**FRESHMAN PROFILE**		% frosh w/ grant	83
% African American	7	**Most Popular Majors**		Range ACT	19-25	Avg. grant	$4,000
% Asian	1	business administration		Average ACT	22	% frosh w/ loan	58
% Caucasian	88	social science		Minimum TOEFL	550	Avg. loan	$1,645
% Hispanic	1	education		Average HS GPA or Avg	3.2		
% Native American	1	**ADMISSIONS**		Graduated top 10% of class	20		
% international	1	Admissions Rating	67	Graduated top 25% of class	46		
# of countries represented	11	# of applicants	769	Graduated top 50% of class	76		

ASSUMPTION COLLEGE

500 Salisbury Street, Worcester, MA 01615 • Admissions: 508-767-7285 • Fax: 508-799-4412
• Financial Aid: 508-767-7158 • E-mail: admissions@assumption.edu • Web Site: www.assumption.edu

Assumption College was founded in 1904 by the Assumptionists, a branch of the Augustinians. The college was the first French Catholic college in the country, and until the mid-1950s most courses were taught in French. Today, Assumption offers twenty-six major programs; among the most popular are social/rehabilitation services, business, and English. The College's 150-acre campus is about an hour from Boston and is residential in feel. The majority of Assumption's students live in campus housing, which is guaranteed to all who desire it. (Options afford the opportunity to live in a variety of theme housing, including a substance-free environment.) Extracurricular offerings include a student volunteer program that features a two-week Mexico mission. Assumption has garnered lots of national recognition for its combination of academic strength and character-building environment.

ADMISSIONS

The admissions committee considers (in descending order of importance): HS record, class rank, test scores, recommendations, essay. *Also considered (in descending order of importance):* personality, alumni relationship, special talents, extracurriculars, geographical distribution. Either the SAT or ACT is required. An interview is recommended. Admissions process is need-blind. *High school units required/recommended:* 15 total units are required; 4 English required, 2 math required, 2 science recommended, 2 foreign language required, 1 history required.

FINANCIAL AID

Students should submit: FAFSA (due March 1), the school's own financial aid form (due March 1), a copy of parents' most recent income tax filing (due May 1). The Princeton Review suggests that all financial aid forms be submitted as soon as possible after January 1. *The following grants/scholarships are offered:* state scholarships. *Students borrow from the following loan programs:* Stafford, PLUS. College Work-Study Program is available. Institutional employment is available. The off-campus job outlook is excellent.

STUDENT BODY

Total undergrad enrollment	2,397
% male/female	40/60
% from out of state	40
% transfers	12
% from catholic high school	30
% live on campus	90
% African American	1
% Asian	2
% Caucasian	94
% Hispanic	3
% international	2
# of countries represented	12

ACADEMICS

Calendar	semester
Student/teacher ratio	12:1
FT faculty	228
% faculty from religious order	9

Most Popular Majors
social/rehabilitation services
business
English

ADMISSIONS

Admissions Rating	80
% of acceptees attending	29

Deadlines

Regular admission	3/1
Regular notification	rolling

FRESHMAN PROFILE

Minimum TOEFL	550

FINANCIAL FACTS

Tuition	$13,700
Room & board	$5,980
Estimated book expense	$500
% frosh receiving aid	60
% undergrads receiving aid	57

Barat College

700 E. Westleigh Road, Lake Forest, IL 60045 • Admissions: 708-295-4260 • Fax: 708-234-1084
• Financial Aid: 847-615-5675

Barat College was founded in 1848 by the Society of the Sacred Heart. The Society was established shortly after the French Revolution by Madeleine Sophie Barat, based on the belief that women should have a strong liberal arts education. It is from her that the college takes its name. As is the case with many small colleges founded as single-sex institutions, Barat eventually became coed (in 1982). The college's 30-acre campus is a twenty-minute walk from Lake Michigan; downtown Chicago is twenty-nine miles to the south and accessible by train. Academic offerings are diverse, covering a range from liberal arts and sciences to business, education, and visual-performing arts. The campus boasts a new $5 million, 30,000 square-foot library.

ADMISSIONS

The admissions committee considers (in descending order of importance): HS record, class rank, test scores, essay, recommendations. *Also considered (in descending order of importance):* extracurriculars, personality, special talents. Either the SAT or ACT is required; ACT is preferred. An interview is recommended. Admissions process is need-blind. *High school units required/recommended:* 16 total units are recommended; 4 English recommended, 2 math recommended, 2 science recommended, 2 foreign language recommended, 2 social studies recommended, 1 history recommended. Minimum composite ACT score of 20 (combined SAT I score of 900), rank in top half of secondary school class, and minimum 2.5 GPA recommended. *Special Requirements:* An RN is required for nursing program applicants. Audition required of dance program applicants.

FINANCIAL AID

Students should submit: FAFSA, the school's own financial aid form, a copy of parents' most recent income tax filing. The Princeton Review suggests that all financial aid forms be submitted as soon as possible after January 1. *The following grants/scholarships are offered:* Pell, SEOG, academic merit, the school's own scholarships, the school's own grants, state scholarships, state grants, private scholarships, private grants, foreign aid. *Students borrow from the following loan programs:* Stafford, unsubsidized Stafford, Perkins, PLUS, the school's own loan fund, supplemental loans, private loans. College Work-Study Program is available. Institutional employment is available. The off-campus job outlook is good.

STUDENT BODY

Total undergrad enrollment	719
% male/female	28/72
% from out of state	19
% transfers	54
% live on campus	57
% African American	7
% Asian	4
% Caucasian	85
% Hispanic	3
% international	6
# of countries represented	16

ACADEMICS

Calendar	semester
Student/teacher ratio	8:1
FT faculty	90
% faculty from religious order	1

Most Popular Majors
management/business
education
psychology

ADMISSIONS

Admissions Rating	67
% of acceptees attending	63

Deadlines

Regular admission	rolling
Regular notification	rolling

FRESHMAN PROFILE

Minimum TOEFL	500
Graduated top 10% of class	15
Graduated top 25% of class	36
Graduated top 50% of class	55

FINANCIAL FACTS

Tuition	$11,970
Room & board	$4,820
Estimated book expense	$400
% frosh receiving aid	70
% undergrads receiving aid	70

BARRY UNIVERSITY

11300 N. E. 2nd Avenue, Miami Shores, FL 33161 • Admissions: 305-899-3110 • Fax: 305-899-3149
• Financial Aid: 305-899-3673 • E-mail: admissions@pcsa01.barry.edu • Web Site: www.barry.edu

Founded in 1940, Barry University is Florida's oldest and largest Catholic university. The University's 90-acre campus is twenty minutes from both Miami Beach and Fort Lauderdale. Affiliated with the Dominican Sisters, Barry's five schools with undergraduate programs (School of Arts and Sciences, Andreas School of Business, Adrian Dominican School of Education, School of Natural and Health Sciences, and School of Nursing) offer over fifty academic majors. The university enrolls students from nearly every state and several dozen foreign countries. The women's volleyball team won the NCAA Division II national championship in 1995. In soccer, Barry's Lady Buccaneers have won three national championships in the past six years. Barry has an active campus ministry, and offers the Dominican scholarship to students who can demonstrate both service to the community and leadership ability. State-of-the-art facilities include the David Brinkley Television Production Studio, a cell biology-biotechnology lab, a human performance lab, and computer imaging labs.

ADMISSIONS

The admissions committee considers (in descending order of importance): HS record, test scores, recommendations, essay, class rank. *Also considered (in descending order of importance):* alumni relationship, extracurriculars, personality, special talents, geographical distribution. Either the SAT or ACT is required. An interview is recommended. Admissions process is need-blind. *High school units required/recommended:* 20 total units are recommended; 4 English recommended, 3 math recommended, 2 science recommended, 3 foreign language recommended, 2 social studies recommended, 2 history recommended. *Special Requirements:* 3-1/2 units of math including algebra, geometry, and trigonometry required of math program applicants. Algebra I and II, biology, and chemistry required of nursing and science program applicants. 1 unit of biology and 1 unit of chemistry required of biology (pre-dental, pre-medical, and pre-veterinary) program applicants.

FINANCIAL AID

Students should submit: FAFSA (due March 1), the school's own financial aid form (due March 1), state aid form, a copy of parents' most recent income tax filing. The Princeton Review suggests that all financial aid forms be submitted as soon as possible after January 1. *The following grants/scholarships are offered:* Pell, SEOG, academic merit, athletic, the school's own scholarships, the school's own grants, state scholarships, state grants, private scholarships, private grants. *Students borrow from the following loan programs:* Stafford, unsubsidized Stafford, Perkins, PLUS, the school's own loan fund, supplemental loans, private loans. College Work-Study Program is available. Institutional employment is available. The off-campus job outlook is fair.

STUDENT BODY	
Total undergrad enrollment	5,756
% male/female	38/62
% from out of state	38
% transfers	47
% live on campus	33
% African American	13
% Asian	2
% Caucasian	53
% Hispanic	31
# of countries represented	57

ACADEMICS

Calendar	semester
Student/teacher ratio	13:1

FT faculty	541
% faculty from religious order	25
% graduate in 4 yrs.	45

Most Popular Majors
accounting
management
nursing

ADMISSIONS

Admissions Rating	67
# of applicants	910
% of applicants accepted	77
% of acceptees attending	37

Deadlines	
Regular admission	7/15

FRESHMAN PROFILE

Average verbal SAT	505
Average math SAT	497
Average ACT	21
Minimum TOEFL	550
Average HS GPA or Avg	3.5
Graduated top 10% of class	29
Graduated top 25% of class	56
Graduated top 50% of class	80

FINANCIAL FACTS	
Tuition	$12,790
Room & board	$5,680
Estimated book expense	$600
% frosh receiving aid	75
% undergrads receiving aid	71
% frosh w/ grant	41
Avg. grant	$1,000
% frosh w/ loan	44
Avg. loan	$2,451

BELLARMINE COLLEGE

2001 Newburg Road, Louisville, KY 40205 • Admissions: 502-452-8131 • Fax: 502-452-8002
• Financial Aid: 502-452-8131

Founded in 1950, Bellarmine College is located on a 120-acre campus seven miles from downtown Louisville. The college was founded under the sponsorship of the Archdiocese of Louisville with the assistance of the Conventual Franciscan Fathers, and is named after a Jesuit, Saint Robert Bellarmine (1542–1621). Saint Robert was an intellectual and person of faith with a passionate commitment to the greater good. Bellarmine was one of the first colleges in Kentucky to admit students of all races. The college offers over two dozen academic programs spread among the liberal arts and sciences, business, education, and nursing; popular majors are business administration, accounting, and nursing. Facilities of note include a nine-hole golf course, a tennis center, a new 72,000-square-foot library, and the Thomas Merton Center, an archive housing over 40,000 items from the works of the famed religious writer and poet. Fifty clubs and organizations are registered on campus, covering both academically-and-socially-oriented pursuits. Students excel in both areas: Bellarmine's mock trial team has gotten national recognition as have the Lady Knights, an NCAA Division II power in women's basketball. In ten years, they have made four appearances in national championship tournament play, finishing fourth in the nation in 1994.

ADMISSIONS

The admissions committee considers (in descending order of importance): HS record, class rank, test scores, recommendations, essay. *Also considered (in descending order of importance):* extracurriculars, alumni relationship, geographical distribution, personality, special talents. Either the SAT or ACT is required. An interview is recommended. *High school units required/recommended:* 4 English required, 3 math required, 4 math recommended, 2 science required, 3 science recommended, 2 foreign language recommended, 2 social studies required. Minimum combined SAT I score of 1000 (composite ACT score of 21), rank in top half of secondary school class, and minimum 2.5 GPA recommended. *Special Requirements:* An audition is required for music program applicants.

FINANCIAL AID

Students should submit: FAFSA (due March 15). The Princeton Review suggests that all financial aid forms be submitted as soon as possible after January 1. *The following grants/scholarships are offered:* Pell, SEOG, academic merit, athletic, the school's own scholarships, the school's own grants, state scholarships, state grants, private scholarships, private grants, United Negro College Fund. *Students borrow from the following loan programs:* Stafford, unsubsidized Stafford, Perkins, PLUS, the school's own loan fund, supplemental loans, private loans. College Work-Study Program is available. Institutional employment is available. The off-campus job outlook is excellent.

STUDENT BODY		ACADEMICS			
Total undergrad enrollment	1,282	Calendar	semester	% of applicants accepted	88
% male/female	42/58	Student/teacher ratio	12:1	% of acceptees attending	47
% from out of state	19	FT faculty	180		
% transfers	19	% faculty from religious order	5	**Deadlines**	
% from catholic high school	50	% graduate in 4 yrs.	59	Regular admission	8/1
% live on campus	33			Regular notification	rolling
% African American	3	**Most Popular Majors**			
% Asian	1	business administration		**FRESHMAN PROFILE**	
% Caucasian	94	accounting		Range verbal SAT	490-610
% Hispanic	1	nursing		Average verbal SAT	550
% international	1			Range math SAT	500-610
# of countries represented	14	**ADMISSIONS**		Average math SAT	547
		Admissions Rating	71	Range ACT	21-26
		# of applicants	799	Average ACT	24
				Minimum TOEFL	550
				Average HS GPA or Avg	3.5

Graduated top 10% of class	36
Graduated top 25% of class	66
Graduated top 50% of class	92
FINANCIAL FACTS	
Tuition	$10,850
Room & board	$3,580
Estimated book expense	$750
% frosh receiving aid	90
% undergrads receiving aid	80
% frosh w/ grant	45
Avg. grant	$2,635
% frosh w/ loan	53
Avg. loan	$2,760

BELMONT ABBEY COLLEGE

100 Belmont-Mt. Holly Rd., Belmont, NC 28012 • *Admissions: 704-825-6665* • *Fax: 704-825-6670*
• *Financial Aid: 800-523-2355* • *E-mail: admissions@bac.edu* • *Web Site: www.bac.edu*

Founded in 1876 by Benedictine Monks, Belmont Abbey is located on a 650-acre campus twelve miles from Charlotte. One of two Catholic colleges in North Carolina, the Abbey offers eighteen majors, mainly in the liberal arts and sciences, business, and education. Among the most popular programs are business administration, education, and biology. Nearly a sixth of the teaching faculty are members of the religious community of the Abbey, and reside in an on-campus monastery. Students are welcome to attend the monastic liturgies on campus, and Belmont Abbey's Christian Fellowship meets once a week. These meetings usually consist of music, guest speakers, or activities that promote discussion, and social time for chat. Extracurriculars include a full range of offerings both academic and social, but sports are perhaps the most popular pursuit. About 80 percent of all students are involved in intramural sports, evidence that Belmont Abbey is a community dedicated to building both body and soul.

ADMISSIONS

The admissions committee considers (in descending order of importance): HS record, test scores, class rank, recommendations, essay. *Also considered (in descending order of importance):* alumni relationship, extracurriculars, personality, special talents. Either the SAT or ACT is required; SAT is preferred. An interview is recommended. Admissions process is need-blind. *High school units required/recommended:* 16 total units are required; 4 English required, 3 math required, 2 science required, 2 foreign language required, 1 social studies required, 1 history required. Minimum combined SAT I score of 850, rank in top quarter of secondary school class, and minimum 2.3 GPA recommended.

FINANCIAL AID

Students should submit: FAFSA (due April 1), state aid form (due April 1), a copy of parents' most recent income tax filing (due April 1). The Princeton Review suggests that all financial aid forms be submitted as soon as possible after January 1. *The following grants/scholarships are offered:* Pell, SEOG, academic merit, athletic, the school's own scholarships, the school's own grants, state grants, private scholarships, private grants, ROTC. *Students borrow from the following loan programs:* Stafford, unsubsidized Stafford, Perkins, PLUS, the school's own loan fund, supplemental loans, federal nursing loans, health professions loans, private loans. College Work-Study Program is available. Institutional employment is available. The off-campus job outlook is good.

STUDENT BODY

Total undergrad enrollment	833
% male/female	48/52
% from out of state	39
% transfers	18
% live on campus	45
% African American	6
% Asian	2
% Caucasian	85
% Hispanic	2
% Native American	1
% international	4
# of countries represented	17

ACADEMICS

Calendar	semester
Student/teacher ratio	11:1
FT faculty	80
% faculty from religious order	12
% graduate in 4 yrs.	44

Most Popular Majors
business administration
education
biology

ADMISSIONS

Admissions Rating	65
# of applicants	777
% of applicants accepted	87
% of acceptees attending	33

Deadlines

Regular admission	8/1
Regular notification	rolling

FRESHMAN PROFILE

Average verbal SAT	492
Average math SAT	473
Minimum TOEFL	550
Average HS GPA or Avg	2.9
Graduated top 10% of class	13
Graduated top 25% of class	53
Graduated top 50% of class	70

FINANCIAL FACTS

Tuition	$9,920
Room & board	$5,346
Estimated book expense	$488
% frosh receiving aid	85
% undergrads receiving aid	81
% frosh w/ grant	51
Avg. grant	$2,800
% frosh w/ loan	70
Avg. loan	$2,625

BENEDICTINE COLLEGE

1020 North 2nd, Atchison, KS 66002 • Admissions: 913-367-5340 • Fax: 913-367-6102
• Financial Aid: 913-367-5340,-ext.-2484 • E-mail: mail@benedictine.edu • Web Site: www.benedictine.edu

Situated on a 200-acre campus forty-five miles from Kansas City, Benedictine College is the largest private college in Kansas. Founded in 1858 as an all-male institution, the College became coed in 1971 through a merger with Mount Saint Scholastica. Thus, both Benedictine Monks and Sisters are a presence on campus. The college offers nearly three dozen majors, ranging from the liberal arts and sciences to business, education, and computer and information sciences. Benedictine participates in the National Undergraduate Research Observatory Consortium, which affords students access to a thirty-one-inch telescope atop Anderson Mesa in Arizona. Activities available on campus run the gamut, ranging from standard offerings like a student newspaper, student government, and yearbook to groups focused on right-to-life and environmental issues. Arts groups, especially those involving music, are abundant. Benedictine's football squad has showcased their talents of late with a recent finish in the NAIA's Division II top twenty. On a more pastoral note, the Sisters offer a program called "Partners in Prayer" in which interested students are paired with a Sister and meet once a week for a meal and liturgy of the hours at the Mount St. Scholastica campus.

ADMISSIONS

The admissions committee considers (in descending order of importance): HS record, test scores, class rank, essay, recommendations. *Also considered (in descending order of importance):* personality, alumni relationship, extracurriculars, special talents. Either the SAT or ACT is required; ACT is preferred. An interview is recommended. Admissions process is need-blind. *High school units required/recommended:* 16 total units are required; 19 total units are recommended; 4 English required, 4 math recommended, 2 science required, 4 science recommended, 2 foreign language required, 4 foreign language recommended, 2 social studies required, 1 history required. Minimum composite ACT score of 18 (combined SAT I score of 840) and rank in top half of secondary school class or minimum 2.0 GPA required. *Special Requirements:* An audition is required for music program applicants.

FINANCIAL AID

Students should submit: FAFSA (due April 15), the school's own financial aid form, state aid form (due March 1), a copy of parents' most recent income tax filing (due April 15). The Princeton Review suggests that all financial aid forms be submitted as soon as possible after January 1. *The following grants/scholarships are offered:* state scholarships. *Students borrow from the following loan programs:* Stafford, PLUS. College Work-Study Program is available. Institutional employment is available. The off-campus job outlook is poor.

STUDENT BODY		ACADEMICS		ADMISSIONS		FINANCIAL FACTS	
Total undergrad enrollment	858	Calendar	semester	Admissions Rating	73	Tuition	$10,600
% male/female	56/44	Student/teacher ratio	12:1	% of acceptees attending	30	Room & board	$4,140
% from out of state	59	FT faculty	71			Estimated book expense	$1,500
% transfers	18	% faculty from religious order	40	**Deadlines**		% frosh receiving aid	93
% from catholic high school	40	% graduate in 4 yrs.	43	Regular admission	8/15	% undergrads receiving aid	93
% live on campus	70			Regular notification	rolling	% frosh w/ grant	86
% African American	2	**Most Popular Majors**				Avg. grant	NR
% Asian	1	business administration		**FRESHMAN PROFILE**		% frosh w/ loan	56
% Caucasian	93	education		Average ACT	22	Avg. loan	$3,941
% Hispanic	3	biology		Minimum TOEFL	500		
% Native American	1			Graduated top 10% of class	9		
% international	3			Graduated top 25% of class	36		
# of countries represented	8			Graduated top 50% of class	65		

BENEDICTINE UNIVERSITY

5700 College Rd., Lisle, IL 60532 • Admissions: 708-960-1500 • Fax: 708-960-1126
• Financial Aid: 630-829-6100 • E-mail: admit@eagle.ibc.edu • Web Site: www.ben.edu

Located twenty-five miles west of Chicago, Benedictine University, was founded by the Benedictine Monks of Saint Procopius Abbey in 1887. The University sits on a 108-acre campus in the heart of a research corridor that includes the Fermi Nuclear Accelerator Laboratories and Argonne National Laboratories. Benedictine offers over fifty majors. The University recently received a $600,000 grant from The Howard Hughes Medical Institute, to be used to strengthen the institution's undergraduate programs in the biological sciences. Selected on the basis of its record in preparing students for careers in the sciences, Benedictine was one of only fifty-two colleges and universities recognized nationwide. The campus ministry involves students, faculty, administrators, and staff members in activities designed to serve both the campus and the surrounding area. Activities outside the classroom are numerous, with a particularly abundant selection of multicultural groups. The opportunity to work with outstanding mentors extends to athletics too. In 1995, Benedictine coaches of four sports (swimming and diving, tennis, women's softball, and men's soccer) received "Coach of the Year" honors from their conference colleagues.

ADMISSIONS

The admissions committee considers (in descending order of importance): HS record, class rank, test scores, recommendations, essay. *Also considered (in descending order of importance):* special talents, extracurriculars, personality. Either the SAT or ACT is required; ACT is preferred. An interview is recommended. Admissions process is need-blind. *High school units required/recommended:* 16 total units are required; 4 English required, 2 math required, 1 science required, 2 foreign language required, 1 history required. Minimum composite ACT score of 21, rank in top half of secondary school class, and minimum 2.0 GPA required. *Special Requirements:* An audition is required for music program applicants. An RN is required for nursing program applicants. 3 units of mathematics (including advanced algebra/trigonometry) strongly recommended of accounting, business economics, computer science, economics, mathematics, and science program applicants. Additional science units recommended of science program applicants. Interview and essay required of Scholars Program applicants.

FINANCIAL AID

Students should submit: FAFSA (due May 1), the school's own financial aid form (due May 1), state aid form (due May 1), a copy of parents' most recent income tax filing (due May 1). The Princeton Review suggests that all financial aid forms be submitted as soon as possible after January 1. *The following grants/scholarships are offered:* state scholarships. *Students borrow from the following loan programs:* Stafford, PLUS. College Work-Study Program is available. Institutional employment is available. The off-campus job outlook is good.

STUDENT BODY
Total undergrad enrollment	1,741
% male/female	48/52
% from out of state	2
% transfers	50
% from catholic high school	48
% live on campus	36
% African American	6
% Asian	7
% Caucasian	79
% Hispanic	3
% Native American	1
% international	1

ACADEMICS
Calendar	semester
Student/teacher ratio	14:1
FT faculty	182
% faculty from religious order	5
% graduate in 4 yrs.	54

Most Popular Majors
biology
economics and business
psychology

ADMISSIONS
Admissions Rating	76
% of acceptees attending	48

Deadlines
Regular admission	rolling
Regular notification	rolling

FRESHMAN PROFILE
Average ACT	23
Minimum TOEFL	550
Graduated top 10% of class	18
Graduated top 25% of class	30
Graduated top 50% of class	71

FINANCIAL FACTS
Tuition	$11,640
Room & board	$4,618
Estimated book expense	$650

% frosh receiving aid	94
% undergrads receiving aid	95
% frosh w/ grant	90
Avg. grant	NR
% frosh w/ loan	62
Avg. loan	$1,987

BOSTON COLLEGE

Chestnut Hill, MA 02167 • Admissions: 617-552-3100 • Fax: 617-552-0798
• Financial Aid: 617-552-3320 • E-mail: undergraduate.admission@bc.edu • Web Site: www.bc.edu

Founded in 1863 to serve the sons of Boston's Irish immigrants, Boston College sits on a 200-acre campus just six miles from downtown Boston. The college is the fourth largest private university in New England, and has the largest full-time undergraduate enrollment of any Catholic university in the United States. Not that the college's stature ends with its student body—BC is also credited with having the largest active teaching community of Jesuits in the world. Bachelor's degrees are offered in fifty fields of study, and the college confers more than 3,500 degrees annually through its eleven schools and colleges. Life outside the classroom is also abuzz at BC. The college plans to break ground for a new student center this year. The Eagles, BC's athletic teams, are known for their competitiveness in football and basketball, and the college is a perennial NCAA Division I hockey powerhouse.

ADMISSIONS

The admissions committee considers (in descending order of importance): HS record, test scores, class rank, essay, recommendations. *Also considered (in descending order of importance):* personality, special talents, alumni relationship, extracurriculars, geographical distribution. Either the SAT or ACT is required. *High school units required/recommended:* 20 total units are recommended; 4 English recommended, 4 math recommended, 3 science recommended, 4 foreign language recommended, 2 social studies recommended. *Special Requirements:* TOEFL is required of all international students. 2 units of lab science including chemistry required of nursing program applicants. 4 units of college-preparatory math strongly recommended of School of Management applicants. *The admissions office says:* "Boston College seeks a student body with a diversity of talents, attitudes, backgrounds, and interests to produce a vital community atmosphere. As a Jesuit institution, Boston College also chooses responsible and concerned students who are interested in the ideals of commitment and service to others."

FINANCIAL AID

Students should submit: FAFSA, the school's own financial aid form, a copy of parents' most recent income tax filing. The Princeton Review suggests that all financial aid forms be submitted as soon as possible after January 1. *The following grants/scholarships are offered:* Pell, SEOG, academic merit, the school's own scholarships, the school's own grants, state scholarships, state grants, private scholarships, private grants. *Students borrow from the following loan programs:* Stafford, unsubsidized Stafford, Perkins, PLUS, the school's own loan fund, supplemental loans, private loans. Applicants will be notified of awards beginning April 1. College Work-Study Program is available. Institutional employment is available. The off-campus job outlook is good.

STUDENT BODY		ACADEMICS		Deadlines		FINANCIAL FACTS	
Total undergrad enrollment	8,958	Calendar	semester	Early decision/action	11/1	Tuition	$19,770
% male/female	47/53	Student/teacher ratio	15:1	Regular admission	1/15	Room & board	$7,770
% from out of state	71	FT faculty	957	Regular notification	4/15	Estimated book expense	$800
% transfers	2					% frosh receiving aid	59
% from catholic high school	29	**Most Popular Majors**		**FRESHMAN PROFILE**		% undergrads receiving aid	55
% live on campus	74	English		Range verbal SAT	580-670	% frosh w/ grant	39
% African American	4	finance		Range math SAT	600-690	Avg. grant	$11,468
% Asian	8	psychology		Minimum TOEFL	550		
% Caucasian	77	**ADMISSIONS**		Graduated top 10% of class	61		
% Hispanic	5	Admissions Rating	95	Graduated top 25% of class	93		
% international	3	# of applicants	16,501	Graduated top 50% of class	100		
# of countries represented	92	% of applicants accepted	41				
		% of acceptees attending	37				

CABRINI COLLEGE

610 King of Prussia Rd., Radnor, PA 19087 • Admissions: 610-902-8552 • Fax: 610-902-8309
• Financial Aid: 610-902-8420 • E-mail: admit@cabrini.edu • Web Site: www.cabrini.edu

Founded in 1957 by the Missionary Sisters of the Sacred Heart of Jesus, Cabrini College is located on a 112-acre campus eighteen miles from Philadelphia. The college is named for Francis Xavier Cabrini, the first American citizen to be proclaimed a saint. Nearly forty majors are offered, mainly in liberal arts and sciences, business, education, and health sciences. Popular programs include education, business, and communications. Co-ops (programs that combine outside work for pay with classroom study) and internships are available in most major programs. A very high percentage of Cabrini students go on to graduate school. Special facilities include a preschool on campus and a 30-acre preserve used for environmental studies. In addition to all the typical clubs and organizations that one can find on campus, students have the opportunity to participate in such social action groups as Prison Literacy, Outreach to the Homeless, and Respect Life. Cabrini's athletic teams participate in the Mid-Atlantic Conference of the NCAA's Division III, and the women's basketball team is particularly strong, finishing with a top-ten ranking last year.

ADMISSIONS

The admissions committee considers (in descending order of importance): HS record, test scores, essay, class rank, recommendations. *Also considered (in descending order of importance):* personality, alumni relationship, extracurriculars, special talents. Either the SAT or ACT is required; SAT is preferred. An interview is recommended. Admissions process is need-blind. *High school units required/recommended:* 17 total units are required; 4 English required, 3 math required, 3 science required, 2 foreign language required, 3 social studies required. Minimum combined SAT I score of 900, rank in top half of secondary school class, and minimum 2.5 GPA recommended.

FINANCIAL AID

Students should submit: FAFSA, the school's own financial aid form, a copy of parents' most recent income tax filing. The Princeton Review suggests that all financial aid forms be submitted as soon as possible after January 1. *The following grants/scholarships are offered:* Pell, SEOG, academic merit, athletic, the school's own scholarships, the school's own grants, state scholarships, state grants, private scholarships, private grants, ROTC. *Students borrow from the following loan programs:* Stafford, unsubsidized Stafford, Perkins, PLUS, the school's own loan fund, supplemental loans, private loans. College Work-Study Program is available. Institutional employment is available. The off-campus job outlook is excellent.

STUDENT BODY		ACADEMICS			% of applicants accepted	88	Graduated top 10% of class	8
Total undergrad enrollment	1,719	Calendar	semester		% of acceptees attending	37	Graduated top 25% of class	28
% male/female	32/68	Student/teacher ratio	12:1				Graduated top 50% of class	69
% from out of state	23	FT faculty	178		**Deadlines**			
% transfers	39	% faculty from religious order	0		Regular admission	rolling	**FINANCIAL FACTS**	
% from catholic high school	52	% graduate in 4 yrs.	57		Regular notification	rolling	Tuition	$11,660
% live on campus	54						Room & board	$6,700
% African American	4	**Most Popular Majors**			**FRESHMAN PROFILE**		Estimated book expense	$600
% Asian	1	education			Range verbal SAT	440-550	% frosh receiving aid	80
% Caucasian	93	business			Average verbal SAT	471	% undergrads receiving aid	77
% Hispanic	1	communications			Range math SAT	10-520		
% international	1	**ADMISSIONS**			Average math SAT	453		
# of countries represented	36	Admissions Rating	63		Minimum TOEFL	550		
		# of applicants	748		Average HS GPA or Avg	2.9		

CALDWELL COLLEGE

9 Ryerson Ave, Caldwell, NJ 07006 • Admissions: 201-228-4424 • Fax: 201-228-2897
• Financial Aid: 201-228-4424 • E-mail: caldadmit@adl.com • Web Site: www.njin.net/~rosmaita

Founded in 1939 by the Sisters of Saint Dominic, Caldwell College became coed in 1985. The college, located twenty miles from New York City on a 100-acre campus in northern New Jersey, is one of the youngest Dominican colleges and universities in the world. Twenty-eight majors are offered at the college, mostly within the liberal arts and sciences but also including programs in business, criminal justice, and education. Among the most popular academic disciplines are business administration, psychology, and education. A very high percentage of Caldwell's students go on to graduate school. Perhaps in an effort to build upon this impressive record, the college will dedicate a new $3.5 million academic building this year. Other facilities of note include an art gallery, a theater, and a television studio. Since most students who attend the college commute, there's little pressure for housing. As a result, on-campus housing is guaranteed to all who seek it. In addition to the usual extracurricular offerings found at most colleges, students at Caldwell produce their own foreign language newspaper.

ADMISSIONS

The admissions committee considers (in descending order of importance): class rank, test scores, HS record, recommendations. *Also considered (in descending order of importance):* alumni relationship, extracurriculars, personality, special talents. Either the SAT or ACT is required; SAT is preferred. An interview is recommended. Admissions process is need-blind. *High school units required/recommended:* 16 total units are required; 4 English required, 2 math required, 2 science required, 2 foreign language required, 1 history required. Minimum combined SAT I score of 900 and rank in top half of secondary school class recommended. *Special Requirements:* A portfolio is required for art program applicants. An audition is required for music program applicants. An RN is required for nursing program applicants.

FINANCIAL AID

Students should submit: FAFSA (due April 1), the school's own financial aid form state aid form, a copy of parents' most recent income tax filing. The Princeton Review suggests that all financial aid forms be submitted as soon as possible after January 1. *The following grants/scholarships are offered:* state scholarships. *Students borrow from the following loan programs:* Stafford, PLUS. College Work-Study Program is available. Institutional employment is available. The off-campus job outlook is excellent.

STUDENT BODY

Total undergrad enrollment	1,646
% male/female	38/62
% from out of state	4
% transfers	26
% from catholic high school	60
% live on campus	34
% African American	11
% Asian	2
% Caucasian	64
% Hispanic	6
# of countries represented	16

ACADEMICS

Calendar	semester
Student/teacher ratio	15:1
FT faculty	113
% faculty from religious order	22
% graduate in 4 yrs.	48

Most Popular Majors
business administration
psychology
education

ADMISSIONS

Admissions Rating	70
# of applicants	1,111
% of applicants accepted	67
% of acceptees attending	27

Deadlines

Regular admission	rolling
Regular notification	rolling

FRESHMAN PROFILE

Range verbal SAT	420-520
Average verbal SAT	415
Range math SAT	440-530
Average math SAT	490
Average HS GPA or Avg	2.5
Graduated top 10% of class	9
Graduated top 25% of class	21
Graduated top 50% of class	50

FINANCIAL FACTS

Tuition	$10,050
Room & board	$5,100
Estimated book expense	$478
% frosh receiving aid	69
% undergrads receiving aid	72
% frosh w/ grant	35
Avg. grant	NR
% frosh w/ loan	57
Avg. loan	$2,425

CALUMET COLLEGE OF SAINT JOSEPH

2400 New York Ave, Whiting, IN 46394 • *Admissions: 219-473-4215* • *Fax: 219-473-4279*
• *Financial Aid: 219-473-4215*

Calumet College of Saint Joseph was founded in 1951 by the Fathers of the Society of the Precious Blood. The college, on a 256-acre campus in northwest Indiana, is just twenty miles from downtown Chicago. Nearly half of the students at Calumet are minorities, one of the largest percentages of minority students of any private college in Indiana. All students are commuters, and most attend college part time. To accommodate the needs of its students, Calumet offers many classes in the early morning, evening hours, and on Saturdays. Twenty-one majors are available in a variety of disciplines, mainly within the liberal arts and sciences, business, and education. Career-oriented programs in paralegal studies, management, and criminal justice are among the most popular choices. Noteworthy facilities include an art gallery, a wetlands area for environmental studies, and an on-campus preschool.

ADMISSIONS

The admissions committee considers (in descending order of importance): HS record, class rank, essay, test scores, recommendations. *Also considered (in descending order of importance):* personality, extracurriculars, special talents. An interview is recommended. *High school units required/recommended:* 15 total units are recommended; 4 English recommended, 3 math recommended, 2 science recommended, 1 foreign language recommended, 2 social studies recommended, 1 history recommended. Rank in top half of secondary school class and minimum 2.0 GPA required. *Special Requirements:* TOEFL is required of all international students.

FINANCIAL AID

Students should submit: FAFSA (due March 1), the school's own financial aid form (due March 1), state aid form (due March 1), a copy of parents' most recent income tax filing. The Princeton Review suggests that all financial aid forms be submitted as soon as possible after January 1. *The following grants/scholarships are offered:* state scholarships. *Students borrow from the following loan programs:* Stafford, PLUS. College Work-Study Program is available. Institutional employment is available. The off-campus job outlook is fair.

STUDENT BODY

Total undergrad enrollment	1,125
% male/female	31/69
% from out of state	15
% transfers	75
% African American	19
% Asian	1
% Caucasian	60
% Hispanic	15
% Native American	1
# of countries represented	3

ACADEMICS

Calendar	semester
Student/teacher ratio	10:1
FT faculty	110
% faculty from religious order	6

Most Popular Majors
paralegal
management
criminal justice

ADMISSIONS

Admissions Rating	64

Deadlines

Regular admission	rolling
Regular notification	rolling

FRESHMAN PROFILE

Minimum TOEFL	550
Graduated top 10% of class	13
Graduated top 25% of class	24
Graduated top 50% of class	59

FINANCIAL FACTS

Tuition	$5,460
Estimated book expense	$250
% frosh receiving aid	58
% undergrads receiving aid	67

CANISIUS COLLEGE

2001 Main Street, Buffalo, NY 14208 • Admissions: 716-888-2200 • Fax: 716-888-2525
• Financial Aid: 716-888-2300 • E-mail: inquiry@gort.canisius.edu • Web Site: www.canisius.edu

Canisius, greater Buffalo's largest private college, was founded by a group of European Jesuits in 1870. Named after Saint Peter Canisius, a sixteenth century Dutch scholar, the college is located on a 25-acre campus. Canisius enjoys a special relationship with the city of Buffalo, best evidenced by the large number of its graduates who have occupied important positions in the professional, educational, commercial, and political life of the city and its surrounding communities. The college offers forty-seven majors, focused mainly within the liberal arts and sciences, business, education, and a variety of career-oriented areas. The most popular major choices are accounting, psychology, and management. More interesting options include art history, criticism, and conservation, athletic training and sports medicine, hotel and restaurant management, and urban studies. There's more than variety to the college's academic offerings—there's strength too. Canisius has produced eight Fulbright Fellowship winners during the past eight years. Extracurricular options are both broad and deep, covering an impressively full range of interests. Facilities of note include a planetarium and new townhouse residences. In order to mitigate against the harsh upstate New York winters, the college uses an underground tunnel network to connect campus buildings.

ADMISSIONS

The admissions committee considers (in descending order of importance): HS record, class rank, test scores, recommendations, essay. *Also considered (in descending order of importance):* extracurriculars, special talents, alumni relationship, personality. Either the SAT or ACT is required; SAT is preferred. An interview is recommended. Admissions process is need-blind. *High school units required/recommended:* 16 total units are required; 4 English required, 3 math required, 1 science required, 2 foreign language required, 2 social studies required. Minimum combined SAT I score of 950, rank in top half of secondary school class, and minimum grade average of 80 recommended.

FINANCIAL AID

Students should submit: FAFSA (due February 1), the school's own financial aid form, state aid form (due May 1), a copy of parents' most recent income tax filing (due June 15). The Princeton Review suggests that all financial aid forms be submitted as soon as possible after January 1. *The following grants/scholarships are offered:* state scholarships, United Negro College Fund. *Students borrow from the following loan programs:* Stafford, PLUS. Applicants will be notified of awards beginning April 1. College Work-Study Program is available. Institutional employment is available. The off-campus job outlook is good.

STUDENT BODY		ACADEMICS		FRESHMAN PROFILE		FINANCIAL FACTS	
Total undergrad enrollment	3,275	Calendar	semester	% of acceptees attending	34	Graduated top 25% of class	44
% male/female	54/46	Student/teacher ratio	12:1	**Deadlines**		Graduated top 50% of class	72
% from out of state	6	FT faculty	383	Regular admission	rolling		
% transfers	27	% faculty from religious order	7	Regular notification	rolling	**FINANCIAL FACTS**	
% from catholic high school	25	% graduate in 4 yrs.	57	**FRESHMAN PROFILE**		Tuition	$12,600
% live on campus	30	**Most Popular Majors**		Range verbal SAT	490-570	Room & board	$5,825
% African American	4	accounting		Average verbal SAT	537	Estimated book expense	$400
% Asian	1	psychology		Range math SAT	480-580	% frosh receiving aid	87
% Caucasian	90	management		Average math SAT	546	% undergrads receiving aid	80
% Hispanic	2	**ADMISSIONS**		Range ACT	19-21	% frosh w/ grant	80
% international	3	Admissions Rating	71	Average ACT	24	Avg. grant	NR
# of countries represented	45	# of applicants	2,424	Minimum TOEFL	500	% frosh w/ loan	76
		% of applicants accepted	84	Average HS GPA or Avg	3.3	Avg. loan	$3,147
				Graduated top 10% of class	19		

CARDINAL STRITCH COLLEGE

6801 North Yates Road, Milwaukee, WI 53217 • Admissions: 414-351-7504 • Fax: 414-351-7516
• Financial Aid: 414-352-5400 • E-mail: admityou@asc.stritch.edu • Web Site: www.stritch.edu

Cardinal Stritch College was founded as Saint Clare College in 1937 by the Sisters of Saint Francis. In 1946 the name was changed in honor of the former archbishop of Milwaukee, Samuel Cardinal Stritch, and the college became coed. Cardinal Stritch, the largest Franciscan college in North America, sits on a 40-acre campus fifteen minutes from Milwaukee. The college offers thirty majors within the areas of liberal arts and sciences, business, education, and nursing; the latter three comprise the most popular areas of study. The majority of students at Cardinal Stritch are commuters; fewer than 15 percent live in campus housing. Still, the college seems to provide a lively social center for its students—a wide range of clubs, organizations, and athletic teams are available. Cardinal Stritch offers a variety of scholarships, based on such considerations as choice of major, academic achievement, artistic talents, athletic ability, and minority status.

ADMISSIONS

The admissions committee considers (in descending order of importance): HS record, test scores, class rank, recommendations, essay. *Also considered (in descending order of importance):* extracurriculars, special talents, alumni relationship, personality. Either the SAT or ACT is required; ACT is preferred. An interview is recommended. *High school units required/recommended:* 18 total units are required; 4 English required, 2 math required, 2 science required, 2 foreign language required, 2 social studies required, 1 history required. Minimum composite ACT score of 20, rank in top half of secondary school class, and minimum 2.0 GPA required. *Special Requirements:* TOEFL is required of all international students.

FINANCIAL AID

Students should submit: FAFSA, the school's own financial aid form. The Princeton Review suggests that all financial aid forms be submitted as soon as possible after January 1. *The following grants/scholarships are offered:* Pell, SEOG, academic merit, athletic, the school's own scholarships, the school's own grants, state scholarships, state grants, private scholarships, private grants, ROTC. *Students borrow from the following loan programs:* Stafford, unsubsidized Stafford, Perkins, PLUS, the school's own loan fund, supplemental loans, state loans, federal nursing loans, private loans. College Work-Study Program is available. Institutional employment is available. The off-campus job outlook is excellent.

STUDENT BODY		ACADEMICS		Deadlines		FINANCIAL FACTS	
Total undergrad enrollment	2,764	Calendar	semester	Regular admission	8/20	Tuition	$8,960
% male/female	38/62	Student/teacher ratio	8:1	Regular notification	rolling	Room & board	$3,880
% from out of state	20	FT faculty	665			Estimated book expense	$500
% transfers	42	% faculty from religious order	5	**FRESHMAN PROFILE**		% frosh receiving aid	80
% from catholic high school	10			Average ACT	22	% undergrads receiving aid	80
% live on campus	10	**Most Popular Majors**		Minimum TOEFL	550		
% African American	8	business		Average HS GPA or Avg	2.8		
% Asian	2	education		Graduated top 10% of class	10		
% Caucasian	80	nursing		Graduated top 25% of class	32		
% Hispanic	3	**ADMISSIONS**		Graduated top 50% of class	55		
% Native American	1	Admissions Rating	71				
% international	1	# of applicants	378				
		% of applicants accepted	78				
		% of acceptees attending	56				

CARLOW COLLEGE

3333 Fifth Avenue, Pittsburgh, PA 15213 • *Admissions: 412-578-6059* • *Fax: 412-578-8710*
• *Financial Aid: 412-578-6058* • *Web Site: www.carlow.edu*

Carlow College was founded in 1929 by the Sisters of Mercy, and takes its name from the Irish town where the Order began. The college's 13-acre campus is three miles from downtown Pittsburgh. Carlow is primarily a women's college, admitting men to its nursing program and evening division only. Residential dorms are for women only, but housing is limited in general as Carlow is essentially a commuter school. The college offers twenty-eight majors within the liberal arts and sciences, business, education, and health sciences. Most popular programs include nursing, biology, and business management. Education majors take note: The college has a preschool and elementary school on campus, providing a built-in laboratory for student-teaching experience.

ADMISSIONS

The admissions committee considers (in descending order of importance): HS record, class rank, test scores, essay, recommendations. *Also considered (in descending order of importance):* personality, alumni relationship, extracurriculars, special talents. Either the SAT or ACT is required; SAT is preferred. An interview is recommended. *High school units required/recommended:* 18 total units are required; 4 English required, 3 math required, 3 science required. Rank in top two-fifths of secondary school class and minimum 3.0 GPA required. *Special Requirements:* A portfolio is required for art program applicants. 3 units of social studies, 2 units of lab science, and 2 units of math (1 unit must be algebra) required of nursing program applicants.

FINANCIAL AID

Students should submit: FAFSA (due May 1), the school's own financial aid form (due May 1), state aid form (due May 1), a copy of parents' most recent income tax filing (due May 1). The Princeton Review suggests that all financial aid forms be submitted as soon as possible after January 1. *Students borrow from the following loan programs:* Stafford, PLUS. Applicants will be notified of awards beginning February 15. College Work-Study Program is available. The off-campus job outlook is excellent.

STUDENT BODY		ACADEMICS		ADMISSIONS		FINANCIAL FACTS	
Total undergrad enrollment	2,085	Calendar	semester	Admissions Rating	68	Tuition	$10,730
% male/female	8/92	Student/teacher ratio	10:1	# of applicants	439	Room & board	$4,692
% from out of state	4	FT faculty	229	% of applicants accepted	79	Estimated book expense	$500
% transfers	61	% faculty from religious order	4	% of acceptees attending	43	% frosh receiving aid	94
% from catholic high school	11	% graduate in 4 yrs.	51			% undergrads receiving aid	88
% live on campus	15			**Deadlines**			
% African American	10	**Most Popular Majors**		Regular admission	rolling		
% Asian	1	nursing		Regular notification	rolling		
% Caucasian	65	biology		**FRESHMAN PROFILE**			
% Hispanic	1	business management		Minimum TOEFL	500		
% Native American	1						
% international	1						
# of countries represented	27						

CARROLL COLLEGE (MT)

N. Benton Ave, Helena, MT 59625 • Admissions: 406-447-4384 • Fax: 406-447-4533
• Financial Aid: 406-447-5425 • E-mail: enroll@carroll.edu • Web Site: www.carroll.edu

Carroll College was founded in 1909 by the Diocese of Helena, and became coed in 1944. The college is located on a 63-acre campus just inside the city limits. Carroll's motto, Non Scholae Sed Vitae (Not For School But For Life), articulates the college's commitment to the continuing development of the intellectual, spiritual, and professional facets of each student. Thirty-three majors are available, mainly within the traditional Catholic college disciplines of the liberal arts and sciences, business, education, and the health professions. Popular majors include biology, nursing, and business administration. Special facilities and equipment include an observatory and a seismograph station. Freshmen and sophomores are required to live on campus. Thankfully, extracurricular activities are abundant, especially those related to music, and Carroll's athletic teams have garnered much recognition of late. Last year the swimming Saints celebrated their eleventh consecutive Frontier Conference championship, and the football team finished fourth within the conference.

ADMISSIONS

The admissions committee considers (in descending order of importance): HS record, test scores, recommendations, class rank, essay. *Also considered (in descending order of importance):* alumni relationship, extracurriculars, personality, special talents. Either the SAT or ACT is required. An interview is recommended. Admissions process is need-blind. *High school units required/recommended:* 4 English recommended, 3 math recommended, 2 science recommended, 2 foreign language recommended, 2 social studies recommended, 2 history recommended. Minimum composite ACT score of 21 (combined SAT I score of 1000) and minimum 2.5 GPA recommended.

FINANCIAL AID

Students should submit: FAFSA (due March 1). The Princeton Review suggests that all financial aid forms be submitted as soon as possible after January 1. *The following grants/scholarships are offered:* Pell, SEOG, academic merit, athletic, the school's own scholarships, the school's own grants, state grants, private scholarships, private grants, ROTC, foreign aid. *Students borrow from the following loan programs:* Stafford, unsubsidized Stafford, Perkins, PLUS, the school's own loan fund, supplemental loans, private loans. College Work-Study Program is available. Institutional employment is available. The off-campus job outlook is good.

STUDENT BODY	
Total undergrad enrollment	1,352
% male/female	37/63
% from out of state	32
% transfers	15
% from catholic high school	30
% live on campus	44
% African American	1
% Asian	4
% Caucasian	91
% Hispanic	1
% Native American	2
% international	6
# of countries represented	14

ACADEMICS	
Calendar	semester
Student/teacher ratio	11:1
FT faculty	125
% faculty from religious order	12
% graduate in 4 yrs.	48

Most Popular Majors
biology
nursing
business administration

ADMISSIONS	
Admissions Rating	72
# of applicants	640

% of applicants accepted	94
% of acceptees attending	47

Deadlines	
Regular admission	6/1
Regular notification	rolling

FRESHMAN PROFILE	
Range verbal SAT	490-610
Average verbal SAT	540
Range math SAT	470-600
Average math SAT	540
Range ACT	21-26
Average ACT	23
Minimum TOEFL	525
Average HS GPA or Avg	3.4

Graduated top 10% of class	28
Graduated top 25% of class	57
Graduated top 50% of class	86

FINANCIAL FACTS	
Tuition	$9,789
Room & board	$3,915
Estimated book expense	$390
% frosh receiving aid	80
% undergrads receiving aid	80
% frosh w/ loan	62
Avg. loan	$3,400

THE CATHOLIC UNIVERSITY OF AMERICA

Cardinal Station, Washington, D.C. 20064 • Admissions: 202-319-5305 • Fax: 202-319-6533
• Financial Aid: 202-319-5307 • E-mail: cua-admissions@cua.edu • Web Site: www.cua.edu

The Catholic University of America is the national university of the Catholic Church, and the only U.S. university with a papal charter. CUA was founded 1884 by the bishops of the United States with the endorsement of Pope Leo XIII, and became coed in 1925. The university is located on a 155-acre campus in the northeast section of the city, and consists of ten schools. Six of them—the schools of Architecture and Planning, Arts and Science, Music, Engineering, Nursing, and Philosophy—offer undergraduate degrees. Fifty-five majors are available; most popular are architecture, nursing, and politics. Drama is also quite strong; CUA's Hartke Theatre is one of the finest regional theaters in the country. Many fine facilities can be found on the campus, including anthropology and art museums, a nuclear reactor, and vitreous-state laboratories. The Shrine of the Immaculate Conception, the eighth largest cathedral in the world, is contiguous to the campus. Through its archdiocesan scholarship program CUA awards more than twenty four-year, full-tuition scholarships to entering freshmen each year.

ADMISSIONS

The admissions committee considers (in descending order of importance): HS record, class rank, recommendations, essay, test scores. *Also considered (in descending order of importance):* extracurriculars, personality, special talents, alumni relationship, geographical distribution. Either the SAT or ACT is required. Admissions process is need-blind. *High school units required/recommended:* 17 total units are required; 21 total units are recommended; 4 English required, 3 math required, 4 math recommended, 3 science required, 4 science recommended, 2 foreign language required, 4 foreign language recommended, 4 social studies required. *Special Requirements:* An audition is required for music program applicants. Biology, chemistry, language, math, and social science required of nursing program applicants. *The admissions office says:* "We are looking for a well-rounded student [who demonstrates a] balance of academics, activities, and community service." CUA also notes that "students are evaluated on the basis of the whole application package."

FINANCIAL AID

Students should submit: FAFSA (due February 28), CSS Profile (due January 15), the school's own financial aid form (due February 28), state aid form (due February 28), a copy of parents' most recent income tax filing (due February 28). The Princeton Review suggests that all financial aid forms be submitted as soon as possible after January 1. *The following grants/scholarships are offered:* state scholarships. *Students borrow from the following loan programs:* Stafford, PLUS. Applicants will be notified of awards beginning April 1. College Work-Study Program is available. Institutional employment is available. The off-campus job outlook is excellent.

STUDENT BODY

Total undergrad enrollment	2,364
% male/female	45/55
% from out of state	95
% transfers	27
% from catholic high school	52
% live on campus	57
% African American	7
% Asian	3
% Caucasian	85
% Hispanic	5
# of countries represented	103

ACADEMICS

Calendar	semester
Student/teacher ratio	9:1
FT faculty	666
% faculty from religious order	4
% graduate in 4 yrs.	76

Most Popular Majors
architecture
nursing
politics

ADMISSIONS

Admissions Rating	85
% of acceptees attending	37

Deadlines

Early decision/action	11/15
Regular admission	2/15
Regular notification	4/1

FRESHMAN PROFILE

Range verbal SAT	550-650
Range math SAT	530-630
Range ACT	23-28
Minimum TOEFL	500
Graduated top 10% of class	25
Graduated top 25% of class	54
Graduated top 50% of class	89

FINANCIAL FACTS

Tuition	$15,562
Room & board	$6,844
Estimated book expense	$480
% frosh receiving aid	77
% undergrads receiving aid	61
% frosh w/ grant	54
Avg. grant	NR
% frosh w/ loan	47
Avg. loan	$972

CHAMINADE UNIVERSITY OF HONOLULU

3140 Waialae Ave., Honolulu, HI 96816 • Admissions: 808-735-4735 • Fax: 808-739-4647
• Financial Aid: 808-735-4780 • Web Site: www.chaminade.edu

Marianist priests and brothers founded Chaminade University in 1955. The university's 53-acre campus is located on the island of Oahu, thirty-five miles from Honolulu. Though primarily a commuter school, Chaminade has four residence halls on campus. Its students represent thirty-five states and thirty-three foreign countries. Academic offerings cover more than twenty-three areas of concentration, focusing in the liberal arts and sciences, business, and education. Popular programs include management, criminal justice, and business administration. The campus boasts a natural history museum and its own planetarium. Unique among the standard extracurricular activities, clubs, and sports available at Chaminade is a men's water polo team.

ADMISSIONS

The admissions committee considers (in descending order of importance): HS record, test scores, essay, recommendations, class rank. *Also considered (in descending order of importance):* extracurriculars, personality, alumni relationship, special talents. Either the SAT or ACT is required. An interview is recommended. *High school units required/recommended:* 16 total units are required; 4 English required, 4 math required, 1 science required, 2 foreign language required, 3 social studies required. Minimum combined SAT I score of 800 (composite ACT score of 19) and minimum 2.0 GPA recommended. *Special Requirements:* TOEFL is required of all international students.

FINANCIAL AID

Students should submit: FAFSA, the school's own financial aid form, state aid form, a copy of parents' most recent income tax filing. The Princeton Review suggests that all financial aid forms be submitted as soon as possible after January 1. *The following grants/scholarships are offered:* Pell, SEOG, academic merit, the school's own scholarships, the school's own grants, state scholarships, state grants, private scholarships, private grants. *Students borrow from the following loan programs:* Stafford, unsubsidized Stafford, Perkins, PLUS, the school's own loan fund, supplemental loans, private loans. Applicants will be notified of awards beginning March 15. College Work-Study Program is available. Institutional employment is available. The off-campus job outlook is fair.

STUDENT BODY		ACADEMICS		ADMISSIONS		FINANCIAL FACTS	
Total undergrad enrollment	1,920	Calendar	semester	Admissions Rating	61	Tuition	$10,600
% male/female	46/54	Student/teacher ratio	14:1	# of applicants	392	Room & board	$5,130
% from out of state	35	FT faculty	160	% of applicants accepted	84	Estimated book expense	$600
% transfers	37	% faculty from religious order	1	% of acceptees attending	19	% undergrads receiving aid	55
% from catholic high school	20	**Most Popular Majors**		**Deadlines**			
% live on campus	25	management		Regular admission	rolling		
% African American	10	criminal justice		Regular notification	rolling		
% Asian	33	business administration					
% Caucasian	53			**FRESHMAN PROFILE**			
% Hispanic	3			Average ACT	21		
% Native American	1			Minimum TOEFL	450		
# of countries represented	33			Average HS GPA or Avg	3.1		

CHESTNUT HILL COLLEGE

9601 Germantown Ave., Philadelphia, PA 19118 • Admissions: 215-248-7001 • Fax: 215-248-7155
• Financial Aid: 215-248-7101

Founded in 1924 by the Sisters of Saint Joseph, Chestnut Hill College began with an enrollment of fifteen women, guided by the conviction that "on the education of women largely depends the future of society." The college's 45-acre campus is fifteen miles from downtown Philadelphia. In its early years, the college offered courses in cookery and millinery; today twenty-nine majors are available from among the liberal arts and sciences, business, and education, including new programs in environmental science, communications and technology, and fine arts and technology. Popular academic choices include biology, elementary education, and psychology. Facilities of note are an observatory, a planetarium, and a nationally recognized Irish literature collection. Campus clubs and organizations cover all the usual bases; most interesting is a foreign-language newspaper. Foreign languages can run to the truly foreign here; the founder of the Klingon Language Institute (not affiliated with the college) is a Chestnut Hill faculty member who also uses Klingon in a linguistics course he teaches at the college.

ADMISSIONS

The admissions committee considers (in descending order of importance): HS record, class rank, test scores, essay, recommendations. *Also considered (in descending order of importance):* personality, alumni relationship, extracurriculars, special talents. Either the SAT or ACT is required. An interview is recommended. *High school units required/recommended:* 16 total units are required; 4 English required, 3 math required, 4 math recommended, 3 science required, 4 science recommended, 2 foreign language required, 3 foreign language recommended, 4 social studies required. Minimum combined SAT I score of 950, rank in top two-fifths of secondary school class, and minimum 3.0 GPA recommended. *Special Requirements:* An audition is required for music program applicants. Portfolio recommended of studio art program applicants.

FINANCIAL AID

Students should submit: FAFSA (due March 15), the school's own financial aid form (due March 15), state aid form, a copy of parents' most recent income tax filing (due March 15). The Princeton Review suggests that all financial aid forms be submitted as soon as possible after January 1. *The following grants/scholarships are offered:* Pell, SEOG, academic merit, the school's own scholarships, the school's own grants, state grants, private scholarships, private grants, foreign aid. *Students borrow from the following loan programs:* Stafford, unsubsidized Stafford, Perkins, PLUS, the school's own loan fund, supplemental loans, private loans. College Work-Study Program is available. Institutional employment is available. The off-campus job outlook is excellent.

STUDENT BODY		ACADEMICS		Deadlines		FINANCIAL FACTS	
Total undergrad enrollment	728	Calendar	semester	Regular admission	rolling	Tuition	$13,000
% male/female	0/100	Student/teacher ratio	10:1	Regular notification	rolling	Room & board	$5,772
% from out of state	23	FT faculty	118			Estimated book expense	$700
% transfers	9	% faculty from religious order	38	**FRESHMAN PROFILE**		% frosh receiving aid	66
% from catholic high school	40	% graduate in 4 yrs.	62	Average verbal SAT	481	% undergrads receiving aid	65
% live on campus	67			Average math SAT	487	% frosh w/ grant	79
% African American	10	**Most Popular Majors**		Minimum TOEFL	550	Avg. grant	$5,273
% Asian	3	biology		Graduated top 10% of class	20	% frosh w/ loan	75
% Caucasian	80	elementary education		Graduated top 25% of class	58	Avg. loan	$2,625
% Hispanic	7	psychology		Graduated top 50% of class	84		
% international	4	**ADMISSIONS**					
# of countries represented	12	Admissions Rating	71				
		% of acceptees attending	54				

CHRISTIAN BROTHERS UNIVERSITY

650 E. Parkway South, Memphis, TN 38104 • *Admissions: 901-321-3200* • *Fax: 901-321-3202*
• *Financial Aid: 901-722-0305* • *E-mail: admissions@bucs.cbu.edu*

Christian Brothers University was founded in 1871 by its namesake Order. The university functioned as a combined elementary school, high school, and college until 1915, granting high school diplomas as well as bachelor's and master's degrees. Christian Brothers is located on a 70-acre campus in a residential area of Memphis. Students of over twenty-five different faiths are enrolled at CBU; only about a third of the university's student body are Catholic. Twenty-five majors are offered by the university in four schools: Liberal Arts, Sciences, Business, and Engineering. Most popular programs include accounting, management, and electrical engineering. The M.K. Gandhi Center for the Study of Peace and Nonviolence, founded by Gandhi's grandson, is based on the CBU campus.

ADMISSIONS

The admissions committee considers (in descending order of importance): test scores, HS record, class rank, essay, recommendations. *Also considered (in descending order of importance):* personality, extracurriculars, geographical distribution, alumni relationship, special talents. Either the SAT or ACT is required. An interview is recommended. Admissions process is need-blind. *High school units required/recommended:* 4 English recommended, 3 math recommended, 3 science recommended. Minimum composite ACT score of 20 (combined SAT I score of 930) and minimum 2.25 GPA required.

FINANCIAL AID

Students should submit: FAFSA (due March 1). The Princeton Review suggests that all financial aid forms be submitted as soon as possible after January 1. *The following grants/scholarships are offered:* Pell, SEOG, academic merit, athletic, the school's own scholarships, the school's own grants, state scholarships, state grants, private scholarships, private grants, ROTC. *Students borrow from the following loan programs:* Stafford, unsubsidized Stafford, Perkins, PLUS, the school's own loan fund, supplemental loans, health professions loans, private loans. College Work-Study Program is available. Institutional employment is available. The off-campus job outlook is excellent.

STUDENT BODY

Total undergrad enrollment	1,454
% male/female	50/50
% from out of state	30
% transfers	12
% from catholic high school	38
% live on campus	35
% African American	16
% Asian	2
% Caucasian	75
% Hispanic	1
% international	5
# of countries represented	19

ACADEMICS

Calendar	semester
Student/teacher ratio	11:1
FT faculty	162
% faculty from religious order	12
% graduate in 4 yrs.	50

Most Popular Majors
accounting
management
electrical engineering

ADMISSIONS

Admissions Rating	79
# of applicants	894
% of applicants accepted	84
% of acceptees attending	44

Deadlines

Regular admission	rolling
Regular notification	rolling

FRESHMAN PROFILE

Range verbal SAT	440-590
Average verbal SAT	560
Range math SAT	500-590
Average math SAT	570
Range ACT	20-26
Average ACT	24
Minimum TOEFL	500
Graduated top 10% of class	49
Graduated top 25% of class	66
Graduated top 50% of class	89

FINANCIAL FACTS

Tuition	$10,700
Room & board	$3,650
Estimated book expense	$800
% frosh receiving aid	79
% undergrads receiving aid	71
% frosh w/ grant	70
Avg. grant	$4,000
% frosh w/ loan	96
Avg. loan	$3,225

CLARKE COLLEGE

*1550 Clarke Drive, Dubuque, IA 52001 • Admissions: 319-588-6300 • Fax: 319-588-6789
• Financial Aid: 319-588-6327 • E-mail: admissions@keller.clarke.edu • Web Site: www.clarke.edu*

Clarke College, the first women's college in Iowa, was established in 1843 by Mary Frances Clarke, founder of the Sisters of Charity of the Blessed Virgin Mary. The college, which became coed in 1979, is on a 60-acre campus in the heart of Dubuque. Students under the age of twenty-three are required to live on campus. Fifty-five majors are offered within the liberal arts and sciences, business, education, and health sciences. Popular majors include physical therapy, nursing, and business. Special features among Clarke campus facilities are a planetarium and an art gallery. A wide range of campus clubs, activities, and intercollegiate sports are available; most noteworthy among them is an alpine ski team.

ADMISSIONS

The admissions committee considers (in descending order of importance): HS record, test scores, essay, recommendations, class rank. Either the SAT or ACT is required; ACT is preferred. An interview is required. Admissions process is need-blind. *High school units required/recommended:* 18 total units are required; 20 total units are recommended; 4 English required, 3 math required, 2 science required, 3 science recommended, 2 foreign language required, 2 social studies required, 3 social studies recommended. Units in social studies should include history. Minimum composite ACT score of 20 (combined SAT I score of 1000), rank in top half of secondary school class, and minimum 2.0 GPA required. *Special Requirements:* TOEFL is required of all international students. Documented shadow/clinical experience required for physical therapy program applicants.

FINANCIAL AID

Students should submit: FAFSA (due March 15). The Princeton Review suggests that all financial aid forms be submitted as soon as possible after January 1. *The following grants/scholarships are offered:* Pell, SEOG, academic merit, the school's own scholarships, the school's own grants, state scholarships, state grants, private scholarships, private grants, foreign aid. *Students borrow from the following loan programs:* Stafford, unsubsidized Stafford, Perkins, PLUS, the school's own loan fund, supplemental loans, private loans. Applicants will be notified of awards beginning April 1. College Work-Study Program is available. Institutional employment is available. The off-campus job outlook is excellent.

STUDENT BODY

Total undergrad enrollment	1,050
% male/female	34/66
% from out of state	49
% transfers	30
% from catholic high school	64
% live on campus	78
% African American	5
% Caucasian	90
% Hispanic	2
% Native American	1
% international	2
# of countries represented	6

ACADEMICS

Calendar	semester
Student/teacher ratio	9:1
FT faculty	122
% faculty from religious order	19
% graduate in 4 yrs.	63

Most Popular Majors
physical therapy
nursing
business

ADMISSIONS

Admissions Rating	74
# of applicants	487

% of applicants accepted	82
% of acceptees attending	51

Deadlines

Regular admission	rolling
Regular notification	rolling

FRESHMAN PROFILE

Range verbal SAT	490-590
Average verbal SAT	513
Range math SAT	500-600
Average math SAT	521
Range ACT	21-26
Average ACT	24
Minimum TOEFL	500
Average HS GPA or Avg	3.4

Graduated top 10% of class	26
Graduated top 25% of class	59
Graduated top 50% of class	85

FINANCIAL FACTS

Tuition	$11,730
Room & board	$4,480
Estimated book expense	$500
% frosh receiving aid	89
% undergrads receiving aid	75
% frosh w/ grant	73
Avg. grant	$4,569
% frosh w/ loan	74
Avg. loan	$2,994

COLLEGE MISERICORDIA

301 Lake Street, Dallas, PA 18612 • *Admissions: 717-675-4449* • *Fax: 717-675-2441*
• *Financial Aid: 717-674-6280* • *E-mail: admiss@miseri.edu* • *Web Site: www.miseri.edu*

College Misericordia was founded in 1924 by the Sisters of Mercy. The college's 100-acre residential campus is located twenty miles from Scranton. Misericordia offers thirty-two majors within the realm of liberal arts and sciences, business, education, and health sciences. Most popular majors include physical therapy, occupational therapy, and education. The college's academic offerings are augmented by the Alternative Learner's Project, a program focused on assisting students with learning disabilities achieve their college goals. Amid Misericordia's relatively standard complement of extracurricular activities, athletic facilities and accomplishments are particularly noteworthy for a college of its size: The college has a 78,000-square-foot sports and health center, which includes a gymnasium and swimming pool, and the women's basketball team finished the 1995–96 season in the top ten of the NCAA's Division III.

ADMISSIONS

The admissions committee considers (in descending order of importance): class rank, HS record, test scores, recommendations. *Also considered (in descending order of importance):* alumni relationship, personality, special talents, extracurriculars. Either the SAT or ACT is required; SAT is preferred. An interview is recommended. Admissions process is need-blind. *High school units required/recommended:* 4 English recommended, 4 math recommended, 4 science recommended, 4 social studies recommended, 4 history recommended. *Special Requirements:* TOEFL is required of all international students. Chemistry or biology recommended of nursing program applicants. Chemistry recommended of occupational therapy program applicants. Biology and physics recommended of radiologic technology program applicants. Chemistry, biology, and trigonometry recommended of pre-medicine program applicants.

FINANCIAL AID

Students should submit: FAFSA (due March 1), the school's own financial aid form (due March 1), state aid form. The Princeton Review suggests that all financial aid forms be submitted as soon as possible after January 1. *Students borrow from the following loan programs:* Stafford, PLUS. College Work-Study Program is available. The off-campus job outlook is good.

STUDENT BODY			
Total undergrad enrollment	1,590	FT faculty	148
% male/female	25/75	% faculty from religious order	6
% from out of state	20	% graduate in 4 yrs.	41
% from catholic high school	12		
% live on campus	53		
% African American	2		
% Caucasian	96		
% Hispanic	1		
% international	1		
# of countries represented	5		

ACADEMICS

Calendar	semester
Student/teacher ratio	12:1

Most Popular Majors

physical therapy
occupational therapy
education

ADMISSIONS

Admissions Rating	80
# of applicants	1,280
% of applicants accepted	61
% of acceptees attending	32

Deadlines

Regular admission	rolling
Regular notification	rolling

FRESHMAN PROFILE

Range verbal SAT	410-610
Average verbal SAT	510
Range math SAT	350-630
Average math SAT	500
Average ACT	23
Minimum TOEFL	500
Average HS GPA or Avg	3.0
Graduated top 10% of class	26
Graduated top 25% of class	52
Graduated top 50% of class	74

FINANCIAL FACTS

Tuition	$12,260
Room & board	$6,050
Estimated book expense	$500
% frosh receiving aid	95
% undergrads receiving aid	95
% frosh w/ grant	82
Avg. grant	NR
% frosh w/ loan	78
Avg. loan	$3,191

CREIGHTON UNIVERSITY

2500 California Plaza, Omaha, NE 68178 • Admissions: 402-280-2703 • Fax: 402-280-2685
• Financial Aid: 402-280-2731 • E-mail: admissions@creighton.edu • Web Site: www.creighton.edu

Founded in 1878 by the Jesuits, Creighton University is on a 78-acre campus sixty miles from Lincoln. The university offers fifty majors within its three undergraduate colleges of arts and sciences, business administration, and nursing. Most popular programs include the health professions, business, and biological sciences. Facilities of note are an observatory and an art gallery. When it comes to extracurricular activities, Creighton offers an abundance of options; over 100 clubs and organizations are registered on campus. These groups help to keep the student body close to campus; though fewer than half of the university's students live on campus, virtually everyone finds themselves there on weekends. Arguably the biggest events on campus each year are the baseball games—Creighton is the permanent host for the NCAA's College World Series.

ADMISSIONS

The admissions committee considers (in descending order of importance): HS record, class rank, test scores, recommendations, essay. *Also considered (in descending order of importance):* extracurriculars, personality, special talents. Either the SAT or ACT is required; ACT is preferred. An interview is recommended. Admissions process is need-blind. *High school units required/recommended:* 16 total units are required; 4 English required, 3 math required, 2 science required, 2 foreign language required, 2 social studies required. Minimum composite ACT score of 20, rank in top half of secondary school class, and minimum 2.5 GPA required. *Special Requirements:* TOEFL is required of all international students.

FINANCIAL AID

Students should submit: FAFSA (due April 1), the school's own financial aid form (due April 1), state aid form, a copy of parents' most recent income tax filing (due April 1). The Princeton Review suggests that all financial aid forms be submitted as soon as possible after January 1. *The following grants/scholarships are offered:* Pell, SEOG, academic merit, athletic, the school's own scholarships, the school's own grants, state scholarships, state grants, private scholarships, private grants, foreign aid. *Students borrow from the following loan programs:* Stafford, unsubsidized Stafford, Perkins, PLUS, the school's own loan fund, supplemental loans, private loans. Applicants will be notified of awards beginning March 1. College Work-Study Program is available. Institutional employment is available. The off-campus job outlook is excellent.

STUDENT BODY

Total undergrad enrollment	3,679
% male/female	41/59
% from out of state	42
% transfers	12
% from catholic high school	30
% live on campus	53
% African American	4
% Asian	5
% Caucasian	84
% Hispanic	3
% Native American	1
% international	3
# of countries represented	54

ACADEMICS

Calendar	semester
Student/teacher ratio	5:1
FT faculty	1323
% faculty from religious order	7
% graduate in 4 yrs.	67

Most Popular Majors
health professions
business
biological sciences

ADMISSIONS

Admissions Rating	73
# of applicants	3,369
% of applicants accepted	92
% of acceptees attending	28

Deadlines

Regular admission	8/1
Regular notification	rolling

FRESHMAN PROFILE

Average ACT	25
Minimum TOEFL	500
Average HS GPA or Avg	3.5
Graduated top 10% of class	35
Graduated top 25% of class	70
Graduated top 50% of class	89

FINANCIAL FACTS

Tuition	$11,746
Room & board	$4,726
Estimated book expense	$600
% frosh receiving aid	80
% undergrads receiving aid	75
% frosh w/ grant	55
Avg. grant	$1,990
% frosh w/ loan	51
Avg. loan	$4,013

D'YOUVILLE COLLEGE

One D'Youville Square, 320 Porter Avenue, Buffalo, NY 14201 • *Admissions: 716-881-1600* • *Fax: 716-881-7790*
• *Financial Aid: 716-881-7691* • *E-mail: admiss@dyc.edu* • *Web Site: www.dyc.edu*

D'Youville College was founded in 1908 as the first college for women in western New York, and went coed in 1971. The college is named after Marguerite D'Youville, a pioneer in social welfare and health care who founded the Grey Nuns of the Sacred Heart. D'Youville's tiny campus is located one mile from downtown Buffalo, and a walkable yet hardy distance from Canada. The college offers thirty majors within the liberal arts and sciences, business, education, and the health sciences. Most popular majors are physical therapy, nursing, and occupational therapy. A D'Youville specialty is their program for those who wish to teach the blind and visually impaired. Extracurriculars include twenty-three registered clubs and organizations, and a modest selection of activities and athletics.

ADMISSIONS

The admissions committee considers (in descending order of importance): HS record, test scores, class rank, recommendations, essay. *Also considered (in descending order of importance):* extracurriculars, personality, alumni relationship, special talents. Either the SAT or ACT is required. An interview is recommended. Admissions process is need-blind. *High school units required/recommended:* 18 total units are recommended; 4 English recommended, 3 math recommended, 3 science recommended, 3 foreign language recommended, 4 social studies recommended. Minimum combined SAT I score of 800, rank in top half of secondary school class, and minimum grade average of 80 required. *Special Requirements:* TOEFL is required of all international students. Biology, chemistry, minimum combined SAT I score of 900, and minimum grade average of 85 required of dietetics, nursing, occupational therapy, and physical therapy program applicants. Minimum combined SAT I score of 1000 required of physician assistant program applicants.

FINANCIAL AID

Students should submit: FAFSA (due April 15), state aid form (due April 15), a copy of parents' most recent income tax filing. The Princeton Review suggests that all financial aid forms be submitted as soon as possible after January 1. *The following grants/scholarships are offered:* state scholarships. *Students borrow from the following loan programs:* Stafford, PLUS. Applicants will be notified of awards beginning April 15. College Work-Study Program is available. Institutional employment is available. The off-campus job outlook is good.

STUDENT BODY

Total undergrad enrollment	1,377
% male/female	25/75
% from out of state	11
% transfers	50
% from catholic high school	10
% live on campus	25
% African American	8
% Asian	1
% Caucasian	72
% Hispanic	3
% Native American	1
# of countries represented	4

ACADEMICS

Calendar	semester
Student/teacher ratio	12:1
FT faculty	164
% faculty from religious order	4
% graduate in 4 yrs.	52

Most Popular Majors
physical therapy
nursing
occupational therapy

ADMISSIONS

Admissions Rating	77
# of applicants	1,036

% of applicants accepted	53
% of acceptees attending	29

Deadlines

Regular admission	rolling
Regular notification	rolling

FRESHMAN PROFILE

Range verbal SAT	490-580
Average verbal SAT	443
Range math SAT	480-570
Average math SAT	486
Range ACT	20-25
Average ACT	23
Minimum TOEFL	500
Graduated top 10% of class	21

Graduated top 25% of class	56
Graduated top 50% of class	90

FINANCIAL FACTS

Tuition	$9,510
Room & board	$4,600
Estimated book expense	$680
% frosh receiving aid	86
% undergrads receiving aid	84

DAEMEN COLLEGE

4380 Main Street, Amherst, NY 14226 • Admissions: 716-839-1820 • Fax: 716-839-8516
• Financial Aid: 716-839-8254 • E-mail: admissions@daemen.edu • Web Site: www.daemen.edu

Daemen College was established in 1947 by the Sisters of Saint Francis of Penance and Christian Charity. Located five miles from Buffalo, the college's campus is 37 acres. Daemen offers fifty majors within the liberal arts and sciences, business, education, and the health professions. Most popular programs include physical therapy, nursing, and education. (Nursing is upper division only; students must complete two years of college prior to entering the program.) Over twenty clubs and organizations are registered on campus. Scholarship opportunities include awards for academic achievement and athletics (even though the college offers just one intercollegiate sport, basketball).

ADMISSIONS

The admissions committee considers (in descending order of importance): HS record, test scores, class rank, recommendations. *Also considered (in descending order of importance):* alumni relationship, extracurriculars, geographical distribution, personality, special talents. Either the SAT or ACT is required. An interview is recommended. Admissions process is need-blind. *High school units required/recommended:* 4 English required, 3 math required, 3 science required, 2 social studies required, 2 history required. *Special Requirements:* A portfolio is required for art program applicants. An RN is required for nursing program applicants. TOEFL is required of all international students.

FINANCIAL AID

Students should submit: FAFSA, the school's own financial aid form, state aid form, a copy of parents' most recent income tax filing. The Princeton Review suggests that all financial aid forms be submitted as soon as possible after January 1. *The following grants/scholarships are offered:* Pell, SEOG, the school's own scholarships, the school's own grants, state scholarships, state grants, private scholarships, private grants, ROTC, foreign aid. *Students borrow from the following loan programs:* Stafford, unsubsidized Stafford, Perkins, PLUS, the school's own loan fund, supplemental loans, private loans. College Work-Study Program is available. Institutional employment is available. The off-campus job outlook is excellent.

STUDENT BODY

Total undergrad enrollment	1,791
% male/female	31/69
% from out of state	6
% live on campus	50
% African American	9
% Asian	1
% Caucasian	85
% Hispanic	2
% Native American	1
% international	1
# of countries represented	7

ACADEMICS

Calendar	semester
Student/teacher ratio	11:1
FT faculty	170
% graduate in 4 yrs.	26

Most Popular Majors
physical therapy
nursing
education

ADMISSIONS

Admissions Rating	62
# of applicants	1,574
% of applicants accepted	75
% of acceptees attending	30

Deadlines

Regular admission	rolling
Regular notification	rolling

FRESHMAN PROFILE

Average verbal SAT	500
Average math SAT	500
Average ACT	21
Minimum TOEFL	500

Average HS GPA or Avg	2.9

FINANCIAL FACTS

Tuition	$9,950
Room & board	$5,200
% frosh receiving aid	92
% undergrads receiving aid	98

UNIVERSITY OF DALLAS

1845 East Northgate, University Station, Irving, TX 75062 • Admissions: 972-721-5000 • Fax: 972-721-4040
• Financial Aid: 972-721-5266 • E-mail: undadmis@acad.udallas.edu • Web Site: www.udallas.edu

Founded in 1956 by the Diocese of Dallas, the University of Dallas is located on an ample 750-acre campus next to Texas Stadium (home of the Dallas Cowboys) and five miles from the city's downtown. The campus is a vast complex of Catholic facilities that extends far beyond the university itself. It includes the Holy Trinity Seminary, the Dominican Priory, the Cistercian Abbey and Preparatory School, the Highlands School (a Catholic primary and secondary school), and four chapels. The university was the first college in the U.S. to be accredited by the American Academy for Liberal Education, an accrediting agency that places a particular focus on the traditional Western civilization-based liberal arts curriculum. Dallas offers twenty-six undergraduate majors within the liberal arts and sciences. The majority of students spend at least a semester at the university's campus in Rome prior to their junior year.

ADMISSIONS

The admissions committee considers (in descending order of importance): HS record, class rank, test scores, essay, recommendations. *Also considered (in descending order of importance):* personality, alumni relationship, extracurriculars, special talents. Either the SAT or ACT is required. An interview is recommended. Admissions process is need-blind. *High school units required/recommended:* 14 total units are required; 18 total units are recommended; 4 English required, 3 math required, 4 math recommended, 3 science required, 4 science recommended, 2 foreign language required, 3 foreign language recommended, 2 social studies required, 3 social studies recommended. *The admissions office says:* "[We pay] attention to the individual record. The review process takes the total student record into consideration, not just standardized test scores. Our typical student is distinguished by a serious nature, and a time commitment to learning, a real desire to read the great books in their entirety and spend time discussing them."

FINANCIAL AID

Students should submit: FAFSA (due March 1), the school's own financial aid form (due March 1). The Princeton Review suggests that all financial aid forms be submitted as soon as possible after January 1. *The following grants/scholarships are offered:* Pell, SEOG, academic merit, the school's own scholarships, the school's own grants, state scholarships, state grants, private scholarships, private grants, ROTC. *Students borrow from the following loan programs:* Stafford, unsubsidized Stafford, Perkins, PLUS, the school's own loan fund, supplemental loans, state loans, federal nursing loans, private loans. Applicants will be notified of awards beginning March 30. College Work-Study Program is available. Institutional employment is available. The off-campus job outlook is good.

STUDENT BODY	
Total undergrad enrollment	1,088
% male/female	37/63
% from out of state	36
% transfers	30
% from catholic high school	35
% live on campus	63
% African American	1
% Asian	10
% Caucasian	71
% Hispanic	13
% Native American	1
% international	3
# of countries represented	15

ACADEMICS	
Calendar	semester
Student/teacher ratio	13:1
FT faculty	220
% faculty from religious order	9
% graduate in 4 yrs.	57

Most Popular Majors
biology
English
politics

ADMISSIONS	
Admissions Rating	78
# of applicants	720

% of applicants accepted	89
% of acceptees attending	40

Deadlines	
Early decision/action	12/1
Regular admission	2/1
Regular notification	rolling

FRESHMAN PROFILE	
Range verbal SAT	540-670
Average verbal SAT	581
Range math SAT	540-660
Average math SAT	603
Range ACT	25-28
Average ACT	27
Minimum TOEFL	550

Average HS GPA or Avg	3.2
Graduated top 10% of class	38
Graduated top 25% of class	70
Graduated top 50% of class	93

FINANCIAL FACTS	
Tuition	$12,920
Room & board	$4,918
Estimated book expense	$500
% frosh receiving aid	93
% undergrads receiving aid	82
% frosh w/ grant	71
Avg. grant	$5,831
% frosh w/ loan	72
Avg. loan	$3,054

UNIVERSITY OF DAYTON

300 College Park Drive, Dayton, OH 45469 • Admissions: 937 229-4411 • Fax: 937-229-4545
• Financial Aid: 937-229-4311 • E-mail: admission@udayton.edu • Web Site: www.udayton.edu

The University of Dayton, the tenth largest Catholic university in the U.S., was founded in 1850 by the Marianists. The university is located on a 110-acre campus two miles from downtown. Seventy majors are available, primarily within the areas of liberal arts and sciences, business administration, education, and engineering. Education, engineering, and communications rank among the most popular majors. With twenty-five active ministers, Dayton's campus ministry is the largest of any Catholic college in the nation. Time spent outside the classroom provides plenty of opportunities for involvement; the university has twenty service organizations, sixty professional clubs, and dozens of other activities and athletic programs. Basketball is a particularly popular sport at Dayton.

ADMISSIONS

The admissions committee considers (in descending order of importance): HS record, test scores, class rank, recommendations, essay. *Also considered (in descending order of importance):* extracurriculars, special talents. Either the SAT or ACT is required. An interview is recommended. Admissions process is need-blind. *High school units required/recommended:* 18 total units are recommended; 4 English recommended, 3 math recommended, 3 science recommended, 2 foreign language recommended, 2 social studies recommended. Rank in top two-thirds of secondary school class recommended; minimum test scores and GPA vary depending on program. *Special Requirements:* An audition is required for music program applicants. Completion of math courses through algebra II and trigonometry recommended of business administration, computer science, engineering, mathematics, and natural sciences program applicants. (4 years of high school math preferred.) *The admissions office says:* "All 6,000+ applications are reviewed individually with attention given to ALL areas—grades, rank, scores, curriculum, activities, personal statement, recommendations, and counselor feedback. All visitors are given the opportunities for an individual admission interview as well as financial aid."

FINANCIAL AID

Students should submit: FAFSA (due March 31), state aid form. The Princeton Review suggests that all financial aid forms be submitted as soon as possible after January 1. *The following grants/scholarships are offered:* Pell, SEOG, academic merit, athletic, the school's own scholarships, the school's own grants, state grants, private scholarships, private grants, ROTC. *Students borrow from the following loan programs:* Stafford, unsubsidized Stafford, Perkins, PLUS, the school's own loan fund, supplemental loans, private loans. Applicants will be notified of awards beginning March 15. College Work-Study Program is available.

STUDENT BODY

Total undergrad enrollment	5,899
% male/female	51/49
% from out of state	43
% transfers	10
% from catholic high school	48
% live on campus	90
% African American	3
% Asian	1
% Caucasian	90
% Hispanic	2
% international	1
# of countries represented	26

ACADEMICS

Calendar	semester
Student/teacher ratio	14:1
FT faculty	822
% faculty from religious order	7
% graduate in 4 yrs.	73

Most Popular Majors
education
engineering
communication

ADMISSIONS

Admissions Rating	74
# of applicants	4,974

% of applicants accepted	90
% of acceptees attending	35

Deadlines

Regular admission	rolling
Regular notification	rolling

FRESHMAN PROFILE

Range verbal SAT	510-620
Range math SAT	510-640
Range ACT	21-27
Minimum TOEFL	500
Graduated top 10% of class	23
Graduated top 25% of class	49
Graduated top 50% of class	78

FINANCIAL FACTS

Tuition	$13,690
Room & board	$4,500
Estimated book expense	$600
% frosh receiving aid	92
% undergrads receiving aid	98
% frosh w/ grant	96
Avg. grant	$8,756
% frosh w/ loan	70
Avg. loan	$2,938

DePaul University

1 East Jackson Boulevard, Chicago, IL 60604 • Admissions: 312-362-8300 • Fax: 312-362-5289
• Financial Aid: 312-362-8526 • E-mail: admitdpu@wppost.depaul.edu • Web Site: www.depaul.edu

Founded in 1898 by the Vincentians, DePaul University is the nation's second largest Catholic university. It is named for Saint Vincent de Paul, the Vincentians' founder. The university's 32-acre main campus is located in the Lincoln Park area north of Chicago's downtown. Though a small amount of university housing is available, DePaul is essentially a commuter school. Sixty-eight majors are offered, focusing mainly on the liberal arts and sciences, business, education, and health sciences. Chicago is apparently a lasting attraction to students who attend DePaul; about 85 percent of the university's 90,000 alumni chose to remain in the city upon graduation. Beyond the natural attractions of the city, nonacademic pursuits are in abundance; the university has over 100 registered clubs and organizations, and a wide range of activities and athletics. DePaul's basketball Blue Demons are a big draw, competing regularly against many of the best teams in the NCAA.

ADMISSIONS

The admissions committee considers (in descending order of importance): HS record, class rank, test scores, recommendations, essay. *Also considered (in descending order of importance):* extracurriculars, personality, alumni relationship, special talents. Either the SAT or ACT is required. An interview is recommended. Admissions process is need-blind. *High school units required/recommended:* 16 total units are required; 4 English required, 2 math required, 2 science required, 2 social studies required, 2 history required. Additional units of math and science recommended. *Special Requirements:* An audition is required for music program applicants. An RN is required for nursing program applicants. Audition required of theater program applicants. *The admissions office says:* "No cutoffs or formulas are used in considering applicants. A student's total academic record and extracurricular or co-curricular activities are considered."

FINANCIAL AID

Students should submit: FAFSA (due May 1). The Princeton Review suggests that all financial aid forms be submitted as soon as possible after January 1. *The following grants/scholarships are offered:* state scholarships. *Students borrow from the following loan programs:* Stafford, PLUS. College Work-Study Program is available. Institutional employment is available. The off-campus job outlook is excellent.

STUDENT BODY

Total undergrad enrollment	9,788
% male/female	43/57
% from out of state	30
% transfers	48
% live on campus	25
% African American	12
% Asian	6
% Caucasian	69
% Hispanic	11
% international	1
# of countries represented	60

ACADEMICS

Calendar	quarter
Student/teacher ratio	15:1
FT faculty	1079

Most Popular Majors
accountancy
finance
marketing

ADMISSIONS

Admissions Rating	74
% of acceptees attending	30

Deadlines

Regular admission	8/15
Regular notification	rolling

FRESHMAN PROFILE

Average verbal SAT	511
Average math SAT	554
Average ACT	25
Minimum TOEFL	550
Graduated top 10% of class	30
Graduated top 25% of class	58
Graduated top 50% of class	89

FINANCIAL FACTS

Tuition	$12,750
Room & board	$5,500
Estimated book expense	$600
% frosh receiving aid	65
% undergrads receiving aid	67
% frosh w/ grant	63
Avg. grant	NR
% frosh w/ loan	71
Avg. loan	$2,625

UNIVERSITY OF DETROIT MERCY

P.O. Box 19900, Detroit, MI 48219 • Admissions: 313-993-1245 • Fax: 313-993-1534
• Financial Aid: 313-993-1350 • E-mail: admissions@udmercy.edu • Web Site: www.udmercy.edu

The University of Detroit Mercy was founded in 1877 by the Jesuits as the University of Detroit. In 1990, the university absorbed Mercy College, and adopted its current name. Detroit Mercy's 70-acre campus is located several miles north of the city's downtown. Fifty-four majors are offered, focusing mainly within the liberal arts and sciences, business, education, engineering, and health sciences. Among the most popular programs are nursing, mechanical engineering, and architecture-environmental design. Jesuits comprise almost 10 percent of the faculty. Extracurricular offerings include seventy registered clubs and organizations, and a variety of activities and athletics.

ADMISSIONS

The admissions committee considers (in descending order of importance): HS record, class rank, recommendations, test scores. *Also considered (in descending order of importance):* extracurriculars, personality, geographical distribution, special talents. Either the SAT or ACT is required. An interview is recommended. College-preparatory program including English, foreign language, laboratory science, math, and social science is strongly recommended.

FINANCIAL AID

Students should submit: FAFSA (due April 15), the school's own financial aid form, state aid form. The Princeton Review suggests that all financial aid forms be submitted as soon as possible after January 1. *The following grants/scholarships are offered:* Pell, SEOG, academic merit, athletic, the school's own scholarships, the school's own grants, state scholarships, state grants, private scholarships, private grants, foreign aid, United Negro College Fund. *Students borrow from the following loan programs:* Stafford, unsubsidized Stafford, Perkins, PLUS, the school's own loan fund, supplemental loans, private loans. Applicants will be notified of awards beginning March 1. College Work-Study Program is available. Institutional employment is available. The off-campus job outlook is good.

STUDENT BODY

Total undergrad enrollment	4,484
% male/female	45/55
% from out of state	5
% transfers	66
% live on campus	14
% African American	41
% Asian	2
% Caucasian	52
% Hispanic	1
% Native American	1
% international	3
# of countries represented	50

ACADEMICS

Calendar	semester
Student/teacher ratio	15:1
FT faculty	482
% graduate in 4 yrs.	36

Most Popular Majors
nursing
mechanical engineering
architecture/environmental design

ADMISSIONS

Admissions Rating	72
# of applicants	1,441
% of applicants accepted	77
% of acceptees attending	39

Deadlines

Regular admission	8/15
Regular notification	rolling

FRESHMAN PROFILE

Range ACT	19-25
Average ACT	22
Average HS GPA or Avg	3.2
Graduated top 10% of class	23
Graduated top 25% of class	55
Graduated top 50% of class	81

FINANCIAL FACTS

Tuition	$12,216
Room & board	$4,560
Estimated book expense	$616
% frosh receiving aid	70
% undergrads receiving aid	62
% frosh w/ grant	80
Avg. grant	$6,800
% frosh w/ loan	60
Avg. loan	$3,003

DOMINICAN COLLEGE OF BLAUVELT

470 Western Highway, Orangeburg, NY 10962 • *Admissions: 914-359-7800* • *Fax: 914-359-2313*
• *Financial Aid: 914-359-7800*

Dominican College of Blauvelt was founded in 1952 by the Dominican Sisters. The predominately commuter college is located on a 14-acre campus seventeen miles from New York City in the lower Hudson Valley. The college offers thirty-four majors in the areas of liberal arts and sciences, business, education, and the health sciences. Popular programs include management, nursing, and occupational therapy. Extracurricular offerings are sparse—athletics, especially basketball, are the most popular recreational pursuits at Dominican. The results speak for themselves; the men's basketball team has won six NAIA district championships in the past eight years, and eleven of the college's baseball players have signed professional contracts since 1988. Dominican offers a fixed tuition plan under which students are not subject to a tuition increase as long as they remain enrolled on a full-time basis at the college.

ADMISSIONS

The admissions committee considers (in descending order of importance): HS record, test scores, recommendations, class rank. *Also considered (in descending order of importance):* personality, special talents, alumni relationship, extracurriculars. Either the SAT or ACT is required; SAT is preferred. An interview is recommended. *High school units required/recommended:* 16 total units are recommended; 4 English recommended, 1 math recommended, 1 science recommended, 2 foreign language recommended, 3 social studies recommended. Minimum combined SAT I score of 800 and minimum 2.0 GPA recommended. *Special Requirements:* R.N. required of nursing program applicants to Weekend Program.

FINANCIAL AID

Students should submit: FAFSA (due July 1), the school's own financial aid form (due July 1), state aid form (due ASAP), a copy of parents' most recent income tax filing (due July 1). The Princeton Review suggests that all financial aid forms be submitted as soon as possible after January 1. *The following grants/scholarships are offered:* state scholarships. *Students borrow from the following loan programs:* Stafford, PLUS. Applicants will be notified of awards beginning March 15. College Work-Study Program is available. Institutional employment is available. The off-campus job outlook is good.

STUDENT BODY

Total undergrad enrollment	1,781
% male/female	29/71
% from out of state	30
% transfers	21
% from catholic high school	50
% live on campus	10
% African American	9
% Asian	3
% Caucasian	81
% Hispanic	7
% international	1

ACADEMICS

Calendar	semester
Student/teacher ratio	10:1
FT faculty	179
% faculty from religious order	10
% graduate in 4 yrs.	40

Most Popular Majors
management
nursing
occupational therapy

ADMISSIONS

Admissions Rating	66
# of applicants	367

% of applicants accepted	75
% of acceptees attending	37

Deadlines

Regular admission	rolling
Regular notification	rolling

FRESHMAN PROFILE

Range verbal SAT	390-490
Average verbal SAT	440
Range math SAT	370-510
Average math SAT	436
Minimum TOEFL	500
Average HS GPA or Avg	7.7
Graduated top 10% of class	4
Graduated top 25% of class	17

Graduated top 50% of class	44

FINANCIAL FACTS

Tuition	$9,750
Room & board	$6,000
Estimated book expense	$600
% frosh receiving aid	71
% undergrads receiving aid	65
% frosh w/ grant	46
Avg. grant	NR
% frosh w/ loan	82
Avg. loan	$7,082

DOMINICAN COLLEGE OF SAN RAFAEL

50 Acacia Ave, San Rafael, CA 94901 • Admissions: 800-788-3522 • Fax: 415-485-3214
• Financial Aid: 415-485-3294 • E-mail: enroll@dominican.edu • Web Site: www.dominican.edu

Dominican College of San Rafael was founded in 1890 by the Dominican Sisters. It was the first Catholic college for women in California to offer four-year degrees. The college's 80-acre campus is located eleven miles from San Francisco and just south of the scenic wine country of the Sonoma and Napa Valleys. True to the tradition of the Order, the curriculum "refuses to accept an artificial distinction between liberal education and education for a career." Dominican offers seventeen majors in the liberal arts and sciences, business, and nursing. Most popular majors are nursing, psychology, and business administration. The campus houses both an art gallery and a natural history museum. The campus is largely a commuter environment; three coed residence halls house less than a quarter of the student body. The college offers several forms of aid not dependent on need, including three particularly generous merit scholarship programs.

ADMISSIONS

The admissions committee considers (in descending order of importance): HS record, test scores, recommendations, essay, class rank. *Also considered (in descending order of importance):* extracurriculars, special talents, personality, geographical distribution. Either the SAT or ACT is required; SAT is preferred. An interview is recommended. Admissions process is need-blind. *High school units required/recommended:* 16 total units are required; 6 total units are recommended; 4 English required, 2 math required, 4 math recommended, 1 science required, 2 science recommended, 2 foreign language required, 1 history required. Minimum combined SAT I score of 800 and minimum 2.5 GPA required. *Special Requirements:* An audition is required for music program applicants. TOEFL is required of all international students.

FINANCIAL AID

Students should submit: FAFSA, the school's own financial aid form, state aid form, a copy of parents' most recent income tax filing. The Princeton Review suggests that all financial aid forms be submitted as soon as possible after January 1. *The following grants/scholarships are offered:* state scholarships. *Students borrow from the following loan programs:* Stafford, PLUS. College Work-Study Program is available. Institutional employment is available. The off-campus job outlook is poor.

STUDENT BODY

Total undergrad enrollment	1,025
% male/female	24/76
% from out of state	3
% transfers	64
% from catholic high school	40
% live on campus	25
% African American	6
% Asian	10
% Caucasian	72
% Hispanic	10
% Native American	1
% international	3
# of countries represented	15

ACADEMICS

Calendar	semester
Student/teacher ratio	8:1
FT faculty	182
% faculty from religious order	7
% graduate in 4 yrs.	45

Most Popular Majors
nursing
psychology
business administration

ADMISSIONS

Admissions Rating	67
# of applicants	225
% of applicants accepted	88
% of acceptees attending	38

Deadlines

Regular admission	8/15
Regular notification	rolling

FRESHMAN PROFILE

Range verbal SAT	480-620
Average verbal SAT	512
Range math SAT	450-570
Average math SAT	496
Minimum TOEFL	550

Average HS GPA or Avg	3.2
Graduated top 10% of class	21
Graduated top 25% of class	47
Graduated top 50% of class	70

FINANCIAL FACTS

Tuition	$14,380
Room & board	$6,370
Estimated book expense	$612
% frosh receiving aid	66
% undergrads receiving aid	72

DOMINICAN UNIVERSITY

7900 West Division, River Forest, IL 60305 • Admissions: 708-524-6800 • Fax: 708-524-5990
• Financial Aid: 708-524-6809 • E-mail: rosadmis@email.rosary.edu • Web Site: www.rosary.edu

Dominican University (named as such in 1996) was founded in 1901 as the single-sex Rosary College, but went coed in 1970. The university's 30-acre campus is located in a residential neighborhood ten miles from downtown Chicago. Thirty-eight academic majors are available, primarily within the liberal arts, sciences, and business. Popular majors include business administration, accounting, and psychology. The university was one of the first in the United States to establish study-abroad programs. Thirty clubs and organizations are registered at Dominican, complemented by a small selection of activities and athletics.

ADMISSIONS

The admissions committee considers (in descending order of importance): HS record, class rank, test scores, recommendations, essay. *Also considered (in descending order of importance):* extracurriculars, personality, alumni relationship, geographical distribution, special talents. Either the SAT or ACT is required. An interview is recommended. Admissions process is need-blind. 14 units from English, math, lab science, foreign language, and social studies and 2 units of electives required. Rank in top half of secondary school class and minimum 2.5 GPA required. *Special Requirements:* A portfolio is required for art program applicants.

FINANCIAL AID

Students should submit: FAFSA, a copy of parents' most recent income tax filing. The Princeton Review suggests that all financial aid forms be submitted as soon as possible after January 1. *The following grants/scholarships are offered:* state scholarships. *Students borrow from the following loan programs:* Stafford, PLUS. College Work-Study Program is available. Institutional employment is available. The off-campus job outlook is excellent.

STUDENT BODY

Total undergrad enrollment	875
% male/female	26/74
% from out of state	7
% transfers	50
% from catholic high school	50
% live on campus	30
% African American	6
% Asian	2
% Caucasian	79
% Hispanic	9
% international	3
# of countries represented	27

ACADEMICS

Calendar	semester
Student/teacher ratio	15:1
FT faculty	121
% faculty from religious order	19

Most Popular Majors
business administration
accounting
psychology

ADMISSIONS

Admissions Rating	72
# of applicants	391
% of applicants accepted	80
% of acceptees attending	49

Deadlines

Regular admission	rolling
Regular notification	rolling

FRESHMAN PROFILE

Range ACT	19-24
Average ACT	22
Minimum TOEFL	550
Average HS GPA or Avg	3.0
Graduated top 10% of class	22
Graduated top 25% of class	60
Graduated top 50% of class	87

FINANCIAL FACTS

Tuition	$12,130
Room & board	$4,740
Estimated book expense	$550
% frosh receiving aid	80
% undergrads receiving aid	70
% frosh w/ grant	76
Avg. grant	NR
% frosh w/ loan	65
Avg. loan	$2,801

DUQUESNE UNIVERSITY

600 Forbes Avenue, Pittsburgh, PA 15282 • *Admissions: 412-395-5000* • *Fax: 412-396-5644*
• *Financial Aid: 412-396-6607* • *E-mail: admissions@duq2.cc.duq.edu* • *Web Site: www.duq.edu*

Duquesne University was founded in 1878 by the Congregation of the Holy Spirit. The University's 40-acre hilltop campus is located on the shores of the Monongahela River. Eighty-one majors are offered within eight undergraduate schools; liberal arts, business administration, education, health sciences, music, natural and environmental sciences, nursing, and pharmacy. Top programs include pharmacy, nursing, and physical therapy. Campus facilities of note are a pharmacy simulation lab, a cultural center, and a phenomenology center. Nonacademic pursuits abound at Duquesne; the university has 127 registered clubs and organizations offering a broad range of activities in the performing arts, social action and volunteer groups, multicultural interests, campus ministry, and academic honor societies and interest groups. NCAA intercollegiate athletics are offered in twelve sports for men, ten for women; intramural and club sports are also available.

ADMISSIONS

The admissions committee considers (in descending order of importance): HS record, class rank, test scores, recommendations, essay. *Also considered (in descending order of importance):* special talents, extracurriculars, personality, alumni relationship, geographical distribution. Either the SAT or ACT is required; SAT is preferred. An interview is recommended. Admissions process is need-blind. *High school units required/recommended:* 16 total units are recommended; 4 English recommended, 2 math recommended, 2 science recommended, 2 foreign language recommended, 2 social studies recommended. Minimum combined SAT I score of 1000, rank in top three-fifths of secondary school class, and minimum 2.5 GPA recommended. *Special Requirements:* An audition is required for music program applicants. TOEFL is required of all international students. *The admissions office says:* "[We have] rolling admissions. We have a strong bond with many high schools and take the counselors' recommendation very seriously."

FINANCIAL AID

Students should submit: FAFSA, the school's own financial aid form. The Princeton Review suggests that all financial aid forms be submitted as soon as possible after January 1. *The following grants/scholarships are offered:* state scholarships. *Students borrow from the following loan programs:* Stafford, PLUS. College Work-Study Program is available. Institutional employment is available. The off-campus job outlook is good.

STUDENT BODY

Total undergrad enrollment	5,751
% male/female	43/57
% from out of state	27
% transfers	13
% live on campus	68
% African American	5
% Asian	3
% Caucasian	81
% Hispanic	3
% international	5
# of countries represented	90

ACADEMICS

Calendar	semester
Student/teacher ratio	16:1
FT faculty	716

Most Popular Majors
business
pharmacy
health sciences

ADMISSIONS

Admissions Rating	75
# of applicants	4,134
% of applicants accepted	65
% of acceptees attending	46

Deadlines

Early decision/action	11/15
Regular admission	7/1
Regular notification	rolling

FRESHMAN PROFILE

Average verbal SAT	570
Average math SAT	540
Average ACT	23
Minimum TOEFL	500
Average HS GPA or Avg	2.9
Graduated top 10% of class	51
Graduated top 25% of class	78
Graduated top 50% of class	93

FINANCIAL FACTS

Tuition	$13,396
Room & board	$5,803
Estimated book expense	$500
% frosh receiving aid	80
% undergrads receiving aid	78
% frosh w/ grant	64
Avg. grant	NR
% frosh w/ loan	70
Avg. loan	$4,512

ELMS COLLEGE

291 Springfield Street, Chicopee, MA 01013 • Admissions: 413-592-2761 • Fax: 413-594-2781
• Financial Aid: 413-594-2761 • E-mail: admissions@elms.edu • Web Site: www.crocker.com/~elmscol

Elms College was founded as a women's college in 1928 by the Sisters of Saint Joseph. The college's 32-acre campus is located two miles north of Springfield and thirty miles from Hartford, Connecticut. Elms is a member of the Cooperating Colleges of Greater Springfield, affording students the opportunity to cross-register at other member schools. Students choose from nearly forty majors offered within the liberal arts and sciences, business, education, and health sciences. Keep an eye on the college's program in speech language pathology/audiology—it's an up-and-coming area of student interest. An unusual academic option affords students the opportunity to minor in coaching. Students and campus ministry work closely in developing nonacademic activities and are active respondents to social issues. In the midst of the quite typical complement of extracurricular offerings found at Elms are new athletic and fitness facilities and an intercollegiate equestrian team.

ADMISSIONS

The admissions committee considers (in descending order of importance): HS record, class rank, test scores, recommendations, essay. *Also considered (in descending order of importance):* extracurriculars, alumni relationship, personality, special talents, geographical distribution. ; SAT is preferred. An interview is recommended. Admissions process is need-blind. *High school units required/recommended:* 12 total units are required; 20 total units are recommended; 4 English required, 2 math required, 4 math recommended, 2 science required, 4 science recommended, 2 foreign language required, 4 foreign language recommended, 1 social studies required, 4 social studies recommended, 1 history required, 2 history recommended. Rank in top half of secondary school class and minimum 2.5 GPA required; minimum combined SAT I score of 900 recommended.

FINANCIAL AID

Students should submit: FAFSA (due February 1), the school's own financial aid form (due February 1), state aid form (due February 1), a copy of parents' most recent income tax filing (due February 1). The Princeton Review suggests that all financial aid forms be submitted as soon as possible after January 1. *The following grants/ scholarships are offered:* Pell, SEOG, the school's own scholarships, the school's own grants, state scholarships, state grants, ROTC. *Students borrow from the following loan programs:* Stafford, unsubsidized Stafford, Perkins, PLUS, the school's own loan fund, supplemental loans. College Work-Study Program is available. Institutional employment is available. The off-campus job outlook is good.

STUDENT BODY		ACADEMICS		Deadlines		FINANCIAL FACTS	
Total undergrad enrollment	944	Calendar	semester	Regular admission	rolling	Tuition	$12,450
% male/female	0/100	Student/teacher ratio	10:1	Regular notification	rolling	Room & board	$5,000
% from out of state	10	FT faculty	103			Estimated book expense	$500
% transfers	38	% graduate in 4 yrs.	60	**FRESHMAN PROFILE**		% frosh receiving aid	92
% live on campus	40			Range verbal SAT	460-560	% undergrads receiving aid	80
% African American	9	**Most Popular Majors**		Average verbal SAT	502	% frosh w/ grant	70
% Asian	3	nursing		Range math SAT	430-540	Avg. grant	$4,088
% Caucasian	72	social work		Average math SAT	488	% frosh w/ loan	89
% Hispanic	11	education		Minimum TOEFL	500	Avg. loan	$2,625
% international	9			Average HS GPA or Avg	3.0		
# of countries represented	7	**ADMISSIONS**		Graduated top 10% of class	22		
		Admissions Rating	66	Graduated top 25% of class	44		
		# of applicants	255	Graduated top 50% of class	87		
		% of applicants accepted	93				
		% of acceptees attending	46				

EMMANUEL COLLEGE (MA)

400 The Fenway, Boston, MA 02115 • *Admissions: 617-735-9715* • *Fax: 617-735-9877*
• *Financial Aid: 617-735-9725* • *E-mail: enroll@emmanuel.edu* • *Web Site: www.emmanuel.edu*

Founded in 1919 by the Sisters of Notre Dame de Namur, Emmanuel College was the first Catholic women's college in New England. The college's 16-acre, tree-lined residential campus is located near the city's downtown on the Fenway. Men are admitted for graduate and continuing education courses only. Thirty-five majors are offered, primarily within the liberal arts and sciences, business, and education. Most popular programs are business administration, nursing, and health care administration. Outside the classroom, thirty clubs and organizations are available at the college; athletic teams are fielded in basketball, softball, tennis, and volleyball. Although Emmanuel remains a women's college, dormitory housing on the college's campus is leased to both male and female students from other local colleges.

ADMISSIONS

The admissions committee considers (in descending order of importance): HS record, class rank, recommendations, test scores, essay. *Also considered (in descending order of importance):* personality, extracurriculars, alumni relationship, special talents. Either the SAT or ACT is required. An interview is required. Admissions process is need-blind. *High school units required/recommended:* 16 total units are required; 4 English required, 3 math required, 2 science required, 3 foreign language required, 2 social studies required. *Special Requirements:* An RN is required for nursing program applicants.

FINANCIAL AID

Students should submit: FAFSA (due March 1), CSS Profile, state aid form (due May 1), a copy of parents' most recent income tax filing (due April 15). The Princeton Review suggests that all financial aid forms be submitted as soon as possible after January 1. *The following grants/scholarships are offered:* Pell, SEOG, academic merit, the school's own scholarships, the school's own grants, state scholarships, state grants, private scholarships, private grants. *Students borrow from the following loan programs:* Stafford, unsubsidized Stafford, Perkins, PLUS, the school's own loan fund, supplemental loans, private loans. College Work-Study Program is available. Institutional employment is available. The off-campus job outlook is excellent.

STUDENT BODY

Total undergrad enrollment	1,201
% male/female	10/90
% from out of state	9
% transfers	16
% live on campus	62
% African American	9
% Asian	5
% Caucasian	73
% Hispanic	4
% international	6
# of countries represented	43

ACADEMICS

Calendar	semester
Student/teacher ratio	14:1
FT faculty	100

Most Popular Majors
business administration
nursing
health care administration

ADMISSIONS

Admissions Rating	64
% of acceptees attending	58

Deadlines

Regular admission	rolling
Regular notification	rolling

FRESHMAN PROFILE

Minimum TOEFL	500
Graduated top 10% of class	16
Graduated top 25% of class	58
Graduated top 50% of class	100

FINANCIAL FACTS

Tuition	$13,700
Room & board	$6,525
Estimated book expense	$500
% frosh receiving aid	76
% undergrads receiving aid	71
% frosh w/ grant	77
Avg. grant	$7,211
% frosh w/ loan	74
Avg. loan	$3,325

FAIRFIELD UNIVERSITY

1073 North Benson Road, Fairfield, CT 06430 • *Admissions: 203-254-4100* • *Fax: 203-254-4007*
• *Financial Aid: 203-254-4000* • *E-mail: admis@fair1.fairfield.edu* • *Web Site: www.fairfield.edu*

Fairfield University was founded by the Jesuits as a single-sex college for males in 1947; it became coed in 1970. The university is located on a 200-acre campus forty-five miles northeast of New York City. Fairfield offers twenty-eight majors within the liberal arts, business, nursing, and engineering. The most popular programs are English, nursing, and biology. Noteworthy facilities include an extensive arts center, a media center, and a television studio. Among Fairfield's sixty registered organizations are a variety of musical ensembles, ethnic and cultural groups, and an Appalachian volunteer group. Athletic outlets are numerous, with teams established in a wide range of sports at the intercollegiate, intramural, and club levels. The men's basketball team was one of the Cinderella stories of the year at the end of the 1996–97 season, winning the Metro Atlantic Athletic Conference title for a surprise automatic trip to the NCAA's March Madness. The underdog of the tournament, the Stags stunned a national television audience by playing the game of their careers before narrowly losing to Dean Smith's North Carolina Tar Heels in the first round.

ADMISSIONS

The admissions committee considers (in descending order of importance): HS record, class rank, test scores, recommendations. *Also considered (in descending order of importance):* personality, alumni relationship, extracurriculars, special talents. Either the SAT or ACT is required; SAT is preferred. An interview is recommended. *High school units required/recommended:* 17 total units are required; 3 English required, 4 English recommended, 3 math required, 2 science required, 2 foreign language required, 3 social studies required, 1 history required. Rank in top two-fifths of secondary school class recommended. *The admissions office says:* "Students at Fairfield University learn that academic achievement should be coupled with social concerns so that 25% of them are involved in serving at area kitchens and shelters for the homeless, working with children whose parents have AIDS, tutoring inner city children and volunteering to assist the needy in Appalachia, Ecuador, Haiti, and Mexico."

FINANCIAL AID

Students should submit: FAFSA, a copy of parents' most recent income tax filing. The Princeton Review suggests that all financial aid forms be submitted as soon as possible after January 1. *The following grants/scholarships are offered:* Pell, SEOG, the school's own scholarships, the school's own grants, state scholarships, state grants. *Students borrow from the following loan programs:* Stafford, unsubsidized Stafford, Perkins, PLUS, the school's own loan fund, supplemental loans. Applicants will be notified of awards beginning April 1. College Work-Study Program is available. Institutional employment is available. The off-campus job outlook is good.

STUDENT BODY		ACADEMICS		% of applicants accepted	71	Graduated top 25% of class	52
Total undergrad enrollment	3,100	Calendar	semester	% of acceptees attending	23	Graduated top 50% of class	85
% male/female	48/52	Student/teacher ratio	13:1	**Deadlines**		**FINANCIAL FACTS**	
% from out of state	77	FT faculty	318	Early decision/action	12/1	Tuition	$17,900
% transfers	2	% faculty from religious order	6	Regular admission	3/1	Room & board	$7,024
% live on campus	80	% graduate in 4 yrs.	83	Regular notification	4/1	Estimated book expense	$450
% African American	2	**Most Popular Majors**				% frosh receiving aid	66
% Asian	4	English		**FRESHMAN PROFILE**		% undergrads receiving aid	65
% Caucasian	88	nursing		Range verbal SAT	510-600	% frosh w/ grant	42
% Hispanic	4	biology		Average verbal SAT	552	Avg. grant	$5,600
% international	2	**ADMISSIONS**		Range math SAT	510-600	% frosh w/ loan	44
# of countries represented	26	Admissions Rating	75	Average math SAT	555	Avg. loan	$2,838
		# of applicants	5,253	Average ACT	25		
				Minimum TOEFL	550		
				Graduated top 10% of class	17		

FELICIAN COLLEGE

262 South Main Street, Lodi, NJ 07644 • Admissions: 201-778-1029 • Fax: 201-778-1029
• Financial Aid: 201-778-1190 • Web Site: www.felician.edu

Felician College was founded by the Felician Sisters in 1923 as the Immaculate Conception Normal School. It became a teacher-training college for religious women in 1935, a junior college in 1942, admitted laywomen in 1964, and changed its name to Felician in 1967. The college's 27-acre campus, on the banks of the Saddle River, is fifteen miles from New York City. Seventeen majors are available within the liberal arts and sciences, education, and health sciences. Among the most popular programs are nursing and elementary education. Felician's facilities include an on-campus elementary school for exceptional children. Twenty-two registered organizations are available to students, as well as a variety of activities and athletic pursuits. No campus housing is available, but the college does offer assistance to those seeking off-campus living arrangements.

ADMISSIONS

The admissions committee considers (in descending order of importance): HS record, test scores, essay, recommendations. *Also considered (in descending order of importance):* geographical distribution, personality, extracurriculars, special talents. Either the SAT or ACT is required; SAT is preferred. An interview is required. Admissions process is need-blind. *High school units required/recommended:* 0 total units are required; 16 total units are recommended; 0 English required, 4 English recommended, 0 math required, 3 math recommended, 0 science required, 2 science recommended, 0 foreign language required, 2 foreign language recommended, 0 social studies required, 2 social studies recommended, 0 history required, 0 history recommended. Minimum grade of C for in-state applicants; minimum 3.4 GPA required of out-of-state applicants. In-state applicants with minimum 3.3 GPA are eligible regardless of test scores. Applicants with minimum combined SAT I score of 1400 (composite ACT score of 31) and minimum combined SAT II scores of 1730 (in-state) or 1850 (out-of-state), with no score below 530 on any one test, are eligible on the basis of test scores alone. *Special Requirements:* Chemistry and biology with lab required of nursing program applicants.

FINANCIAL AID

Students should submit: FAFSA. The Princeton Review suggests that all financial aid forms be submitted as soon as possible after January 1. *The following grants/scholarships are offered:* Pell, SEOG, academic merit, the school's own scholarships, the school's own grants, state scholarships, state grants, private scholarships, private grants. *Students borrow from the following loan programs:* Stafford, unsubsidized Stafford, Perkins, PLUS, the school's own loan fund, supplemental loans, state loans, private loans. College Work-Study Program is available. The off-campus job outlook is good.

STUDENT BODY

Total undergrad enrollment	978
% male/female	15/85
% from out of state	2
% transfers	58
% African American	7
% Asian	7
% Caucasian	75
% Hispanic	10
% Native American	1
% international	1
# of countries represented	11

ACADEMICS

Calendar	semester
Student/teacher ratio	11:1
FT faculty	97

Most Popular Majors
nursing
elementary education

ADMISSIONS

Admissions Rating	61
% of acceptees attending	64

Deadlines

Regular admission	rolling
Regular notification	3/15

FRESHMAN PROFILE

Average verbal SAT	362
Average math SAT	394
Minimum TOEFL	500
Graduated top 10% of class	4
Graduated top 25% of class	38
Graduated top 50% of class	69

FINANCIAL FACTS

Tuition	$8,550
Estimated book expense	$500
% frosh receiving aid	55
% undergrads receiving aid	28
% frosh w/ grant	25
Avg. grant	NR
% frosh w/ loan	15
Avg. loan	$2,000

FONTBONNE COLLEGE

6800 Wydown Boulevard, Saint Louis, MO 63105 • *Admissions: 314-889-1400* • *Fax: 314-889-1451*
• *Financial Aid: 314-889-1414* • *E-mail: pmusen@fontbonne.edu* • *Web Site: www.fontbonne.edu*

Founded in 1923 by the Sisters of Saint Joseph of Carondelet, Fontbonne College is on a 13-acre campus six miles from downtown Saint Louis. Although the college maintains a steadfast liberal arts tradition, it also focuses on careers. Fontbonne offers forty-nine majors, the majority from the realm of liberal arts and sciences, business, and education. Business administration, education, and communications arts are the most popular of these options. Special features of the campus include an art museum. The speech and hearing clinic is especially noteworthy for students considering enrolling in the college's program for communication disorders. There are twenty registered clubs and organizations at Fontbonne, along with a small variety of activities and athletic teams.

ADMISSIONS

The admissions committee considers (in descending order of importance): HS record, test scores, class rank, recommendations, essay. *Also considered (in descending order of importance):* extracurriculars, personality, special talents, alumni relationship, geographical distribution. Either the SAT or ACT is required; ACT is preferred. An interview is recommended. Admissions process is need-blind. *High school units required/ recommended:* 20 total units are recommended; 4 English required, 3 math required, 3 science required, 3 social studies required, 3 history recommended. Electives must include foreign language. Minimum composite ACT score of 20, rank in top half of secondary school class, and minimum 2.5 GPA recommended. *Special Requirements:* A portfolio is required for art program applicants. Audition required of theatre program applicants.

FINANCIAL AID

Students should submit: FAFSA (due Open), the school's own financial aid form (due Open), state aid form (due Open). The Princeton Review suggests that all financial aid forms be submitted as soon as possible after January 1. *The following grants/scholarships are offered:* Pell, SEOG, academic merit, athletic, the school's own scholarships, the school's own grants, state scholarships, state grants, foreign aid. *Students borrow from the following loan programs:* Stafford, unsubsidized Stafford, Perkins, PLUS, the school's own loan fund, supplemental loans. College Work-Study Program is available. Institutional employment is available. The off-campus job outlook is excellent.

STUDENT BODY		ACADEMICS		ADMISSIONS		FINANCIAL FACTS	
Total undergrad enrollment	1,294	Calendar	semester	Admissions Rating	70	Tuition	$9,500
% male/female	26/74	Student/teacher ratio	13:1	# of applicants	360	Room & board	$4,400
% from out of state	15	FT faculty	143	% of applicants accepted	84	Estimated book expense	$300
% transfers	43	% faculty from religious order	1	% of acceptees attending	50	% frosh receiving aid	80
% from catholic high school	50	% graduate in 4 yrs.	55			% undergrads receiving aid	86
% live on campus	33			**Deadlines**		% frosh w/ grant	80
% African American	22	**Most Popular Majors**		Regular admission	8/1	Avg. grant	$4,200
% Asian	1	business administration		Regular notification	rolling	% frosh w/ loan	90
% Caucasian	72	education				Avg. loan	$2,450
% Hispanic	1	communications arts		**FRESHMAN PROFILE**			
% international	5			Average ACT	22		
# of countries represented	10			Minimum TOEFL	500		
				Graduated top 10% of class	17		
				Graduated top 25% of class	47		
				Graduated top 50% of class	74		

FORDHAM UNIVERSITY

441 East Fordham Road, New York, NY 10458 • Admissions: 800-FORDHAM • Fax: 718-367-9404
• Financial Aid: 718-817-3800 • E-mail: buckley@lars.fordham.edu • Web Site: www.fordham.edu

Fordham University was founded in 1841 by the Jesuits. The university is based on two campuses: The Rose Hill campus in the Bronx and the Lincoln Center campus in Manhattan. Rose Hill is an 80-acre traditional, residential campus, while the Lincoln Center location sits on one acre and caters to commuting students. The tradition of excellence at Fordham is recognized by both Catholics and non-Catholics alike. Fifty countries are represented in the student body. Sixty-six majors are available in Fordham's three undergraduate schools. A new library is scheduled to open soon on the Rose Hill campus. Extracurriculars are abundant—the university has 130 registered organizations and a wide variety of activities. WFUV, Fordham's radio station, is perpetually regarded as one of the best in college radio. While no longer the national athletic power it once was, the university continues to offer a very broad range of intercollegiate and intramural sports.

ADMISSIONS

The admissions committee considers (in descending order of importance): HS record, class rank, test scores, recommendations, essay. *Also considered (in descending order of importance):* alumni relationship, extracurriculars, geographical distribution, personality, special talents. Either the SAT or ACT is required. An interview is recommended. Admissions process is need-blind. *High school units required/recommended:* 18 total units are required; 22 total units are recommended; 4 English required, 3 math required, 4 math recommended, 1 science required, 2 science recommended, 2 foreign language recommended, 3 social studies required, 4 social studies recommended. *Special Requirements:* TOEFL is required of all international students. 4 units of math and 1 unit each of chemistry and physics required of science program applicants. Stronger math background required of applicants to College of Business.

FINANCIAL AID

Students should submit: FAFSA (due February 1), CSS Profile (due February 1), the school's own financial aid form (due February 1). The Princeton Review suggests that all financial aid forms be submitted as soon as possible after January 1. *The following grants/scholarships are offered:* state scholarships. *Students borrow from the following loan programs:* Stafford, PLUS. Applicants will be notified of awards beginning April 1. College Work-Study Program is available. The off-campus job outlook is excellent.

STUDENT BODY

Total undergrad enrollment	4,474
% male/female	49/51
% from out of state	30
% transfers	7
% from catholic high school	40
% live on campus	50
% African American	6
% Asian	5
% Caucasian	71
% Hispanic	15
% Native American	1
% international	2
# of countries represented	50

ACADEMICS

Calendar	semester
Student/teacher ratio	17:1
FT faculty	765
% faculty from religious order	5
% graduate in 4 yrs.	79

Most Popular Majors
business administration
communications/media studies
English/comparative literature

ADMISSIONS

Admissions Rating	77
# of applicants	5,357

% of applicants accepted	70
% of acceptees attending	34

Deadlines

Early decision/action	11/1
Regular admission	2/1
Regular notification	3/15

FRESHMAN PROFILE

Range verbal SAT	520-620
Average verbal SAT	583
Range math SAT	500-590
Average math SAT	558
Minimum TOEFL	550
Average HS GPA or Avg	3.2
Graduated top 10% of class	26

Graduated top 25% of class	58
Graduated top 50% of class	88

FINANCIAL FACTS

Tuition	$16,800
Room & board	$7,800
Estimated book expense	$600
% frosh receiving aid	80
% undergrads receiving aid	80
% frosh w/ grant	77
Avg. grant	NR
% frosh w/ loan	66
Avg. loan	NR

FRANCISCAN UNIVERSITY OF STEUBENVILLE

University Blvd., P.O. Box 7200, Steubenville, OH 43952 • Admissions: 614-283-6226 • Fax: 614-283-6472
• Financial Aid: 614-283-6211 • E-mail: admissions@francisc.edu • Web Site: www.franuniv.edu

Franciscan University, founded in 1946, is located on 100 acres overlooking the Ohio River, forty-two miles from Pittsburgh. Sponsored by the Third Order Regulars (Franciscans), the university is a nationally recognized campus for Christian renewal. Although the university's original purpose was to serve the local community, its students now come from as far away as Hawaii, as well as forty countries. Franciscan offers thirty-five majors among the liberal arts and sciences, business, education, engineering, and health sciences. Popular majors include theology, education, and nursing. Students are encouraged to spend a semester during sophomore year at the university's branch campus in Gaming, Austria. Franciscan counts some twenty-eight registered organizations on campus and a variety of artistic and social groups, including a community volunteer program and human life concerns (a pro-life group). Intramural and club sports are offered, but there are no intercollegiate athletic teams.

ADMISSIONS

The admissions committee considers (in descending order of importance): HS record, test scores, class rank, essay, recommendations. *Also considered (in descending order of importance):* extracurriculars, personality, special talents. Either the SAT or ACT is required. An interview is recommended. Admissions process is need-blind. *High school units required/recommended:* 15 total units are required; 4 English required, 2 math required, 2 science required, 2 foreign language required, 2 social studies required. Additional units of science and mathematics recommended. Minimum combined SAT I score of 970 (composite ACT score of 19), rank in top half of secondary school class, and minimum 2.4 GPA required. *Special Requirements:* TOEFL is required of all international students.

FINANCIAL AID

Students should submit: FAFSA (due March 1), the school's own financial aid form (due March 15), state aid form. The Princeton Review suggests that all financial aid forms be submitted as soon as possible after January 1. *The following grants/scholarships are offered:* Pell, SEOG, academic merit, athletic, the school's own scholarships, the school's own grants, state scholarships, state grants, private scholarships, private grants, ROTC. *Students borrow from the following loan programs:* Stafford, unsubsidized Stafford, Perkins, PLUS, the school's own loan fund, supplemental loans, private loans. College Work-Study Program is available. Institutional employment is available. The off-campus job outlook is fair.

STUDENT BODY

Total undergrad enrollment	1,538
% male/female	41/59
% from out of state	63
% transfers	32
% from catholic high school	59
% live on campus	50
% African American	1
% Asian	3
% Caucasian	84
% Hispanic	4
% Native American	1
% international	9

ACADEMICS

Calendar	semester
Student/teacher ratio	14:1
FT faculty	139
% faculty from religious order	11
% graduate in 4 yrs.	58

Most Popular Majors
theology
education
nursing

ADMISSIONS

Admissions Rating	75
% of acceptees attending	42

Deadlines

Regular admission	6/30
Regular notification	rolling

FRESHMAN PROFILE

Range verbal SAT	420-570
Average verbal SAT	498
Range math SAT	440-580
Average math SAT	508
Range ACT	20-26
Average ACT	23
Minimum TOEFL	500
Graduated top 10% of class	22
Graduated top 25% of class	49
Graduated top 50% of class	75

FINANCIAL FACTS

Tuition	$10,590
Room & board	$4,500
Estimated book expense	$500
% frosh receiving aid	80
% undergrads receiving aid	82
% frosh w/ grant	60
Avg. grant	$1,500
% frosh w/ loan	61
Avg. loan	$2,669

GANNON UNIVERSITY

University Square, Erie, PA 16541 • Admissions: 814-871-7240 • Fax: 814-871-5803
• Financial Aid: 814-871-7337 • E-mail: admissions@cluster.gannon.edu • Web Site: www.gannon.edu

Gannon University was founded in 1925 by the Diocese of Erie. The university's 50-acre campus is ninety miles from Cleveland. On-campus facilities of note include laser and spectrographic labs, and a metallurgy institute. Sixty-one undergraduate majors are offered at Gannon, centered within the liberal arts and sciences, business, education, engineering, and health sciences. Popular majors include nursing, engineering, and biology. Opportunities outside the classroom include sixty-five registered clubs and organizations, and eleven honor societies. Activities run the gamut from arts and media activities to social-action groups and volunteer programs. Intercollegiate, intramural, and club sports are abundant; the university fields nine intercollegiate teams each for men and women.

ADMISSIONS

The admissions committee considers (in descending order of importance): HS record, test scores, class rank, recommendations, essay. *Also considered (in descending order of importance):* personality, alumni relationship, extracurriculars. Either the SAT or ACT is required; SAT is preferred. An interview is recommended. Admissions process is need-blind. *High school units required/recommended:* 16 total units are required; 4 English required, 2 math required, 4 math recommended, 2 science required, 4 science recommended, 2 foreign language required, 2 social studies required, 4 social studies recommended. Rank in top half of secondary school class and minimum 2.5 GPA required; minimum required test scores vary by program. Minimum secondary school unit requirements vary by program.

FINANCIAL AID

Students should submit: FAFSA (due March 1), the school's own financial aid form, state aid form (due March 1). The Princeton Review suggests that all financial aid forms be submitted as soon as possible after January 1. *The following grants/scholarships are offered:* Pell, SEOG, the school's own scholarships, the school's own grants, state scholarships, state grants, private scholarships, private grants, federal nursing scholarship, foreign aid. *Students borrow from the following loan programs:* Stafford, unsubsidized Stafford, Perkins, PLUS, the school's own loan fund, supplemental loans, private loans. College Work-Study Program is available. Institutional employment is available. The off-campus job outlook is good.

STUDENT BODY

Total undergrad enrollment	2,826
% male/female	44/56
% from out of state	18
% transfers	18
% from catholic high school	20
% live on campus	40
% African American	4
% Asian	1
% Caucasian	94
% Hispanic	1
% international	1
# of countries represented	16

ACADEMICS

Calendar	semester
Student/teacher ratio	11:1
FT faculty	290
% faculty from religious order	7
% graduate in 4 yrs.	64

Most Popular Majors

professional nursing
engineering
biology

ADMISSIONS

Admissions Rating	72
# of applicants	2,274

% of applicants accepted	76
% of acceptees attending	31

Deadlines

Regular admission	rolling
Regular notification	rolling

FRESHMAN PROFILE

Range verbal SAT	500-590
Average verbal SAT	550
Range math SAT	500-590
Average math SAT	550
Range ACT	22-26
Average ACT	24
Minimum TOEFL	550

Average HS GPA or Avg	3.3
Graduated top 10% of class	24
Graduated top 25% of class	58
Graduated top 50% of class	89

FINANCIAL FACTS

Tuition	$11,410
Room & board	$4,760
Estimated book expense	$600
% frosh receiving aid	86
% undergrads receiving aid	86

GEORGETOWN UNIVERSITY

37th and O Streets, NW, Washington, D.C. 20057 • Admissions: 202-687-5055 • Fax: 202-687-5084 • Financial Aid: 202-687-4547 • E-mail: guadmiss@gunet.georgetown.edu • Web Site: www.georgetown.edu

Founded in 1789 by the Jesuits, Georgetown University is the oldest Catholic institution of higher learning in the United States. The university's 110-acre campus is in a residential neighborhood minutes from Washington, D.C.'s downtown. Students may choose from over thirty-five majors offered within five schools: arts and sciences, business administration, foreign service, and language and linguistics. Noteworthy facilities include a seismological observatory, a fine arts gallery, and a satellite link for foreign language broadcasts. There's no shortage of extracurriculars here; Georgetown counts an impressive 100 registered clubs and organizations on campus. The university fields thirteen men's and eleven women's athletic teams; the men's basketball team is a perennial power in the Big East Conference. Georgetown has the most selective admissions process of all Catholic universities.

ADMISSIONS

The admissions committee considers (in descending order of importance): HS record, test scores, class rank, recommendations, essay. *Also considered (in descending order of importance):* extracurriculars, alumni relationship, geographical distribution, personality, special talents. Either the SAT or ACT is required. An interview is required. Admissions process is need-blind. *High school units required/recommended:* 4 English recommended, 3 math recommended, 2 science recommended, 2 foreign language recommended, 2 social studies recommended. *Special Requirements:* TOEFL is required of all international students. 4 units of math and 3 units of science required of math and science program applicants. Chemistry, biology, and physics required of nursing program applicants. Language background required of foreign service and language program applicants. *The admissions office says:* "Students who plan a program in mathematics or science should include four years of math and at least three years of science. Candidates for the nursing program (are recommended to include) one year of biology, one year of chemistry, and one year of physics."

FINANCIAL AID

Students should submit: FAFSA, a copy of parents' most recent income tax filing. The Princeton Review suggests that all financial aid forms be submitted as soon as possible after January 1. *The following grants/scholarships are offered:* Pell, SEOG, academic merit, the school's own scholarships, the school's own grants, state scholarships, state grants, private scholarships, private grants, ROTC. *Students borrow from the following loan programs:* Stafford, unsubsidized Stafford, Perkins, PLUS, the school's own loan fund, supplemental loans, private loans. Applicants will be notified of awards beginning April 1. College Work-Study Program is available. Institutional employment is available. The off-campus job outlook is excellent.

STUDENT BODY		ACADEMICS				FINANCIAL FACTS	
Total undergrad enrollment	6,051	Calendar	semester	% of applicants accepted	23	Tuition	$21,206
% male/female	48/52	Student/teacher ratio	12:1	% of acceptees attending	47	Room & board	$8,091
% from out of state	98	FT faculty	1995			Estimated book expense	$715
% transfers	20	% faculty from religious order	7	**Deadlines**		% frosh receiving aid	41
% from catholic high school	20	% graduate in 4 yrs.	87	Regular admission	1/10	% undergrads receiving aid	50
% live on campus	80			Regular notification	4/1	% frosh w/ grant	43
% African American	6	**Most Popular Majors**				Avg. grant	$9,624
% Asian	8	international affairs		**FRESHMAN PROFILE**		% frosh w/ loan	42
% Caucasian	67	government		Range verbal SAT	620-720	Avg. loan	$2,385
% Hispanic	6	English		Range math SAT	610-710		
% international	10			Range ACT	26-31		
# of countries represented	116	**ADMISSIONS**		Minimum TOEFL	550		
		Admissions Rating	98	Graduated top 10% of class	79		
		# of applicants	13,010	Graduated top 25% of class	95		
				Graduated top 50% of class	99		

GEORGIAN COURT COLLEGE

900 Lakewood Avenue, Lakewood, NJ 08701 • Admissions: 908-364-2200 • Fax: 908-367-3920
• Financial Aid: 908-364-2200,-ext.-258 • E-mail: admissions-ugrad@georgian.edu • Web Site:
www.georgian.edu

Georgian Court College was founded as a women's college in 1908 by the Sisters of Mercy. Sixty miles from Philadelphia, the college's 150-acre campus is located on the George Gould estate, a national historic landmark within a half-hour's drive of the New Jersey shore. Georgian Court offers twenty-one majors, primarily within the liberal arts and sciences, business, and education. Popular majors include business administration, psychology, and accounting. Among facilities of note are an art gallery and an arboretum. There are thirty-six registered clubs and organizations at the college, and twelve honor societies. Athletic teams are fielded in four sports. Thanks to the college's concerted effort to keep tuition increases in check, Georgian Court is one of the most inexpensive independent colleges in New Jersey.

ADMISSIONS

The admissions committee considers (in descending order of importance): HS record, class rank, test scores, essay, recommendations. *Also considered (in descending order of importance):* personality, special talents, extracurriculars, alumni relationship. Either the SAT or ACT is required; SAT is preferred. An interview is recommended. Admissions process is need-blind. *High school units required/recommended:* 16 total units are required; 4 English required, 2 math required, 1 science required, 2 foreign language required, 1 history required. Minimum combined SAT I score of 860 (composite ACT score of 19) and rank in top half of secondary school class required. *Special Requirements:* An audition is required for music program applicants.

FINANCIAL AID

Students should submit: FAFSA CSS Profile, the school's own financial aid form, state aid form, a copy of parents' most recent income tax filing. The Princeton Review suggests that all financial aid forms be submitted as soon as possible after January 1. *The following grants/scholarships are offered:* Pell, SEOG, the school's own scholarships, the school's own grants, state scholarships, state grants, private scholarships, private grants, federal nursing scholarship. *Students borrow from the following loan programs:* Stafford, unsubsidized Stafford, PLUS, the school's own loan fund, supplemental loans, state loans, private loans. Applicants will be notified of awards beginning March 1. College Work-Study Program is available. Institutional employment is available. The off-campus job outlook is good.

STUDENT BODY		ACADEMICS			
Total undergrad enrollment	1,667	Calendar	semester	% of applicants accepted	94
% male/female	5/95	Student/teacher ratio	12:1	% of acceptees attending	49
% from out of state	1	FT faculty	194		
% transfers	59	% faculty from religious order	11	**Deadlines**	
% live on campus	26	% graduate in 4 yrs.	68	Regular admission	8/1
% African American	4			Regular notification	rolling
% Asian	1	**Most Popular Majors**			
% Caucasian	87	business administration		**FRESHMAN PROFILE**	
% Hispanic	4	psychology		Range verbal SAT	420-520
% international	1	accounting		Average verbal SAT	478
				Range math SAT	410-520
		ADMISSIONS		Average math SAT	466
		Admissions Rating	62	Minimum TOEFL	550
		# of applicants	286	Graduated top 10% of class	6
				Graduated top 25% of class	28

Graduated top 50% of class	70
FINANCIAL FACTS	
Tuition	$10,332
Room & board	$4,500
Estimated book expense	$350
% frosh receiving aid	81
% undergrads receiving aid	65

GONZAGA UNIVERSITY

East 502 Boone Avenue, Spokane, WA 99258 • Admissions: 800-322-2584 • Fax: 509-324-5780
• Financial Aid: 800-793-1716 • E-mail: ballinger@gu.gonzaga.edu • Web Site: www.gonzaga.edu

The Society of Jesus (the Jesuits) founded Gonzaga University in 1887; women were first admitted in 1948. The university is situated on an 83-acre campus on the Spokane River in eastern Washington. Gonzaga awards degrees in fifty-two majors in five undergraduate schools: arts and sciences, business administration, engineering, education, and professional studies. Psychology, business administration, and biology are the most popular academic programs. Campus facilities and equipment of note include two scanning electron microscopes, a computer-aided design center, an information and technology center, and an art center and museum. The university's fifty-eight registered clubs and organizations offer a wide range of options for activities outside the classroom. Gonzaga fields athletic teams in eight sports for men, seven for women. Special scholarships are offered for academic merit, graduates of Catholic high schools, and additional considerations.

ADMISSIONS

The admissions committee considers (in descending order of importance): HS record, test scores, recommendations, essay, class rank. *Also considered (in descending order of importance):* personality, alumni relationship, extracurriculars, special talents. Either the SAT or ACT is required. An interview is recommended. Admissions process is need-blind. *High school units required/recommended:* 17 total units are required; 4 English required, 3 math required, 1 science required, 2 foreign language required, 1 history required. Minimum SAT I scores of 530 in verbal and 500 in math and minimum 2.8 GPA required. *Special Requirements:* A portfolio is required for art program applicants. An audition is required for music program applicants. An R.N. is required for nursing program applicants. R.N., A.D.N., or L.P.N. required of nursing program applicants. *The admissions office says:* "We are real people with whom applicants can talk. We want to 'meet' them by phone if not in person. It helps us if they take the time to become 'real' to us."

FINANCIAL AID

Students should submit: FAFSA (due February 1), the school's own financial aid form. The Princeton Review suggests that all financial aid forms be submitted as soon as possible after January 1. *The following grants/ scholarships are offered:* Pell, SEOG, academic merit, athletic, the school's own scholarships, the school's own grants, state scholarships, state grants, private scholarships, private grants, ROTC, foreign aid. *Students borrow from the following loan programs:* Stafford, unsubsidized Stafford, Perkins, PLUS, the school's own loan fund, supplemental loans, private loans. Applicants will be notified of awards beginning April 1. College Work-Study Program is available. Institutional employment is available. The off-campus job outlook is excellent.

STUDENT BODY		ACADEMICS		Deadlines		FINANCIAL FACTS	
Total undergrad enrollment	3,008	Calendar	semester	Early decision/action	12/1	Tuition	$14,900
% male/female	47/53	Student/teacher ratio	17:1	Regular admission	3/1	Room & board	$4,950
% from out of state	49	FT faculty	279	Regular notification	rolling	Estimated book expense	$600
% transfers	26	% faculty from religious order	60			% frosh receiving aid	82
% from catholic high school	35	% graduate in 4 yrs.	58	**FRESHMAN PROFILE**		% undergrads receiving aid	81
% live on campus	47			Average verbal SAT	596	% frosh w/ grant	38
% African American	1	**Most Popular Majors**		Average math SAT	581	Avg. grant	$4,500
% Asian	5	psychology		Average ACT	26	% frosh w/ loan	48
% Caucasian	80	business administration		Minimum TOEFL	520	Avg. loan	$3,813
% Hispanic	4	biology		Graduated top 10% of class	36		
% Native American	1	**ADMISSIONS**		Graduated top 25% of class	67		
% international	5	Admissions Rating	75	Graduated top 50% of class	91		
# of countries represented	46	% of acceptees attending	42				

UNIVERSITY OF GREAT FALLS

1301 - 20th Street South, Great Falls, MT 59405 • Admissions: 406-761-8210 • Fax: 406-791-5395
• Financial Aid: 406-791-5235 • E-mail: adminrec@ugf.edu • Web Site: www.ugf.edu

The University of Great Falls was founded in 1932 by the Sisters of Providence, and became coed in 1937. The university is located on a 44-acre campus near the quintuple falls of the Missouri River in the heartland of Montana. The university offers twenty-nine academic majors, primarily within the liberal arts and sciences, business, and education. Among the most popular majors are criminal justice, human services, and counseling psychology. The university is a commuter campus; fewer than 10 percent of the student body live on campus. A variety of standard activities—student government, a newspaper, a literary magazine, and several musical ensembles—are available; of special interest is the United Tribes Club. Athletic offerings are intramural only.

ADMISSIONS

The admissions committee considers (in descending order of importance): HS record, test scores, class rank, recommendations. *Also considered (in descending order of importance):* personality, extracurriculars, special talents. An interview is recommended. Admissions process is need-blind. *High school units required/recommended:* 19 total units are recommended; 4 English recommended, 3 math recommended, 2 science recommended, 1 social studies recommended, 1 history recommended.

FINANCIAL AID

Students should submit: FAFSA, the school's own financial aid form. The Princeton Review suggests that all financial aid forms be submitted as soon as possible after January 1. *The following grants/scholarships are offered:* Pell, SEOG, academic merit, the school's own scholarships, the school's own grants, state grants, private scholarships, private grants, foreign aid. *Students borrow from the following loan programs:* Stafford, unsubsidized Stafford, Perkins, PLUS, the school's own loan fund, supplemental loans, state loans, federal nursing loans, private loans. Applicants will be notified of awards beginning April 15. College Work-Study Program is available. Institutional employment is available. The off-campus job outlook is fair.

STUDENT BODY		ACADEMICS		ADMISSIONS		FINANCIAL FACTS	
Total undergrad enrollment	1,237	Calendar	semester	Admissions Rating	81	Tuition	$6,900
% male/female	32/68	Student/teacher ratio	10:1	% of acceptees attending	68	Room & board	$1,320
% from out of state	11	FT faculty	139	**Deadlines**		Estimated book expense	$600
% transfers	46	% faculty from religious order	6	Regular admission	rolling	% frosh receiving aid	80
% live on campus	9			Regular notification	rolling	% undergrads receiving aid	80
% African American	1	**Most Popular Majors**					
% Caucasian	89	criminal justice		**FRESHMAN PROFILE**			
% Hispanic	1	human services		Minimum TOEFL	500		
% Native American	5	counseling psychology					
% international	4						
# of countries represented	6						

GWYNEDD-MERCY COLLEGE

Sumneytown Pike, Gwynedd Valley, PA 19437 • Admissions: 215-641-5510 • Fax: 215-641-5556
• Financial Aid: 215-641-5570 • E-mail: admissions@gmc.edu • Web Site: www.gmc.edu

Gwynedd-Mercy College was founded in 1948 by the Sisters of Mercy. The college sits on a 170-acre residential campus twenty miles from Philadelphia. Twenty-seven majors are offered in the liberal arts and sciences, business, education, and health sciences. Among the most popular majors are nursing, education, and business. The College's health and nursing programs are affiliated with seventy-four hospitals and medical centers throughout the region. Special academic facilities include an on-campus nursery school. Gwynedd-Mercy counts twenty-one registered clubs and organizations, offering a variety of arts, media, social, and cultural groups. A new multimillion-dollar athletic complex provides the home for intercollegiate athletic teams in four sports for men, five for women.

ADMISSIONS

The admissions committee considers (in descending order of importance): HS record, test scores, class rank, recommendations. *Also considered (in descending order of importance):* alumni relationship, extracurriculars. Either the SAT or ACT is required; SAT is preferred. An interview is recommended. Admissions process is need-blind. *High school units required/recommended:* 17 total units are required; 4 English required, 3 math required, 3 science required, 2 foreign language required, 1 history required. Minimum combined SAT I score of 900 required; rank in top third of secondary school class recommended. *Special Requirements:* Chemistry required of biology, cardiovascular technology, and nursing program applicants. Physics required of radiation therapy technology program applicants. Chemistry or physics required of respiratory care program applicants.

FINANCIAL AID

Students should submit: FAFSA (due March 15), the school's own financial aid form (due March 15), state aid form (due March 15), a copy of parents' most recent income tax filing (due March 15). The Princeton Review suggests that all financial aid forms be submitted as soon as possible after January 1. *The following grants/ scholarships are offered:* academic merit, the school's own scholarships, the school's own grants, state scholarships, state grants, private scholarships, private grants, foreign aid. *Students borrow from the following loan programs:* Stafford, unsubsidized Stafford, PLUS, the school's own loan fund, supplemental loans, state loans, private loans. Applicants will be notified of awards beginning March 15. College Work-Study Program is available. Institutional employment is available. The off-campus job outlook is excellent.

STUDENT BODY

Total undergrad enrollment	1,824
% male/female	17/83
% from out of state	7
% transfers	90
% from catholic high school	55
% live on campus	9
% African American	4
% Asian	5
% Caucasian	88
% Hispanic	2
% Native American	1
% international	4
# of countries represented	30

ACADEMICS

Calendar	semester
Student/teacher ratio	9:1
FT faculty	227
% faculty from religious order	5

Most Popular Majors
nursing
education
business

ADMISSIONS

Admissions Rating	71
% of acceptees attending	44

Deadlines

Regular admission	rolling
Regular notification	rolling

FRESHMAN PROFILE

Range verbal SAT	390-510
Average verbal SAT	470
Range math SAT	420-530
Average math SAT	500
Minimum TOEFL	500
Graduated top 10% of class	30
Graduated top 25% of class	56
Graduated top 50% of class	90

FINANCIAL FACTS

Tuition	$11,794
Room & board	$5,800
Estimated book expense	$1,000
% frosh receiving aid	80
% undergrads receiving aid	86
% frosh w/ grant	62
Avg. grant	$5,500
% frosh w/ loan	53
Avg. loan	$2,664

COLLEGE OF THE HOLY CROSS

College Street, Worcester, MA 01610 • Admissions: 508-793-2011 • Fax: 508-793-2336
• Financial Aid: 508-793-2265 • E-mail: admissions@holycross.edu • Web Site: www.holycross.edu

The College of the Holy Cross was founded in 1843 by the Jesuits. The college is situated on a 174-acre campus forty-five miles from Boston. Students may choose from twenty-five majors within the liberal arts and sciences. Most popular among academic options are English, economics, and history. Among facilities and equipment worth noting are three scanning electron microscopes, an art gallery, a greenhouse, and a facility for aquatic research. As for extracurriculars, Holy Cross counts seventy-five registered clubs and organizations on campus, among them many musical ensembles, political groups, and a variety of specific ethnic cultural activities. The college offers a wide variety of men's and women's intercollegiate athletic teams, including men's water polo. Intramural and club sports are also abundant.

ADMISSIONS

The admissions committee considers (in descending order of importance): HS record, class rank, test scores, recommendations, essay. *Also considered (in descending order of importance):* personality, special talents, alumni relationship, extracurriculars, geographical distribution. Either the SAT or ACT is required; SAT is preferred. An interview is recommended. Admissions process is need-blind. *High school units required/recommended:* 22 total units are recommended; 4 English recommended, 4 math recommended, 4 science recommended, 4 foreign language recommended, 3 social studies recommended, 3 history recommended. *Special Requirements:* TOEFL is required of all international students. *The admissions office says:* "The Holy Cross admissions process is distinguished by the presence of two Early Decision options; the ability to admit the class without regard to family finances; recognition of the applicants' energy and time commitment beyond the classroom."

FINANCIAL AID

Students should submit: FAFSA (due February 1), CSS Profile (due February 1), state aid form, Divorced Parents form (due February 1), a copy of parents' most recent income tax filing (due May 1). The Princeton Review suggests that all financial aid forms be submitted as soon as possible after January 1. *The following grants/scholarships are offered:* Pell, SEOG, the school's own scholarships, the school's own grants, state scholarships, state grants, private scholarships, private grants, ROTC, foreign aid. *Students borrow from the following loan programs:* Stafford, unsubsidized Stafford, Perkins, PLUS, the school's own loan fund, supplemental loans, private loans. Applicants will be notified of awards beginning April 1. College Work-Study Program is available. Institutional employment is available. The off-campus job outlook is fair.

STUDENT BODY		ACADEMICS							
Total undergrad enrollment	2,656	Calendar	semester	% of applicants accepted	44	Graduated top 25% of class	91
% male/female	47/53	Student/teacher ratio	10:1	% of acceptees attending	38	Graduated top 50% of class	100
% from out of state	62	FT faculty	259	**Deadlines**		**FINANCIAL FACTS**	
% transfers	2	% faculty from religious order	8	Early decision/action	12/15	Tuition	$19,700
% from catholic high school	40	% graduate in 4 yrs.	90	Regular admission	1/15	Room & board	$6,750
% live on campus	85			Regular notification	4/1	Estimated book expense	$400
% African American	3	**Most Popular Majors**				% frosh receiving aid	50
% Asian	2	English		**FRESHMAN PROFILE**		% undergrads receiving aid	56
% Caucasian	90	economics		Range verbal SAT	570-650	% frosh w/ grant	60
% Hispanic	3	history		Average verbal SAT	631	Avg. grant	$8,672
% Native American	1			Range math SAT	550-650	% frosh w/ loan	63
% international	1	**ADMISSIONS**		Average math SAT	618	Avg. loan	$3,421
# of countries represented	13	Admissions Rating	90	Minimum TOEFL	550		
		# of applicants	4,185	Graduated top 10% of class	64		

HOLY FAMILY COLLEGE

Grant and Frankford Avenues, Philadelphia, PA 19114 • Admissions: 215-637-3050 • Fax: 215-637-3787 • Financial Aid: 215-637-5538

Holy Family College was founded in 1954 by the Sisters of the Holy Family of Nazareth. Located fifteen miles from downtown Philadelphia, the college's campus comprises 47 acres. Forty-nine majors are offered at Holy Family, the majority within the disciplines of liberal arts and sciences, business, education, and nursing. Most popular of these offerings are nursing, elementary education, and business. Facilities of note include an on-campus nursery school and kindergarten. A small selection of clubs and organizations include student government, a variety of publications, musical ensembles, and social groups. The college fields three athletic teams for men, four for women.

ADMISSIONS

The admissions committee considers (in descending order of importance): class rank, HS record, test scores, recommendations, essay. *Also considered (in descending order of importance):* alumni relationship, extracurriculars, geographical distribution, personality, special talents. Either the SAT or ACT is required. An interview is recommended. *High school units required/recommended:* 16 total units are required; 4 English required, 3 math required, 2 science required, 2 foreign language required, 2 social studies required, 2 history required. Rank in top three-fifths of secondary school class required; rank in top two-fifths recommended. *Special Requirements:* TOEFL is required of all international students.

FINANCIAL AID

Students should submit: FAFSA (due February 15), the school's own financial aid form (due February 15), state aid form (due February 15), a copy of parents' most recent income tax filing (due February 15). The Princeton Review suggests that all financial aid forms be submitted as soon as possible after January 1. *The following grants/scholarships are offered:* state scholarships. *Students borrow from the following loan programs:* Stafford, PLUS. College Work-Study Program is available. Institutional employment is available. The off-campus job outlook is good.

STUDENT BODY

Total undergrad enrollment	2,162
% male/female	24/76
% from out of state	6
% transfers	51
% from catholic high school	55
% African American	2
% Asian	1
% Caucasian	94
% Hispanic	2
% international	2
# of countries represented	9

ACADEMICS

Calendar	semester
Student/teacher ratio	10:1
FT faculty	253
% faculty from religious order	13
% graduate in 4 yrs.	65

Most Popular Majors
nursing
elementary education
business

ADMISSIONS

Admissions Rating	63
# of applicants	471
% of applicants accepted	78
% of acceptees attending	44

Deadlines

Regular admission	7/1
Regular notification	rolling

FRESHMAN PROFILE

Average verbal SAT	454
Average math SAT	436
Minimum TOEFL	500
Graduated top 10% of class	14
Graduated top 25% of class	41
Graduated top 50% of class	88

FINANCIAL FACTS

Tuition	$10,120
Estimated book expense	$500
% frosh receiving aid	89
% undergrads receiving aid	86
% frosh w/ grant	20
Avg. grant	NR
% frosh w/ loan	35
Avg. loan	NR

HOLY NAMES COLLEGE

3500 Mountain Blvd., Oakland, CA 94619 • Admissions: 510-436-1321 • Fax: 510-436-1325
• Financial Aid: 510-436-1327 • Web Site: www.hnc.edu

Founded in 1868 by the Sisters of the Holy Names, Holy Names College is one of the oldest colleges in the Bay area. The college is situated on a 60-acre campus twenty miles from San Francisco. Holy Names offers seventeen majors in the liberal arts and sciences, business, and nursing. Facilities of note include the Valley Center for the Performing Arts, housing a 400-seat concert hall and a studio theater. A variety of clubs and organizations are registered at the college, offering a range of extracurricular options including music and arts activities, cultural groups, and volunteer/community service. Holy Names is a relative newcomer to intercollegiate athletics, joining the NAIA just three years ago in men's and women's basketball and volleyball. The impressive women's volleyball team was California Coastal Conference champion one year later.

ADMISSIONS

The admissions committee considers (in descending order of importance): HS record, test scores, essay, recommendations, class rank. *Also considered (in descending order of importance):* extracurriculars, personality, special talents. Either the SAT or ACT is required. An interview is recommended. Admissions process is need-blind. *High school units required/recommended:* 15 total units are required; 4 English required, 3 math required, 1 science required, 2 foreign language required, 3 foreign language recommended, 1 history required. Minimum combined SAT I score of 880 and minimum 2.8 GPA required. *Special Requirements:* An R.N. is required for nursing program applicants. TOEFL is required of all international students.

FINANCIAL AID

Students should submit: FAFSA (due March 2), the school's own financial aid form (due March 2), state aid form. The Princeton Review suggests that all financial aid forms be submitted as soon as possible after January 1. *The following grants/scholarships are offered:* Pell, SEOG, academic merit, the school's own scholarships, the school's own grants, state grants, private scholarships, private grants, ROTC. *Students borrow from the following loan programs:* Stafford, unsubsidized Stafford, Perkins, PLUS, the school's own loan fund, supplemental loans, private loans. Applicants will be notified of awards beginning April 1. College Work-Study Program is available. Institutional employment is available. The off-campus job outlook is good.

STUDENT BODY		ACADEMICS				FINANCIAL FACTS	
Total undergrad enrollment	600	Calendar	semester	Regular admission	8/1	Tuition	$13,150
% male/female	32/68	Student/teacher ratio	9:1	Regular notification	rolling	Room & board	$5,522
% from out of state	3	FT faculty	112	**FRESHMAN PROFILE**		Estimated book expense	$612
% transfers	39	% graduate in 4 yrs.	35	Average verbal SAT	422	% frosh receiving aid	80
% live on campus	45			Average math SAT	448	% undergrads receiving aid	80
% African American	25	**Most Popular Majors**		Minimum TOEFL	500	% frosh w/ grant	89
% Asian	7	nursing		Graduated top 10% of class	21	Avg. grant	NR
% Caucasian	35	business administration/economics		Graduated top 25% of class	38	% frosh w/ loan	82
% Hispanic	9	human services		Graduated top 50% of class	72	Avg. loan	$2,625
% Native American	1	**ADMISSIONS**					
# of countries represented	14	Admissions Rating	62				
		% of acceptees attending	26				
		Deadlines					
		Early decision/action	11/30				

IMMACULATA COLLEGE

Immaculata, PA 19345 • Admissions: 610-647-4400 • Fax: 610-251-1668
• Financial Aid: 610-647-4400, ext. 3025 • E-mail: admission@immaculate.edu • Web Site: www.immaculata.edu

Immaculata College was founded in 1920 by the Sisters of the Immaculate Heart of Mary, and was the Philadelphia area's first Catholic college for women. The college is located on a 375-acre campus, twenty miles from the city's downtown. Thirty majors within the liberal arts and sciences, business, nursing, and a variety of career-oriented disciplines are available at Immaculata. Most popular of these academic offerings are psychology, business, and English. Special academic facilities include a children's school on campus. A variety of clubs and organizations are registered on campus: musical groups, a newspaper, a magazine, and yearbook are among the favorites. Athletic teams are fielded in five sports each for men and women.

ADMISSIONS

The admissions committee considers (in descending order of importance): HS record, class rank, test scores, recommendations, essay. *Also considered (in descending order of importance):* extracurriculars, alumni relationship, personality, special talents. Either the SAT or ACT is required; SAT is preferred. An interview is recommended. Admissions process is need-blind. *High school units required/recommended:* 19 total units are required; 4 English required, 2 math required, 2 science required, 2 foreign language required, 3 social studies required, 1 history required. Minimum SAT I scores of 400 in both verbal and math, rank in top three-fifths of secondary school class, and minimum 2.3 GPA required. *Special Requirements:* An audition is required for music program applicants. An R.N. is required for nursing program applicants.

FINANCIAL AID

Students should submit: FAFSA (due March 1), the school's own financial aid form (due May 1), state aid form, a copy of parents' most recent income tax filing (due May 1). The Princeton Review suggests that all financial aid forms be submitted as soon as possible after January 1. *The following grants/scholarships are offered:* Pell, SEOG, the school's own scholarships, the school's own grants, state scholarships, state grants, private scholarships, private grants, foreign aid. *Students borrow from the following loan programs:* Stafford, unsubsidized Stafford, Perkins, PLUS, the school's own loan fund, supplemental loans, private loans. Applicants will be notified of awards beginning March 1. College Work-Study Program is available. Institutional employment is available. The off-campus job outlook is good.

STUDENT BODY

Total undergrad enrollment	1,414
% male/female	8/92
% from out of state	9
% transfers	16
% from catholic high school	48
% live on campus	76
% African American	5
% Asian	3
% Caucasian	85
% Hispanic	4
# of countries represented	24

ACADEMICS

Calendar	semester
Student/teacher ratio	13:1
FT faculty	164
% faculty from religious order	49
% graduate in 4 yrs.	52

Most Popular Majors
psychology
business
English

ADMISSIONS

Admissions Rating	65
# of applicants	259
% of applicants accepted	91
% of acceptees attending	44

Deadlines

Regular admission	rolling
Regular notification	rolling

FRESHMAN PROFILE

Range verbal SAT	450-570
Average verbal SAT	506
Range math SAT	400-530
Average math SAT	472
Minimum TOEFL	550
Average HS GPA or Avg	3.0
Graduated top 10% of class	15
Graduated top 25% of class	45
Graduated top 50% of class	66

FINANCIAL FACTS

Tuition	$11,400
Room & board	$5,855
Estimated book expense	$400
% frosh receiving aid	75
% undergrads receiving aid	68
% frosh w/ grant	70
Avg. grant	$4,900
% frosh w/ loan	73
Avg. loan	$2,625

UNIVERSITY OF THE INCARNATE WORD

4301 Broadway, San Antonio, TX 78209 • Admissions: 210-829-6005 • Fax: 210-829-3921
• Financial Aid: 210-829-6008 • E-mail: briand@the.college.iwctx.edu • Web Site: www.iwctx.edu

University of the Incarnate Word was founded in 1881 by the Sisters of Charity. The university's 100-acre campus is located five miles from downtown San Antonio. Incarnate Word offers forty majors within the areas of liberal arts and sciences, business, education, and nursing. Among the most popular of majors are business, nursing, and education. Special facilities and equipment include a black-box theater, archaeological digs, and an electron microscope. The university counts twenty-five registered clubs and organizations among its extracurricular offerings, which also includes athletic teams in six sports each for men and women.

ADMISSIONS

The admissions committee considers (in descending order of importance): HS record, class rank, test scores, essay. *Also considered (in descending order of importance):* special talents, extracurriculars, personality. Either the SAT or ACT is required. An interview is recommended. Admissions process is need-blind. *High school units required/recommended:* 16 total units are required; 4 English required, 2 math required, 2 science required, 2 foreign language required, 2 social studies required, 2 history required. Minimum composite ACT score of 18 (combined SAT I score of 920), rank in top half of secondary school class, and minimum 2.0 GPA required. *Special Requirements:* Science prerequisites and minimum 2.5 GPA required of nursing program applicants. Passing score on TASP Test and minimum 2.5 GPA required of education program applicants.

FINANCIAL AID

Students should submit: FAFSA, the school's own financial aid form, a copy of parents' most recent income tax filing. The Princeton Review suggests that all financial aid forms be submitted as soon as possible after January 1. *The following grants/scholarships are offered:* Pell, SEOG, academic merit, the school's own scholarships, the school's own grants, state grants, private scholarships, private grants, federal nursing scholarship, ROTC. *Students borrow from the following loan programs:* Stafford, unsubsidized Stafford, Perkins, PLUS, the school's own loan fund, supplemental loans, state loans, federal nursing loans, private loans. College Work-Study Program is available. Institutional employment is available. The off-campus job outlook is good.

STUDENT BODY

Total undergrad enrollment	2,241
% male/female	30/70
% from out of state	2
% transfers	33
% from catholic high school	19
% live on campus	26
% African American	9
% Asian	2
% Caucasian	41
% Hispanic	47
% international	1
# of countries represented	11

ACADEMICS

Calendar	semester
Student/teacher ratio	12:1
FT faculty	235
% faculty from religious order	6

Most Popular Majors
business
nursing
education

ADMISSIONS

Admissions Rating	65
% of acceptees attending	42

Deadlines

Regular admission	rolling
Regular notification	rolling

FRESHMAN PROFILE

Range verbal SAT	390-490
Average verbal SAT	441
Range math SAT	420-530
Average math SAT	480
Range ACT	18-23
Average ACT	21
Minimum TOEFL	550
Graduated top 10% of class	16
Graduated top 25% of class	49
Graduated top 50% of class	83

FINANCIAL FACTS

Tuition	$10,060
Room & board	$4,467
Estimated book expense	$300
% frosh receiving aid	62
% undergrads receiving aid	67
% frosh w/ grant	63
Avg. grant	$2,170
% frosh w/ loan	76
Avg. loan	$2,958

IONA COLLEGE

715 North Avenue, New Rochelle, NY 10801 • *Admissions: 914-633-2502* • *Fax: 914-633-2182*
• *Financial Aid: 914-633-2497* • *E-mail: tdelahunt@iona.edu* • *Web Site: www.iona.edu*

Iona College was founded in 1940 by the Christian Brothers. Its 35-acre campus is twenty miles from New York City. Iona describes itself as "an ecumenical community bonded by belief, the refreshing difference offered by American Catholic higher education." The college offers fifty majors in three divisions: The School of Arts and Science, the Hagan School of Business, and the Columba School for Adults. Iona has seventy-three registered clubs and organizations, and twenty-five honor societies. Notably, their far-reaching selection of activities includes a bagpipe band. Iona's Gaels athletic teams compete in a broad range of sports. The college's cross-country team is nationally ranked; men's basketball is a strong competitor in the Metropolitan Athletic Conference.

ADMISSIONS

The admissions committee considers (in descending order of importance): HS record, test scores, recommendations, class rank. *Also considered (in descending order of importance):* alumni relationship, extracurriculars, personality, special talents. Either the SAT or ACT is required; SAT is preferred. An interview is recommended. *High school units required/recommended:* 16 total units are recommended; 4 English recommended, 3 math recommended, 2 foreign language recommended, 1 social studies recommended, 1 history recommended. Rank in top half of secondary school class and minimum 2.5 GPA recommended. *Special Requirements:* 2 units of lab science required of science program applicants.

FINANCIAL AID

Students should submit: FAFSA, the school's own financial aid form, state aid form, a copy of parents' most recent income tax filing. The Princeton Review suggests that all financial aid forms be submitted as soon as possible after January 1. *The following grants/scholarships are offered:* Pell, SEOG, academic merit, athletic, the school's own scholarships, the school's own grants, state scholarships, state grants, private scholarships, private grants, ROTC. *Students borrow from the following loan programs:* Stafford, unsubsidized Stafford, Perkins, PLUS, the school's own loan fund, supplemental loans, health professions loans, private loans. Applicants will be notified of awards beginning February 1. College Work-Study Program is available. Institutional employment is available. The off-campus job outlook is excellent.

STUDENT BODY				FRESHMAN PROFILE			
Total undergrad enrollment	4,626	FT faculty	425	Range verbal SAT	289-505	% frosh receiving aid	89
% male/female	47/53	% graduate in 4 yrs.	56	Average verbal SAT	407	% undergrads receiving aid	89
% from out of state	8	**Most Popular Majors**		Range math SAT	313-563	% frosh w/ grant	72
% transfers	15	mass communication		Average math SAT	466	Avg. grant	$2,000
% live on campus	9	criminal justice		Average ACT	19	% frosh w/ loan	66
% African American	17	psychology		Minimum TOEFL	550	Avg. loan	$2,981
% Asian	2	**ADMISSIONS**		Graduated top 10% of class	9		
% Caucasian	68	Admissions Rating	60	Graduated top 25% of class	28		
% Hispanic	13	% of acceptees attending	25	Graduated top 50% of class	55		
% international	2	**Deadlines**		**FINANCIAL FACTS**			
ACADEMICS		Regular admission	rolling	Tuition	$12,200		
Calendar	4-1-4	Regular notification	rolling	Room & board	$7,400		
Student/teacher ratio	15:1			Estimated book expense	$600		

JOHN CARROLL UNIVERSITY

20700 North Park Boulevard, University Heights, OH 44118 • Admissions: 216-397-4294 • Fax: 216-397-4256
• Financial Aid: 216-397-4248 • E-mail: tfanning@jcvaya.jcu.edu • Web Site: www.jcu.edu

John Carroll University was founded in 1886 by the Jesuits. Named after the first Catholic bishop in the United States, the university's 60-acre campus is ten miles from Cleveland. Thirty-three majors are available within the liberal arts, sciences, and business. Among the most popular majors are communications, English, and marketing. Noteworthy facilities include an international studies center and a broadcast archive. Sixty-five registered clubs and organizations are available, providing a diverse selection of activities in media, the arts, politics, and social activism. Athletic teams are fielded in eleven sports for men, nine for women. John Carroll is a powerhouse in Division III men's basketball, consistently ranking among the top teams in the nation; the wrestling program is also quite strong.

ADMISSIONS

The admissions committee considers (in descending order of importance): HS record, test scores, class rank, recommendations, essay. *Also considered (in descending order of importance):* extracurriculars, personality, alumni relationship, geographical distribution, special talents. Either the SAT or ACT is required. An interview is recommended. Admissions process is need-blind. *High school units required/recommended:* 16 total units are required; 4 English recommended, 3 math recommended, 2 science recommended, 2 foreign language recommended, 1 social studies recommended, 2 history recommended.

FINANCIAL AID

Students should submit: FAFSA (due March 1), state aid form. The Princeton Review suggests that all financial aid forms be submitted as soon as possible after January 1. *The following grants/scholarships are offered:* Pell, SEOG, academic merit, the school's own scholarships, the school's own grants, state scholarships, state grants, private scholarships, private grants. *Students borrow from the following loan programs:* Stafford, unsubsidized Stafford, Perkins, PLUS, the school's own loan fund, supplemental loans, private loans. College Work-Study Program is available. Institutional employment is available. The off-campus job outlook is good.

STUDENT BODY		ACADEMICS		Deadlines		FINANCIAL FACTS	
Total undergrad enrollment	3,482	Calendar	semester	Regular admission	6/1	Tuition	$13,122
% male/female	50/50	Student/teacher ratio	13:1	Regular notification	rolling	Room & board	$5,550
% from out of state	35	FT faculty	347			Estimated book expense	$600
% transfers	14	% faculty from religious order	5	**FRESHMAN PROFILE**		% frosh receiving aid	75
% from catholic high school	50	% graduate in 4 yrs.	77	Range verbal SAT	470-590	% undergrads receiving aid	75
% live on campus	57			Average verbal SAT	512	% frosh w/ grant	83
% African American	4	**Most Popular Majors**		Range math SAT	540-650	Avg. grant	$3,500
% Asian	2	communications		Average math SAT	566	% frosh w/ loan	68
% Caucasian	91	English		Range ACT	21-27	Avg. loan	$2,349
% Hispanic	1	marketing		Average ACT	23		
% international	1			Minimum TOEFL	550		
# of countries represented	15	**ADMISSIONS**		Graduated top 10% of class	27		
		Admissions Rating	80	Graduated top 25% of class	57		
		% of acceptees attending	38	Graduated top 50% of class	85		

KING'S COLLEGE (PA)

133 North River Street, Wilkes Barre, PA 18711 • *Admissions: 717-826-5900* • *Fax: 717-825-9049*
• *Financial Aid: 717-826-5868* • *E-mail: admssns@rs01.kings.edu* • *Web Site: www.kings.edu*

The Congregation of the Holy Cross founded King's College in 1946. The college is located on a nine-acre campus on the edge of downtown Wilkes-Barre. Forty majors are available mainly from within the liberal arts and sciences, business, and education, the most popular majors being biology, accounting, and criminal justice. Facilities of note include a rooftop greenhouse, molecular biology lab, and a computer graphics lab. King's offers more than fifty registered clubs and organizations, and thirteen honor societies on campus; activities range from political and social groups to musical ensembles, radio and television. Athletic teams are fielded in eleven sports for men, and ten for women.

ADMISSIONS

The admissions committee considers (in descending order of importance): HS record, class rank, recommendations, test scores, essay. *Also considered (in descending order of importance):* alumni relationship, extracurriculars, personality, geographical distribution, special talents. Either the SAT or ACT is required. An interview is recommended. Admissions process is need-blind. *High school units required/recommended:* 17 total units are required; 4 English recommended, 3 math recommended, 2 science recommended, 2 foreign language recommended, 3 social studies recommended, 3 history recommended.

FINANCIAL AID

Students should submit: FAFSA, the school's own financial aid form (due March 1), state aid form (due March 1), a copy of parents' most recent income tax filing (due March 1). The Princeton Review suggests that all financial aid forms be submitted as soon as possible after January 1. *The following grants/scholarships are offered:* Pell, SEOG, academic merit, the school's own scholarships, the school's own grants, state scholarships, state grants. *Students borrow from the following loan programs:* Stafford, unsubsidized Stafford, Perkins, PLUS, the school's own loan fund, supplemental loans, state loans. Applicants will be notified of awards beginning February 1. College Work-Study Program is available. Institutional employment is available. The off-campus job outlook is good.

STUDENT BODY

Total undergrad enrollment	2,151
% male/female	53/47
% from out of state	26
% transfers	23
% from catholic high school	30
% live on campus	39
% African American	2
% Asian	1
% Caucasian	95
% Hispanic	1
# of countries represented	8

ACADEMICS

Calendar	semester
Student/teacher ratio	13:1
FT faculty	176
% faculty from religious order	8
% graduate in 4 yrs.	79

Most Popular Majors
biology
accounting
criminal justice

ADMISSIONS

Admissions Rating	75
# of applicants	1,611
% of applicants accepted	74
% of acceptees attending	37

Deadlines

Regular admission	8/15
Regular notification	rolling

FRESHMAN PROFILE

Range verbal SAT	470-581
Average verbal SAT	522
Range math SAT	468-579
Average math SAT	517
Minimum TOEFL	525
Graduated top 10% of class	19
Graduated top 25% of class	47
Graduated top 50% of class	80

FINANCIAL FACTS

Tuition	$12,400
Room & board	$5,780
Estimated book expense	$500
% frosh receiving aid	71
% undergrads receiving aid	80
% frosh w/ grant	63
Avg. grant	$4,263
% frosh w/ loan	60
Avg. loan	$3,008

LaRoche College

9000 Babcock Blvd., Pittsburgh, PA 15237 • *Admissions: 412-367-9241* • *Fax: 412-367-9368*
• *Financial Aid: Call-Admissions*

LaRoche College was founded in 1963 by the Sisters of Divine Providence, and became coed in 1969. The college is situated on a 90-acre campus ten miles from Pittsburgh's downtown. Thirty-six majors are available at LaRoche, focused mainly within the liberal arts and sciences, business, education, and health sciences. Among the most popular disciplines are health sciences, business, and psychology. Noteworthy facilities include an art gallery. The college offers thirty-two clubs and organizations covering a fairly standard selection of activities including student government, a newspaper, a magazine, and a multicultural group. Athletic teams are fielded in four sports for men, five for women.

ADMISSIONS

Special Requirements: TOEFL is required of all international students.

FINANCIAL AID

Students should submit: FAFSA (due February 15), the school's own financial aid form (due February 15), state aid form (due February 15). The Princeton Review suggests that all financial aid forms be submitted as soon as possible after January 1. *Students borrow from the following loan programs:* Stafford, PLUS. College Work-Study Program is available.

STUDENT BODY

% from out of state	10
% from catholic high school	33
% live on campus	40
% African American	2
% Asian	1
% Caucasian	96
% Hispanic	1
% international	1

ACADEMICS

Calendar	semester
Student/teacher ratio	14:1
FT faculty	126
% faculty from religious order	5

ADMISSIONS

Admissions Rating	61
% of acceptees attending	53

Deadlines

Regular admission	rolling

FRESHMAN PROFILE

Average verbal SAT	380

Average math SAT	408
Minimum TOEFL	500
Graduated top 10% of class	10
Graduated top 25% of class	41
Graduated top 50% of class	70

FINANCIAL FACTS

Tuition	$9,712

Room & board	$5,198
Estimated book expense	$600
% frosh receiving aid	91
% undergrads receiving aid	75
% frosh w/ grant	67
Avg. grant	NR
% frosh w/ loan	77
Avg. loan	$2,625

LaSalle University

Olney Avenue at 20th Street, Philadelphia, PA 19141 • *Admissions: 215-591-1500* • *Fax: 215-951-1656*
• *Financial Aid: 215-951-1070* • *E-mail: admiss@lasalle.edu* • *Web Site: www.lasalle.edu/home.html*

In 1863 LaSalle University was founded by the Christian Brothers. The university is set on a 100-acre residential campus in the northwest section of Philadelphia, six miles from downtown. LaSalle offers nearly fifty majors within the liberal arts and sciences, business, education, and nursing. Most popular disciplines include accounting, communication arts, and finance. Noteworthy facilities include an art museum, a child development center, and an urban studies center. The university has a whopping 115 registered clubs and organizations offering just about every activity imaginable, including a nonalcoholic nightclub open seven days a week. Over 1000 LaSalle students participate in the Center for Community Learning, a volunteer organization active both locally and far afield. Five freshmen per year are awarded half-tuition scholarships in recognition of their community service. Intercollegiate athletic teams are fielded in ten sports for men, eleven for women. Division IAA football will commence play for the 1997 season. The university also offers an extensive selection of intramural and club sports. The men's basketball team at LaSalle ranks thirteenth with the most wins of any program in NCAA history.

ADMISSIONS

The admissions committee considers (in descending order of importance): HS record, class rank, test scores, essay, recommendations. *Also considered (in descending order of importance):* extracurriculars, alumni relationship, personality, special talents. Either the SAT or ACT is required; SAT is preferred. An interview is recommended. Admissions process is need-blind. *High school units required/recommended:* 16 total units are required; 4 English required, 3 math required, 1 science required, 2 foreign language required, 1 history required. Rank in top half of secondary school class and minimum C average recommended. Open admissions policy for women over age 25 and for veterans.

FINANCIAL AID

Students should submit: FAFSA (due February 15), state aid form. The Princeton Review suggests that all financial aid forms be submitted as soon as possible after January 1. *The following grants/scholarships are offered:* Pell, SEOG, academic merit, athletic, the school's own scholarships, the school's own grants, state grants, private scholarships, private grants, ROTC, foreign aid. *Students borrow from the following loan programs:* Stafford, unsubsidized Stafford, Perkins, PLUS, the school's own loan fund, supplemental loans, state loans, private loans. Applicants will be notified of awards beginning March 15. College Work-Study Program is available. Institutional employment is available. The off-campus job outlook is excellent.

STUDENT BODY		ACADEMICS		Deadlines		FINANCIAL FACTS	
Total undergrad enrollment	4,129	Calendar	semester	Regular admission	4/1	Tuition	$13,770
% male/female	46/54	Student/teacher ratio	16:1	Regular notification	rolling	Room & board	$5,990
% from out of state	34	FT faculty	352			Estimated book expense	$500
% transfers	15	% graduate in 4 yrs.	73	**FRESHMAN PROFILE**		% frosh receiving aid	85
% live on campus	63			Range verbal SAT	440-540	% undergrads receiving aid	85
% African American	7	**Most Popular Majors**		Average verbal SAT	507	% frosh w/ grant	75
% Asian	4	accounting		Range math SAT	480-590	Avg. grant	$4,500
% Caucasian	85	communication arts		Average math SAT	547	% frosh w/ loan	69
% Hispanic	4	finance		Minimum TOEFL	500	Avg. loan	$3,348
% international	1	**ADMISSIONS**		Graduated top 10% of class	21		
# of countries represented	25	Admissions Rating	76	Graduated top 25% of class	51		
		% of acceptees attending	27	Graduated top 50% of class	88		

LeMoyne College

Syracuse, NY 13214 • Admissions: 315-445-4100 • Fax: 315-445-4540
• Financial Aid: 315-445-4400 • E-mail: admissions@maple.lemoyne.edu • Web Site: www.lemoyne.edu

LeMoyne College was founded in 1946 by the Jesuits, and is named for Simon LeMoyne, a seventeenth-century Jesuit who was an emissary of the French government to the Iroquois Confederacy. The college rests on a 150-acre residential campus located two miles from downtown Syracuse. Nineteen majors are offered within the liberal arts and sciences, business, and education. Most popular academic options include accounting, business administration, and psychology. There are sixty-one registered clubs and organizations at LeMoyne; activities cover a broad spectrum, including a newspaper and other media groups, musical ensembles, and a variety of social action and cultural organizations. Athletic teams are fielded in eight sports each for men and women.

ADMISSIONS

The admissions committee considers (in descending order of importance): HS record, test scores, class rank, recommendations, essay. *Also considered (in descending order of importance):* extracurriculars, personality, special talents, alumni relationship. Either the SAT or ACT is required. An interview is recommended. *High school units required/recommended:* 16 total units are required; 4 English required, 3 math required, 3 science required, 3 foreign language required, 3 social studies required. *Special Requirements:* TOEFL is required of all international students.

FINANCIAL AID

Students should submit: FAFSA (due April 15), CSS Profile (due April 15), the school's own financial aid form, a copy of parents' most recent income tax filing (due May 1). The Princeton Review suggests that all financial aid forms be submitted as soon as possible after January 1. *The following grants/scholarships are offered:* Pell, SEOG, academic merit, athletic, the school's own scholarships, the school's own grants, state scholarships, state grants, private scholarships, private grants, ROTC, foreign aid. *Students borrow from the following loan programs:* Stafford, unsubsidized Stafford, Perkins, PLUS. Applicants will be notified of awards beginning March 15. College Work-Study Program is available. Institutional employment is available. The off-campus job outlook is excellent.

STUDENT BODY

Total undergrad enrollment	1,730
% male/female	42/58
% from out of state	6
% transfers	19
% from catholic high school	45
% live on campus	74
% African American	4
% Asian	1
% Caucasian	89
% Hispanic	4
% international	1
# of countries represented	10

ACADEMICS

Calendar	semester
Student/teacher ratio	13:1
FT faculty	119
% faculty from religious order	20
% graduate in 4 yrs.	63

Most Popular Majors
accounting
business administration
psychology

ADMISSIONS

Admissions Rating	75
# of applicants	1,719
% of applicants accepted	78
% of acceptees attending	30

Deadlines

Regular admission	3/15
Regular notification	rolling

FRESHMAN PROFILE

Average verbal SAT	550
Average math SAT	550
Average ACT	25
Minimum TOEFL	550
Average HS GPA or Avg	86.0

FINANCIAL FACTS

Tuition	$11,650
Room & board	$5,035
Estimated book expense	$400
% frosh receiving aid	93
% undergrads receiving aid	90
% frosh w/ grant	87
Avg. grant	$8,000
% frosh w/ loan	80
Avg. loan	$2,625

LEWIS UNIVERSITY

Route 53, Romeoville, IL 60441 • *Admissions: 815-838-0500* • *Fax: 815-838-9456*
• *Financial Aid: 815-836-5263*

The Christian Brothers founded Lewis University in 1932. The university is situated on a 450-acre campus thirty miles from Chicago. Fifty-three majors are offered, primarily aviation, the liberal arts and sciences, business, education, and nursing. Most popular academic programs include aviation, business administration, and nursing. Noteworthy facilities include a campus airport and an aeronautical training center. Forty-four registered clubs and organizations, and ten honor societies are available at the University. Activities are available in a variety of pursuits; most noteworthy are a chapter of Amnesty International, a cultural-awareness council, and a full range of musical ensembles. Athletic teams are fielded in eight sports each for men and women.

ADMISSIONS

The admissions committee considers (in descending order of importance): HS record, test scores, class rank, recommendations, essay. *Also considered (in descending order of importance):* alumni relationship, extracurriculars, personality, special talents. Either the SAT or ACT is required. An interview is recommended. Admissions process is need-blind. *High school units required/recommended:* 18 total units are required; 4 English recommended, 3 math recommended, 3 science recommended, 2 foreign language recommended, 3 social studies recommended. Rank in top half of secondary school class and minimum 2.0 GPA required. Open admissions policy for undergraduate applicants over age 23. *Special Requirements:* TOEFL is required of all international students.

FINANCIAL AID

Students should submit: FAFSA. The Princeton Review suggests that all financial aid forms be submitted as soon as possible after January 1. *The following grants/scholarships are offered:* state scholarships. *Students borrow from the following loan programs:* Stafford, PLUS. College Work-Study Program is available. Institutional employment is available. The off-campus job outlook is good.

STUDENT BODY

Total undergrad enrollment	3,148
% male/female	44/56
% from out of state	4
% transfers	13
% live on campus	30
% African American	13
% Asian	2
% Caucasian	80
% Hispanic	4
% international	1
# of countries represented	25

ACADEMICS

Calendar	semester
Student/teacher ratio	16:1
FT faculty	243

Most Popular Majors
aviation
business administration
nursing

ADMISSIONS

Admissions Rating	62
% of acceptees attending	38

Deadlines

Regular admission	9/1
Regular notification	rolling

FRESHMAN PROFILE

Minimum TOEFL	500
Graduated top 10% of class	12
Graduated top 25% of class	28
Graduated top 50% of class	58

FINANCIAL FACTS

Tuition	$10,016
Room & board	$4,400
Estimated book expense	$200
% frosh receiving aid	85
% undergrads receiving aid	85

LORAS COLLEGE

1450 Alta Vista, Dubuque, IA 52004 • *Admissions: 319-588-7100* • *Fax: 319-588-7964*
• *Financial Aid: 319-588-7166* • *E-mail: adms@loras.edu*

Loras College was founded in 1839 by the Archdiocese of Dubuque. The sixty-acre campus is the second oldest Catholic college west of the Mississippi. The college offers sixty majors within the liberal arts and sciences, business, and education. Most popular academic disciplines are accounting, English, and psychology. Special facilities include a television studio, an observatory, a planetarium, and a residential arts complex. An extensive selection of extracurricular activities focus on student government, musical ensembles and other arts groups, a student newspaper and magazine, an environmental organization, and film, television, and radio groups. Athletic teams are fielded in ten sports each for men and women.

ADMISSIONS

The admissions committee considers (in descending order of importance): class rank, HS record, test scores, recommendations, essay. *Also considered (in descending order of importance):* alumni relationship, personality. Either the SAT or ACT is required. An interview is recommended. Admissions process is need-blind. *High school units required/recommended:* 17 total units are recommended; 4 English recommended, 3 math recommended, 3 science recommended, 2 foreign language recommended, 3 social studies recommended, 2 history recommended. Minimum composite ACT score of 20 and rank in top half of secondary school class recommended.

FINANCIAL AID

Students should submit: FAFSA. The Princeton Review suggests that all financial aid forms be submitted as soon as possible after January 1. *The following grants/scholarships are offered:* Pell, SEOG, the school's own scholarships, the school's own grants, state scholarships, state grants, private scholarships, private grants, foreign aid. *Students borrow from the following loan programs:* Stafford, unsubsidized Stafford, Perkins, PLUS, the school's own loan fund, supplemental loans, private loans. College Work-Study Program is available. Institutional employment is available. The off-campus job outlook is good.

STUDENT BODY		ACADEMICS					
Total undergrad enrollment	1,736	Calendar	semester	% of applicants accepted	81	Average HS GPA or Avg	3.5
% male/female	48/52	Student/teacher ratio	13:1	% of acceptees attending	37	Graduated top 10% of class	21
% from out of state	44	FT faculty	136			Graduated top 25% of class	42
% transfers	16	% faculty from religious order	7	**Deadlines**		Graduated top 50% of class	87
% from catholic high school	70	% graduate in 4 yrs.	54	Regular admission	8/15		
% live on campus	62			Regular notification	rolling	**FINANCIAL FACTS**	
% African American	2	**Most Popular Majors**				Tuition	$11,800
% Asian	1	accounting		**FRESHMAN PROFILE**		Room & board	$4,000
% Caucasian	95	English		Range verbal SAT	470-620	Estimated book expense	$600
% Hispanic	1	psychology		Average verbal SAT	536	% frosh receiving aid	75
% international	3			Range math SAT	500-650	% undergrads receiving aid	80
# of countries represented	15	**ADMISSIONS**		Average math SAT	564		
		Admissions Rating	75	Range ACT	20-26		
		# of applicants	1,180	Average ACT	23		
				Minimum TOEFL	500		

LOURDES COLLEGE

6832 Convent Road, Sylvania, OH 43560 • *Admissions: 419-885-5291* • *Fax: 419-882-3987*
• *Financial Aid: Call-Admissions*

Lourdes College was founded in 1958 by the Sisters of Saint Francis. With the 89-acres of campus only ten miles from Toledo, Lourdes is a commuter school. Twenty-six majors are available within the liberal arts and sciences, business, and nursing. Among the most popular disciplines are business administration and management, nursing, and psychology. Noteworthy facilities include a planetarium and a nature preserve. Lourdes offers a selection of clubs and organizations that include student government, a variety of musical ensembles, a student newspaper, and several honor societies. Basketball and volleyball are offered as intramural sports; the college does not compete in intercollegiate athletics.

ADMISSIONS
Special Requirements: TOEFL is required of all international students.

FINANCIAL AID
Students should submit: FAFSA (due March 1), the school's own financial aid form (due March 1). The Princeton Review suggests that all financial aid forms be submitted as soon as possible after January 1. *The following grants/scholarships are offered:* Pell, SEOG, academic merit, athletic, the school's own scholarships, the school's own grants, state grants, private scholarships, private grants. *Students borrow from the following loan programs:* Stafford, unsubsidized Stafford, Perkins, PLUS, the school's own loan fund, supplemental loans, private loans. College Work-Study Program is available.

STUDENT BODY		ADMISSIONS		FINANCIAL FACTS	
% from out of state	11	Admissions Rating	69	Tuition	$7,700
% from catholic high school	19	% of acceptees attending	65	Estimated book expense	$564
% African American	4			% frosh receiving aid	25
% Caucasian	94	**Deadlines**		% undergrads receiving aid	25
% Hispanic	1	Regular admission	rolling	% frosh w/ grant	35
% international	1	**FRESHMAN PROFILE**		Avg. grant	$1,500
		Range ACT	18-22	% frosh w/ loan	40
ACADEMICS		Minimum TOEFL	500	Avg. loan	$2,500
Calendar	semester	Graduated top 10% of class	17		
Student/teacher ratio	12:1	Graduated top 25% of class	48		
FT faculty	140	Graduated top 50% of class	72		
% faculty from religious order	20				
% graduate in 4 yrs.	21				

LOYOLA COLLEGE (MD)

4501 North Charles Street, Baltimore, MD 21210 • Admissions: 410-617-5012 • Fax: 410-617-2176 • Financial Aid: 410-617-2576 • Web Site: www.loyola.edu

Loyola College was founded in 1852 by the Jesuits, and became coed in 1971. The college is located on a 65-acre residential campus. Thirty-one majors are available within the liberal arts and sciences, business, education, and engineering. Most popular disciplines are business, biology, and psychology. Facilities worth noting include an art gallery, a speech pathology lab, and audiology center. Fifty student-run clubs and organizations are offered on campus, including a chapter of Amnesty International, a broad range of musical ensembles, media opportunities, and political and social-action groups. Athletic teams are fielded in seven sports each for men and women. Perpetually strong, the men's lacrosse team was the runner-up in the 1990 NCAA Championship.

ADMISSIONS

The admissions committee considers (in descending order of importance): HS record, test scores, class rank, essay, recommendations. *Also considered (in descending order of importance):* extracurriculars, alumni relationship, personality, special talents. An interview is recommended. Admissions process is need-blind. *High school units required/recommended:* 20 total units are recommended; 4 English recommended, 3 math recommended, 4 science recommended, 4 foreign language recommended, 3 social studies recommended, 2 history recommended. Maximum of 3 commercial, industrial, or technical courses may be counted. Basic guidelines are a B or higher in academic classes, 1100 on Sat-I and class rank in the top 30%. *Special Requirements:* TOEFL is required of all international students.

FINANCIAL AID

Students should submit: FAFSA, CSS Profile. The Princeton Review suggests that all financial aid forms be submitted as soon as possible after January 1. *The following grants/scholarships are offered:* Pell, SEOG, athletic, the school's own scholarships, the school's own grants, state scholarships, state grants, private scholarships, private grants, ROTC. *Students borrow from the following loan programs:* Stafford, unsubsidized Stafford, Perkins, PLUS, supplemental loans, private loans. Applicants will be notified of awards beginning April 1. College Work-Study Program is available. Institutional employment is available. The off-campus job outlook is excellent.

STUDENT BODY

Total undergrad enrollment	3,205
% male/female	45/55
% from out of state	69
% transfers	12
% live on campus	77
% African American	4
% Asian	3
% Caucasian	90
% Hispanic	2
% international	2
# of countries represented	10

ACADEMICS

Calendar	semester
Student/teacher ratio	14:1
FT faculty	442
% faculty from religious order	4
% graduate in 4 yrs.	78

Most Popular Majors
business
biology
psychology

ADMISSIONS

Admissions Rating	80
# of applicants	5,431
% of applicants accepted	66

Deadlines

Regular admission	1/15
Regular notification	4/15

FRESHMAN PROFILE

Range verbal SAT	540-640
Average verbal SAT	591
Range math SAT	530-640
Average math SAT	583
Minimum TOEFL	550
Average HS GPA or Avg	3.3
Graduated top 10% of class	27
Graduated top 25% of class	63
Graduated top 50% of class	92

FINANCIAL FACTS

Tuition	$16,300
Room & board	$7,240
Estimated book expense	$700
% frosh receiving aid	68
% undergrads receiving aid	65
% frosh w/ grant	55
Avg. grant	$8,170
% frosh w/ loan	48
Avg. loan	$3,090

LOYOLA MARYMOUNT UNIVERSITY

7900 Loyola Boulevard, Los Angeles, CA 90045 • *Admissions: 310-338-2700* • *Fax: 310-338-7738*
• *Financial Aid: 310-338-2753* • *E-mail: fhorvath@lmumail.lmu.edu* • *Web Site: www.lmu.edu*

Loyola Marymount University was founded by the Jesuits in 1911, and became coed in 1973. The university's 110-acre campus is fifteen miles from downtown Los Angeles. Students may choose from over thirty-eight majors, most of which are found within the liberal arts and sciences, business, and engineering. Among the most popular academic options are business administration, communications, and psychology. Loyola Marymount's facilities include a fine arts complex with a recital hall, recording studio, and art gallery. The university offers a remarkable 117 registered clubs and organizations on campus, covering a range of social service, academic, political, ethnic, and religious activities. Athletic teams are fielded in ten sports for men, including water polo, and eight for women; a variety of intramural and club sports are also available. Men's basketball is the most recognized of Loyola Marymount's teams.

ADMISSIONS

The admissions committee considers (in descending order of importance): HS record, test scores, essay, recommendations, class rank. *Also considered (in descending order of importance):* special talents, alumni relationship, extracurriculars, personality. Either the SAT or ACT is required; SAT is preferred. An interview is recommended. Admissions process is need-blind. *High school units required/recommended:* 16 total units are recommended; 4 English recommended, 3 math recommended, 2 science recommended, 3 foreign language recommended, 3 social studies recommended. *Special Requirements:* An audition is required for music program applicants. TOEFL is required of all international students. 4 units of mathematics required of computer science, engineering, and mathematics program applicants.

FINANCIAL AID

Students should submit: FAFSA (due February 15), CSS Profile, state aid form, a copy of parents' most recent income tax filing (due April 16). The Princeton Review suggests that all financial aid forms be submitted as soon as possible after January 1. *The following grants/scholarships are offered:* Pell, SEOG, academic merit, the school's own scholarships, the school's own grants, state grants, private scholarships, private grants. *Students borrow from the following loan programs:* Stafford, unsubsidized Stafford, Perkins, PLUS, the school's own loan fund, supplemental loans, private loans. Applicants will be notified of awards beginning April 1. College Work-Study Program is available. Institutional employment is available. The off-campus job outlook is excellent.

STUDENT BODY
Total undergrad enrollment	4,164
% male/female	43/57
% from out of state	12
% transfers	30
% live on campus	48
% African American	6
% Asian	16
% Caucasian	55
% Hispanic	19
% Native American	1
% international	5
# of countries represented	73

ACADEMICS
Calendar	semester
Student/teacher ratio	11:1
FT faculty	599
% faculty from religious order	9
% graduate in 4 yrs.	74

Most Popular Majors
business administration
communication arts
psychology

ADMISSIONS
Admissions Rating	73
# of applicants	4,855
% of applicants accepted	66
% of acceptees attending	26

Deadlines
Regular admission	2/1
Regular notification	rolling

FRESHMAN PROFILE
Range verbal SAT	500-600
Average verbal SAT	552
Range math SAT	500-610
Average math SAT	554
Minimum TOEFL	550
Average HS GPA or Avg	3.3
Graduated top 10% of class	28
Graduated top 25% of class	53
Graduated top 50% of class	85

FINANCIAL FACTS
Tuition	$15,446
Room & board	$6,492
Estimated book expense	$550
% frosh receiving aid	66
% undergrads receiving aid	60
% frosh w/ grant	49
Avg. grant	$6,407
% frosh w/ loan	71
Avg. loan	$2,596

LOYOLA UNIVERSITY NEW ORLEANS ▫

6363 St. Charles Avenue, New Orleans, LA 70118 • Admissions: 504-865-3240 • Fax: 504-865-3383
• Financial Aid: 504-865-3231 • E-mail: admit@loyno.beta.edu • Web Site: www.loyno.edu

Loyola University New Orleans was founded by the Jesuits in 1912, and is the largest Catholic university in the South. The 23-acre campus is located across the street from the lovely Audubon Park and a short five miles from downtown New Orleans. Loyola has three undergraduate colleges—arts and sciences, business administration, and music—that collectively offer sixty majors and preprofessional programs. Popular majors include psychology, communications, and biology. Special campus features include an art gallery, an electron microscope, a concert hall, a small-business development center, an experimental theater, psychology research labs, and an institute of politics. Among extracurricular offerings are a variety of clubs and organizations ranging from an opera company and a symphony orchestra to media groups and community-action organizations. Loyola fields eight intercollegiate athletic teams each for men and women; intramural and club teams also exist.

ADMISSIONS

The admissions committee considers (in descending order of importance): HS record, test scores, recommendations, essay, resume of activities. *Also considered (in descending order of importance):* extracurriculars, special talents, alumni relationship. Either the SAT or ACT is required. An interview is recommended. Admissions process is need-blind. *High school units required/recommended:* 17 total units are required; 4 English required, 3 math required, 2 science required, 2 foreign language recommended, 2 social studies required. *Special Requirements:* A portfolio is required for art program applicants. An audition is required for music program applicants. An R.N. is required for nursing program applicants. *The admissions office says:* "Because of the diversity of high school curricula, cultural influences on test results, the various abilities required in collegiate programs, and the unique background of applicants, each applicant's admissions portfolio is reviewed individually."

FINANCIAL AID

Students should submit: FAFSA. The Princeton Review suggests that all financial aid forms be submitted as soon as possible after January 1. *The following grants/scholarships are offered:* Pell, SEOG, academic merit, the school's own scholarships, the school's own grants, state grants, private scholarships, private grants, federal nursing scholarship, ROTC. *Students borrow from the following loan programs:* Perkins, PLUS, supplemental loans, private loans. Applicants will be notified of awards beginning early March. College Work-Study Program is available. The off-campus job outlook is good.

STUDENT BODY
Total undergrad enrollment	2,595
% male/female	40/60
% from out of state	46
% transfers	19
% from catholic high school	45
% live on campus	24
% African American	12
% Asian	4
% Caucasian	63
% Hispanic	11
% Native American	1
% international	5
# of countries represented	44

ACADEMICS
Calendar	semester
Student/teacher ratio	12:1
FT faculty	406
% faculty from religious order	7
% graduate in 4 yrs.	56

Most Popular Majors
business
communications
psychology

ADMISSIONS
Admissions Rating	74
# of applicants	1,725
% of applicants accepted	86
% of acceptees attending	36

Deadlines
Regular admission	8/1
Regular notification	rolling

FRESHMAN PROFILE
Range verbal SAT	530-650
Average verbal SAT	585
Range math SAT	500-620
Average math SAT	554
Range ACT	22-27
Average ACT	25
Minimum TOEFL	500
Average HS GPA or Avg	3.5

Graduated top 10% of class	33
Graduated top 25% of class	57
Graduated top 50% of class	83

FINANCIAL FACTS
Tuition	$13,274
Room & board	$5,850
Estimated book expense	$650
% frosh receiving aid	50
% undergrads receiving aid	50
% frosh w/ grant	68
Avg. grant	$7,615
% frosh w/ loan	44
Avg. loan	NR

LOYOLA UNIVERSITY OF CHICAGO

820 North Michigan Avenue, Chicago, IL 60611 • Admissions: 312-915-6500 • Fax: 312-915-6449
• Financial Aid: 312-915-6639 • E-mail: admission@luc.edu • Web Site: www.luc.edu

Loyola University of Chicago was founded in 1870 by the Jesuits. The university's 105-acre campus is located on Lake Michigan, just north of downtown Chicago. Facilities and equipment of note on campus include a gallery of medieval and renaissance art, a seismograph station, and a scanning electron microscope. The university has two branch campuses in greater Chicago, and another in Rome. Forty undergraduate majors are offered at Loyola, centered within the liberal arts and sciences, business, education, and nursing. Popular majors include psychology, business, and biology. Opportunities outside the classroom include an astonishing 136 registered clubs and organizations; activities run the gamut from arts and media activities to social-action groups and volunteer programs. Intercollegiate athletic teams are fielded in six sports for men, seven for women; intramural and club sports are also available.

ADMISSIONS

The admissions committee considers (in descending order of importance): HS record, test scores, class rank, recommendations. *Also considered (in descending order of importance):* extracurriculars, personality, special talents. Either the SAT or ACT is required. An interview is recommended. Admissions process is need-blind. *High school units required/recommended:* 15 total units are required; 4 English required, 2 math required, 4 math recommended, 1 science required, 2 science recommended, 4 foreign language recommended, 1 social studies required, 3 social studies recommended. Minimum 2.0 GPA required. *Special Requirements:* TOEFL is required of all international students. Biology and chemistry with labs required of nursing program applicants. *The admissions office says:* "We review student files on a rolling basis once they are complete with an application for admission, official transcripts, and ACT or SAT I scores."

FINANCIAL AID

Students should submit: FAFSA (due April 1), CSS Profile (due). The Princeton Review suggests that all financial aid forms be submitted as soon as possible after January 1. *The following grants/scholarships are offered:* Pell, SEOG, state scholarships, state grants, private scholarships, private grants, foreign aid. *Students borrow from the following loan programs:* Stafford, unsubsidized Stafford, Perkins, PLUS, supplemental loans, private loans. College Work-Study Program is available. Institutional employment is available. The off-campus job outlook is excellent.

STUDENT BODY

Total undergrad enrollment	8,106
% male/female	39/61
% from out of state	18
% transfers	29
% from catholic high school	39
% live on campus	29
% African American	5
% Asian	13
% Caucasian	69
% Hispanic	7
% international	1
# of countries represented	72

ACADEMICS

Calendar	semester
Student/teacher ratio	7:1
FT faculty	2098
% faculty from religious order	5
% graduate in 4 yrs.	62

Most Popular Majors
psychology
business
biology

ADMISSIONS

Admissions Rating	73
% of acceptees attending	38

Deadlines

Regular admission	4/1
Regular notification	rolling

FRESHMAN PROFILE

Range verbal SAT	420-540
Average verbal SAT	472
Range math SAT	470-610
Average math SAT	534
Range ACT	22-27
Average ACT	24
Minimum TOEFL	500
Graduated top 10% of class	32

Graduated top 25% of class	58
Graduated top 50% of class	88

FINANCIAL FACTS

Tuition	$14,400
Room & board	$6,210
Estimated book expense	$670
% frosh receiving aid	80
% undergrads receiving aid	80
% frosh w/ grant	54
Avg. grant	$3,141
% frosh w/ loan	53
Avg. loan	$2,948

MADONNA UNIVERSITY

36600 Schoolcraft Road, Livonia, MI 48150 • Admissions: 313-591-5052 • Fax: 313-432-5393
• Financial Aid: 313-432-5663 • E-mail: brohl@smtp.munet.edu • Web Site: www.munet.edu

Madonna University was founded in 1947 by the Felician Sisters as a women's college, and became coed in 1972. The university's 49-acre campus is located eighteen miles from downtown Detroit. Madonna awards degrees in fifty-one majors, primarily within the liberal arts and sciences, business, education, and health sciences. Nursing, business, and criminal justice are among the most popular academic programs. The University offers a wide range of options for activities outside the classroom. The available clubs and organizations include student government, a variety of musical ensembles, student-faculty academic clubs, and multicultural groups. Madonna fields athletic teams in basketball and baseball for men; basketball, softball, and volleyball for women. Special scholarships are offered for academic merit and a broad range of additional considerations.

ADMISSIONS

The admissions committee considers (in descending order of importance): HS record, test scores, class rank, recommendations, essay. *Also considered (in descending order of importance):* alumni relationship, extracurriculars, personality, special talents, geographical distribution. . An interview is recommended. *High school units required/recommended:* 19 total units are required; 3 English required, 2 math required, 2 science required, 2 foreign language recommended, 3 social studies required. Minimum composite ACT score of 20 and minimum 2.5 GPA required. *Special Requirements:* 1 unit each of algebra, biology, and chemistry required of nursing, medical and radiologic technology program applicants. Audition recommended of music program applicants. Portfolio recommended of art program applicants.

FINANCIAL AID

Students should submit: FAFSA, the school's own financial aid form. The Princeton Review suggests that all financial aid forms be submitted as soon as possible after January 1. *The following grants/scholarships are offered:* Pell, SEOG, academic merit, the school's own scholarships, the school's own grants, state grants, private scholarships, private grants. *Students borrow from the following loan programs:* Stafford, unsubsidized Stafford, Perkins, PLUS, the school's own loan fund, supplemental loans, state loans, private loans. College Work-Study Program is available. Institutional employment is available. The off-campus job outlook is good.

STUDENT BODY
Total undergrad enrollment	4,029
% male/female	24/76
% from out of state	2
% live on campus	5
% African American	10
% Asian	2
% Caucasian	85
% Hispanic	2
% Native American	1
% international	1

ACADEMICS
Calendar	semester
Student/teacher ratio	17:1
FT faculty	254
% faculty from religious order	3

Most Popular Majors
nursing
business
criminal justice

ADMISSIONS
Admissions Rating	65
% of acceptees attending	59

Deadlines
Regular admission	8/1
Regular notification	rolling

FRESHMAN PROFILE
Minimum TOEFL	540
Graduated top 10% of class	13
Graduated top 25% of class	27
Graduated top 50% of class	90

FINANCIAL FACTS
Tuition	$5,670
Room & board	$5,986
Estimated book expense	$430
% frosh receiving aid	25
% undergrads receiving aid	25

MANHATTAN COLLEGE

Manhattan College Parkway, Riverdale, NY 10471 • Admissions: 718-862-8000 • Fax: 718-862-8019
• Financial Aid: 718-862-7381 • E-mail: admit@manhattan.edu • Web Site: www.manhattan.edu

The Christian Brothers founded Manhattan College in 1853. The college sits on a 47-acre campus in the Bronx, fifteen miles from midtown Manhattan. Students may choose from sixty-four majors primarily within the liberal arts and sciences, business, education, and engineering. One shining star is a program in nuclear medical technology. Most popular among academic options are civil engineering, biology, and accounting. Among the notable facilities and equipment are a nuclear reactor and a plant morphogenesis lab. Manhattan counts seventy registered clubs and organizations, and twenty-six honor societies on campus, among them many music and arts organizations, political groups, and a variety of specific ethnic cultural activities. The college offers eight intercollegiate sports each for men and women; a variety of intramural and club sports are also available.

ADMISSIONS

The admissions committee considers (in descending order of importance): HS record, test scores, recommendations, class rank, essay. *Also considered (in descending order of importance):* alumni relationship, extracurriculars, geographical distribution, personality, special talents. Either the SAT or ACT is required; SAT is preferred. An interview is recommended. Admissions process is need-blind. *High school units required/recommended:* 16 total units are required; 4 English required, 3 math required, 4 math recommended, 2 science required, 3 science recommended, 2 foreign language required, 3 foreign language recommended, 3 social studies required. Rank in top half of secondary school class and minimum grade average of 80 recommended.

FINANCIAL AID

Students should submit: FAFSA (due February 15), the school's own financial aid form (due February 15), state aid form, Divorced Parents form, a copy of parents' most recent income tax filing (due April 30). The Princeton Review suggests that all financial aid forms be submitted as soon as possible after January 1. *The following grants/scholarships are offered:* Pell, SEOG, academic merit, athletic, the school's own scholarships, the school's own grants, state scholarships, state grants, private scholarships, private grants, foreign aid. *Students borrow from the following loan programs:* Stafford, unsubsidized Stafford, Perkins, PLUS, the school's own loan fund, supplemental loans, private loans. Applicants will be notified of awards beginning April 1. College Work-Study Program is available. Institutional employment is available. The off-campus job outlook is good.

STUDENT BODY		ACADEMICS		Deadlines		FINANCIAL FACTS	
Total undergrad enrollment	2,602	Calendar	semester	Early decision/action	12/1	Tuition	$13,800
% male/female	50/50	Student/teacher ratio	11:1	Regular admission	3/1	Room & board	$7,150
% from out of state	17	FT faculty	272	Regular notification	rolling	Estimated book expense	$500
% transfers	30	% graduate in 4 yrs.	85			% frosh receiving aid	85
% live on campus	50			**FRESHMAN PROFILE**		% undergrads receiving aid	65
% African American	5	**Most Popular Majors**		Average verbal SAT	514	% frosh w/ grant	91
% Asian	8	civil engineering		Average math SAT	516	Avg. grant	$4,000
% Caucasian	75	biology		Minimum TOEFL	520	% frosh w/ loan	73
% Hispanic	12	accounting		Average HS GPA or Avg	3.0	Avg. loan	$2,625
% international	2	**ADMISSIONS**		Graduated top 10% of class	23		
# of countries represented	50	Admissions Rating	76	Graduated top 25% of class	67		
		# of applicants	2,986	Graduated top 50% of class	77		
		% of applicants accepted	69				
		% of acceptees attending	28				

Marian College

3200 Cold Spring Road, Indianapolis, IN 46222 • Admissions: 317-929-0321 • Fax: 317-929-0323
• Financial Aid: 317-929-0234 • Web Site: marian.creighton.edu/~marian-w/college/ccenter.html

Marian College was founded in 1851 by the Sisters of Saint Francis Third Order Regular. The college's campus is six miles from the center of Indianapolis and extends over 114 acres. A 35-acre tract including a lake and waterfall has been designated a wetlands ecology laboratory. Twenty-eight majors are offered at Marian, the majority within the disciplines of liberal arts and sciences, business, education, and nursing. Of note is a program in sports administration. Most popular of Marian's offerings are nursing, business, and elementary education. Forty-one registered clubs and organizations include student government, a variety of publications, musical ensembles, and service groups. The college fields seven athletic teams each for men and women; intramural sports are also offered.

ADMISSIONS

The admissions committee considers (in descending order of importance): test scores, HS record, class rank, recommendations, essay. *Also considered (in descending order of importance):* special talents, extracurriculars, personality. Either the SAT or ACT is required; SAT is preferred. *High school units required/recommended:* 3 English required, 2 math required, 1 science required, 1 social studies required. 2 units of foreign language recommended. Minimum combined SAT I score of 800, rank in top half of secondary school class, and minimum 2.3 GPA recommended. *Special Requirements:* Nursing program applicants must meet additional requirements.

FINANCIAL AID

Students should submit: FAFSA (due April 15), the school's own financial aid form (due April 15), state aid form, a copy of parents' most recent income tax filing. The Princeton Review suggests that all financial aid forms be submitted as soon as possible after January 1. *The following grants/scholarships are offered:* state scholarships. *Students borrow from the following loan programs:* Stafford, PLUS. The off-campus job outlook is good.

STUDENT BODY
Total undergrad enrollment	1,352
% male/female	34/66
% from out of state	6
% transfers	27
% live on campus	42
% African American	12
% Asian	1
% Caucasian	81
% Hispanic	1
% international	2
# of countries represented	21

ACADEMICS
Calendar	semester
Student/teacher ratio	8:1
FT faculty	152
% graduate in 4 yrs.	53

Most Popular Majors
nursing
business administration
elementary education

ADMISSIONS
Admissions Rating	64
% of acceptees attending	46

Deadlines
Regular admission	rolling
Regular notification	rolling

FRESHMAN PROFILE
Average verbal SAT	508
Average math SAT	497
Minimum TOEFL	550
Average HS GPA or Avg	3.1
Graduated top 10% of class	19
Graduated top 25% of class	42
Graduated top 50% of class	77

FINANCIAL FACTS
Tuition	$11,440
Room & board	$4,212
Estimated book expense	$550
% frosh receiving aid	78
% undergrads receiving aid	85

MARIAN COLLEGE OF FOND DU LAC

45 S. National Ave., Fond du Lac, WI 54935 • Admissions: 414-923-7650 • Fax: 414-923-7154
• Financial Aid: 414-923-7614 • E-mail: admit@mariancoll.edu

The Sisters of the Congregation of Saint Agnes founded Marian College of Fond Du Lac in 1936. The college's 40-acre campus is located sixty-two miles from Milwaukee. Marian offers forty-two majors in the liberal arts and sciences, business, education, and nursing. The programs that fill up quickly are nursing, business, and education. Facilities of note include an on-campus child-care center. A variety of clubs and organizations are registered at the college, offering a range of extracurricular options, including music and arts activities, cultural groups, a variety of publications, and volunteer community service. In addition to their academic record, graduates can also get a community-service transcript. Marian offers intercollegiate athletic teams in eight sports for men, and seven for women.

ADMISSIONS

The admissions committee considers (in descending order of importance): HS record, test scores, class rank, recommendations. *Also considered (in descending order of importance):* personality, special talents, extracurriculars, alumni relationship, geographical distribution. Either the SAT or ACT is required; ACT is preferred. An interview is recommended. Admissions process is need-blind. *High school units required/recommended:* 16 total units are required; 3 English required, 4 English recommended, 2 math required, 2 science recommended, 2 foreign language recommended, 2 social studies recommended. Minimum composite ACT score of 18, rank in top half of secondary school class, and minimum 2.0 GPA required. *Special Requirements:* 1 unit of chemistry and 1 unit of biology required of nursing program applicants.

FINANCIAL AID

Students should submit: FAFSA (due April 15), the school's own financial aid form (due April 15). The Princeton Review suggests that all financial aid forms be submitted as soon as possible after January 1. *The following grants/scholarships are offered:* state scholarships. *Students borrow from the following loan programs:* Stafford, PLUS. College Work-Study Program is available. Institutional employment is available. The off-campus job outlook is good.

STUDENT BODY		ACADEMICS		Deadlines		Room & board	$3,800
Total undergrad enrollment	1,856	Calendar	semester	Regular admission	7/1	Estimated book expense	$500
% male/female	33/67	Student/teacher ratio	7:1	Regular notification	rolling	% frosh receiving aid	85
% from out of state	20	FT faculty	372			% undergrads receiving aid	85
% from catholic high school	30	% faculty from religious order	2	**FRESHMAN PROFILE**			
% live on campus	55			Average ACT	20		
% African American	3	**Most Popular Majors**		Minimum TOEFL	525		
% Asian	2	nursing		Graduated top 10% of class	15		
% Caucasian	88	business		Graduated top 25% of class	41		
% Hispanic	1	education		Graduated top 50% of class	70		
% Native American	1	**ADMISSIONS**		**FINANCIAL FACTS**			
% international	1	Admissions Rating	68	Tuition	$10,560		
# of countries represented	5	% of acceptees attending	51				

MARIST COLLEGE

North Road, Poughkeepsie, NY 12601 • Admissions: 914-575-3000 • Fax: 800-436-5483
• Financial Aid: 914-575-3230 • E-mail: HWW@ musica.marista.edu • Web Site: www.marist.edu

Marist College was founded by the Marist Brothers in 1929 as a religious training school. The college is located on a 134-acre campus in Poughkeepsie, seventy-five miles from New York City. Marist seeks to explore ways in which academic excellence may be enhanced with state-of-the-art information and communications technology. Forty-six majors within the liberal arts and sciences, business, education, and a variety of career-oriented disciplines are available at the college. Special academic facilities include the Lowell Thomas Communications Center, a management studies center, a river laboratory for environmental studies, and the Marist Institute for Public Opinion—a nationally respected political polling group. There are seventy-four clubs and organizations registered at the college, offering a diverse selection of activities in the arts, multicultural concerns, journalistic activities, political groups, and volunteer and social-action clubs. Marist fields an impressive array of seventeen intercollegiate athletic teams for men and fourteen for women, including sailing. Men's basketball is the most prominent of the college's teams.

ADMISSIONS

The admissions committee considers (in descending order of importance): HS record, class rank, test scores, recommendations, essay. *Also considered (in descending order of importance):* geographical distribution, personality, special talents, alumni relationship, extracurriculars. Either the SAT or ACT is required. An interview is recommended. Admissions process is need-blind. *High school units required/recommended:* 16 total units are required; 4 English recommended, 3 math recommended, 2 science recommended, 2 foreign language recommended, 3 social studies recommended, 2 history recommended. Minimum combined SAT I score of 900, rank in top two-fifths of secondary school class, and minimum grade average of 80 required. *Special Requirements:* 4 units of math recommended for computer science and science program applicants.

FINANCIAL AID

Students should submit: FAFSA (due February 15), state aid form, a copy of parents' most recent income tax filing (due June 1). The Princeton Review suggests that all financial aid forms be submitted as soon as possible after January 1. *The following grants/scholarships are offered:* Pell, SEOG, athletic, the school's own scholarships, the school's own grants, state scholarships, state grants, private scholarships, private grants, ROTC. *Students borrow from the following loan programs:* Stafford, unsubsidized Stafford, Perkins, PLUS, the school's own loan fund, supplemental loans, private loans. College Work-Study Program is available. Institutional employment is available. The off-campus job outlook is good.

STUDENT BODY

Total undergrad enrollment	3,935
% male/female	43/57
% from out of state	40
% transfers	14
% from catholic high school	24
% live on campus	70
% African American	8
% Asian	2
% Caucasian	84
% Hispanic	5
% Native American	1
% international	1
# of countries represented	11

ACADEMICS

Calendar	semester
Student/teacher ratio	11:1
FT faculty	392
% faculty from religious order	1
% graduate in 4 yrs.	64

Most Popular Majors
communication arts
business administration
psychology

ADMISSIONS

Admissions Rating	84
# of applicants	4,710

% of applicants accepted	64
% of acceptees attending	29

Deadlines

Early decision/action	12/1
Regular admission	3/1
Regular notification	rolling

FRESHMAN PROFILE

Average verbal SAT	541
Average math SAT	533
Average ACT	25
Minimum TOEFL	550

FINANCIAL FACTS

Tuition	$11,400
Room & board	$6,300
Estimated book expense	$550
% frosh receiving aid	73
% undergrads receiving aid	68
% frosh w/ grant	66
Avg. grant	$2,431
% frosh w/ loan	75
Avg. loan	$3,715

MARQUETTE UNIVERSITY

P.O. Box 1881, Milwaukee, WI 53201 • Admissions: 414-288-7250 • Fax: 414-288-7179
• Financial Aid: 414-288-7390 • E-mail: go2marquette@marquette.edu • Web Site: www.marquette.edu

Marquette University was founded in 1881 by the Jesuits. Originally called Saint Aloysius College, the name was later changed to honor Father Jacques Marquette, a French Jesuit missionary and explorer. The university's 80-acre campus is located in downtown Milwaukee. Marquette offers sixty-two majors within the areas of liberal arts and sciences, business, education, engineering, and health sciences. Among the most popular of majors are mechanical engineering, accounting, and electrical engineering. Special facilities and equipment include an electron microscope, an art museum, a speech and hearing clinic, a chromatography lab, and a sports law center. Marquette is designated by the Department of Education as a national resource center for international studies. When it comes to extracurricular activities, if you can't find it at Marquette it probably doesn't exist; the university has a huge selection of 160 registered clubs and organizations. Marquette fields intercollegiate athletic teams in seventeen sports for men, and twelve for women. Intramural and club sports are equally as extensive. The men's basketball team is nationally competitive, regularly appearing in post season tournament play.

ADMISSIONS

The admissions committee considers (in descending order of importance): HS record, class rank, test scores, recommendations, essay. Either the SAT or ACT is required. An interview is recommended. Admissions process is need-blind. *High school units required/recommended:* 16 total units are recommended; 4 English recommended, 3 math recommended, 2 science recommended, 2 foreign language recommended, 2 social studies recommended. Minimum composite ACT score of 21 (combined SAT I score of 800) and minimum 2.0 GPA required. *Special Requirements:* Additional math and/or science units required for business, engineering, and health profession program applicants.

FINANCIAL AID

Students should submit: FAFSA (due March 1). The Princeton Review suggests that all financial aid forms be submitted as soon as possible after January 1. *The following grants/scholarships are offered:* Pell, SEOG, academic merit, the school's own scholarships, the school's own grants, state scholarships, state grants, private scholarships, private grants. *Students borrow from the following loan programs:* Stafford, unsubsidized Stafford, Perkins, PLUS, the school's own loan fund, supplemental loans, private loans. College Work-Study Program is available. Institutional employment is available. The off-campus job outlook is excellent.

STUDENT BODY		ACADEMICS	
Total undergrad enrollment	7,462	Calendar	semester
% male/female	47/53	Student/teacher ratio	12:1
% from out of state	52	FT faculty	914
% transfers	15	% faculty from religious order	4
% from catholic high school	37	% graduate in 4 yrs.	75
% live on campus	41		
% African American	4	**Most Popular Majors**	
% Asian	5	mechanical engineering	
% Caucasian	88	accounting	
% Hispanic	3	electrical engineering	
% international	1	**ADMISSIONS**	
# of countries represented	80	Admissions Rating	74
		# of applicants	5,323

% of applicants accepted	86	Graduated top 10% of class	33
% of acceptees attending	31	Graduated top 25% of class	64
		Graduated top 50% of class	91
Deadlines			
Regular admission	rolling	**FINANCIAL FACTS**	
Regular notification	rolling	Tuition	$14,710
FRESHMAN PROFILE		Room & board	$5,350
Range verbal SAT	520-620	Estimated book expense	$600
Average verbal SAT	571	% frosh receiving aid	92
Range math SAT	530-630	% undergrads receiving aid	80
Average math SAT	580	% frosh w/ grant	43
Range ACT	23-28	Avg. grant	$5,500
Average ACT	25	% frosh w/ loan	61
Minimum TOEFL	500	Avg. loan	$4,519
Average HS GPA or Avg	3.0		

UNIVERSITY OF MARY

7500 University Drive, Bismarck, ND 58504 • Admissions: 701-255-7500 • Fax: 701-255-7687
• Financial Aid: 701-255-7500 • E-mail: steph@umary.edu • Web Site: umary.edu

The Benedictine Sisters founded the University of Mary in 1959. Located six miles from the state capital's downtown, the university's 107-acre campus overlooks the Missouri River. UM offers twenty-three majors within the liberal arts and sciences, business, education, and health sciences. Among the most popular of these programs are biology, nursing, and business administration. Construction planning is underway for a new library-technology center. The university offers sixty clubs and service organizations; most noteworthy is its vast array of activities in the arts, especially music. Nearly all of the men's and women's intercollegiate athletic teams are powers in the NAIA, fielding perennial championship-contending (and title-winning) teams in football, cross-country, volleyball, basketball, wrestling, track and field, tennis, and softball.

ADMISSIONS

The admissions committee considers (in descending order of importance): HS record, test scores, class rank, recommendations. Either the SAT or ACT is required; ACT is preferred. Admissions process is need-blind. *High school units required/recommended:* 4 English recommended, 2 math recommended, 2 science recommended, 3 social studies recommended. Minimum composite ACT score of 18, rank in top half of secondary school class, and minimum 2.5 GPA recommended. *Special Requirements:* An audition is required for music program applicants. TOEFL is required of all international students.

FINANCIAL AID

Students should submit: FAFSA, the school's own financial aid form. The Princeton Review suggests that all financial aid forms be submitted as soon as possible after January 1. *The following grants/scholarships are offered:* state scholarships. *Students borrow from the following loan programs:* Stafford, PLUS. College Work-Study Program is available. Institutional employment is available. The off-campus job outlook is good.

STUDENT BODY		ACADEMICS		ADMISSIONS		FINANCIAL FACTS	
Total undergrad enrollment	1,867	Calendar	4-4-1	Admissions Rating	75	Tuition	$7,230
% male/female	38/62	Student/teacher ratio	13:1	% of acceptees attending	58	Room & board	$2,890
% from out of state	27	FT faculty	153			Estimated book expense	$500
% from catholic high school	3	% faculty from religious order	12	**Deadlines**		% frosh receiving aid	83
% live on campus	40	% graduate in 4 yrs.	50	Regular admission	8/1	% undergrads receiving aid	78
% African American	1			Regular notification	rolling		
% Asian	1	**Most Popular Majors**					
% Caucasian	93	biology		**FRESHMAN PROFILE**			
% Hispanic	1	nursing		Average ACT	22		
% Native American	4	business administration		Average HS GPA or Avg	3.2		
% international	1			Graduated top 10% of class	13		
				Graduated top 25% of class	38		
				Graduated top 50% of class	71		

MARYGROVE COLLEGE

8425 West McNichols Rd., Detroit, MI 48221 • *Admissions: 313-862-5200* • *Fax: 313-864-6670*
• *Financial Aid: 313-862-8000*

Marygrove College was founded in 1910 by the Servants of the Immaculate Heart of Mary. It became coed in 1971. The college's 68-acre campus is located six miles from downtown Detroit. Marygrove awards degrees in forty-seven majors, primarily within the liberal arts and sciences, business, education, and health sciences. Business, education, and social work are among the most popular academic programs. There are sixteen available clubs and organizations, including student government, a newspaper and magazine, performing arts and academic organizations. Marygrove does not compete in intercollegiate athletics. Distinguished Scholar Awards ranging from $500 to full tuition are presented to thirty-five new students each year in recognition of achievement in academics or visual and performing arts.

ADMISSIONS

The admissions committee considers (in descending order of importance): HS record, recommendations, test scores, class rank. *Also considered (in descending order of importance):* special talents, alumni relationship, personality, extracurriculars. Either the SAT or ACT is required; ACT is preferred. An interview is recommended. Admissions process is need-blind. *High school units required/recommended:* 25 total units are recommended; 8 English recommended, 4 math recommended, 1 science recommended, 1 foreign language recommended, 4 social studies recommended, 5 history recommended. Minimum 2.7 GPA required. *Special Requirements:* A portfolio is required for art program applicants. An audition is required for music program applicants. TOEFL is required of all international students. Separate requirements for allied health program applicants.

FINANCIAL AID

Students should submit: FAFSA, the school's own financial aid form, state aid form, a copy of parents' most recent income tax filing. The Princeton Review suggests that all financial aid forms be submitted as soon as possible after January 1. *The following grants/scholarships are offered:* state scholarships. *Students borrow from the following loan programs:* Stafford, PLUS. Applicants will be notified of awards beginning May 1. College Work-Study Program is available. The off-campus job outlook is fair.

STUDENT BODY
Total undergrad enrollment	1,087
% male/female	15/85
% from out of state	2
% transfers	52
% live on campus	8
% African American	72
% Asian	1
% Caucasian	19
% Hispanic	1
% international	1

ACADEMICS
Calendar	semester
Student/teacher ratio	43:1
FT faculty	58
% faculty from religious order	12
% graduate in 4 yrs.	10

Most Popular Majors
business
education
social work

ADMISSIONS
Admissions Rating	70
# of applicants	173

% of applicants accepted	64
% of acceptees attending	71

Deadlines
Regular admission	rolling
Regular notification	rolling

FRESHMAN PROFILE
Minimum TOEFL	550
Average HS GPA or Avg	2.7
Graduated top 10% of class	10
Graduated top 25% of class	75
Graduated top 50% of class	100

FINANCIAL FACTS
Tuition	$8,836

Room & board	$4,330
% frosh receiving aid	92
% undergrads receiving aid	98

MARYMOUNT COLLEGE

100 Marymount Avenue, Tarrytown, NY 10591 • Admissions: 914-631-3451 • Fax: 914-332-4956
• Financial Aid: 914-332-8345 • E-mail: admiss@mms.marymt.edu • Web Site: www.marymt.edu

Marymount College was founded in 1907 by the Religious of the Sacred Heart of Mary. Men are admitted to the college's weekend program only. Its 25-acre campus overlooks the Hudson River, twenty-five miles from New York City. Forty majors are offered at Marymount, the majority within the disciplines of liberal arts and sciences, business, and education. Of note are programs in fashion design and illustration, and clothing and textile studies. Most popular of Marymount's offerings are business, education, and psychology. Twenty-eight registered clubs and organizations include student government, a variety of publications, musical ensembles, cultural and international organizations, and service groups. The college fields seven intercollegiate athletic teams, including an equestrian team, and a diverse selection of intramural sports.

ADMISSIONS
The admissions committee considers (in descending order of importance): HS record, recommendations, test scores, essay, class rank. *Also considered (in descending order of importance):* personality, extracurriculars, alumni relationship, geographical distribution, special talents. Either the SAT or ACT is required; SAT is preferred. An interview is recommended. Admissions process is need-blind. *High school units required/ recommended:* 16 total units are required; 4 English recommended, 3 math recommended, 3 science recommended, 3 foreign language recommended, 3 social studies recommended. Minimum 2.5 GPA recommended. *Special Requirements:* TOEFL is required of all international students.

FINANCIAL AID
Students should submit: FAFSA (due February 15), the school's own financial aid form (due February 15), a copy of parents' most recent income tax filing (due February 15). The Princeton Review suggests that all financial aid forms be submitted as soon as possible after January 1. *The following grants/scholarships are offered:* Pell, SEOG, academic merit, athletic, the school's own scholarships, the school's own grants, state scholarships, state grants, private scholarships, private grants. *Students borrow from the following loan programs:* Stafford, unsubsidized Stafford, Perkins, PLUS, the school's own loan fund, supplemental loans, private loans. Applicants will be notified of awards beginning February. College Work-Study Program is available. Institutional employment is available. The off-campus job outlook is good.

STUDENT BODY		ACADEMICS		Deadlines		FINANCIAL FACTS	
Total undergrad enrollment	947	Calendar	semester	Regular admission	8/15	Tuition	$12,500
% male/female	6/94	Student/teacher ratio	7:1	Regular notification	rolling	Room & board	$7,200
% from out of state	30	FT faculty	147			Estimated book expense	$555
% transfers	34	% faculty from religious order	8	**FRESHMAN PROFILE**		% frosh receiving aid	63
% from catholic high school	19	% graduate in 4 yrs.	45	Average verbal SAT	455	% undergrads receiving aid	57
% live on campus	70			Average math SAT	460	% frosh w/ grant	59
% African American	13	**Most Popular Majors**		Minimum TOEFL	500	Avg. grant	NR
% Asian	4	business		Average HS GPA or Avg	3.0	% frosh w/ loan	31
% Caucasian	49	education		Graduated top 10% of class	10	Avg. loan	$3,825
% Hispanic	12	psychology		Graduated top 25% of class	36		
% international	5	**ADMISSIONS**		Graduated top 50% of class	76		
# of countries represented	13	Admissions Rating	64				
		% of acceptees attending	34				

MARYMOUNT MANHATTAN COLLEGE

221 East 71st Street, New York, NY 10021 • Admissions: 212-517-0555 • Fax: 212-517-0413
• Financial Aid: 212-517-0463

The Religious of the Sacred Heart of Mary founded Marymount Manhattan College in 1936. Men are admitted only for the college's bachelor of fine arts degree. The college's main facility is an eight-story building on the East Side of Manhattan; a freshman residence hall with recreational facilities is located within a short distance. Twenty-five majors within the liberal arts and sciences, business, and education are available at the college. Most popular of these academic offerings are business management, psychology, and theater. Special academic facilities include clinical facilities for speech pathology and audiology, an art gallery, a theater and a dance studio. Marymount Manhattan offers a diverse selection of activities in the arts, multicultural concerns, journalistic activities, political groups, and volunteer and social-action clubs.

ADMISSIONS

The admissions committee considers (in descending order of importance): HS record, class rank, recommendations, test scores, essay. *Also considered (in descending order of importance):* extracurriculars, personality, special talents, alumni relationship. Either the SAT or ACT is required. An interview is recommended. Admissions process is need-blind. *High school units required/recommended:* 20 total units are recommended; 4 English recommended, 3 math recommended, 3 science recommended, 3 foreign language recommended, 3 social studies recommended. Minimum SAT I scores of 450 in both verbal and math, and 2.0 GPA recommended. *Special Requirements:* A portfolio is required for art program applicants. Audition required of dance and theatre program applicants.

FINANCIAL AID

Students should submit: FAFSA. The Princeton Review suggests that all financial aid forms be submitted as soon as possible after January 1. *The following grants/scholarships are offered:* state scholarships. *Students borrow from the following loan programs:* Stafford, PLUS. College Work-Study Program is available. Institutional employment is available. The off-campus job outlook is excellent.

STUDENT BODY

Total undergrad enrollment	1,973
% male/female	23/77
% from out of state	16
% transfers	29
% live on campus	23
% African American	20
% Asian	5
% Caucasian	54
% Hispanic	17
% international	3
# of countries represented	35

ACADEMICS

Calendar	4-1-4
Student/teacher ratio	8:1
FT faculty	233
% graduate in 4 yrs.	39

Most Popular Majors
business management
psychology
theatre

ADMISSIONS

Admissions Rating	69
% of acceptees attending	44

Deadlines

Regular admission	rolling
Regular notification	rolling

FRESHMAN PROFILE

Average verbal SAT	460
Average math SAT	500
Average ACT	23
Minimum TOEFL	550
Graduated top 10% of class	22
Graduated top 25% of class	50
Graduated top 50% of class	80

FINANCIAL FACTS

Tuition	$11,650
Room & board	$5,300
Estimated book expense	$500
% frosh receiving aid	80
% undergrads receiving aid	85

MARYMOUNT UNIVERSITY

2807 North Glebe Road, Arlington, VA 22207 • *Admissions: 703-284-1500* • *Fax: 703-522-0349*
• *Financial Aid: 703-284-1530* • *E-mail: admissions@marymount.edu* • *Web Site: www.marymount.edu*

Founded in 1950 by the Religious of the Sacred Heart of Mary, Marymount University became coed in 1987. The university is situated on a 21-acre campus minutes from Washington, D.C. Marymount offers thirty-three majors in the liberal arts and sciences, business, education, nursing, and a selection of career-oriented disciplines. Most popular academic programs include psychology, interior design, and nursing. Twenty-six clubs and organizations are registered at the college, offering a range of extracurricular options including music and arts activities, a variety of publications, political groups, and professional organizations. Marymount sponsors intercollegiate athletic teams in five sports each for men and women.

ADMISSIONS

The admissions committee considers (in descending order of importance): HS record, test scores, recommendations, class rank. *Also considered (in descending order of importance):* extracurriculars, personality, alumni relationship. Either the SAT or ACT is required. An interview is recommended. *High school units required/recommended:* 16 total units are recommended; 4 English recommended, 3 math recommended, 2 science recommended, 3 foreign language recommended, 3 social studies recommended. Minimum combined SAT I score of 800 and minimum 2.5 GPA in academic courses required.

FINANCIAL AID

Students should submit: FAFSA (due March 1), the school's own financial aid form (due March 1). The Princeton Review suggests that all financial aid forms be submitted as soon as possible after January 1. *The following grants/scholarships are offered:* Pell, SEOG, academic merit, the school's own scholarships, the school's own grants, yes scholarships, state grants, private scholarships, private grants. *Students borrow from the following loan programs:* Stafford, unsubsidized Stafford, Perkins, PLUS, the school's own loan fund, supplemental loans, private loans. Applicants will be notified of awards beginning March 15. College Work-Study Program is available. Institutional employment is available. The off-campus job outlook is excellent.

STUDENT BODY		ACADEMICS		Deadlines		FINANCIAL FACTS	
Total undergrad enrollment	2,023	Calendar	semester	Regular admission	rolling	Tuition	$12,400
% male/female	24/76	Student/teacher ratio	10:1	Regular notification	rolling	Room & board	$5,640
% from out of state	36	FT faculty	385			Estimated book expense	$500
% transfers	14			**FRESHMAN PROFILE**		% frosh receiving aid	74
% live on campus	26	**Most Popular Majors**		Range verbal SAT	400-500	% undergrads receiving aid	80
% African American	14	psychology		Average verbal SAT	440	% frosh w/ grant	51
% Asian	7	interior design		Range math SAT	420-530	Avg. grant	$7,500
% Caucasian	73	nursing		Average math SAT	467	% frosh w/ loan	72
% Hispanic	6	**ADMISSIONS**		Minimum TOEFL	500	Avg. loan	$1,432
# of countries represented	64	Admissions Rating	64	Graduated top 10% of class	10		
		% of acceptees attending	28	Graduated top 25% of class	30		
				Graduated top 50% of class	63		

MARYWOOD COLLEGE

2300 Adams Avenue, Scranton, PA 18509 • *Admissions: 717-348-6234* • *Fax: 717-348-1899*
• *Financial Aid: 717-348-6225* • *E-mail: ugadm@ac.marywood.edu* • *Web Site: www.marywood.edu*

Marywood College was founded by the Servants of the Immaculate Heart of Mary in 1915. The college, located on a 152-acre campus, offers seventy-nine majors among the liberal arts and sciences, business, education, and health sciences. Popular majors include elementary education and business administration. Noteworthy facilities include art galleries, a museum, an early childhood center, a greenhouse, and a computer music laboratory. Marywood counts some forty-one registered organizations on campus and a variety of artistic and social groups, including a community volunteer program and numerous journalistic outlets, from publications to television and radio. Intercollegiate athletic teams at Marywood compete in four sports for men, five for women.

ADMISSIONS

The admissions committee considers (in descending order of importance): HS record, class rank, test scores, recommendations, essay. *Also considered (in descending order of importance):* alumni relationship, extracurriculars, personality, special talents. Either the SAT or ACT is required; SAT is preferred. An interview is recommended. Admissions process is need-blind. *High school units required/recommended:* 16 total units are required; 4 English required, 2 math required, 1 science required, 3 social studies required. Minimum combined SAT I score of 900, rank in top half of secondary school class, and minimum 2.5 GPA recommended. Minimum combined SAT I score of 970 (composite ACT score of 20) required of nursing program applicants. Minimum combined SAT I score of 970 (composite ACT score of 21) required of education and special education program applicants. *Special Requirements:* A portfolio is required for art program applicants. An audition is required for music program applicants.

FINANCIAL AID

Students should submit: FAFSA (due February 15), the school's own financial aid form (due February 15), a copy of parents' most recent income tax filing (due May 1). The Princeton Review suggests that all financial aid forms be submitted as soon as possible after January 1. *The following grants/scholarships are offered:* Pell, SEOG, academic merit, athletic, the school's own scholarships, the school's own grants, state scholarships, state grants, private scholarships, private grants, ROTC, foreign aid. *Students borrow from the following loan programs:* Stafford, unsubsidized Stafford, Perkins, PLUS, the school's own loan fund, supplemental loans, private loans. Applicants will be notified of awards beginning March 1. College Work-Study Program is available. The off-campus job outlook is good.

STUDENT BODY		ACADEMICS		Deadlines		FINANCIAL FACTS	
Total undergrad enrollment	1,758	Calendar	semester	Regular admission	rolling	Tuition	$12,640
% male/female	22/78	Student/teacher ratio	12:1	Regular notification	rolling	Room & board	$5,200
% from out of state	21	FT faculty	250			Estimated book expense	$600
% transfers	42	% faculty from religious order	20	**FRESHMAN PROFILE**		% frosh receiving aid	90
% live on campus	30	% graduate in 4 yrs.	59	Range verbal SAT	480-570	% undergrads receiving aid	80
% African American	1			Average verbal SAT	533		
% Asian	1	**Most Popular Majors**		Range math SAT	460-560		
% Caucasian	95	elementary education		Average math SAT	512		
% Hispanic	2	business administration		Range ACT	20-25		
% international	1			Minimum TOEFL	500		
# of countries represented	16	**ADMISSIONS**		Average HS GPA or Avg	3.2		
		Admissions Rating	73	Graduated top 10% of class	19		
		# of applicants	992	Graduated top 25% of class	47		
		% of applicants accepted	76	Graduated top 50% of class	83		
		% of acceptees attending	33				

MERCYHURST COLLEGE

Glenwood Hills, Erie, PA 16546 • *Admissions: 814-824-2202* • *Fax: 814-824-2071*
• *Financial Aid: 814-824-2287* • *E-mail: roth@paradise.mercy.edu* • *Web Site: eden.mercy.edu*

Founded in 1926 by the Sisters of Mercy, Mercyhurst College became coed in 1969. The college's 75-acre campus overlooks Lake Erie, 100 miles from Pittsburgh and ninety miles from Buffalo. The campus is home to an observatory, an art gallery, and archeological and culinary institutes. Mercyhurst offers nearly 100 majors in a wide variety of academic disciplines and career-oriented programs; among the most popular are business, natural sciences, and music. Thirty-one clubs and organizations are registered at the college, offering a range of extracurricular options, including music and arts activities, a variety of publications, radio, and television. Mercyhurst competes in intercollegiate athletics in eleven sports for men, nine for women; a range of intramural and club sports are also offered. Housing on campus is guaranteed.

ADMISSIONS

The admissions committee considers (in descending order of importance): HS record, recommendations, essay, class rank, test scores. *Also considered (in descending order of importance):* personality, extracurriculars, special talents, alumni relationship, geographical distribution. Either the SAT or ACT is required. An interview is recommended. Admissions process is need-blind. *High school units required/recommended:* 18 total units are recommended; 4 English recommended, 3 math recommended, 3 science recommended, 2 foreign language recommended, 1 social studies recommended, 2 history recommended. Minimum combined SAT I score of 800, rank in top half of secondary school class, or minimum 2.5 GPA recommended. *Special Requirements:* A portfolio is required for art program applicants. An audition is required for music program applicants. Audition required of dance program applicants.

FINANCIAL AID

Students should submit: FAFSA (due May 1), the school's own financial aid form (due March 15), a copy of parents' most recent income tax filing (due May 1). The Princeton Review suggests that all financial aid forms be submitted as soon as possible after January 1. *The following grants/scholarships are offered:* Pell, SEOG, academic merit, the school's own scholarships, the school's own grants, state scholarships, state grants, private scholarships, private grants, ROTC, foreign aid. *Students borrow from the following loan programs:* Stafford, unsubsidized Stafford, Perkins, PLUS, the school's own loan fund, supplemental loans, state loans, private loans. College Work-Study Program is available. Institutional employment is available. The off-campus job outlook is good.

STUDENT BODY

Total undergrad enrollment	2,635
% male/female	48/52
% from out of state	37
% transfers	25
% from catholic high school	19
% live on campus	78
% African American	3
% Asian	2
% Caucasian	88
% Hispanic	2
% Native American	1
% international	7
# of countries represented	17

ACADEMICS

Calendar	other
Student/teacher ratio	16:1
FT faculty	172
% faculty from religious order	3
% graduate in 4 yrs.	60

Most Popular Majors
business
natural sciences
music

ADMISSIONS

Admissions Rating	75
# of applicants	1,761

% of applicants accepted	77
% of acceptees attending	34

Deadlines

Regular admission	rolling
Regular notification	rolling

FRESHMAN PROFILE

Range verbal SAT	500-600
Average verbal SAT	549
Range math SAT	480-580
Average math SAT	532
Range ACT	21-26
Average ACT	23
Minimum TOEFL	550
Average HS GPA or Avg	3.4

Graduated top 10% of class	16
Graduated top 25% of class	42
Graduated top 50% of class	85

FINANCIAL FACTS

Tuition	$10,920
Room & board	$4,500
Estimated book expense	$1,000
% frosh receiving aid	88
% undergrads receiving aid	85
% frosh w/ grant	80
Avg. grant	$4,530
% frosh w/ loan	75
Avg. loan	$2,387

MERRIMACK COLLEGE

315 Turnpike Street, North Andover, MA 01845 • *Admissions: 508-837-5100* • *Fax: 508-837-5222*
• *Financial Aid: 508-837-5186* • *E-mail: mretelle@merrimack.edu*

Merrimack College was founded in 1947 by the Fathers of the Order of Saint Augustine. The college's 220-acre campus is located next to the rambling Merrimack River and is twenty-five miles north of Boston. Merrimack offers forty-two majors, primarily within the liberal arts and sciences, business, and engineering. Notable campus features are a microscale chemistry institute, an art gallery, and an observatory. The college offers fifty-four clubs and organizations, providing a range of extracurricular options including music and arts activities, cultural groups, a variety of publications, and volunteer community service. Athletic teams at Merrimack compete in intercollegiate athletics in nine sports for men, eight for women. Housing is guaranteed to all who wish to live on campus.

ADMISSIONS

The admissions committee considers (in descending order of importance): HS record, class rank, test scores, recommendations, essay. *Also considered (in descending order of importance):* alumni relationship, extracurriculars, geographical distribution, personality, special talents. Either the SAT or ACT is required; SAT is preferred. An interview is recommended. Admissions process is need-blind. *High school units required/recommended:* 16 total units are required; 4 English required, 3 math required, 4 math recommended, 1 science required, 3 science recommended, 2 foreign language recommended, 2 social studies required, 1 history recommended. 4 units of math and 3 units of science required of engineering and science program applicants. Physics required of engineering program applicants. Minimum combined SAT I score of 800, rank in top half of secondary school class, and minimum 2.5 GPA recommended.

FINANCIAL AID

Students should submit: FAFSA (due March 1), state aid form (due April 1), a copy of parents' most recent income tax filing (due June 1). The Princeton Review suggests that all financial aid forms be submitted as soon as possible after January 1. *The following grants/scholarships are offered:* Pell, SEOG, the school's own scholarships, the school's own grants, state scholarships, state grants, private scholarships, private grants. *Students borrow from the following loan programs:* Stafford, unsubsidized Stafford, Perkins, PLUS, the school's own loan fund, supplemental loans, health professions loans, private loans. Applicants will be notified of awards beginning March 15. College Work-Study Program is available. Institutional employment is available. The off-campus job outlook is good.

STUDENT BODY		ACADEMICS		Deadlines		FINANCIAL FACTS	
Total undergrad enrollment	30	Calendar	semester	Regular admission	3/1	Tuition	$13,980
% male/female	50/50	% faculty from religious order	5	**FRESHMAN PROFILE**		Room & board	$6,900
% from out of state	29	% graduate in 4 yrs.	70	Average verbal SAT	510	Estimated book expense	$400
% transfers	9			Average math SAT	520	% frosh receiving aid	62
% from catholic high school	40	**Most Popular Majors**		Average ACT	22	% undergrads receiving aid	65
% live on campus	60	psychology		Minimum TOEFL	500	% frosh w/ grant	29
% African American	1	sports medicine				Avg. grant	$6,000
% Asian	3	accounting				% frosh w/ loan	53
% Caucasian	92	**ADMISSIONS**				Avg. loan	$3,735
% Hispanic	3	Admissions Rating	76				
% international	3	# of applicants	500				
# of countries represented	16						

MOLLOY COLLEGE

1000 Hempstead Avenue, Rockville Center, NY 11570 • *Admissions: 516-678-5000* • *Fax: 516-257-2247*
• *Financial Aid: 516-256-2217* • *E-mail: admissions@molloy.edu* • *Web Site: www.molloy.edu*

Founded in 1955 by the Sisters of Saint Dominic, Molloy College first admitted men in 1982. The college's 25-acre commuter campus is located on Long Island, twenty miles east of New York City. Molloy offers thirty major programs in the liberal arts, business, and health sciences; among the most popular are nursing, psychology, and business management. Noteworthy campus features include a professional repertory theater company-in-residence, an institute of cross-cultural and ethnic studies, an institute of gerontology, and a cable studio. Extracurricular offerings include thirty registered clubs and organizations and several publications; noteworthy are the college's numerous musical groups, a community service program, and a women's center. Five intercollegiate athletic teams for men and seven for women are fielded, including an equestrian team. In 1995, Molloy's women's softball team won the Eastern College Athletic Conference championship.

ADMISSIONS

The admissions committee considers (in descending order of importance): HS record, test scores, recommendations, essay, class rank. *Also considered (in descending order of importance):* extracurriculars, special talents, alumni relationship, personality. Either the SAT or ACT is required. An interview is recommended. Admissions process is need-blind. *High school units required/recommended:* 13 total units are required; 4 English required, 2 math required, 2 science required, 2 foreign language required, 3 social studies required. Minimum combined SAT I score of 800 and minimum grade average of 80 required. *Special Requirements:* A portfolio is required for art program applicants. An audition is required for music program applicants.

FINANCIAL AID

Students should submit: FAFSA (due April 15), the school's own financial aid form (due April 15), state aid form, a copy of parents' most recent income tax filing (due April 15). The Princeton Review suggests that all financial aid forms be submitted as soon as possible after January 1. *The following grants/scholarships are offered:* Pell, SEOG, athletic, the school's own scholarships, the school's own grants, state scholarships, state grants. *Students borrow from the following loan programs:* Stafford, unsubsidized Stafford, PLUS, the school's own loan fund, supplemental loans. College Work-Study Program is available. Institutional employment is available. The off-campus job outlook is excellent.

STUDENT BODY

Total undergrad enrollment	1,981
% male/female	19/81
% transfers	71
% from catholic high school	40
% African American	10
% Asian	2
% Caucasian	84
% Hispanic	4

ACADEMICS

Calendar	4-1-4
Student/teacher ratio	8:1
FT faculty	250

Most Popular Majors

nursing
psychology
business management

ADMISSIONS

Admissions Rating	65
% of acceptees attending	46

Deadlines

Regular admission	rolling
Regular notification	rolling

FRESHMAN PROFILE

Average verbal SAT	435
Average math SAT	468
Minimum TOEFL	500
Graduated top 10% of class	16
Graduated top 25% of class	40
Graduated top 50% of class	80

FINANCIAL FACTS

Tuition	$9,600
Estimated book expense	$700
% frosh receiving aid	75
% undergrads receiving aid	86
% frosh w/ grant	58

Avg. grant	$2,552
% frosh w/ loan	82
Avg. loan	$4,083

MOUNT MARTY COLLEGE

1105 West Eighth Street, Yankton, SD 57078 • *Admissions: 605-668-1545* • *Fax: 605-668-1357*
• *Financial Aid: 800-658-4552* • *Web Site: www.mtmc.edu*

Founded in 1936 by the Benedictine Sisters, Mount Marty College takes its name from Bishop Martin Marty, a Benedictine missionary to the Indians and the first Catholic bishop of the Dakota Territory. The college's 80-acre campus overlooks the Missouri River sixty miles from Sioux City and minutes from Lewis and Clark Lake, one of South Dakota's most popular recreational areas. Mount Marty offers over two dozen academic programs, spread among the liberal arts and sciences, business, education, and nursing; with nursing, business, and education ranking among the more popular majors. Academic facilities include Sacred Heart Hospital, located adjacent to the campus, which functions as the main clinical facility for health sciences students. The college offers a wide range of options for activities outside the classroom; available clubs and organizations include student government, a variety of musical ensembles, student-faculty academic clubs, religious organizations, and multicultural groups. Athletic teams compete for Mount Marty in five sports each for men and women. Students under the age of twenty-one must live on campus if they do not live at home.

ADMISSIONS

The admissions committee considers (in descending order of importance): HS record, test scores, class rank, recommendations, essay. *Also considered (in descending order of importance):* alumni relationship, extracurriculars, special talents. Either the SAT or ACT is required. An interview is recommended. Admissions process is need-blind. Minimum composite ACT score of 18 and minimum 2.0 GPA required. *Special Requirements:* TOEFL is required of all international students.

FINANCIAL AID

Students should submit: FAFSA (due March 1). The Princeton Review suggests that all financial aid forms be submitted as soon as possible after January 1. *The following grants/scholarships are offered:* Pell, SEOG, academic merit, athletic, the school's own scholarships, the school's own grants, state scholarships, state grants, private scholarships, private grants. *Students borrow from the following loan programs:* Stafford, unsubsidized Stafford, Perkins, PLUS, the school's own loan fund, supplemental loans, state loans, private loans. College Work-Study Program is available. Institutional employment is available. The off-campus job outlook is good.

STUDENT BODY		ACADEMICS		Deadlines		FINANCIAL FACTS	
Total undergrad enrollment	1,052	Calendar	4-1-4	Regular admission	9/1	Tuition	$7,988
% male/female	30/70	Student/teacher ratio	1:1	Regular notification	rolling	Room & board	$3,470
% from out of state	30	FT faculty	928			Estimated book expense	$600
% from catholic high school	20	% faculty from religious order	40	**FRESHMAN PROFILE**		% frosh receiving aid	94
% live on campus	70			Average ACT	22	% undergrads receiving aid	96
% African American	1	**Most Popular Majors**		Minimum TOEFL	500	% frosh w/ grant	89
% Asian	1	nursing		Graduated top 10% of class	41	Avg. grant	$2,796
% Caucasian	97	business		Graduated top 25% of class	71	% frosh w/ loan	79
% Native American	1	education		Graduated top 50% of class	85	Avg. loan	$2,885
% international	1	**ADMISSIONS**					
# of countries represented	4	Admissions Rating	81				
		% of acceptees attending	53				

MOUNT MERCY COLLEGE

1330 Elmhurst Drive N.E., Cedar Rapids, IA 52402 • *Admissions: 319-363-8213* • *Fax: 319-363-5270*
• *Financial Aid: 319-368-6467* • *Web Site: www.mtmercy.edu*

Mount Mercy College was founded as a two-year college for women in 1928 by the Sisters of Mercy. It began offering four-year degrees in 1957, and became coed in 1968. The college's 36-acre hilltop campus boasts a spectacular view of the city of Cedar Rapids. A network of tunnels connects nearly all campus buildings, an especially effective way to deal with the Midwest's raw winters. Mount Mercy offers nearly three dozen majors ranging from the liberal arts and sciences to business, education, and nursing. Arts groups, especially those involving music, are abundant. Nineteen clubs and organizations are registered at the college, offering a range of extracurricular options including music and arts activities, a chapter of Amnesty International, and a community service organization. Mount Mercy fields six intercollegiate athletic teams each for men and women, and offers a range of seasonal intramural sports on campus.

ADMISSIONS

The admissions committee considers (in descending order of importance): HS record, class rank, essay, recommendations, test scores. *Also considered (in descending order of importance):* alumni relationship, extracurriculars, geographical distribution, personality, special talents. Either the SAT or ACT is required. An interview is recommended. *High school units required/recommended:* 17 total units are recommended; 4 English recommended, 4 math recommended, 3 science recommended, 2 foreign language recommended, 2 social studies recommended, 2 history recommended. Minimum composite ACT score of 19, rank in top half of secondary school class, and minimum 2.5 GPA required.

FINANCIAL AID

Students should submit: FAFSA (due March 1), the school's own financial aid form (due March 1), a copy of parents' most recent income tax filing. The Princeton Review suggests that all financial aid forms be submitted as soon as possible after January 1. *The following grants/scholarships are offered:* state scholarships. *Students borrow from the following loan programs:* Stafford, PLUS. College Work-Study Program is available. Institutional employment is available. The off-campus job outlook is excellent.

STUDENT BODY

Total undergrad enrollment	1,348
% male/female	27/73
% from out of state	3
% transfers	57
% live on campus	50
% African American	1
% Asian	1
% Caucasian	97
% international	1
# of countries represented	7

ACADEMICS

Calendar	4-1-4
Student/teacher ratio	11:1
FT faculty	124
% faculty from religious order	1

Most Popular Majors
administrative management
education
nursing

ADMISSIONS

Admissions Rating	69
% of acceptees attending	50

Deadlines

Regular admission	8/15
Regular notification	rolling

FRESHMAN PROFILE

Minimum TOEFL	500
Graduated top 10% of class	12
Graduated top 25% of class	36
Graduated top 50% of class	78

FINANCIAL FACTS

Tuition	$11,370
Room & board	$3,800
% frosh receiving aid	85
% undergrads receiving aid	85
% frosh w/ grant	30
Avg. grant	NR
% frosh w/ loan	80
Avg. loan	$3,000

MOUNT SAINT CLARE COLLEGE

400 North Bluff Boulevard, Clinton, IA 52732 • Admissions: 319-242-4153 • Fax: 319-924-2203
• Financial Aid: 319-242-4023 • Web Site: www.clare.edu

Mount Saint Clare College was founded in 1895 by the Sisters of Saint Francis. The college's 124-acre campus is located thirty-five miles from Davenport, one of the quad cities of eastern Iowa and western Illinois. Mount Saint Clare offers academic programs in a wide variety of disciplines; among the most popular are liberal arts, elementary and secondary education, and business administration. Facilities include a preschool on campus and planning is under way for a new multipurpose educational center. Extracurricular opportunities are numerous; among available activities are Circle K (a service club), several music and arts groups, multicultural and ethnic organizations, academic honor societies, and the Student Iowa State Education Association (SISEA). Intercollegiate athletic teams are fielded in seven sports for men, eight for women. Mount Saint Clare holds an annual academic scholarship competition to give talented students an opportunity to win renewable scholarship awards that range up to full tuition.

ADMISSIONS

The admissions committee considers (in descending order of importance): test scores, HS record, recommendations, class rank. *Also considered (in descending order of importance):* extracurriculars, personality, alumni relationship, special talents. Either the SAT or ACT is required; ACT is preferred. An interview is recommended. Admissions process is need-blind. *High school units required/recommended:* 3 English required, 4 English recommended, 2 math required, 3 math recommended, 2 science required, 3 science recommended, 1 foreign language recommended, 3 social studies required. History units recommended. Minimum composite ACT score of 17, rank in top half of secondary school class, or minimum 2.0 GPA required. *Special Requirements:* TOEFL is required of all international students.

FINANCIAL AID

Students should submit: FAFSA, state aid form, a copy of parents' most recent income tax filing. The Princeton Review suggests that all financial aid forms be submitted as soon as possible after January 1. *The following grants/scholarships are offered:* state scholarships. *Students borrow from the following loan programs:* Stafford, PLUS. Applicants will be notified of awards beginning March 1. College Work-Study Program is available. Institutional employment is available. The off-campus job outlook is good.

STUDENT BODY

% male/female	35/65
% from out of state	29
% transfers	44
% live on campus	35
% African American	8
% Asian	3
% Caucasian	87
% Hispanic	1
% Native American	1
% international	3
# of countries represented	14

ACADEMICS

Calendar	semester
% faculty from religious order	8

Most Popular Majors
liberal arts
elementary and secondary education
business administration

ADMISSIONS

Admissions Rating	66

Deadlines

Regular admission	8/15
Regular notification	rolling

FRESHMAN PROFILE

Minimum TOEFL	450

FINANCIAL FACTS

Tuition	$10,900
Room & board	$3,870
Estimated book expense	$500
% frosh receiving aid	95
% undergrads receiving aid	95

COLLEGE OF MOUNT SAINT JOSEPH

*5701 Delhi Road, Cincinnati, OH 45233 • Admissions: 513-244-4200 • Fax: 513-244-4629
• Financial Aid: 513-244-4418 • E-mail: edward eckel@mail.msj.edu • Web Site: www.msj.edu*

The College of Mount Saint Joseph was founded in 1920 by the Sisters of Charity. Its 75-acre hilltop campus overlooks the Ohio River, seven miles from downtown Cincinnati. Among noteworthy features are a 1000-seat theater, a music therapy clinic, and an art gallery. The college offers forty majors among liberal arts, business, education, and health sciences. Popular majors include business, education, and art. Mount Saint Joseph offers thirty clubs and organizations, providing a range of extracurricular options including music and arts activities, career-oriented professional organizations, a variety of publications, and volunteer community service groups. Athletic teams compete in intercollegiate athletics in four men's and five women's sports.

ADMISSIONS

The admissions committee considers (in descending order of importance): HS record, test scores, class rank, recommendations, essay. *Also considered (in descending order of importance):* extracurriculars, special talents, alumni relationship, personality. Either the SAT or ACT is required. Admissions process is need-blind. *High school units required/recommended:* 13 total units are required; 4 English required, 2 math required, 4 math recommended, 2 science required, 4 science recommended, 2 foreign language required, 4 foreign language recommended, 1 social studies required, 3 social studies recommended, 1 history required. Minimum composite ACT score of 19 (SAT I scores of 400 verbal and 440 math), rank in top three-fifths of secondary school class, and minimum 2.25 GPA required. *Special Requirements:* An audition is required for music program applicants. Chemistry required of science and nursing program applicants.

FINANCIAL AID

Students should submit: FAFSA (due April 15), the school's own financial aid form (due April 15). The Princeton Review suggests that all financial aid forms be submitted as soon as possible after January 1. *The following grants/scholarships are offered:* Pell, SEOG, academic merit, athletic, state scholarships, state grants, private scholarships, private grants. *Students borrow from the following loan programs:* Stafford, unsubsidized Stafford, Perkins, PLUS, supplemental loans, private loans. College Work-Study Program is available. Institutional employment is available. The off-campus job outlook is good.

STUDENT BODY
Total undergrad enrollment	1,383
% male/female	32/68
% from out of state	15
% transfers	15
% from catholic high school	38
% live on campus	30
% African American	6
% Asian	2
% Caucasian	90
% international	4
# of countries represented	16

ACADEMICS
Calendar	semester
Student/teacher ratio	7:1
FT faculty	301
% faculty from religious order	5
% graduate in 4 yrs.	68

Most Popular Majors
business
education
art

ADMISSIONS
Admissions Rating	72
# of applicants	745
% of applicants accepted	80
% of acceptees attending	38

Deadlines
Regular admission	8/15
Regular notification	rolling

FRESHMAN PROFILE
Range verbal SAT	450-590
Average verbal SAT	520
Range math SAT	470-610
Average math SAT	540
Range ACT	19-24
Average ACT	22
Minimum TOEFL	450
Average HS GPA or Avg	3.2

Graduated top 10% of class	20
Graduated top 25% of class	52
Graduated top 50% of class	85

FINANCIAL FACTS
Tuition	$11,300
Room & board	$4,730
Estimated book expense	$400
% frosh receiving aid	70
% undergrads receiving aid	73
% frosh w/ grant	79
Avg. grant	$3,000
% frosh w/ loan	84
Avg. loan	$3,484

Mount Saint Mary College

Powell Avenue, Newburgh, NY 12550 • Admissions: 914-569-3248 • Fax: 914-562-6762
• Financial Aid: 914-569-3195 • Web Site: www.msmc.edu

Mount Saint Mary College was founded in 1954 by the Dominican Sisters. Its 70-acre campus overlooks the Hudson River, twelve miles from the United States Military Academy at West Point and fifty-eight miles north of New York City. The college offers a total of thirty majors in disciplines within the liberal arts and sciences, business, education, and nursing. Facilities of note include an on-campus Montessori elementary school and a 47,000- square-foot recreation center, which holds a cardiovascular fitness center, a dance studio, and an elevated track. Thirty registered clubs and organizations offer a range of activities, among them music and arts ensembles, multicultural groups, a variety of publications, and volunteer community service groups. Mount Saint Mary's Knights compete in four intercollegiate sports for men and five for women. College teams are current or recent conference champions in women's soccer, volleyball, and basketball, and men's baseball. The men's basketball team finished the 1996–97 season ranked in the top ten in the country in NCAA Division III.

ADMISSIONS

The admissions committee considers (in descending order of importance): HS record, class rank, test scores, recommendations, essay. *Also considered (in descending order of importance):* alumni relationship, extracurriculars, geographical distribution, personality, special talents. Either the SAT or ACT is required. An interview is required. Admissions process is need-blind. *High school units required/recommended:* 24 total units are recommended; 4 English recommended, 3 math recommended, 3 science recommended, 3 foreign language recommended, 4 social studies recommended, 4 history recommended. Minimum combined SAT I score of 900, rank in top half of secondary school class, and minimum grade average of 80 recommended. *Special Requirements:* Biology and chemistry required of nursing program applicants.

FINANCIAL AID

Students should submit: FAFSA, state aid form, a copy of parents' most recent income tax filing. The Princeton Review suggests that all financial aid forms be submitted as soon as possible after January 1. *The following grants/scholarships are offered:* state scholarships. *Students borrow from the following loan programs:* Stafford, PLUS. Applicants will be notified of awards beginning March 1. College Work-Study Program is available. Institutional employment is available. The off-campus job outlook is good.

STUDENT BODY		ACADEMICS		ADMISSIONS	
Total undergrad enrollment	1,599	Calendar	4-1-4	Admissions Rating	64
% male/female	32/68	Student/teacher ratio	13:1	% of acceptees attending	37
% from out of state	28	FT faculty	160		
% transfers	33	% faculty from religious order	3	**Deadlines**	
% live on campus	67	% graduate in 4 yrs.	62	Regular admission	rolling
% African American	7			Regular notification	rolling
% Asian	2	**Most Popular Majors**			
% Caucasian	86	education		**FRESHMAN PROFILE**	
% Hispanic	3	nursing		Range verbal SAT	370-480
% Native American	1	business management/		Average verbal SAT	450
% international	1	administration		Range math SAT	390-560
# of countries represented	10			Average math SAT	450
				Minimum TOEFL	500
				Graduated top 10% of class	14

Graduated top 25% of class	48
Graduated top 50% of class	76
FINANCIAL FACTS	
Tuition	$9,150
Room & board	$5,125
Estimated book expense	$400
% frosh receiving aid	80
% undergrads receiving aid	74

MOUNT SAINT MARY'S COLLEGE (CA)

12001 Chalon Rd., Los Angeles, CA 90049 • Admissions: 310-471-9516 • Fax: 310-471-3258
• Financial Aid: 310-471-9505 • E-mail: admissons@msmc.la.edu • Web Site: msmc.la.edu

The Sisters of Saint Joseph of Carondelet founded Mount Saint Mary's College in 1925. The college's two campuses total fifty-six acres in the heart of Los Angeles. Men are admitted only for nursing, music, and physical therapy assistant programs; housing is available for women only. Nearly forty majors are offered, organized into three groupings: social sciences, arts and humanities, and the sciences. Popular programs include nursing, biology, and business. Special facilities include an art gallery. Mount Saint Mary's has thirty-five clubs and organizations on campus; most numerous among them are a wide variety of cultural groups and professional career associations. Intercollegiate athletics are not available. The college is a member of PLEN—the Public Leadership in Education Network—a consortium of fourteen women's colleges that offers annual seminars and paid internships in Washington, D.C.

ADMISSIONS

The admissions committee considers (in descending order of importance): HS record, test scores, class rank, essay, recommendations. *Also considered (in descending order of importance):* extracurriculars, personality, alumni relationship, geographical distribution, special talents. Either the SAT or ACT is required; SAT is preferred. An interview is recommended. Admissions process is need-blind. *High school units required/ recommended:* 16 total units are recommended; 4 English recommended, 3 math recommended, 3 science recommended, 2 foreign language recommended, 2 social studies recommended, 2 history recommended. Combined SAT I score of 900, rank in top quarter of secondary school class, and minimum 3.0 GPA recommended.

FINANCIAL AID

Students should submit: FAFSA (due March 2). The Princeton Review suggests that all financial aid forms be submitted as soon as possible after January 1. *The following grants/scholarships are offered:* state scholarships. *Students borrow from the following loan programs:* Stafford, PLUS. College Work-Study Program is available. Institutional employment is available. The off-campus job outlook is good.

STUDENT BODY

Total undergrad enrollment	1,054
% male/female	2/98
% from out of state	16
% transfers	36
% live on campus	52
% African American	9
% Asian	17
% Caucasian	29
% Hispanic	35
% Native American	1
% international	3
# of countries represented	3

ACADEMICS

Calendar	semester
Student/teacher ratio	4:1
FT faculty	254

Most Popular Majors
nursing
biology
business

ADMISSIONS

Admissions Rating	71
# of applicants	481
% of applicants accepted	63
% of acceptees attending	21

Deadlines

Regular admission	3/1
Regular notification	rolling

FRESHMAN PROFILE

Average verbal SAT	540
Average math SAT	516
Average ACT	21
Minimum TOEFL	500
Average HS GPA or Avg	3.5
Graduated top 10% of class	66
Graduated top 25% of class	91
Graduated top 50% of class	96

FINANCIAL FACTS

Tuition	$14,050
Room & board	$5,800
Estimated book expense	$400
% frosh receiving aid	75
% undergrads receiving aid	77

MOUNT SAINT MARY'S COLLEGE (MD)

16300 Old Emmitsburg Rd., Emmitsburg, MD 21727 • Admissions: 301-447-5214 • Fax: 301-447-5755
• Financial Aid: 301-447-5207 • E-mail: admiss@msmary.edu • Web Site: www.msmary.edu

Founded in 1808, Mount Saint Mary's College is the second oldest Catholic college in the country. The college's rural 1400-acre campus is sixty-five miles from Washington and fifty miles from Baltimore. Forty majors are offered at Mount Saint Mary's within the liberal arts and sciences, business, and education. Among the most popular academic disciplines are business, biology, and elementary education. Campus features of note include an art collection reflecting Catholic history in America, 300 acres of mountain forest, and the Grotto of Our Lady of Lourdes, a national shrine. Over seventy registered clubs and organizations offer a full complement of extracurriculars, including an array of community service opportunities, academic and cultural clubs, publications, and arts groups. The college has a long history of championship-caliber intercollegiate athletic teams, competing in seventeen sports in the NCAA, eight for men, nine for women. Men's basketball coach Jim Phelan is the fourth-winningest coach in NCAA history; women's basketball coach Bill Sheahan boasts one of the sport's top career-winning percentages.

ADMISSIONS

The admissions committee considers (in descending order of importance): HS record, class rank, test scores, recommendations, essay. *Also considered (in descending order of importance):* alumni relationship, extracurriculars, personality, special talents. Either the SAT or ACT is required; SAT is preferred. An interview is recommended. Admissions process is need-blind. *High school units required/recommended:* 16 total units are required; 4 English required, 3 math required, 3 science required, 2 foreign language required, 3 social studies required. Rank in top half of secondary school class and minimum 3.0 GPA required. *Special Requirements:* TOEFL is required of all international students.

FINANCIAL AID

Students should submit: FAFSA, CSS Profile (due March 15). The Princeton Review suggests that all financial aid forms be submitted as soon as possible after January 1. *The following grants/scholarships are offered:* Pell, SEOG, academic merit, athletic, the school's own scholarships, the school's own grants, state scholarships, state grants, private scholarships, private grants, ROTC. *Students borrow from the following loan programs:* Stafford, unsubsidized Stafford, Perkins, PLUS, the school's own loan fund, supplemental loans, private loans. Applicants will be notified of awards beginning mid February. College Work-Study Program is available. Institutional employment is available. The off-campus job outlook is fair.

STUDENT BODY
Total undergrad enrollment	1,390
% male/female	47/53
% from out of state	54
% transfers	14
% from catholic high school	62
% live on campus	86
% African American	6
% Asian	2
% Caucasian	90
% Hispanic	2
% international	1
# of countries represented	11

ACADEMICS
Calendar	semester
Student/teacher ratio	13:1
FT faculty	145
% faculty from religious order	5
% graduate in 4 yrs.	72

Most Popular Majors
business
biology
elementary education

ADMISSIONS
Admissions Rating	69
% of acceptees attending	36

Deadlines
Regular admission	3/1
Regular notification	rolling

FRESHMAN PROFILE
Average verbal SAT	460
Average math SAT	500
Minimum TOEFL	550
Graduated top 10% of class	13
Graduated top 25% of class	34
Graduated top 50% of class	68

FINANCIAL FACTS
Tuition	$14,120
Room & board	$6,250
Estimated book expense	$600
% frosh receiving aid	65
% undergrads receiving aid	66

COLLEGE OF MOUNT SAINT VINCENT

6301 Riverdale Avenue, Riverdale, NY 10471 • Admissions: 718-405-3400 • Fax: 718-495-7945
• Financial Aid: 718-405-3290

Founded in 1847 by the Sisters of Charity as an academy for women, the College of Mount Saint Vincent became coed in 1973. The College's 70-acre campus overlooking the Hudson River is the largest privately-owned property within the boundaries of New York City. Noteworthy facilities and equipment are a computer graphics and animation center, a new fitness center, a television studio, and an electron microscope. Twenty-seven majors are available in a variety of disciplines, mainly within the liberal arts and sciences, business, and education. Nursing, business, and communications are among the most popular choices. Mount Saint Vincent offers twenty-five clubs and organizations, and fourteen honor societies. Activities include publications, television and radio, music and arts organizations, multicultural groups, and a variety of community service/social-action clubs. Intercollegiate athletics at the Mount are offered in five sports for men, six for women. The men's basketball team was among the top ten teams in the NCAA Division III's Atlantic region last year.

ADMISSIONS

The admissions committee considers (in descending order of importance): HS record, test scores, class rank, recommendations, essay. *Also considered (in descending order of importance):* extracurriculars, personality, alumni relationship, geographical distribution, special talents. Either the SAT or ACT is required. An interview is recommended. Admissions process is need-blind. *High school units required/recommended:* 16 total units are required; 17 total units are recommended; 4 English required, 2 math required, 2 science required, 2 foreign language required, 1 social studies required, 1 history required, 2 history recommended. Minimum SAT I scores of 480 verbal and 440 math, rank in top half of secondary school class, and minimum 2.5 GPA recommended. *Special Requirements:* Biology and chemistry required of nursing program applicants.

FINANCIAL AID

Students should submit: FAFSA (due March 15), the school's own financial aid form (due March 15), state aid form (due March 15). The Princeton Review suggests that all financial aid forms be submitted as soon as possible after January 1. *The following grants/scholarships are offered:* state scholarships. *Students borrow from the following loan programs:* Stafford, PLUS. Applicants will be notified of awards beginning March 30. College Work-Study Program is available. Institutional employment is available. The off-campus job outlook is excellent.

STUDENT BODY		ACADEMICS		Deadlines		FINANCIAL FACTS	
Total undergrad enrollment	1,139	Calendar	semester	Regular admission	rolling	Tuition	$13,000
% male/female	21/79	Student/teacher ratio	12:1	Regular notification	rolling	Room & board	$6,240
% from out of state	11	FT faculty	97			Estimated book expense	$500
% transfers	37			**FRESHMAN PROFILE**		% frosh receiving aid	86
% live on campus	59	**Most Popular Majors**		Range verbal SAT	377-464	% undergrads receiving aid	82
% African American	13	nursing		Average verbal SAT	454	% frosh w/ grant	67
% Asian	4	business		Range math SAT	431-535	Avg. grant	NR
% Caucasian	59	communication		Average math SAT	474	% frosh w/ loan	78
% Hispanic	14	**ADMISSIONS**		Average ACT	23	Avg. loan	$2,600
% international	1	Admissions Rating	65	Minimum TOEFL	500		
# of countries represented	9	% of acceptees attending	27	Graduated top 10% of class	23		
				Graduated top 25% of class	46		
				Graduated top 50% of class	76		

NAZARETH COLLEGE OF ROCHESTER

4245 East Avenue, Rochester, NY 14618 • Admissions: 716-586-2525 • Fax: 716-586-2431
• Financial Aid: 716-389-2310 • E-mail: tkdarin@naz.edu • Web Site: www.naz.edu

Nazareth College of Rochester was founded in 1924 by the Sisters of Saint Joseph. The college's 75-acre campus is located seven miles from Rochester's downtown. Academic offerings cover more than three dozen majors. Among the most popular are business administration, psychology, and English. Nazareth belongs to Rochester Area Colleges (RAC), a fifteen-member consortium that allows students to cross-register at such institutions as the University of Rochester and Rochester Institute of Technology. Thirty clubs and activities cover a full range, from standard offerings such as a student newspaper and performing arts organizations to community volunteer groups and fifteen honor societies. Intercollegiate athletics, especially women's basketball and men's lacrosse, are popular as well as successful—the women's basketball program ranks in the top 10 in NCAA Division III, and the men's lacrosse team were the 1992 champions. A total of six sports for men and nine for women are available.

ADMISSIONS

The admissions committee considers (in descending order of importance): HS record, test scores, class rank, recommendations, essay. *Also considered (in descending order of importance):* alumni relationship, extracurriculars, geographical distribution, special talents, personality. Either the SAT or ACT is required. An interview is recommended. Admissions process is need-blind. *High school units required/recommended:* 19 total units are recommended; 4 English recommended, 3 math recommended, 3 science recommended, 3 foreign language recommended, 4 social studies recommended. Minimum combined SAT I score of 850 (composite ACT score of 20), rank in top third of secondary school class, and minimum 2.75 GPA recommended. *Special Requirements:* A portfolio is required for art program applicants. An audition is required for music program applicants. An R.N. is required for nursing program applicants.

FINANCIAL AID

Students should submit: FAFSA (due March 30), a copy of parents' most recent income tax filing (due May). The Princeton Review suggests that all financial aid forms be submitted as soon as possible after January 1. *The following grants/scholarships are offered:* Pell, SEOG, academic merit, athletic, the school's own scholarships, the school's own grants, state scholarships, state grants, private scholarships, private grants, federal nursing scholarship, ROTC. *Students borrow from the following loan programs:* Stafford, unsubsidized Stafford, Perkins, PLUS, the school's own loan fund, supplemental loans, federal nursing loans, private loans. College Work-Study Program is available. Institutional employment is available. The off-campus job outlook is excellent.

STUDENT BODY

Total undergrad enrollment	1,764
% male/female	27/73
% from out of state	5
% transfers	33
% live on campus	63
% African American	4
% Asian	1
% Caucasian	93
% Hispanic	1
% Native American	1
% international	1
# of countries represented	6

ACADEMICS

Calendar	semester
Student/teacher ratio	18:1
FT faculty	154
% faculty from religious order	4
% graduate in 4 yrs.	63

Most Popular Majors
business administration
psychology
English

ADMISSIONS

Admissions Rating	74
# of applicants	1,099
% of applicants accepted	79
% of acceptees attending	39

Deadlines

Regular admission	3/1
Regular notification	2/1

FRESHMAN PROFILE

Range verbal SAT	504-622
Average verbal SAT	553
Range math SAT	500-612
Average math SAT	550
Range ACT	22-26
Average ACT	24
Minimum TOEFL	550
Average HS GPA or Avg	3.3
Graduated top 10% of class	20
Graduated top 25% of class	50
Graduated top 50% of class	93

FINANCIAL FACTS

Tuition	$11,926
Room & board	$5,690
Estimated book expense	$550
% frosh receiving aid	79
% undergrads receiving aid	82
% frosh w/ grant	76
Avg. grant	$4,890
% frosh w/ loan	74
Avg. loan	$3,118

NEUMANN COLLEGE

Concord Rd., Aston, PA 19014 • *Admissions: 610-558-5616* • *Fax: 610-558-5652*
• *Financial Aid: 610-558-5521* • *E-mail: hfoch@smtpgatc.neumann.edu* • *Web Site: www.neumann.edu*

Neumann College was established in 1965 by the Sisters of Saint Francis of Philadelphia as a liberal arts college for women, but went coed in 1980. Named in honor of Saint John Neumann, who was instrumental in the founding of the Sisters of Saint Francis, the college offers an education based on the concept that knowledge—while valuable in itself—is to be used in the service of others, and that learning is a lifelong process. Neumann's 14-acre commuter campus is located twelve miles from Philadelphia; housing is not available. The college offers fourteen major programs in a variety of academic disciplines. Among the most popular are nursing, liberal studies, and education. Extracurricular offerings include several performing arts organizations, student government, a newspaper, and a variety of academically focused clubs. Four intercollegiate athletic teams are fielded for men, and five for women.

ADMISSIONS

The admissions committee considers (in descending order of importance): HS record, class rank, test scores, recommendations. *Also considered (in descending order of importance):* extracurriculars, alumni relationship, personality. Either the SAT or ACT is required. An interview is recommended. Admissions process is need-blind. *High school units required/recommended:* 18 total units are required; 4 English required, 2 math required, 2 science required, 2 foreign language recommended, 2 social studies required, 2 history required.

FINANCIAL AID

Students should submit: FAFSA, the school's own financial aid form, a copy of parents' most recent income tax filing. The Princeton Review suggests that all financial aid forms be submitted as soon as possible after January 1. *The following grants/scholarships are offered:* Pell, SEOG, academic merit, the school's own scholarships, the school's own grants, state grants, private scholarships, private grants, ROTC, foreign aid. *Students borrow from the following loan programs:* Stafford, unsubsidized Stafford, Perkins, PLUS, the school's own loan fund, supplemental loans, state loans, private loans. Applicants will be notified of awards beginning February. College Work-Study Program is available. Institutional employment is available. The off-campus job outlook is good.

STUDENT BODY
Total undergrad enrollment	1,126
% male/female	23/77
% from out of state	20
% from catholic high school	60
% African American	6
% Caucasian	92
% Hispanic	1

ACADEMICS
Calendar	semester
Student/teacher ratio	11:1
FT faculty	107
% faculty from religious order	14

Most Popular Majors
nursing
liberal studies
education

ADMISSIONS
Admissions Rating	65
% of acceptees attending	38

Deadlines
Regular admission	rolling
Regular notification	rolling

FRESHMAN PROFILE
Minimum TOEFL	550

Graduated top 10% of class	17
Graduated top 25% of class	23
Graduated top 50% of class	53

FINANCIAL FACTS
Tuition	$11,700
% frosh receiving aid	69
% undergrads receiving aid	68

COLLEGE OF NEW ROCHELLE

29 Castle Place, New Rochelle, NY 10801 • Admissions: 914-654-5452 • Fax: 914-654-5554
• Financial Aid: 914-654-5224

The College of New Rochelle was founded in 1904 by the Order of Saint Ursula; it was the first Catholic college for women in New York State. Today, New Rochelle's School of Arts and Sciences continues the tradition of enrolling only women, while its other three schools—the graduate school, School of New Resources (for adult learners), and school of nursing—also admit men. Resting on 20 acres, the campus is sixteen miles north of Manhattan. The college offers twenty-seven undergraduate degree programs, mostly within the liberal arts and sciences, business, education, and nursing. Among the most popular majors are psychology, art, and business; the college's education programs are also quite strong. New Rochelle has numerous impressive facilities, among them Leland Castle (a National Historic Site), art galleries, an institute for entrepreneurial studies, and rare book collections of James Joyce, Thomas More, and the Ursuline Order. Twenty-six clubs and organizations offer the standard complement of college activities, including student government, music and arts groups, and a number of international and ethnic organizations. Athletic teams compete at the intercollegiate level in five women's sports; the basketball team is regionally powerful.

ADMISSIONS

The admissions committee considers (in descending order of importance): HS record, class rank, test scores, recommendations, essay. *Also considered (in descending order of importance):* alumni relationship, extracurriculars, personality, special talents. Either the SAT or ACT is required; SAT is preferred. An interview is recommended. Admissions process is need-blind. *High school units required/recommended:* 16 total units are required; 4 English recommended, 3 math recommended, 3 science recommended, 2 foreign language recommended, 3 social studies recommended. Minimum combined SAT I score of 850, rank in top half of secondary school class, and minimum 2.0 GPA recommended. *Special Requirements:* A portfolio is required for art program applicants. Minimum SAT I scores of 480 verbal and 440 math required of School of Nursing applicants.

FINANCIAL AID

Students should submit: FAFSA, the school's own financial aid form, state aid form, a copy of parents' most recent income tax filing. The Princeton Review suggests that all financial aid forms be submitted as soon as possible after January 1. *The following grants/scholarships are offered:* state scholarships. *Students borrow from the following loan programs:* Stafford, PLUS. Institutional employment is available. The off-campus job outlook is excellent.

STUDENT BODY

Total undergrad enrollment	1,121
% male/female	2/98
% from out of state	1
% transfers	29
% live on campus	65
# of countries represented	4

ACADEMICS

Calendar	semester
Student/teacher ratio	9:1
FT faculty	483
% graduate in 4 yrs.	30

Most Popular Majors

psychology
art
business

ADMISSIONS

Admissions Rating	66
# of applicants	1,700
% of applicants accepted	88
% of acceptees attending	61

Deadlines

Regular admission	rolling
Regular notification	rolling

FINANCIAL FACTS

Tuition	$11,000
Room & board	$5,700
Estimated book expense	$600

NIAGARA UNIVERSITY

Niagara University, NY 14109 • Admissions: 716-286-8700 • Fax: 716-286-8422
• Financial Aid: 716-286-8686 • E-mail: admissions@niagara.edu • Web Site: www.niagara.edu

Niagara University was founded in 1856 by the Vincentians. Situated on 160 acres overlooking Niagara Gorge, minutes away from world-famous Niagara Falls, the university is twenty miles north of Buffalo. Niagara offers over fifty academic majors; most popular among them are accounting, travel and tourism management, and education. Extracurriculars of all types are abundant. Seventy clubs and organizations offer activities on campus, and there are fourteen honor societies. Sports are quite popular at Niagara; the university was once nationally competitive in men's basketball, and both the men's and women's teams are once again poised to become more than simply regional athletic powers. Membership in the Metro Atlantic Athletic Conference has served to increase the university's visibility. A generous selection of academic, athletic, and arts scholarships ranging up to full tuition are offered annually.

ADMISSIONS

The admissions committee considers (in descending order of importance): HS record, class rank, test scores, recommendations. *Also considered (in descending order of importance):* alumni relationship, extracurriculars, personality, special talents. Either the SAT or ACT is required. An interview is recommended. Admissions process is need-blind. *High school units required/recommended:* 16 total units are required; 4 English required, 2 math required, 3 math recommended, 2 science required, 3 science recommended, 2 foreign language required, 2 social studies required, 3 social studies recommended. Minimum SAT I scores of 500 in both verbal and math (composite ACT score of 21), rank in top half of secondary school class, and minimum B average recommended. *Special Requirements:* 3 units each of science and math required of computer/information sciences, mathematics, nursing, and science program applicants.

FINANCIAL AID

Students should submit: FAFSA (due February 15), a copy of parents' most recent income tax filing. The Princeton Review suggests that all financial aid forms be submitted as soon as possible after January 1. *The following grants/scholarships are offered:* Pell, SEOG, academic merit, the school's own scholarships, the school's own grants, state scholarships, state grants, private scholarships, private grants, federal nursing scholarship, ROTC, foreign aid. *Students borrow from the following loan programs:* Stafford, unsubsidized Stafford, Perkins, PLUS, the school's own loan fund, supplemental loans, federal nursing loans, health professions loans, private loans. Applicants will be notified of awards beginning March 15. College Work-Study Program is available. Institutional employment is available. The off-campus job outlook is excellent.

STUDENT BODY		ACADEMICS					
Total undergrad enrollment	2,291	Calendar	semester	% of applicants accepted	81	Graduated top 10% of class	20
% male/female	38/62	Student/teacher ratio	12:1	% of acceptees attending	29	Graduated top 25% of class	42
% from out of state	8	FT faculty	244			Graduated top 50% of class	76
% transfers	24	% faculty from religious order	1	**Deadlines**			
% live on campus	55	% graduate in 4 yrs.	48	Regular admission	8/15	**FINANCIAL FACTS**	
% African American	5			Regular notification	rolling	Tuition	$11,800
% Asian	1	**Most Popular Majors**				Room & board	$5,388
% Caucasian	86	accounting		**FRESHMAN PROFILE**		Estimated book expense	$500
% Hispanic	2	travel/tourism/hotel/restaurant		Range verbal SAT	470-570	% frosh receiving aid	81
% Native American	1	education		Average verbal SAT	519	% undergrads receiving aid	83
% international	3			Range math SAT	460-570	% frosh w/ grant	84
		ADMISSIONS		Average math SAT	518	Avg. grant	$3,500
		Admissions Rating	70	Range ACT	19-26	% frosh w/ loan	75
		# of applicants	2,359	Average ACT	22	Avg. loan	$3,507
				Minimum TOEFL	500		

COLLEGE OF NOTRE DAME (CA)

1500 Ralston Avenue, Belmont, CA 94002 • Admissions: 415-508-3607 • Fax: 415-637-0493
• Financial Aid: 415-508-3509 • E-mail: admiss@cnd.du • Web Site: www.cnd.edu

Founded in 1851 by the Sisters of Notre Dame de Namur, the College of Notre Dame is located on an 80-acre campus twenty-five miles from San Francisco. Twenty-seven majors, mainly in the liberal arts and sciences, business, and nursing, are offered at the college. Among the most popular programs are business administration, liberal studies, and psychology. Noteworthy facilities include an art gallery, a modern Christian art archive, and an on-campus elementary school. Extracurriculars include twenty-seven clubs and organizations sponsoring a full range of offerings both academic and social; activities include an opera company, a symphony orchestra, a chapter of Amnesty International, and numerous ethnic and cultural groups. Five teams each for men and women represent the college in intercollegiate athletic competition.

ADMISSIONS

The admissions committee considers (in descending order of importance): HS record, test scores, essay, recommendations, class rank. *Also considered (in descending order of importance):* special talents, alumni relationship, extracurriculars, personality. Either the SAT or ACT is required; SAT is preferred. Admissions process is need-blind. *High school units required/recommended:* 14 total units are required; 4 English required, 2 math required, 3 math recommended, 1 science required, 2 science recommended, 2 foreign language required, 3 foreign language recommended, 2 social studies required, 3 social studies recommended. *Special Requirements:* An audition is required for music program applicants.

FINANCIAL AID

Students should submit: FAFSA (due March 2), CSS Profile (due), state aid form. The Princeton Review suggests that all financial aid forms be submitted as soon as possible after January 1. *The following grants/scholarships are offered:* Pell, SEOG, state scholarships, state grants. *Students borrow from the following loan programs:* Stafford, unsubsidized Stafford, Perkins, PLUS, supplemental loans. Applicants will be notified of awards beginning April 15. College Work-Study Program is available. Institutional employment is available. The off-campus job outlook is excellent.

STUDENT BODY

Total undergrad enrollment	973
% male/female	29/71
% from out of state	20
% transfers	59
% from catholic high school	50
% live on campus	37
% African American	7
% Asian	15
% Caucasian	48
% Hispanic	15
% Native American	1
# of countries represented	27

ACADEMICS

Calendar	semester
Student/teacher ratio	9:1
FT faculty	194
% faculty from religious order	5
% graduate in 4 yrs.	52

Most Popular Majors
business administration
liberal studies
psychology

ADMISSIONS

Admissions Rating	68
# of applicants	479

% of applicants accepted	77
% of acceptees attending	35

Deadlines

Regular admission	6/1
Regular notification	rolling

FRESHMAN PROFILE

Range verbal SAT	410-520
Average verbal SAT	465
Range math SAT	410-530
Average math SAT	470
Average ACT	18
Minimum TOEFL	450
Average HS GPA or Avg	3.2

Graduated top 10% of class	19
Graduated top 25% of class	38
Graduated top 50% of class	71

FINANCIAL FACTS

Tuition	$14,400
Room & board	$6,000
Estimated book expense	$630
% frosh receiving aid	85
% undergrads receiving aid	67
% frosh w/ grant	64
Avg. grant	$6,359
% frosh w/ loan	63
Avg. loan	$2,625

NOTRE DAME COLLEGE

2321 Elm Street, Manchester, NH 03104 • Admissions: 603-669-4298 • Fax: 603-644-8316
• Financial Aid: Call-Admissions • E-mail: admissions@nd.edu • Web Site: nd.edu

Founded by the Sisters of the Holy Cross in 1950, the commuter campus of Notre Dame College is located fifty miles from Boston. The college is one of only four New England colleges to be recognized by the John Templeton Foundation as a "character-building college." Clubs and activities cover a full range, from standard offerings such as a newspaper and college theater, to a campus ministry that offers a chapter of Amnesty International, Habitat for Humanity, and several other community service groups. Athletic teams are fielded in three teams each for men and women. A variety of special scholarships are available, including those for academic talent, leadership, artistic talent, children of alumni, and athletics.

ADMISSIONS

Special Requirements: TOEFL is required of all international students.

FINANCIAL AID

Students should submit: FAFSA (due March 15), the school's own financial aid form (due March 15), a copy of parents' most recent income tax filing (due May 1). The Princeton Review suggests that all financial aid forms be submitted as soon as possible after January 1. *The following grants/scholarships are offered:* Pell, SEOG, academic merit, athletic, the school's own scholarships, the school's own grants, state grants, private scholarships, private grants, foreign aid. *Students borrow from the following loan programs:* Stafford, PLUS, the school's own loan fund, private loans. College Work-Study Program is available.

STUDENT BODY		ACADEMICS		Graduated top 10% of class	15	% frosh w/ loan	90
% from out of state	23	Calendar	semester	Graduated top 25% of class	37	Avg. loan	$2,412
% from catholic high school	25	Student/teacher ratio	10:1	Graduated top 50% of class	74		
% live on campus	34	FT faculty	128				
% African American	1	% faculty from religious order	15	**FINANCIAL FACTS**			
% Caucasian	94			Tuition	$11,440		
% Hispanic	1	**ADMISSIONS**		Room & board	$5,295		
% Native American	1	Admissions Rating	69	Estimated book expense	$400		
% international	2	% of acceptees attending	41	% frosh receiving aid	80		
				% undergrads receiving aid	90		
		Deadlines		% frosh w/ grant	60		
		Regular admission	rolling	Avg. grant	$2,400		
		FRESHMAN PROFILE					
		Minimum TOEFL	500				

NOTRE DAME COLLEGE OF OHIO

4545 College Road, South Euclid, OH 44121 • Admissions: 216-381-5766 • Fax: 216-381-3802
• Financial Aid: Call-Admissions • Web Site: ndc.edu

Notre Dame College of Ohio was founded as a women's college in 1922 by the Sisters of Notre Dame. Ten miles from downtown Cleveland, the college is located on a 53-acre residential campus. Notre Dame offers thirty-six academic programs, mainly within the liberal arts and sciences, business, education, and health sciences; these offerings include a broad selection of career-oriented programs. Business programs are by far the most popular, but education is also highly regarded. The college recently opened a new science research center. Extracurricular opportunities include a campus newspaper and magazine, performing arts groups, and organizations devoted to multicultural concerns, religion, and current affairs. Intercollegiate athletics are offered in seven sports; intramurals are also available.

ADMISSIONS

Special Requirements: TOEFL is required of all international students.

FINANCIAL AID

Students should submit: FAFSA (due April 15), the school's own financial aid form (due April 15). The Princeton Review suggests that all financial aid forms be submitted as soon as possible after January 1. *The following grants/scholarships are offered:* Pell, SEOG, academic merit, the school's own scholarships, the school's own grants, state grants, private scholarships, private grants, foreign aid. *Students borrow from the following loan programs:* Stafford, unsubsidized Stafford, Perkins, PLUS, the school's own loan fund, supplemental loans, private loans. College Work-Study Program is available.

STUDENT BODY		ACADEMICS		FRESHMAN PROFILE		FINANCIAL FACTS	
% from out of state	2	Calendar	semester	Range verbal SAT	470-570	Tuition	$11,000
% live on campus	42	Student/teacher ratio	6:1	Average verbal SAT	483	Room & board	$4,095
% African American	27	FT faculty	101	Range math SAT	450-550	Estimated book expense	$650
% Asian	1	% faculty from religious order	24	Average math SAT	508	% frosh receiving aid	95
% Caucasian	63			Range ACT	18-24	% undergrads receiving aid	84
% Hispanic	2	**ADMISSIONS**		Average ACT	21	% frosh w/ loan	63
% Native American	1	Admissions Rating	67	Minimum TOEFL	500	Avg. loan	$1,900
% international	1	# of applicants	223	Average HS GPA or Avg	3.1		
		% of applicants accepted	90				
		% of acceptees attending	29				
		Deadlines					
		Regular admission	6/30				

COLLEGE OF NOTRE DAME OF MARYLAND

4701 N. Charles Street, Baltimore, MD 21210 • Admissions: 410-532-5330 • Fax: 410-532-6287
• Financial Aid: 800-435-0300

Founded in 1873 by the Sisters of Notre Dame de Namur, the College of Notre Dame was the first Catholic college for women in the United States. Its campus sits on 58 acres four miles from downtown Baltimore and thirty-seven miles from Washington. Twenty-four majors are offered, mainly in liberal arts and sciences, business, education, and nursing. Popular programs include business, communications, and education. Dual degree programs in engineering and nursing are offered in conjunction with Johns Hopkins University. Special facilities include an art gallery, television and radio studios, and a planetarium. Notre Dame offers twenty-four clubs and organizations, and seven honor societies. Eight sports teams represent the college in intercollegiate athletic competition.

ADMISSIONS

The admissions committee considers (in descending order of importance): HS record, test scores, recommendations, essay, class rank. *Also considered (in descending order of importance):* extracurriculars, special talents, alumni relationship, geographical distribution, personality. Either the SAT or ACT is required; SAT is preferred. An interview is recommended. Admissions process is need-blind. *High school units required/recommended:* 18 total units are required; 4 English required, 3 math required, 2 science required, 3 foreign language required, 2 history required. Minimum combined SAT I score of 800, minimum 2.5 GPA for college preparatory courses, and strong recommendations required. *Special Requirements:* An R.N. is required for nursing program applicants.

FINANCIAL AID

Students should submit: FAFSA (due February 15), state aid form, a copy of parents' most recent income tax filing (due April 15). The Princeton Review suggests that all financial aid forms be submitted as soon as possible after January 1. *The following grants/scholarships are offered:* state scholarships. *Students borrow from the following loan programs:* Stafford, PLUS. Applicants will be notified of awards beginning April 1. College Work-Study Program is available. Institutional employment is available. The off-campus job outlook is excellent.

STUDENT BODY
Total undergrad enrollment	2,650
% male/female	0/100
% from out of state	30
% transfers	18
% from catholic high school	32
% live on campus	65
% African American	12
% Asian	6
% Caucasian	73
% Hispanic	3
% international	6

ACADEMICS
Calendar	quarter
Student/teacher ratio	15:1
FT faculty	208

Most Popular Majors
business
communication arts
education

ADMISSIONS
Admissions Rating	75
% of acceptees attending	50

Deadlines
Regular admission	2/15
Regular notification	rolling

FRESHMAN PROFILE
Average verbal SAT	470
Average math SAT	500
Minimum TOEFL	500
Graduated top 10% of class	35
Graduated top 25% of class	61
Graduated top 50% of class	88

FINANCIAL FACTS
Tuition	$11,740

Room & board	$5,845
% frosh receiving aid	80
% undergrads receiving aid	78
% frosh w/ grant	72
Avg. grant	NR
% frosh w/ loan	50
Avg. loan	$2,625

UNIVERSITY OF NOTRE DAME

*113 Main Building, Notre Dame, IN 46556 • Admissions: 219-631-7505 • Fax: 219-631-8865
• Financial Aid: 219-631-6436 • E-mail: admissions.admissio.1@nd.edu • Web Site: www.nd.edu*

The University of Notre Dame, one of the nation's premier universities, was founded in 1842 by a twenty-eight-year-old French priest from the Congregation of the Holy Cross with an investment of $310. It has paid off handsomely—today the university's endowment is about $1.1 billion, the eighteenth-largest in the United States. Notre Dame sits on a sprawling 1,250-acre campus in northern Indiana, ninety miles from Chicago. Bachelor's degrees are offered in fifty-six fields of study across a broad spectrum of academic subjects; the university confers nearly 2,000 degrees annually. Impressive facilities include an art museum, a germ-free research lab, a radiation laboratory, an international studies center, and an accelerator lab. The university's football stadium is undergoing a complete renovation and expansion. You'd be hard-pressed to find a university that has more to do than Notre Dame; it offers 200 clubs and organizations, and a behemoth intramural athletics program that attracts over 300 basketball teams alone. The university's athletic teams, the Fighting Irish, have accomplished so much across their history that a discussion of intercollegiate sports simply won't fit here.

ADMISSIONS

The admissions committee considers (in descending order of importance): HS record, class rank, test scores, recommendations, essay. *Also considered (in descending order of importance):* extracurriculars, personality, special talents, alumni relationship. Either the SAT or ACT is required. Admissions process is need-blind. *High school units required/recommended:* 16 total units are required; 20 total units are recommended; 4 English required, 4 English recommended, 3 math required, 4 math recommended, 2 science required, 4 science recommended, 2 foreign language required, 4 foreign language recommended, 2 history required, 4 history recommended. *Special Requirements:* A portfolio is required for art program applicants. An audition is required for music program applicants. TOEFL is required of all international students.

FINANCIAL AID

Students should submit: FAFSA (due February 28), CSS Profile, state aid form, Divorced Parents form, a copy of parents' most recent income tax filing (due March 31). The Princeton Review suggests that all financial aid forms be submitted as soon as possible after January 1. *The following grants/scholarships are offered:* Pell, SEOG, academic merit, athletic, the school's own scholarships, the school's own grants, state scholarships, state grants, private scholarships, private grants, foreign aid. *Students borrow from the following loan programs:* Stafford, unsubsidized Stafford, Perkins, PLUS, the school's own loan fund, supplemental loans, federal nursing loans, private loans. College Work-Study Program is available. Institutional employment is available. The off-campus job outlook is good.

STUDENT BODY		ACADEMICS		% of applicants accepted	40	Graduated top 10% of class	80
Total undergrad enrollment	7,857	Calendar	semester	% of acceptees attending	51	Graduated top 25% of class	96
% male/female	55/45	Student/teacher ratio	11:1			Graduated top 50% of class	99
% from out of state	91	FT faculty	927	**Deadlines**			
% transfers	7	% faculty from religious order	4	Early decision/action	11/1	**FINANCIAL FACTS**	
% from catholic high school	38	% graduate in 4 yrs.	93	Regular admission	1/9	Tuition	$20,000
% live on campus	84			Regular notification	4/7	Room & board	$4,850
% African American	4	**Most Popular Majors**				Estimated book expense	$700
% Asian	4	accountancy		**FRESHMAN PROFILE**		% frosh receiving aid	78
% Caucasian	83	government		Range verbal SAT	600-690	% undergrads receiving aid	74
% Hispanic	7	pre-professional studies in sciences		Average verbal SAT	641	% frosh w/ grant	58
% international	2			Range math SAT	620-710	Avg. grant	$10,346
# of countries represented	39	**ADMISSIONS**		Average math SAT	662	% frosh w/ loan	49
		Admissions Rating	98	Range ACT	27-31	Avg. loan	$4,000
		# of applicants	9,452	Average ACT	29		
				Minimum TOEFL	550		

OHIO DOMINICAN COLLEGE

1216 Sunbury Road, Columbus, OH 43219 • Admissions: 614-251-4500 • Fax: 614-252-0776
• Financial Aid: 614-251-4640 • Web Site: www.odc.edu

Ohio Dominican College was founded in 1911 by the Sisters of Saint Dominic. The college is located four miles from downtown Columbus on a 54-acre campus. Thirty majors are offered at the college, mostly within the liberal arts and sciences but also including programs in business, education, and health care administration. Among the most popular academic disciplines are education, business administration, and criminal justice. Facilities of note include an art gallery. Most students who attend the college commute; about one-fifth live in on-campus housing. Ohio Dominican's on-campus clubs and organizations offer a standard complement of college activities, including student government, music and arts groups, a radio station, and a number of international and ethnic organizations. Intercollegiate athletics are offered in three sports for men, five for women.

ADMISSIONS
The admissions committee considers (in descending order of importance): HS record, test scores, essay, class rank, recommendations. *Also considered (in descending order of importance):* extracurriculars, personality. Either the SAT or ACT is required. An interview is required. Admissions process is need-blind. *High school units required/recommended:* 15 total units are required; 4 English required, 3 math required, 3 science required, 2 foreign language required, 3 social studies required. Minimum 2.3 GPA required.

FINANCIAL AID
Students should submit: FAFSA. The Princeton Review suggests that all financial aid forms be submitted as soon as possible after January 1. *The following grants/scholarships are offered:* state scholarships. *Students borrow from the following loan programs:* Stafford, PLUS. Applicants will be notified of awards beginning February. College Work-Study Program is available. Institutional employment is available. The off-campus job outlook is excellent.

STUDENT BODY
Total undergrad enrollment	1,713
% male/female	37/63
% from out of state	14
% transfers	45
% live on campus	19
% African American	14
% Asian	1
% Caucasian	78
% Hispanic	2
% international	7
# of countries represented	22

ACADEMICS
Calendar	semester
Student/teacher ratio	16:1
FT faculty	107
% faculty from religious order	9

Most Popular Majors
education
business administration
criminal justice

ADMISSIONS
Admissions Rating	67

Deadlines
Regular admission	rolling
Regular notification	rolling

FINANCIAL FACTS
Tuition	$8,490
Room & board	$4,450
Estimated book expense	$650
% frosh receiving aid	88
% undergrads receiving aid	80

OUR LADY OF HOLY CROSS COLLEGE

4123 Woodland Drive, New Orleans, LA 70114 • *Admissions: 504-394-7744* • *Fax: 504-391-2421*
• *Financial Aid: 504-398-2164*

Our Lady of Holy Cross College was founded in 1916 by the Congregation of Marianite Sisters of the Holy Cross, and became coed in 1967. The 75-acre campus is three miles from downtown New Orleans. Most students are nontraditional; the average age of students at Our Lady of Holy Cross is twenty-six. All are commuters; no housing is available. Nineteen majors are available in a variety of disciplines, mainly within the liberal arts and sciences, business, education, and health sciences. Programs in education, nursing, and business are among the most popular choices. Athletics are intramural only, offering softball and volleyball.

ADMISSIONS

The admissions committee considers (in descending order of importance): HS record, class rank, recommendations, test scores. Either the SAT or ACT is required; ACT is preferred. *High school units required/ recommended:* 24 total units are required. *Special Requirements:* TOEFL is required of all international students.

FINANCIAL AID

Students should submit: FAFSA (due April 15), the school's own financial aid form (due April 15), a copy of parents' most recent income tax filing (due April 15). The Princeton Review suggests that all financial aid forms be submitted as soon as possible after January 1. *The following grants/scholarships are offered:* Pell, SEOG, academic merit, athletic, the school's own scholarships, the school's own grants, state grants, ROTC. *Students borrow from the following loan programs:* Stafford, unsubsidized Stafford, Perkins, PLUS, the school's own loan fund, supplemental loans, federal nursing loans. Applicants will be notified of awards beginning July 1. College Work-Study Program is available. The off-campus job outlook is good.

STUDENT BODY

Total undergrad enrollment	1,178
% male/female	24/76
% from out of state	1
% African American	19
% Asian	2
% Caucasian	73
% Hispanic	4

ACADEMICS

Calendar	semester
Student/teacher ratio	14:1
FT faculty	93

Most Popular Majors

education
nursing
business

ADMISSIONS

Admissions Rating	80
% of acceptees attending	79

Deadlines

Regular admission	7/20
Regular notification	rolling

FRESHMAN PROFILE

Minimum TOEFL	500

FINANCIAL FACTS

Tuition	$4,400
Estimated book expense	$534
% frosh receiving aid	61
% undergrads receiving aid	58

OUR LADY OF THE LAKE UNIVERSITY

411 S. W. 24th Street, San Antonio, TX 78207 • Admissions: 210-434-6711 • Fax: 210-431-4048
• Financial Aid: 210-434-3960 • E-mail: scott@lake.ollura.edu • Web Site: www.ollusa.edu

Founded by the Congregation of Divine Providence in 1895 as a women's college, Our Lady of the Lake University became coed in 1969. The university is located on a 72-acre Gothic campus three miles from downtown San Antonio, and is primarily a commuter school; little more than 10 percent of the student body lives on campus. Our Lady of the Lake offers thirty undergraduate majors in four colleges: arts and sciences, business and public administration, education and clinical studies, and the Worden School of Social Service. The most popular majors are business and liberal studies. Extracurricular options offer a student newspaper, performing arts groups, religious organizations, and service clubs. Facilities of note include a laboratory school for children with language and learning disabilities, an elementary school, and an intercultural institute.

ADMISSIONS

The admissions committee considers (in descending order of importance): HS record, test scores, class rank. *Also considered (in descending order of importance):* extracurriculars, personality, alumni relationship, geographical distribution. Either the SAT or ACT is required. *High school units required/recommended:* 16 total units are required; 4 English required, 2 math required, 2 science required, 2 foreign language required, 2 social studies required. Additional units may be required of applicants to some departments and particular majors.

FINANCIAL AID

Students should submit: FAFSA (due April 15), the school's own financial aid form (due April 15), state aid form, a copy of parents' most recent income tax filing (due April 15). The Princeton Review suggests that all financial aid forms be submitted as soon as possible after January 1. *The following grants/scholarships are offered:* Pell, SEOG, academic merit, athletic, the school's own scholarships, the school's own grants, state scholarships, state grants, private scholarships, private grants, federal nursing scholarship. *Students borrow from the following loan programs:* Stafford, unsubsidized Stafford, Perkins, PLUS, the school's own loan fund, supplemental loans, state loans, private loans. College Work-Study Program is available. Institutional employment is available. The off-campus job outlook is good.

STUDENT BODY		ACADEMICS		Deadlines		FINANCIAL FACTS	
Total undergrad enrollment	2,365	Calendar	semester	Regular admission	rolling	Tuition	$9,540
% male/female	23/77	Student/teacher ratio	16:1	Regular notification	rolling	Room & board	$3,916
% from out of state	2	FT faculty	217			Estimated book expense	$750
% live on campus	25	% graduate in 4 yrs.	31	**FRESHMAN PROFILE**		% frosh receiving aid	83
% African American	6			Average verbal SAT	492	% undergrads receiving aid	61
% Asian	1	**Most Popular Majors**		Average math SAT	481	% frosh w/ grant	75
% Caucasian	30	business		Average ACT	21	Avg. grant	$2,100
% Hispanic	60	liberal studies		Minimum TOEFL	525	% frosh w/ loan	77
% international	1	**ADMISSIONS**		Average HS GPA or Avg	3.3	Avg. loan	$2,952
# of countries represented	7	Admissions Rating	71	Graduated top 10% of class	27		
		# of applicants	1,953	Graduated top 25% of class	52		
		% of applicants accepted	74	Graduated top 50% of class	78		
		% of acceptees attending	25				

UNIVERSITY OF PORTLAND

5000 North Willamette Blvd., Portland, OR 97203 • Admissions: 503-283-7911 • Fax: 503-283-7399
• Financial Aid: 503-283-7311 • E-mail: admissio@uofport.edu • Web Site: www.uofport.edu

The University of Portland was founded as a university for men in 1901 by the Congregation of the Holy Cross, and became coed in 1934. The 90-acre residential campus is four miles from Portland's city center. Portland offers fifty majors within the liberal arts and sciences, business, education, engineering, and nursing. Most popular programs include nursing, elementary education, and biology. University facilities of note are a new academic building, a 5,000-seat athletic and convention facility, an art gallery, and an observatory. Forty registered clubs and organizations offer a range of activities that include numerous music and arts groups, cultural organizations, publications, and volunteer services. Seven teams for men and six teams for women compete in intercollegiate athletics; several intramural and club sports are also available.

ADMISSIONS

The admissions committee considers (in descending order of importance): HS record, test scores, essay, recommendations, class rank. *Also considered (in descending order of importance):* alumni relationship, extracurriculars, personality, special talents. Either the SAT or ACT is required. Admissions process is need-blind. *High school units required/recommended:* 14 total units are recommended; 4 English recommended, 3 math recommended, 2 science recommended, 2 foreign language recommended, 3 social studies recommended. Minimum combined SAT I score of 800 or minimum 2.6 GPA required. *Special Requirements:* Minimum combined SAT I score of 900 required of engineering, math, and science program applicants.

FINANCIAL AID

Students should submit: FAFSA (due March 15), the school's own financial aid form (due March 15). The Princeton Review suggests that all financial aid forms be submitted as soon as possible after January 1. *The following grants/scholarships are offered:* Pell, SEOG, academic merit, athletic, the school's own scholarships, the school's own grants, state scholarships, state grants, private scholarships, private grants, ROTC, foreign aid. *Students borrow from the following loan programs:* Stafford, unsubsidized Stafford, Perkins, PLUS, the school's own loan fund, supplemental loans, federal nursing loans, private loans. Applicants will be notified of awards beginning April 10. College Work-Study Program is available. Institutional employment is available. The off-campus job outlook is good.

STUDENT BODY

Total undergrad enrollment	2,078
% male/female	44/56
% from out of state	47
% live on campus	41
% African American	2
% Asian	7
% Caucasian	84
% Hispanic	3
% Native American	1
# of countries represented	47

ACADEMICS

Calendar	semester
Student/teacher ratio	11:1
FT faculty	240
% faculty from religious order	15
% graduate in 4 yrs.	60

Most Popular Majors
nursing
elementary education
biology

ADMISSIONS

Admissions Rating	76
# of applicants	1,603

% of applicants accepted	92
% of acceptees attending	36

Deadlines

Regular admission	8/15
Regular notification	rolling

FRESHMAN PROFILE

Range verbal SAT	510-620
Average verbal SAT	561
Range math SAT	510-640
Average math SAT	565
Minimum TOEFL	500
Average HS GPA or Avg	3.5
Graduated top 10% of class	36

Graduated top 25% of class	64
Graduated top 50% of class	91

FINANCIAL FACTS

Tuition	$13,200
Room & board	$4,240
Estimated book expense	$600
% frosh receiving aid	83
% undergrads receiving aid	75
% frosh w/ grant	58
Avg. grant	$5,280
% frosh w/ loan	44
Avg. loan	$2,877

PROVIDENCE COLLEGE

River Avenue and Eaton Street, Providence, RI 02918 • *Admissions: 401-865-2535* • *Fax: 401-865-2826*
• *Financial Aid: 401-865-2286* • *E-mail: pcadmission@providence.edu* • *Web Site: www.providence.edu*

Founded in 1917 by the Dominicans, Providence College became coed in 1971. The college is located on a 105-acre campus five miles from downtown Providence. Thirty-five majors are available within the liberal arts and sciences, business, and education. Facilities of note on the campus are the Blackfriars Theater, an art gallery, and a science complex. Extracurriculars of all types are abundant; sixty-three clubs and organizations offer activities on campus, and there are twelve honor societies. Providence athletic teams, the Friars, compete in the Big East Conference. The college fields teams in thirteen sports each for men and women, several of which are nationally competitive. The women's cross-country team won the 1995 NCAA championship; the men's basketball team was one of the last eight teams left in last year's NCAA championship tournament, losing in that round to the eventual national champions, the University of Arizona Wildcats.

ADMISSIONS

The admissions committee considers (in descending order of importance): HS record, test scores, class rank, essay, recommendations. *Also considered (in descending order of importance):* extracurriculars, personality, special talents, alumni relationship, geographical distribution. Either the SAT or ACT is required. An interview is recommended. Admissions process is need-blind. *High school units required/recommended:* 18 total units are required; 4 English required, 3 math required, 3 math recommended, 2 science required, 3 science recommended, 3 foreign language required, 4 foreign language recommended, 2 social studies required, 1 history required. Minimum SAT I scores of 510 verbal and 550 math (composite ACT score of 25), rank in top third of secondary school class, and minimum 3.0 GPA recommended. *Special Requirements:* TOEFL is required of all international students. 4 units each of math and science recommended for biology, chemistry, and pre-engineering program applicants.

FINANCIAL AID

Students should submit: FAFSA (due February 1), CSS Profile (due February 1). The Princeton Review suggests that all financial aid forms be submitted as soon as possible after January 1. *The following grants/scholarships are offered:* Pell, SEOG, academic merit, athletic, the school's own scholarships, the school's own grants, state scholarships, state grants, private scholarships, private grants, ROTC. *Students borrow from the following loan programs:* Perkins, PLUS, supplemental loans, private loans. Applicants will be notified of awards beginning April 1. College Work-Study Program is available. Institutional employment is available. The off-campus job outlook is good.

STUDENT BODY		ACADEMICS		Deadlines		Graduated top 50% of class	94
Total undergrad enrollment	3,638	Calendar	semester	Early decision/action	11/15	**FINANCIAL FACTS**	
% male/female	42/58	Student/teacher ratio	13:1	Regular admission	2/1	Tuition	$16,350
% from out of state	85	FT faculty	312	Regular notification	4/1	Room & board	$6,919
% transfers	7	% faculty from religious order	18			Estimated book expense	$400
% live on campus	72			**FRESHMAN PROFILE**		% frosh receiving aid	75
% African American	2	**Most Popular Majors**		Range verbal SAT	520-630	% undergrads receiving aid	74
% Asian	1	business		Average verbal SAT	576	% frosh w/ grant	60
% Caucasian	92	education		Range math SAT	530-620	Avg. grant	$6,550
% Hispanic	2	political science		Average math SAT	571	% frosh w/ loan	34
% international	1	**ADMISSIONS**		Range ACT	25-28	Avg. loan	$6,385
# of countries represented	14	Admissions Rating	77	Average ACT	26		
		# of applicants	4,354	Minimum TOEFL	550		
		% of applicants accepted	71	Graduated top 10% of class	30		
		% of acceptees attending	30	Graduated top 25% of class	69		

QUINCY UNIVERSITY

1800 College Avenue, Quincy, IL 62301 • Admissions: 217-228-5210 • Fax: 217-228-5376
• Financial Aid: 217-228-5260 • E-mail: laytham@quincy.edu • Web Site: www.quincy.edu

Quincy University was founded in 1860 by the Franciscans. The university is located on a 75-acre residential campus two hours from Saint Louis. Thirty-four majors, mainly in the liberal arts and sciences, business, and education, are offered at the college. Among the most popular programs are elementary education, management, and accounting. Noteworthy facilities include an art gallery, the Ameritech Center for Communications, and a biological field station. Extracurriculars include forty-one clubs and organizations sponsoring a full range of offerings both academic and social; activities include a variety of publications, a symphony orchestra, film, television, and radio, and numerous cultural and service groups. Seven teams for men and six for women represent the college in intercollegiate athletic competition, housed at home in an impressive athletic complex that includes football, baseball, and soccer stadiums, a gymnasium, practice fields, and a clubhouse.

ADMISSIONS

The admissions committee considers (in descending order of importance): HS record, test scores, class rank, recommendations. *Also considered (in descending order of importance):* alumni relationship, extracurriculars, special talents, geographical distribution, personality. Either the SAT or ACT is required. An interview is recommended. Admissions process is need-blind. *High school units required/recommended:* 16 total units are recommended; 4 English recommended, 3 math recommended, 3 science recommended, 2 foreign language recommended, 2 social studies recommended, 2 history recommended. Minimum composite ACT score of 20, rank in top half of secondary school class, and minimum 2.0 GPA required. *Special Requirements:* A portfolio is required for art program applicants. An audition is required for music program applicants.

FINANCIAL AID

Students should submit: FAFSA (due March 31), the school's own financial aid form, state aid form. The Princeton Review suggests that all financial aid forms be submitted as soon as possible after January 1. *The following grants/scholarships are offered:* state scholarships. *Students borrow from the following loan programs:* Stafford, PLUS. College Work-Study Program is available. Institutional employment is available. The off-campus job outlook is good.

STUDENT BODY	
Total undergrad enrollment	1,050
% male/female	49/51
% from out of state	30
% transfers	25
% from catholic high school	60
% live on campus	70
% African American	5
% Asian	1
% Caucasian	91
% Hispanic	1
% Native American	1
% international	1
# of countries represented	11

ACADEMICS	
Calendar	semester
Student/teacher ratio	12:1
FT faculty	96
% faculty from religious order	10
% graduate in 4 yrs.	59

Most Popular Majors
elementary education
management
accounting

ADMISSIONS	
Admissions Rating	78
# of applicants	1,208

% of applicants accepted	71
% of acceptees attending	33

Deadlines

Regular admission	rolling
Regular notification	rolling

FRESHMAN PROFILE

Range ACT	21-26
Average ACT	23
Minimum TOEFL	550
Average HS GPA or Avg	3.1
Graduated top 10% of class	23
Graduated top 25% of class	64
Graduated top 50% of class	90

FINANCIAL FACTS	
Tuition	$11,240
Room & board	$4,370
% frosh receiving aid	98
% undergrads receiving aid	95
% frosh w/ grant	79
Avg. grant	NR
% frosh w/ loan	63
Avg. loan	$2,383

REGIS COLLEGE

235 Wellesley Street, Weston, MA 02193 • *Admissions: 617-768-7000* • *Fax: 617-768-7071*
• *Financial Aid: 617-768-7180* • *E-mail: admission@regiscollege.edu*

Regis College was established in 1927 as a women's college by the Sisters of Saint Joseph. The college is on a 168-acre campus twelve miles from Boston. Regis offers nineteen majors within the liberal arts and sciences, and business. Popular majors include communications, political science, and English. The college participates in a cross-registration program with Boston College, Bentley College, and Babson College. Special features among Regis' campus facilities are a philatelic (stamp) museum and a fine arts center with a 650-seat theater. Thirty-six clubs and organizations offer a variety of college activities, including student government, music and arts groups, radio, and a number of religious, cultural, political, and social organizations. Regis competes in intercollegiate athletics in twelve sports; its basketball team is ranked among the top ten in the Atlantic Region of NCAA Division III.

ADMISSIONS

The admissions committee considers (in descending order of importance): HS record, class rank, recommendations, test scores, essay. *Also considered (in descending order of importance):* extracurriculars, personality, special talents, alumni relationship. Either the SAT or ACT is required; SAT is preferred. An interview is required. Admissions process is need-blind. *High school units required/recommended:* 16 total units are required; 4 English required, 3 math required, 2 science required, 2 foreign language required, 2 social studies required, 3 social studies recommended. Minimum SAT I scores of 440 verbal and 430 math (composite ACT score of 22), rank in top third of secondary school class, and minimum grade average of 85 required. *Special Requirements:* An R.N. is required for nursing program applicants.

FINANCIAL AID

Students should submit: FAFSA (due February 15), CSS Profile (due), the school's own financial aid form (due April 1), Divorced Parents form, a copy of parents' most recent income tax filing (due April 1). The Princeton Review suggests that all financial aid forms be submitted as soon as possible after January 1. *The following grants/scholarships are offered:* state scholarships. *Students borrow from the following loan programs:* Stafford, PLUS. College Work-Study Program is available. Institutional employment is available. The off-campus job outlook is good.

STUDENT BODY		ACADEMICS	
Total undergrad enrollment	1,063	Calendar	semester
% male/female	0/100	Student/teacher ratio	10:1
% from out of state	15	FT faculty	141
% transfers	14	% faculty from religious order	19
% from catholic high school	44	% graduate in 4 yrs.	62
% live on campus	77		
% African American	3	**Most Popular Majors**	
% Asian	2	communications	
% Caucasian	69	political science	
% Hispanic	3	English	
% international	3	**ADMISSIONS**	
		Admissions Rating	65
		# of applicants	661

% of applicants accepted	91	Graduated top 50% of class	77
% of acceptees attending	34		
Deadlines		**FINANCIAL FACTS**	
Regular admission	rolling	Tuition	$14,500
Regular notification	rolling	Room & board	$6,600
		Estimated book expense	$450
FRESHMAN PROFILE		% frosh receiving aid	69
Range verbal SAT	470-580	% undergrads receiving aid	67
Average verbal SAT	521	% frosh w/ grant	76
Range math SAT	430-540	Avg. grant	NR
Average math SAT	487	% frosh w/ loan	77
Minimum TOEFL	500	Avg. loan	$3,349
Graduated top 10% of class	14		
Graduated top 25% of class	40		

REGIS UNIVERSITY

3333 Regis Boulevard, Denver, CO 80221 • *Admissions: 303-458-4900* • *Fax: 303-964-5534*
• *Financial Aid: 303-458-4066* • *E-mail: regisadm@regis.edu* • *Web Site: www.regis.edu*

Founded by the Jesuits in 1877, Regis University is named in honor of Saint John Francis Regis, an eighteenth-century French Jesuit. The university's 90-acre residential campus is located ten miles from downtown Denver. Regis offers twenty-six majors within the realm of liberal arts and sciences, business, education, and health sciences. Most popular majors include business administration, communications, and nursing. Nineteen registered clubs and organizations at Regis offer a relatively standard complement of extracurricular activities including a variety of publications, music and arts groups; particularly noteworthy are a mock trial club, a Middle Eastern concerns organization, Christian Life Community, and Circle K International. Six men's and seven women's teams compete in intercollegiate athletics, and a full range of intramural sports are also offered. Both Pope John Paul II and President Clinton have visited the Regis campus.

ADMISSIONS

The admissions committee considers (in descending order of importance): HS record, test scores, recommendations, essay, class rank. *Also considered (in descending order of importance):* extracurriculars, personality, alumni relationship, special talents. Either the SAT or ACT is required. An interview is required. Admissions process is need-blind. *High school units required/recommended:* 16 total units are recommended; 4 English recommended, 2 math recommended, 2 science recommended, 2 foreign language recommended, 2 social studies recommended, 1 history recommended. Minimum 2.5 GPA recommended.

FINANCIAL AID

Students should submit: FAFSA (due March 15), the school's own financial aid form (due March 15). The Princeton Review suggests that all financial aid forms be submitted as soon as possible after January 1. *The following grants/scholarships are offered:* Pell, SEOG, academic merit, athletic, the school's own scholarships, the school's own grants, state scholarships, state grants, private scholarships, private grants. *Students borrow from the following loan programs:* Stafford, unsubsidized Stafford, Perkins, PLUS, the school's own loan fund, supplemental loans, private loans. Applicants will be notified of awards beginning January. College Work-Study Program is available. Institutional employment is available. The off-campus job outlook is good.

STUDENT BODY

Total undergrad enrollment	1,160
% male/female	44/56
% from out of state	40
% live on campus	48
% African American	2
% Asian	3
% Caucasian	80
% Hispanic	9
% Native American	1
% international	3
# of countries represented	7

ACADEMICS

Calendar	semester
Student/teacher ratio	11:1
FT faculty	109
% graduate in 4 yrs.	48

Most Popular Majors
business administration
communications
nursing

ADMISSIONS

Admissions Rating	75
# of applicants	1,104
% of applicants accepted	77
% of acceptees attending	32

Deadlines

Regular admission	8/1
Regular notification	rolling

FRESHMAN PROFILE

Range verbal SAT	470-590
Average verbal SAT	530
Range math SAT	450-580
Average math SAT	521
Range ACT	20-28
Average ACT	22
Minimum TOEFL	550
Average HS GPA or Avg	3.3

FINANCIAL FACTS

Tuition	$14,100
Room & board	$5,980
Estimated book expense	$600
% frosh receiving aid	68
% undergrads receiving aid	73
% frosh w/ grant	50
Avg. grant	$5,580
% frosh w/ loan	49
Avg. loan	$3,500

RIVIER COLLEGE

420 Main Street, Nashua, NH 03060 • Admissions: 603-888-1311 • Fax: 603-891-1799
• Financial Aid: 603-888-1311 • E-mail: rivadmit@mightyriv.edu • Web Site: www.rivier.edu

Rivier College was established in 1933 by the Sisters of the Presentation of Mary. Located forty-five minutes from Boston, the college is situated on a 60-acre residential campus in the foothills of the White Mountains. Housing is guaranteed. Rivier offers fifty-three majors within the liberal arts and sciences, business, education, and the health professions. Most popular programs include business, education, and behavioral sciences. Over twenty clubs and organizations are registered on campus, offering a range of activities that include a variety of publications, music and arts ensembles, preprofessional interest clubs, and religious and volunteer organizations. Intercollegiate athletic teams are available in five sports each for men and women. Intramural competition is offered in six sports. Facilities of note on the Rivier campus include a multilevel studio/art complex, a paralegal/law library, and an electronic imaging laboratory.

ADMISSIONS

The admissions committee considers (in descending order of importance): HS record, recommendations, test scores, essay, class rank. *Also considered (in descending order of importance):* extracurriculars, personality, alumni relationship, special talents. Either the SAT or ACT is required; SAT is preferred. An interview is recommended. Admissions process is need-blind. *High school units required/recommended:* 16 total units are required; 4 English required, 2 math required, 1 science required, 2 foreign language required, 2 social studies required, 1 history recommended. *Special Requirements:* A portfolio is required for art program applicants. An R.N. is required for nursing program applicants. Algebra and chemistry required of nursing program applicants.

FINANCIAL AID

Students should submit: FAFSA (due April 1), the school's own financial aid form (due April 1), a copy of parents' most recent income tax filing. The Princeton Review suggests that all financial aid forms be submitted as soon as possible after January 1. *The following grants/scholarships are offered:* state scholarships. *Students borrow from the following loan programs:* Stafford, PLUS. College Work-Study Program is available. Institutional employment is available. The off-campus job outlook is good.

STUDENT BODY		ACADEMICS		Deadlines		FINANCIAL FACTS	
Total undergrad enrollment	1,728	Calendar	semester	Regular admission	rolling	Tuition	$11,700
% male/female	16/84	Student/teacher ratio	15:1	Regular notification	rolling	Room & board	$5,250
% from out of state	23	FT faculty	190			Estimated book expense	$300
% transfers	36	**Most Popular Majors**		**FRESHMAN PROFILE**		% frosh receiving aid	85
% live on campus	35	business		Minimum TOEFL	500	% undergrads receiving aid	85
% African American	1	education		Graduated top 10% of class	10	% frosh w/ grant	65
% Asian	1	behavioral sciences		Graduated top 25% of class	34	Avg. grant	NR
% Caucasian	78	**ADMISSIONS**		Graduated top 50% of class	71	% frosh w/ loan	91
% Hispanic	2	Admissions Rating	63			Avg. loan	$2,384
% international	2	% of acceptees attending	41				
# of countries represented	6						

ROCKHURST COLLEGE

1100 Rockhurst Rd., Kansas City, MO 64110 • *Admissions: 816-926-4100* • *Fax: 816-501-4588*
• *Financial Aid: 816-501-4100* • *E-mail: admission@vax2.rockhurst.edu* • *Web Site: vax1.rockhurst.edu*

Founded in 1910 by the Jesuits, Rockhurst College is located on a 30-acre residential campus five miles from Kansas City's downtown. Rockhurst offers forty-eight undergraduate majors within the liberal arts and sciences, business, education, and nursing; popular majors include nursing, psychology, and accounting. Special facilities include three art galleries—the Van Ackeren Gallery of Religious Art, the Massman Art Gallery, and the Nelson-Atkins Museum of Art. Activities outside the classroom include over forty registered clubs and organizations; beyond the usual range of extracurriculars such as student government, music and arts groups, and publications are a chapter of Amnesty International, Appalachian Service Project, and several other service clubs. Athletic competition at the intercollegiate level is offered in four sports each for men and women; numerous intramurals are also available.

ADMISSIONS

The admissions committee considers (in descending order of importance): HS record, test scores, class rank, recommendations, essay. *Also considered (in descending order of importance):* extracurriculars, personality, special talents, alumni relationship. Either the SAT or ACT is required; ACT is preferred. An interview is recommended. Admissions process is need-blind. *High school units required/recommended:* 18 total units are recommended; 4 English recommended, 3 math recommended, 3 science recommended, 2 foreign language recommended, 2 social studies recommended, 2 history recommended. Minimum composite ACT score of 20 (combined SAT I score of 960) and rank in top two-fifths of secondary school class required. *Special Requirements:* TOEFL is required of all international students.

FINANCIAL AID

Students should submit: FAFSA (due April 1), the school's own financial aid form (due April 1). The Princeton Review suggests that all financial aid forms be submitted as soon as possible after January 1. *The following grants/scholarships are offered:* state scholarships. *Students borrow from the following loan programs:* Stafford, PLUS. Applicants will be notified of awards beginning February 15. College Work-Study Program is available. Institutional employment is available. The off-campus job outlook is good.

STUDENT BODY		ACADEMICS	
Total undergrad enrollment	2,157	Calendar	semester
% male/female	45/55	Student/teacher ratio	12:1
% from out of state	30	FT faculty	236
% transfers	41	% faculty from religious order	15
% from catholic high school	54	% graduate in 4 yrs.	61
% live on campus	54		
% African American	8	**Most Popular Majors**	
% Asian	2	nursing	
% Caucasian	57	psychology	
% Hispanic	5	accounting	
% Native American	1	**ADMISSIONS**	
% international	1	Admissions Rating	74
# of countries represented	12	# of applicants	1,055

% of applicants accepted	91	Graduated top 10% of class	30
% of acceptees attending	38	Graduated top 25% of class	58
		Graduated top 50% of class	83
Deadlines			
Regular admission	6/30	**FINANCIAL FACTS**	
Regular notification	rolling	Tuition	$11,000
FRESHMAN PROFILE		Room & board	$4,350
Range verbal SAT	520-630	Estimated book expense	$500
Average verbal SAT	569	% frosh receiving aid	87
Range math SAT	510-620	% undergrads receiving aid	80
Average math SAT	566	% frosh w/ grant	84
Range ACT	21-27	Avg. grant	NR
Average ACT	24	% frosh w/ loan	76
Minimum TOEFL	550	Avg. loan	$2,426

ROSEMONT COLLEGE

1400 Montgomery Avenue, Rosemont, PA 19010 • *Admissions: 610-526-2966* • *Fax: 610-527-1041*
• *Financial Aid: 610-526-2966* • *E-mail: roscoladmit@rosemont.edu*

Rosemont College was founded in 1921 by the Society of the Holy Child Jesus. The college is located on a beautiful 56-acre residential campus eleven miles from Philadelphia. On-campus housing is guaranteed. Twenty-three majors are available, primarily within the areas of liberal arts and sciences, and business. English, psychology, and business rank among the most popular majors. There are plenty of opportunities for involvement outside the classroom at Rosemont; the college has twenty-two clubs and organizations, including such groups as the Down-to-Earth Club (an environmental club), several publications, a women's forum, music and arts ensembles, academic interest groups, and multicultural organizations. Athletic competition at the intercollegiate level is offered in basketball, field hockey, softball, tennis, and volleyball. Additional activities are available through a relationship with nearby Villanova University.

ADMISSIONS

The admissions committee considers (in descending order of importance): HS record, class rank, test scores, recommendations, essay. *Also considered (in descending order of importance):* personality, extracurriculars, alumni relationship, special talents. An interview is recommended. Admissions process is need-blind. *High school units required/recommended:* 17 total units are required; 4 English required, 2 math required, 2 science required, 2 foreign language required, 2 social studies required.

FINANCIAL AID

Students should submit: FAFSA, state aid form, a copy of parents' most recent income tax filing. The Princeton Review suggests that all financial aid forms be submitted as soon as possible after January 1. *The following grants/scholarships are offered:* Pell, SEOG, athletic, the school's own scholarships, the school's own grants, state scholarships, state grants, private scholarships, private grants, ROTC. *Students borrow from the following loan programs:* Stafford, unsubsidized Stafford, Perkins, PLUS, the school's own loan fund, supplemental loans, state loans, private loans. College Work-Study Program is available. Institutional employment is available. The off-campus job outlook is good.

STUDENT BODY		ACADEMICS				FINANCIAL FACTS	
Total undergrad enrollment	736	Calendar	semester	% of applicants accepted	67	Graduated top 25% of class	55
% male/female	0/100	Student/teacher ratio	7:1	% of acceptees attending	51	Graduated top 50% of class	84
% from out of state	33	FT faculty	123	**Deadlines**			
% live on campus	80	% graduate in 4 yrs.	68	Regular admission	rolling	**FINANCIAL FACTS**	
% African American	5			Regular notification	rolling	Tuition	$12,460
% Asian	4	**Most Popular Majors**				Room & board	$6,500
% Caucasian	90	English		**FRESHMAN PROFILE**		Estimated book expense	$600
% Hispanic	1	psychology		Range verbal SAT	460-610	% frosh receiving aid	48
% international	3	business		Average verbal SAT	535	% undergrads receiving aid	50
# of countries represented	7	**ADMISSIONS**		Range math SAT	440-570		
		Admissions Rating	81	Average math SAT	500		
		# of applicants	320	Minimum TOEFL	500		
				Average HS GPA or Avg	3.1		
				Graduated top 10% of class	27		

SACRED HEART UNIVERSITY

5151 Park Avenue, Fairfield, CT 06432 • Admissions: 203-371-7880 • Fax: 203-365-7607
• Financial Aid: 203-371-7981 • E-mail: enroll@sacredheart.edu • Web Site: www.sacredheart.edu

Founded in 1963, Sacred Heart University is the third largest university in New England. The university sits on a 56-acre campus one hour from New York City and about two hours from Boston. Sacred Heart was founded by its local diocese, and the administration is staffed primarily by laypeople. Over the past five years, the Sacred Heart campus has undergone a huge expansion program, with over $40 million in new construction. Students may choose from over twenty-five majors, most of which are found within the liberal arts and sciences, business, education, and the health sciences. Most popular among academic options are business administration, accounting, and psychology. As far as extracurricular activities go, Sacred Heart counts fifty-six registered clubs and organizations on campus, among them many musical ensembles, political groups, and a variety of specific ethnic cultural activities. Especially impressive is the University's array of men's and women's athletic teams, constituting the largest NCAA Division II athletic program in the country.

ADMISSIONS

The admissions committee considers (in descending order of importance): HS record, class rank, recommendations, test scores, essay. *Also considered (in descending order of importance):* extracurriculars, special talents, geographical distribution, personality, alumni relationship. Either the SAT or ACT is required. An interview is recommended. Admissions process is need-blind. *High school units required/recommended:* 17 total units are required; 24 total units are recommended; 4 English required, 3 math required, 4 math recommended, 3 science required, 4 science recommended, 2 foreign language required, 4 foreign language recommended, 1 social studies required, 3 social studies recommended, 2 history required, 3 history recommended. Minimum SAT I scores of 450 in both verbal and math, rank in top two-fifths of secondary school class, and minimum 3.0 GPA recommended.

FINANCIAL AID

Students should submit: FAFSA (due March 1), CSS Profile, the school's own financial aid form, state aid form, a copy of parents' most recent income tax filing (due March 1). The Princeton Review suggests that all financial aid forms be submitted as soon as possible after January 1. *The following grants/scholarships are offered:* state scholarships. *Students borrow from the following loan programs:* Stafford, PLUS. College Work-Study Program is available. Institutional employment is available. The off-campus job outlook is good.

STUDENT BODY

Total undergrad enrollment	3,843
% male/female	45/55
% from out of state	27
% transfers	20
% from catholic high school	45
% live on campus	60
% African American	8
% Asian	3
% Caucasian	77
% Hispanic	7
% Native American	1
% international	4
# of countries represented	59

ACADEMICS

Calendar	semester
Student/teacher ratio	14:1
FT faculty	392
% faculty from religious order	1
% graduate in 4 yrs.	73

Most Popular Majors
business administration
accounting
psychology

ADMISSIONS

Admissions Rating	64
# of applicants	2,697
% of applicants accepted	85
% of acceptees attending	26

Deadlines

Regular admission	4/15
Regular notification	rolling

FRESHMAN PROFILE

Range verbal SAT	400-490
Average verbal SAT	520
Range math SAT	400-540
Average math SAT	500
Minimum TOEFL	500
Average HS GPA or Avg	3.0
Graduated top 10% of class	17
Graduated top 25% of class	50
Graduated top 50% of class	87

FINANCIAL FACTS

Tuition	$12,212
Room & board	$6,380
Estimated book expense	$400
% frosh receiving aid	92
% undergrads receiving aid	80
% frosh w/ grant	9
Avg. grant	NR
% frosh w/ loan	88
Avg. loan	NR

SAINT AMBROSE UNIVERSITY

518 West Locust Street, Davenport, IA 52803 • Admissions: 319-383-8888 • Fax: 319-333-6297
• Financial Aid: 319-333-6314 • E-mail: poconnor@saimck.sai.edu • Web Site: www.sau.edu

Saint Ambrose Univeristy, founded in 1882, was established by the first bishop of Davenport as a seminary for young men. Today, Saint Ambrose is coeducational and is the largest Catholic university in Iowa. The university is located in a residential area of Davenport, the largest of the quad cities (Davenport, Rock Island, Moline, and Bettendorf) of eastern Iowa and western Illinois. Saint Ambrose has three colleges—arts and sciences, business, and human services—that collectively offer over fifty undergraduate majors and preprofessional programs. Popular majors include business administration, biology, and occupational therapy. Special campus features include an art gallery, transmission electron microscope, observatory, radio station, and cable television channel. Among extracurricular offerings are ten registered clubs and organizations, a variety of musical groups including a music ministry, and eight intercollegiate athletic teams each for men and women. The university's football program finished in the top twenty in the NAIA's Division II last year.

ADMISSIONS

The admissions committee considers (in descending order of importance): HS record, test scores, class rank, recommendations. *Also considered (in descending order of importance):* alumni relationship, extracurriculars, personality, special talents. Either the SAT or ACT is required; ACT is preferred. An interview is recommended. Admissions process is need-blind. *High school units required/recommended:* 16 total units are required; 4 English required, 2 math required, 2 science required, 1 foreign language required, 2 social studies required, 1 history required. Minimum composite ACT score of 20 (combined SAT I score of 780), rank in top half of secondary school class, and minimum 2.5 GPA required.

FINANCIAL AID

Students should submit: FAFSA (due March 15), the school's own financial aid form (due March 15), state aid form, a copy of parents' most recent income tax filing (due March 15). The Princeton Review suggests that all financial aid forms be submitted as soon as possible after January 1. *The following grants/scholarships are offered:* Pell, SEOG, state scholarships, state grants, private scholarships, private grants, foreign aid. *Students borrow from the following loan programs:* Stafford, unsubsidized Stafford, Perkins, PLUS, supplemental loans, private loans. College Work-Study Program is available. Institutional employment is available. The off-campus job outlook is good.

STUDENT BODY		ACADEMICS		Deadlines		Room & board	$4,420
Total undergrad enrollment	1,735	Calendar	semester	Regular admission	rolling	Estimated book expense	$500
% male/female	45/55	Student/teacher ratio	15:1	Regular notification	rolling	% frosh receiving aid	94
% from out of state	32	FT faculty	173			% undergrads receiving aid	90
% transfers	35	% faculty from religious order	0	**FRESHMAN PROFILE**			
% from catholic high school	42			Range ACT	16-24		
% live on campus	47	**Most Popular Majors**		Average ACT	22		
% African American	4	business administration		Minimum TOEFL	500		
% Asian	1	biology		Graduated top 10% of class	12		
% Caucasian	92	occupational therapy		Graduated top 25% of class	48		
% Hispanic	3	**ADMISSIONS**		Graduated top 50% of class	91		
% international	1	Admissions Rating	73	**FINANCIAL FACTS**			
# of countries represented	8	% of acceptees attending	38	Tuition	$11,740		

SAINT ANSELM COLLEGE

100 Saint Anselm Drive, Manchester, NH 03102 • Admissions: 603-641-7000 • Fax: 603-641-7550
• Financial Aid: 603-641-7110 • E-mail: admissions@anslem.edu • Web Site: www.anselm.edu

Saint Anselm College was founded in 1889 by Benedictine monks. Situated fifty miles north of Boston on a 440-acre hilltop campus overlooking New Hampshire's largest city, many regard the college as one of New England's prettiest. Saint Anselm observes and promotes Christian and Catholic standards of value and conduct, and expects its students to respect and observe those standards. Twenty-seven majors are available, primarily within the liberal arts and sciences, business, and health sciences. Nursing, biology, and psychology are the most popular academic options. Noteworthy on campus is the Izart Observatory, which provides facilities for celestial observation and instruction in astronomy. The college counts fifty-four registered clubs and organizations providing a broad selection of activities ranging from a jazz band and choral groups to the Organization for Life. A very active volunteer center and campus ministry provide opportunities for service on campus and in the surrounding area, with projects serving the homeless, elderly, children, and Special Olympics. Saint Anselm offers a variety of sports across all seasons; men's basketball and ice hockey are perennially competitive on both the regional and national levels in the NCAA's Division II. The college is currently completing the single most costly construction project in its history, a $9 million expansion and reconstruction of its science center.

ADMISSIONS

The admissions committee considers (in descending order of importance): HS record, class rank, test scores, essay, recommendations. *Also considered (in descending order of importance):* personality, extracurriculars, special talents, alumni relationship, geographical distribution. Either the SAT or ACT is required; SAT is preferred. An interview is recommended. Admissions process is need-blind. *High school units required/recommended:* 16 total units are required; 4 English required, 3 math required, 3 science required, 2 foreign language required, 1 social studies required, 1 history required. *Special Requirements:* TOEFL is required of all international students.

FINANCIAL AID

Students should submit: FAFSA (due April 15), a copy of parents' most recent income tax filing (due April 15). The Princeton Review suggests that all financial aid forms be submitted as soon as possible after January 1. *The following grants/scholarships are offered:* state scholarships. *Students borrow from the following loan programs:* Stafford, PLUS. Applicants will be notified of awards beginning March 15. College Work-Study Program is available. Institutional employment is available. The off-campus job outlook is good.

STUDENT BODY		ACADEMICS				FINANCIAL FACTS	
Total undergrad enrollment	1,928	Calendar	semester	% of applicants accepted	84	Graduated top 50% of class	83
% male/female	43/57	Student/teacher ratio	13:1	% of acceptees attending	36		
% from out of state	80	FT faculty	159			Tuition	$14,550
% transfers	5	% faculty from religious order	10	**Deadlines**		Room & board	$5,710
% from catholic high school	22	% graduate in 4 yrs.	79	Regular admission	rolling	Estimated book expense	$600
% live on campus	65			Regular notification	rolling	% frosh receiving aid	64
% Caucasian	97	**Most Popular Majors**				% undergrads receiving aid	62
% Hispanic	1	nursing		**FRESHMAN PROFILE**		% frosh w/ grant	64
% international	1	biology		Range verbal SAT	500-600	Avg. grant	NR
# of countries represented	15	psychology		Average verbal SAT	543	% frosh w/ loan	52
				Range math SAT	480-580	Avg. loan	$3,072
		ADMISSIONS		Average math SAT	529		
		Admissions Rating	73	Minimum TOEFL	600		
		# of applicants	1,950	Graduated top 10% of class	15		
				Graduated top 25% of class	43		

COLLEGE OF SAINT BENEDICT

37 South College Ave., Saint Joseph, MN 56374 • Admissions: 612-363-5308 • Fax: 612-363-5010
• Financial Aid: 320-363-5388 • E-mail: admissions@csbsju.edu • Web Site: www.csbsju.edu/index.html

The College of Saint Benedict was founded by the Sisters of the Order of Saint Benedict in 1887, and was one of the first Catholic women's colleges in the upper Midwest. It currently operates in very close cooperation, both academically and socially, with nearby Saint John's University, a men's college, rendering both institutions coed for all practical purposes. Saint Benedict is situated on a 700-acre campus seventy-five miles from Minneapolis and Saint Paul. New academic programs are available in Asian, Latin, and African studies. Nearly 30 percent of Saint Benedict juniors study abroad, one of the highest percentages of all colleges in the nation. Community outreach is an academic function at the college; in this case, the community extends to such locales as Ghana and the Dominican Republic. The campus residential program includes the active participation of many Benedictine and lay professionals who live and interact with the students they advise. As if there were still time left in the typical student's day, Saint Benedict counts 110 registered organizations on campus. As at its male counterpart Saint John's, the college's athletic teams are quite competitive—particularly the basketball program, which ranks among the best in Division III.

ADMISSIONS

The admissions committee considers (in descending order of importance): HS record, class rank, test scores, essay. *Also considered (in descending order of importance):* extracurriculars, personality, special talents. Either the SAT or ACT is required. An interview is recommended. Admissions process is need-blind. *High school units required/ recommended:* 17 total units are recommended; 4 English recommended, 3 math recommended, 2 science recommended, 2 foreign language recommended, 2 social studies recommended. Minimum composite ACT score of 20 (combined SAT I score of 1000), rank in top two-fifths of secondary school class, and minimum 2.8 GPA in college-preparatory courses recommended. *Special Requirements:* TOEFL is required of all international students. Portfolio required of art scholarship applicants. Audition required of music scholarship applicants. Interview required of theatre scholarship applicants.

FINANCIAL AID

Students should submit: FAFSA (due August 15), the school's own financial aid form (due August 15), state aid form, a copy of parents' most recent income tax filing (due August 15). The Princeton Review suggests that all financial aid forms be submitted as soon as possible after January 1. *Students borrow from the following loan programs:* Stafford, PLUS. Applicants will be notified of awards beginning March 15. College Work-Study Program is available. Institutional employment is available. The off-campus job outlook is fair.

STUDENT BODY		ACADEMICS		% of applicants accepted	92	Graduated top 10% of class	34
Total undergrad enrollment	1,958	Calendar	4-1-4	% of acceptees attending	56	Graduated top 25% of class	68
% male/female	0/100	Student/teacher ratio	11:1			Graduated top 50% of class	93
% from out of state	15	FT faculty	177	**Deadlines**			
% transfers	15	% faculty from religious order	15	Regular admission	rolling	**FINANCIAL FACTS**	
% from catholic high school	20	% graduate in 4 yrs.	71	Regular notification	rolling	Tuition	$13,858
% live on campus	77					Room & board	$4,543
% African American	1	**Most Popular Majors**		**FRESHMAN PROFILE**		Estimated book expense	$600
% Asian	2	elementary education		Range verbal SAT	430-550	% frosh receiving aid	85
% Caucasian	95	nursing		Average verbal SAT	574	% undergrads receiving aid	85
% Hispanic	1	business management		Range math SAT	430-610	% frosh w/ grant	72
% Native American	1			Average math SAT	570	Avg. grant	NR
% international	2	**ADMISSIONS**		Range ACT	21-26	% frosh w/ loan	63
# of countries represented	11	Admissions Rating	77	Average ACT	24	Avg. loan	$3,324
		# of applicants	930	Minimum TOEFL	550		
				Average HS GPA or Avg	3.6		

SAINT BONAVENTURE UNIVERSITY

P.O. Box D, St. Bonaventure, NY 14778 • Admissions: 716-375-2400 • Fax: 716-375-2005
• Financial Aid: 716-375-2528 • E-mail: Anaz@sbu.edu • Web Site: www.sbu.edu

Saint Bonaventure University was founded in 1858 by the Franciscans. The University's 600-acre campus is located near the Pennsylvania border seventy-five miles from Buffalo. Facilities of note on campus include a $7 million arts center, an observatory, and the Franciscan Institute, the principle center for Franciscan research in the United States. Twenty-seven undergraduate majors are offered at Saint Bonnie's, centered within the liberal arts and sciences, business, and education. Popular majors include elementary education, journalism and mass communications, and accounting. Opportunities outside the classroom include fifty-eight registered clubs and organizations, and activities run the gamut from arts and media activities to social-action groups and volunteer programs. Intercollegiate, intramural, and club sports are abundant; men's NCAA basketball is traditionally strong.

ADMISSIONS

The admissions committee considers (in descending order of importance): HS record, test scores, recommendations, class rank, essay. *Also considered (in descending order of importance):* alumni relationship, extracurriculars, personality, special talents. Either the SAT or ACT is required. An interview is recommended. Admissions process is need-blind. *High school units required/recommended:* 16 total units are required; 4 English required, 3 math required, 3 science required, 2 foreign language required, 4 social studies required. Minimum combined SAT I score of 1050, rank in top two-fifths of secondary school class, and minimum 3.0 GPA recommended. *The admissions office says:* "[We] highly encourage students to submit a personal essay—it is an excellent opportunity to point out individual uniqueness or experiences, and situations that have affected academic performance."

FINANCIAL AID

Students should submit: FAFSA, the school's own financial aid form. The Princeton Review suggests that all financial aid forms be submitted as soon as possible after January 1. *The following grants/scholarships are offered:* state scholarships. *Students borrow from the following loan programs:* Stafford, PLUS. Applicants will be notified of awards beginning April 1. College Work-Study Program is available. Institutional employment is available. The off-campus job outlook is fair.

STUDENT BODY

Total undergrad enrollment	1,839
% male/female	48/52
% from out of state	22
% transfers	16
% live on campus	76
% African American	2
% Asian	1
% Caucasian	95
% Hispanic	1
% Native American	1
% international	1
# of countries represented	16

ACADEMICS

Calendar	semester
Student/teacher ratio	18:1
FT faculty	138
% faculty from religious order	1
% graduate in 4 yrs.	72

Most Popular Majors
elementary education
journalism/mass communication
accounting

ADMISSIONS

Admissions Rating	69
# of applicants	1,840
% of applicants accepted	90
% of acceptees attending	36

Deadlines

Regular admission	4/15
Regular notification	rolling

FRESHMAN PROFILE

Average verbal SAT	532
Average math SAT	532
Average ACT	23
Minimum TOEFL	550

Graduated top 10% of class	19
Graduated top 25% of class	44
Graduated top 50% of class	73

FINANCIAL FACTS

Tuition	$11,919
Room & board	$5,326
Estimated book expense	$500
% frosh receiving aid	79
% undergrads receiving aid	80

THE COLLEGE OF SAINT CATHERINE

2004 Randolph Avenue, Saint Paul, MN 55105 • Admissions: 612-690-6505 • Fax: 612-690-8880
• Financial Aid: 612-690-6540 • E-mail: stkate@stkate.edu

Founded in 1905 by the Sisters of Saint Joseph of Carondelet, the College of Saint Catherine is the third largest women's college in the U.S. The college's 110-acre main campus sits midway between the Twin Cities. The campus features an art gallery, an observatory, a recital hall, an experimental psychology lab, and a women's research center. Sixty-nine major programs are available at Saint Catherine, offered mainly within the liberal arts and sciences, business, education, and health sciences. A small branch campus in Minneapolis offers two-year programs specifically in the health sciences. Among the most popular programs are nursing, business, and occupational therapy. The College counts twenty-five registered clubs and organizations among its extracurricular offerings, and fields intercollegiate athletic teams in seven sports.

ADMISSIONS

The admissions committee considers (in descending order of importance): HS record, test scores, class rank, recommendations. *Also considered (in descending order of importance):* extracurriculars, personality. Either the SAT or ACT is required. An interview is recommended. *High school units required/recommended:* 19 total units are recommended; 4 English recommended, 3 math recommended, 3 science recommended, 2 foreign language recommended, 3 social studies recommended, 1 history recommended.

FINANCIAL AID

Students should submit: FAFSA (due April 1), the school's own financial aid form (due April 1). The Princeton Review suggests that all financial aid forms be submitted as soon as possible after January 1. *The following grants/scholarships are offered:* Pell, SEOG, the school's own scholarships, the school's own grants, state scholarships, state grants, private scholarships, private grants. *Students borrow from the following loan programs:* Stafford, unsubsidized Stafford, Perkins, PLUS, the school's own loan fund, supplemental loans, state loans, private loans. Applicants will be notified of awards beginning March 15. College Work-Study Program is available. Institutional employment is available. The off-campus job outlook is excellent.

STUDENT BODY

Total undergrad enrollment	2,198
% male/female	0/100
% from out of state	14
% transfers	58
% from catholic high school	12
% live on campus	39
% African American	1
% Asian	2
% Caucasian	92
% Hispanic	1
% Native American	1
% international	2
# of countries represented	23

ACADEMICS

Calendar	4-1-4
Student/teacher ratio	10:1
FT faculty	245
% faculty from religious order	7
% graduate in 4 yrs.	51

Most Popular Majors
nursing
business
occupational therapy

ADMISSIONS

Admissions Rating	72
# of applicants	612

% of applicants accepted	90
% of acceptees attending	36

Deadlines

Regular admission	8/15
Regular notification	rolling

FRESHMAN PROFILE

Range verbal SAT	525-630
Average verbal SAT	580
Range math SAT	505-600
Average math SAT	549
Range ACT	20-26
Average ACT	23
Minimum TOEFL	500
Average HS GPA or Avg	3.4

Graduated top 10% of class	21
Graduated top 25% of class	41
Graduated top 50% of class	80

FINANCIAL FACTS

Tuition	$12,960
Room & board	$4,282
Estimated book expense	$300
% frosh receiving aid	77
% undergrads receiving aid	68
% frosh w/ grant	84
Avg. grant	$5,593
% frosh w/ loan	70
Avg. loan	$2,857

SAINT EDWARD'S UNIVERSITY

3001 South Congress Avenue, Austin, TX 78704 • Admissions: 512-448-8500 • Fax: 512-448-8492
• Financial Aid: 512-448-8520 • E-mail: seu.admit@admin.stedwrds.edu • Web Site: www.stedwards.edu

Saint Edward's University was founded as a college for men in 1885 by Rev. Edward Sorin, superior general of the Congregation of the Holy Cross, and became coed in 1966. The university's 180-acre campus is located on the southern end of the capital city of Texas, and serves as the summer training site of the Dallas Cowboys. Saint Edward's is largely a commuter college housing only a fifth of its enrollment; thus the representation of fifty-eight foreign countries within the student body is particularly impressive. The university offers a choice of twenty-six undergraduate majors, primarily within the liberal arts and sciences and business. Among the most popular programs are psychology, biology, and criminal justice. A cooperative agreement enables Saint Edward's students to spend a semester at the University of Dallas's campus in Rome. Extracurricular options include thirty-eight registered clubs and organizations, and five athletic teams each for men and women.

ADMISSIONS

The admissions committee considers (in descending order of importance): class rank, test scores, HS record, recommendations. *Also considered (in descending order of importance):* alumni relationship, extracurriculars, personality, special talents. Either the SAT or ACT is required. An interview is recommended. Admissions process is need-blind. *High school units required/recommended:* 11 total units are required; 4 English required, 3 math required, 2 science required, 2 social studies required. Minimum combined SAT I score of 800 (composite ACT score of 17) and rank in top half of secondary school class recommended.

FINANCIAL AID

Students should submit: FAFSA (due March 1), the school's own financial aid form. The Princeton Review suggests that all financial aid forms be submitted as soon as possible after January 1. *The following grants/scholarships are offered:* state scholarships. *Students borrow from the following loan programs:* Stafford, PLUS. College Work-Study Program is available. Institutional employment is available. The off-campus job outlook is excellent.

STUDENT BODY

Total undergrad enrollment	2,649
% male/female	44/56
% from out of state	4
% transfers	35
% from catholic high school	25
% live on campus	25
% African American	4
% Asian	2
% Caucasian	62
% Hispanic	25
% Native American	1
% international	5
# of countries represented	58

ACADEMICS

Calendar	semester
Student/teacher ratio	14:1
FT faculty	221
% faculty from religious order	9
% graduate in 4 yrs.	43

Most Popular Majors

psychology
biology
criminal justice

ADMISSIONS

Admissions Rating	65
% of acceptees attending	35

Deadlines

Regular admission	8/1
Regular notification	rolling

FRESHMAN PROFILE

Average verbal SAT	443
Average math SAT	480
Minimum TOEFL	500
Graduated top 10% of class	20
Graduated top 25% of class	46
Graduated top 50% of class	77

FINANCIAL FACTS

Tuition	$10,400
Room & board	$4,568
Estimated book expense	$650
% frosh receiving aid	73
% undergrads receiving aid	55
% frosh w/ grant	62
Avg. grant	NR
% frosh w/ loan	63
Avg. loan	$2,100

COLLEGE OF SAINT ELIZABETH

2 Convent Road, Morristown, NJ 07960 • *Admissions: 201-605-7000* • *Fax: 201-605-7070*
• *Financial Aid: 201-605-7445* • *E-mail: apply@liza.stelizabeth.edu*

The College of Saint Elizabeth was founded in 1899 by the Sisters of Charity, and was the first four-year college in New Jersey to grant degrees to women. The college's 200-acre campus is located forty miles from New York City. Noteworthy facilities include on-campus nursery and secondary schools, a volunteer services center, a television studio, a Greek theater, and a Shakespeare garden. Saint Elizabeth offers twenty-two majors within the liberal arts and sciences, business, education, and health sciences. The most popular programs are business, psychology, and elementary education. There are nineteen registered clubs and organizations at the college, and six sports are offered. Among the activities available is Students Take Action, a club that encourages volunteerism and coordinates many campus ministry events. Other ministry services include trips to Appalachia, blood drives, walkathons, peer support groups, and hospital and day-care center visits. Students who find life a bit too quiet on campus can hop aboard a train to New York City at the railroad station located adjacent to the college.

ADMISSIONS

The admissions committee considers (in descending order of importance): HS record, test scores, class rank, recommendations, essay. *Also considered (in descending order of importance):* alumni relationship, extracurriculars, personality, geographical distribution, special talents. Either the SAT or ACT is required; SAT is preferred. An interview is recommended. Admissions process is need-blind. *High school units required/recommended:* 16 total units are required; 3 English required, 4 English recommended, 3 math recommended, 2 foreign language required, 1 history required, 2 history recommended. Minimum combined SAT I score of 800, rank in top half of secondary school class, and minimum 2.5 GPA recommended. *Special Requirements:* An RN is required for nursing program applicants.

FINANCIAL AID

Students should submit: FAFSA (due March 1), a copy of parents' most recent income tax filing (due April 15). The Princeton Review suggests that all financial aid forms be submitted as soon as possible after January 1. *The following grants/scholarships are offered:* state scholarships. *Students borrow from the following loan programs:* Stafford, PLUS. College Work-Study Program is available. Institutional employment is available. The off-campus job outlook is good.

STUDENT BODY

Total undergrad enrollment	1,385
% male/female	0/100
% from out of state	2
% transfers	24
% from catholic high school	26
% live on campus	70
% African American	8
% Asian	3
% Caucasian	74
% Hispanic	11
% Native American	1
% international	3
# of countries represented	10

ACADEMICS

Calendar	semester
Student/teacher ratio	10:1
FT faculty	167
% faculty from religious order	18
% graduate in 4 yrs.	44

Most Popular Majors
business
psychology
elementary education

ADMISSIONS

Admissions Rating	70
# of applicants	419

% of applicants accepted	83
% of acceptees attending	36

Deadlines

Regular admission	8/15
Regular notification	rolling

FRESHMAN PROFILE

Range verbal SAT	480-600
Average verbal SAT	541
Range math SAT	450-570
Average math SAT	510
Minimum TOEFL	500
Graduated top 10% of class	17
Graduated top 25% of class	43

Graduated top 50% of class	66

FINANCIAL FACTS

Tuition	$11,400
Room & board	$5,400
Estimated book expense	$500
% frosh receiving aid	75
% undergrads receiving aid	81
% frosh w/ grant	69
Avg. grant	$5,000
% frosh w/ loan	48
Avg. loan	$2,469

SAINT FRANCIS COLLEGE (IN)

2701 Spring Street, Fort Wayne, IN 46808 • *Admissions: 219-434-3279* • *Fax: 219-434-3183*
• *Financial Aid: 219-434-3283* • *E-mail: sflanagan@sfc.edu* • *Web Site: sfc.edu*

The Sisters of Saint Francis of Perpetual Adoration founded Saint Francis College in 1890 as a teacher-training school for their own members. The college is situated on a 70-acre campus located 125 miles from Indianapolis and 150 miles from Chicago. Saint Francis awards degrees in twenty-nine majors in the liberal arts and sciences, business, education, and health sciences. Education, business administration, and nursing are the most popular academic programs. Campus facilities of note include a library housed in a castlelike mansion, a science hall with a telescopic observation deck and planetarium, a nature preserve, and an art gallery. The college has some clubs and activities, and fields athletic teams in five sports for men and four for women. A range of special scholarships are offered for academic merit, artistic ability, athletic talents, and alumni affiliation.

ADMISSIONS

The admissions committee considers (in descending order of importance): HS record, test scores, class rank, essay, recommendations. Either the SAT or ACT is required. Admissions process is need-blind. *High school units required/recommended:* 16 total units are recommended; 4 English recommended, 3 math recommended, 2 science recommended, 2 foreign language recommended, 2 social studies recommended, 2 history recommended. Minimum combined SAT I score of 920 (composite ACT score of 19), rank in top half of secondary school class, and minimum 2.0 GPA required. *Special Requirements:* 1 unit each of algebra, biology, and chemistry required of nursing program applicants.

FINANCIAL AID

Students should submit: FAFSA (due March 1), the school's own financial aid form (due March 1), state aid form. The Princeton Review suggests that all financial aid forms be submitted as soon as possible after January 1. *The following grants/scholarships are offered:* Pell, SEOG, state scholarships, state grants, private scholarships, private grants, ROTC. *Students borrow from the following loan programs:* Stafford, unsubsidized Stafford, Perkins, PLUS, supplemental loans, private loans. College Work-Study Program is available. Institutional employment is available. The off-campus job outlook is good.

STUDENT BODY

Total undergrad enrollment	746
% male/female	29/71
% from out of state	19
% transfers	30
% live on campus	23
% African American	3
% Asian	3
% Caucasian	88
% Hispanic	2
% Native American	1
% international	5

ACADEMICS

Calendar	semester
Student/teacher ratio	10:1
FT faculty	92
% faculty from religious order	5

Most Popular Majors

education
business administration
nursing

ADMISSIONS

Admissions Rating	74
# of applicants	301
% of applicants accepted	68
% of acceptees attending	67

Deadlines

Regular admission	rolling
Regular notification	rolling

FRESHMAN PROFILE

Range verbal SAT	420-540
Average verbal SAT	480
Range math SAT	420-530
Average math SAT	470
Range ACT	19-23
Average ACT	21
Minimum TOEFL	500
Average HS GPA or Avg	3.0
Graduated top 10% of class	13
Graduated top 25% of class	37
Graduated top 50% of class	80

FINANCIAL FACTS

Tuition	$9,820
Room & board	$4,070
Estimated book expense	$500
% frosh receiving aid	80
% undergrads receiving aid	88
% frosh w/ loan	75
Avg. loan	$2,373

SAINT FRANCIS COLLEGE (NY)

180 Remsen Street, Brooklyn Heights, NY 11201 • Admissions: 718-522-2300 • Fax: 718-522-1274
• Financial Aid: 718-522-2300, ext. 255

Saint Francis College was founded in 1884 by the Irish Congregation of the Franciscan Brothers of the Third Order Regular, and became coed in 1960. The college's campus is located in a national historic district in Brooklyn Heights, just across the East River from Manhattan's Wall Street financial district. Saint Francis is home to the Institute of Local Historical Studies, one of New York's largest collections of primary source documents on local history. Among the institute's holdings are Native American deeds and the original charters of the early Dutch and English governors. The college offers twenty-eight academic majors in the liberal arts and sciences, business, education, and health sciences, including programs in aviation administration, aviation business studies, and airway science. Among the most popular majors are management and accounting. Twenty-nine registered clubs and organizations are available on campus, along with twelve honor societies. Saint Francis fields eleven athletic teams for men and nine for women, and has a long tradition of strength in men's basketball.

ADMISSIONS

The admissions committee considers (in descending order of importance): HS record, recommendations, class rank, test scores, essay. *Also considered (in descending order of importance):* personality, alumni relationship, extracurriculars, special talents. SAT is preferred. An interview is recommended. *High school units required/ recommended:* 16 total units are required; 4 English required, 2 math required, 1 science required, 3 social studies required. *Special Requirements:* TOEFL is required of all international students.

FINANCIAL AID

Students should submit: FAFSA (due February 15), the school's own financial aid form (due February 15), state aid form (due February 15). The Princeton Review suggests that all financial aid forms be submitted as soon as possible after January 1. *The following grants/scholarships are offered:* Pell, SEOG, academic merit, athletic, the school's own scholarships, the school's own grants, state scholarships, state grants, private scholarships, private grants, ROTC, foreign aid. *Students borrow from the following loan programs:* Stafford, unsubsidized Stafford, Perkins, PLUS, the school's own loan fund, supplemental loans, private loans. Applicants will be notified of awards beginning March 15. College Work-Study Program is available. Institutional employment is available. The off-campus job outlook is good.

STUDENT BODY		ACADEMICS		ADMISSIONS		FINANCIAL FACTS	
Total undergrad enrollment	2,257	Calendar	semester	Admissions Rating	69	Tuition	$6,930
% male/female	43/57	Student/teacher ratio	15:1	% of acceptees attending	44	Estimated book expense	$550
% from out of state	1	FT faculty	151	**Deadlines**		% frosh receiving aid	73
% transfers	22	% faculty from religious order	1	Regular admission	9/1	% undergrads receiving aid	80
% from catholic high school	60			Regular notification	rolling	% frosh w/ grant	74
% African American	23	**Most Popular Majors**				Avg. grant	$3,000
% Asian	2	management		**FRESHMAN PROFILE**		% frosh w/ loan	22
% Caucasian	54	accounting		Minimum TOEFL	500	Avg. loan	$1,875
% Hispanic	15	special studies					
% Native American	1						
% international	5						
# of countries represented	35						

SAINT FRANCIS COLLEGE (PA)

P.O. Box 600, Loretto, PA 15940 • Admissions: 814-472-3000 • Fax: 814-472-3044
• Financial Aid: 814-472-3010 • E-mail: admissions@sfcpa.edu • Web Site: www.sfcpa.edu

Saint Francis College was founded in 1847 by the Third Order Regular Franciscans. Located eighty miles east of Pittsburgh, the college's campus spreads out on 600 acres. Twenty-five majors are offered at Saint Francis, centered on a general education program that serves as the foundation of the academic experience. The majority of academic programs are in the disciplines of liberal arts and sciences, business, education, and health sciences; the most popular of these offerings are management, elementary education, and accounting. Facilities of note include an art museum, a cadaver lab, and a physical therapy lab. There are forty-five registered clubs and organizations at Saint Francis; available activities run the gamut in the arts, media, multicultural interests, and social activism. In the Franciscan tradition, the campus ministry encourages students to become involved with the poor, elderly, and disadvantaged of the area. The college fields a variety of athletic teams for men and women each season. Men's basketball was once quite competitive nationally; though no longer a major NCAA power, the team continues a tradition of strength on a regional level.

ADMISSIONS

The admissions committee considers (in descending order of importance): HS record, class rank, test scores, recommendations, essay. *Also considered (in descending order of importance):* extracurriculars, personality, alumni relationship, geographical distribution, special talents. Either the SAT or ACT is required. An interview is recommended. *High school units required/recommended:* 16 total units are required; 4 English required, 2 math required, 1 science required, 2 social studies required. Minimum combined SAT I score of 900, rank in top half of secondary school class, and minimum 3.0 GPA recommended. *Special Requirements:* TOEFL is required of all international students. 4 units of math and 2 units of lab science required of math, physician assistant, and science program applicants. 4 units of math and 4 units of science required of physical therapy program applicants.

FINANCIAL AID

Students should submit: FAFSA (due July 30), the school's own financial aid form (due July 30), state aid form, a copy of parents' most recent income tax filing. The Princeton Review suggests that all financial aid forms be submitted as soon as possible after January 1. *The following grants/scholarships are offered:* Pell, SEOG, academic merit, athletic, the school's own scholarships, the school's own grants, state scholarships, state grants, private scholarships, private grants, foreign aid. *Students borrow from the following loan programs:* Stafford, Perkins, PLUS, the school's own loan fund, state loans. Applicants will be notified of awards beginning November 15. College Work-Study Program is available. Institutional employment is available. The off-campus job outlook is fair.

STUDENT BODY
Total undergrad enrollment	1,211
% male/female	46/54
% from out of state	19
% transfers	24
% live on campus	63
% African American	2
% Asian	1
% Caucasian	95
% Hispanic	1
# of countries represented	4

ACADEMICS
Calendar	semester
Student/teacher ratio	15:1
FT faculty	74
% faculty from religious order	3
% graduate in 4 yrs.	50

Most Popular Majors
management
elementary education
accounting

ADMISSIONS
Admissions Rating	77
# of applicants	1,049
% of applicants accepted	71
% of acceptees attending	39

Deadlines
Regular admission	6/1
Regular notification	rolling

FRESHMAN PROFILE
Average verbal SAT	530
Average math SAT	510
Minimum TOEFL	500
Average HS GPA or Avg	3.4

FINANCIAL FACTS
Tuition	$11,680
Room & board	$5,350
Estimated book expense	$400
% frosh receiving aid	94
% undergrads receiving aid	88
% frosh w/ grant	95
Avg. grant	$7,450
% frosh w/ loan	80
Avg. loan	$1,790

COLLEGE OF SAINT FRANCIS

500 Wilcox Street, Joliet, IL 60435 • Admissions: 815-740-3400 • Fax: 815-740-4285
• Financial Aid: 815-740-3403 • Web Site: www.stfrancis.edu

Founded in 1920 by the Sisters of Saint Francis of Mary Immaculate, the College of Saint Francis became coed in 1971. Forty-five miles from downtown Chicago, the college's 14-acre campus is located in a residential neighborhood of Joliet. Saint Francis offers twenty-two majors within the liberal arts and sciences, business, education, and health sciences. Popular majors include business, education, and computer science. There are twenty registered clubs and organizations at the college, and ten honor societies. Athletic teams are fielded in six sports each for men and women. Both academic and athletic merit scholarships are available.

ADMISSIONS
The admissions committee considers (in descending order of importance): HS record, class rank, test scores, essay, recommendations. *Also considered (in descending order of importance):* geographical distribution, special talents, alumni relationship, extracurriculars, personality. Either the SAT or ACT is required; ACT is preferred. An interview is recommended. Admissions process is need-blind. *High school units required/ recommended:* 20 total units are recommended; 4 English recommended, 3 math recommended, 2 science recommended, 2 foreign language recommended, 2 social studies recommended, 2 history recommended. Minimum composite ACT score of 20, rank in top half of secondary school class, and minimum 2.5 GPA required. *Special Requirements:* TOEFL is required of all international students.

FINANCIAL AID
Students should submit: FAFSAstate aid form. The Princeton Review suggests that all financial aid forms be submitted as soon as possible after January 1. *The following grants/scholarships are offered:* Pell, SEOG, academic merit, athletic, the school's own scholarships, the school's own grants, state scholarships, state grants, private scholarships, private grants, ROTC. *Students borrow from the following loan programs:* Stafford, unsubsidized Stafford, Perkins, PLUS, the school's own loan fund, supplemental loans, federal nursing loans, private loans. Applicants will be notified of awards beginning February 15. College Work-Study Program is available. Institutional employment is available. The off-campus job outlook is good.

STUDENT BODY
Total undergrad enrollment	1,028
% male/female	48/52
% from out of state	9
% transfers	39
% from catholic high school	60
% live on campus	45
% African American	3
% Asian	1
% Caucasian	92
% Hispanic	4
% international	1
# of countries represented	4

ACADEMICS
Calendar	semester
Student/teacher ratio	20:1
FT faculty	94
% faculty from religious order	0

Most Popular Majors
business
education
computer science

ADMISSIONS
Admissions Rating	74
% of acceptees attending	50

Deadlines
Regular admission	5/1
Regular notification	rolling

FRESHMAN PROFILE
Minimum TOEFL	550
Graduated top 10% of class	20
Graduated top 25% of class	46
Graduated top 50% of class	80

FINANCIAL FACTS
Tuition	$10,790
Room & board	$4,340
Estimated book expense	$400
% frosh receiving aid	85
% undergrads receiving aid	86
% frosh w/ grant	62
Avg. grant	$6,026
% frosh w/ loan	65
Avg. loan	$2,921

SAINT JOHN FISHER COLLEGE

3690 East Avenue, Rochester, NY 14618 • Admissions: 716-385-8064 • Fax: 716-385-8386
• Financial Aid: 716-385-8042 • E-mail: admissions@sjfc.edu • Web Site: www.sjfc.edu

Founded in 1948 by the Basilian Fathers, Saint John Fisher College is located on a 125-acre campus six miles from Rochester's downtown. The Basilians, or Order of Saint Basil, is an international teaching community. The college offers fifty-three majors in the liberal arts and sciences, business, education, and nursing. Most popular academic programs include management, accounting, and journalism and mass communications. Facilities and equipment of note are extensive; among them are two scanning electron microscopes, a greenhouse, a semiprofessional theater, radiation and animal laboratories, and a marine aquarium. Fifty-two clubs and organizations are registered at Saint John Fisher, offering an impressive range of extracurricular options. An impressive selection of intercollegiate, intramural, and club athletics can be found here. In particular, both the men's and women's basketball programs are eastern powerhouses in NCAA Division III. The college is supremely confident in its ability to provide first-class preparation for life after college—the "Fisher Commitment" offers to pay students $417 per month, up to a total of $5,000, if they aren't offered a job that requires a college degree within six months after graduation.

ADMISSIONS

The admissions committee considers (in descending order of importance): HS record, class rank, test scores, recommendations, essay. *Also considered (in descending order of importance):* personality, extracurriculars, alumni relationship, geographical distribution, special talents. Either the SAT or ACT is required. An interview is recommended. Admissions process is need-blind. *High school units required/recommended:* 16 total units are required; 4 English required, 3 math recommended, 3 science recommended, 2 foreign language recommended, 4 history required.

FINANCIAL AID

Students should submit: FAFSA (due March 1), state aid form (due March 1). The Princeton Review suggests that all financial aid forms be submitted as soon as possible after January 1. *The following grants/scholarships are offered:* Pell, SEOG, academic merit, athletic, the school's own scholarships, the school's own grants, state scholarships, state grants. *Students borrow from the following loan programs:* Stafford, unsubsidized Stafford, Perkins, PLUS, the school's own loan fund, supplemental loans. College Work-Study Program is available. Institutional employment is available. The off-campus job outlook is excellent.

STUDENT BODY		ACADEMICS	
Total undergrad enrollment	2,000	Calendar	semester
% male/female	45/55	Student/teacher ratio	13:1
% from out of state	5	FT faculty	186
% transfers	43	% faculty from religious order	3
% live on campus	53	% graduate in 4 yrs.	56
% African American	5		
% Asian	2	**Most Popular Majors**	
% Caucasian	86	management	
% Hispanic	2	accounting	
% Native American	1	communication/journalism	
% international	1	**ADMISSIONS**	
# of countries represented	7	Admissions Rating	72
		# of applicants	1,164

% of applicants accepted	78	Graduated top 10% of class	19
% of acceptees attending	32	Graduated top 25% of class	47
Deadlines		Graduated top 50% of class	81
Regular admission	rolling	**FINANCIAL FACTS**	
Regular notification	rolling	Tuition	$11,760
FRESHMAN PROFILE		Room & board	$5,870
Range verbal SAT	411-514	Estimated book expense	$500
Average verbal SAT	531	% frosh receiving aid	82
Range math SAT	464-583	% undergrads receiving aid	82
Average math SAT	527	% frosh w/ grant	64
Range ACT	20-26	Avg. grant	$4,300
Average ACT	22	% frosh w/ loan	90
Minimum TOEFL	500	Avg. loan	$3,083

SAINT JOHN'S UNIVERSITY (MN)

P.O. Box 7155, Collegeville, MN 56321 • Admissions: 612-363-2196 • Fax: 612-363-5010
• Financial Aid: 320-363-3664 • E-mail: admissions@csbsju.edu • Web Site: www.csbsju.edu/index.html

Saint John's University was founded in 1857 by Benedictine monks in order to serve the needs of German Catholic immigrants. The university, one of the oldest institutions of higher education in the Midwest, is located on a huge 2,400-acre campus noted for its natural and architectural beauty, twenty-five miles from Minneapolis. It operates in close cooperation both academically and socially with the College of Saint Benedict, a nearby women's college, rendering both institutions coed for all practical purposes. Forty-four majors are available to undergraduates at Saint John's. Facilities worthy of note are the world's largest medieval library, an art gallery, a biology museum, an observatory, and a nature preserve. Life is abuzz outside the classroom—the university reports 110 registered clubs and organizations on campus. The football team hasn't suffered a losing season since 1967, winning three national championships and placing coach John Gagliardi number two on the NCAA all-time coaching victories list, after Alabama's Bear Bryant. The ice hockey and wrestling programs are also especially strong, if not quite as prominent as the football team.

ADMISSIONS

The admissions committee considers (in descending order of importance): HS record, class rank, test scores, essay. *Also considered (in descending order of importance):* extracurriculars, personality. Either the SAT or ACT is required. An interview is recommended. Admissions process is need-blind. *High school units required/recommended:* 17 total units are recommended; 4 English recommended, 3 math recommended, 2 science recommended, 2 foreign language recommended, 2 social studies recommended. Minimum composite ACT score of 20 (combined SAT I score of 1000), rank in top two-fifths of secondary school class, and minimum 2.8 GPA required. *Special Requirements:* TOEFL is required of all international students. Portfolio required of art scholarship applicants. Audition required of music scholarship applicants. Interview required of theatre scholarship applicants.

FINANCIAL AID

Students should submit: FAFSA (due March 1), a copy of parents' most recent income tax filing. The Princeton Review suggests that all financial aid forms be submitted as soon as possible after January 1. *The following grants/scholarships are offered:* Pell, SEOG, academic merit, athletic, the school's own scholarships, the school's own grants, state grants, private scholarships, private grants, ROTC. *Students borrow from the following loan programs:* Stafford, unsubsidized Stafford, Perkins, PLUS, the school's own loan fund, supplemental loans, state loans, private loans. Applicants will be notified of awards beginning March 1. College Work-Study Program is available. Institutional employment is available. The off-campus job outlook is good.

STUDENT BODY		ACADEMICS			
Total undergrad enrollment	1,687	Calendar	4-1-4	% of applicants accepted	87	Graduated top 50% of class	86
% male/female	100/0	Student/teacher ratio	11:1	% of acceptees attending	56	**FINANCIAL FACTS**	
% from out of state	23	FT faculty	167	**Deadlines**		Tuition	$13,858
% transfers	15	% faculty from religious order	27	Regular admission	rolling	Room & board	$2,334
% from catholic high school	19	% graduate in 4 yrs.	67	Regular notification	rolling	Estimated book expense	$600
% live on campus	75					% frosh receiving aid	70
% African American	1	**Most Popular Majors**		**FRESHMAN PROFILE**		% undergrads receiving aid	70
% Asian	2	business management		Average verbal SAT	583	% frosh w/ grant	69
% Caucasian	95	biology		Average math SAT	606	Avg. grant	NR
% Hispanic	1	psychology		Range ACT	21-26	% frosh w/ loan	70
% Native American	1			Average ACT	25	Avg. loan	$2,625
% international	2	**ADMISSIONS**		Minimum TOEFL	550		
# of countries represented	25	Admissions Rating	75	Average HS GPA or Avg	3.5		
		# of applicants	893	Graduated top 10% of class	21		
				Graduated top 25% of class	50		

SAINT JOHN'S UNIVERSITY (NY)

8000 Utopia Parkway, Jamaica, NY 11439 • Admissions: 718-990-6114 • Fax: 718-990-5886
• Financial Aid: 718-990-6403 • E-mail: hallc@stjohns.edu • Web Site: www.stjohns.edu

Founded in 1870 by the Vincentians, Saint John's University is the largest Catholic university in the United States. Saint John's is situated on a 100-acre campus in the New York City borough of Queens, ten miles from Manhattan. The university's nine undergraduate colleges offer over sixty majors, the most popular of which are pharmacy (the largest such program in the nation), criminal justice, and accounting. Saint John's is a commuter college, and no university housing is available. An art gallery, a speech and hearing clinic, and an Asian cultural center are among facilities of note on campus. Over 143 registered clubs and organizations are available at the university; among these are many social-action and cultural groups. Sports are available at the intercollegiate, intramural, and club levels; fifteen men's and eleven women's teams compete in the NCAA's Big East Conference. Men's basketball is the most prominent sport at Saint John's; most games are played at the university's Alumni Hall, but especially significant home matchups are often played at Madison Square Garden, home of the New York Knicks.

ADMISSIONS

The admissions committee considers (in descending order of importance): HS record, test scores, recommendations, class rank. *Also considered (in descending order of importance):* special talents, extracurriculars. Either the SAT or ACT is required; SAT is preferred. An interview is recommended. Admissions process is need-blind. *High school units required/recommended:* 16 total units are required; 4 English required, 2 math required, 1 science required, 3 social studies required. Minimum combined SAT I score of 1000 or minimum 3.0 GPA required. Secondary school unit requirements vary by college; 3 units of math, 2 units of science, 2 years of foreign language required of many. *Special Requirements:* A portfolio is required for art program applicants. TOEFL is required of all international students.

FINANCIAL AID

Students should submit: FAFSA, the school's own financial aid form, a copy of parents' most recent income tax filing. The Princeton Review suggests that all financial aid forms be submitted as soon as possible after January 1. *The following grants/scholarships are offered:* state scholarships. *Students borrow from the following loan programs:* Stafford, PLUS. Applicants will be notified of awards beginning May 1. College Work-Study Program is available. Institutional employment is available. The off-campus job outlook is excellent.

STUDENT BODY

Total undergrad enrollment	14,091
% male/female	47/53
% from out of state	4
% transfers	24
% African American	11
% Asian	9
% Caucasian	66
% Hispanic	11
% international	3
# of countries represented	75

ACADEMICS

Calendar	semester
Student/teacher ratio	17:1
FT faculty	1063
% faculty from religious order	1
% graduate in 4 yrs.	63

Most Popular Majors
pharmacy
criminal justice
accounting

ADMISSIONS

Admissions Rating	68
# of applicants	7,730
% of applicants accepted	87
% of acceptees attending	34

Deadlines

Regular admission	rolling
Regular notification	rolling

FRESHMAN PROFILE

Range verbal SAT	450-570
Average verbal SAT	514
Range math SAT	460-580
Average math SAT	525

Minimum TOEFL	500
Average HS GPA or Avg	3.0
Graduated top 10% of class	23
Graduated top 25% of class	54
Graduated top 50% of class	90

FINANCIAL FACTS

Tuition	$10,950
Estimated book expense	$600
% frosh receiving aid	62
% undergrads receiving aid	75

SAINT JOSEPH COLLEGE

1678 Asylum Avenue, West Hartford, CT 06117 • Admissions: 203-232-4571 • Fax: 203-233-5695
• Financial Aid: 860-232-4571 • E-mail: admissions@mercy.sjc.edu • Web Site: www.sjc.edu

Founded in 1932 by the Sisters of Mercy, Saint Joseph College is the only remaining four-year college for women in Connecticut. The college sits on an 84-acre residential campus three miles from Hartford. Thirty majors are offered primarily in the liberal arts and sciences, business, education, and nursing; the latter and social work being the most popular. Special academic facilities include an on-campus nursery school, kindergarten, and school for exceptional children. Saint Joseph is part of a consortium in the greater Hartford area that enables students to cross-register at five other area colleges and universities. The college counts over thirty registered clubs and organizations, offering a variety of arts, media, social, and cultural groups. Intercollegiate athletic teams are fielded in six sports, competing in the New England Women's Athletic Conference.

ADMISSIONS

The admissions committee considers (in descending order of importance): HS record, class rank, test scores, recommendations, essay. *Also considered (in descending order of importance):* alumni relationship, extracurriculars, geographical distribution, personality, special talents. Either the SAT or ACT is required. An interview is recommended. Admissions process is need-blind. *High school units required/recommended:* 16 total units are required; 4 English recommended, 3 math recommended, 3 science recommended, 2 foreign language recommended, 2 social studies recommended, 2 history recommended. Rank in top half of secondary school class and college preparatory coursework recommended.

FINANCIAL AID

Students should submit: FAFSA (due February 15), the school's own financial aid form (due February 15), state aid form, Divorced Parents form, a copy of parents' most recent income tax filing (due February 15). The Princeton Review suggests that all financial aid forms be submitted as soon as possible after January 1. *The following grants/scholarships are offered:* state scholarships. *Students borrow from the following loan programs:* Stafford, PLUS. College Work-Study Program is available. Institutional employment is available. The off-campus job outlook is good.

STUDENT BODY

Total undergrad enrollment	1,200
% male/female	1/99
% from out of state	7
% transfers	31
% live on campus	50
% African American	8
% Asian	3
% Caucasian	84
% Hispanic	4
% Native American	1
# of countries represented	3

ACADEMICS

Calendar	semester
Student/teacher ratio	14:1
FT faculty	140
% faculty from religious order	6
% graduate in 4 yrs.	73

Most Popular Majors
nursing
child study
social work

ADMISSIONS

Admissions Rating	66
% of acceptees attending	44

Deadlines

Regular admission	5/1
Regular notification	rolling

FRESHMAN PROFILE

Minimum TOEFL	530
Graduated top 10% of class	19
Graduated top 25% of class	44
Graduated top 50% of class	85

FINANCIAL FACTS

Tuition	$13,800
Room & board	$5,300
Estimated book expense	$500
% frosh receiving aid	74
% undergrads receiving aid	69
% frosh w/ grant	82
Avg. grant	$5,972
% frosh w/ loan	84
Avg. loan	$3,944

SAINT JOSEPH'S COLLEGE (BROOKLYN)

*245 Clinton Avenue, Brooklyn, NY 11205 • Admissions: 718-636-6868 • Fax: 718-398-4936
• Financial Aid: 718-636-6800*

Saint Joseph's College was founded in 1916 as a women's college, and became coed in 1970. The college's main campus covers two acres in the historic residential section of Clinton Hill, eight miles from Manhattan. A second campus is located on twenty-five acres in Patchogue, Long Island, fifty miles from New York City. All students from both campuses of Saint Joe's commute. Thirty majors are offered, primarily in the liberal arts and sciences, business, education, and nursing. Popular among these programs are early childhood education, psychology, and business administration. Facilities of note include an on-campus preschool. More than twenty clubs and organizations are registered at the college. Athletic teams are fielded in men's basketball and women's softball and volleyball; students who attend the Long Island campus have the opportunity to participate in several additional intercollegiate sports.

ADMISSIONS

The admissions committee considers (in descending order of importance): HS record, test scores, class rank, recommendations, essay. *Also considered (in descending order of importance):* extracurriculars, personality, special talents. Either the SAT or ACT is required; SAT is preferred. An interview is required. Admissions process is need-blind. *High school units required/recommended:* 18 total units are required; 4 English required, 3 math required, 2 science required, 2 foreign language required. Minimum combined SAT I score of 900 and minimum grade average of 80 required. *Special Requirements:* An R.N. is required for nursing program applicants.

FINANCIAL AID

Students should submit: FAFSA (due February 25), the school's own financial aid form (due February 25), state aid form (due February 25), a copy of parents' most recent income tax filing (due February 25). The Princeton Review suggests that all financial aid forms be submitted as soon as possible after January 1. *The following grants/scholarships are offered:* state scholarships. *Students borrow from the following loan programs:* Stafford, PLUS. Applicants will be notified of awards beginning April 1. College Work-Study Program is available. Institutional employment is available. The off-campus job outlook is excellent.

STUDENT BODY

Total undergrad enrollment	3,183
% male/female	21/79
% from out of state	1
% transfers	34
% African American	15
% Asian	3
% Caucasian	76
% Hispanic	6

ACADEMICS

Calendar	semester
Student/teacher ratio	11:1
FT faculty	287

Most Popular Majors

child study
psychology
business administration

ADMISSIONS

Admissions Rating	65
% of acceptees attending	43

Deadlines

Regular admission	rolling
Regular notification	rolling

FRESHMAN PROFILE

Range verbal SAT	350-433
Average verbal SAT	442
Range math SAT	380-480
Average math SAT	475
Average ACT	19
Minimum TOEFL	500
Graduated top 10% of class	17
Graduated top 25% of class	44
Graduated top 50% of class	77

FINANCIAL FACTS

Tuition	$7,350
Estimated book expense	$600
% frosh receiving aid	90
% undergrads receiving aid	77
% frosh w/ grant	68
Avg. grant	NR
% frosh w/ loan	55
Avg. loan	$2,473

SAINT JOSEPH'S COLLEGE (IN)

P.O. Box 815, Rensselaer, IN 47978 • *Admissions: 219-866-6000* • *Fax: 219-866-6100*
• *Financial Aid: 219-866-6163* • *E-mail: admissions@saintjoe.edu* • *Web Site: www.saintjoe.edu*

Saint Joseph's College was founded in 1889 by the Society of the Precious Blood for the purpose of educating Native American boys. Now coed, the college is located on a 340-acre campus, eighty miles from Chicago and ninety miles from Indianapolis. Forty majors within the liberal arts and sciences, business, and nursing are available at Saint Joseph's. Most popular of these academic offerings are business administration, psychology, and biological sciences. Forty-three clubs and organizations are registered on campus, among them are political and social groups, a volunteer corps, Habitat for Humanity, and a variety of musical organizations. Athletic teams are fielded in eight sports each for men and women. Saint Joe's baseball team were runners-up in the 1996 NCAA Division II championship.

ADMISSIONS

The admissions committee considers (in descending order of importance): HS record, test scores, class rank, recommendations, essay. *Also considered (in descending order of importance):* alumni relationship, extracurriculars, personality, special talents. Either the SAT or ACT is required. An interview is recommended. Admissions process is need-blind. *High school units required/recommended:* 20 total units are required; 4 English required, 4 math required, 3 science required, 2 foreign language required. Rank in top half of secondary school class and minimum 2.0 GPA recommended.

FINANCIAL AID

Students should submit: FAFSA (due March 1), the school's own financial aid form, state aid form (due March 1), a copy of parents' most recent income tax filing. The Princeton Review suggests that all financial aid forms be submitted as soon as possible after January 1. *The following grants/scholarships are offered:* Pell, SEOG, academic merit, athletic, the school's own scholarships, the school's own grants, state scholarships, state grants, private scholarships, private grants. *Students borrow from the following loan programs:* Stafford, unsubsidized Stafford, Perkins, PLUS, the school's own loan fund, supplemental loans, private loans. Applicants will be notified of awards beginning February. College Work-Study Program is available. Institutional employment is available. The off-campus job outlook is fair.

STUDENT BODY

Total undergrad enrollment	870
% male/female	47/53
% from out of state	30
% transfers	11
% live on campus	95
% African American	5
% Caucasian	92
% Hispanic	3
% international	1
# of countries represented	5

ACADEMICS

Calendar	semester
Student/teacher ratio	10:1

FT faculty	89
% faculty from religious order	15
% graduate in 4 yrs.	47

Most Popular Majors
business administration
psychology
biological sciences

ADMISSIONS

Admissions Rating	67
# of applicants	1,028
% of applicants accepted	85
% of acceptees attending	25

Deadlines

Regular admission	rolling
Regular notification	rolling

FRESHMAN PROFILE

Range verbal SAT	430-550
Average verbal SAT	500
Range math SAT	440-560
Average math SAT	500
Range ACT	18-24
Average ACT	21
Minimum TOEFL	550
Average HS GPA or Avg	2.7
Graduated top 10% of class	19
Graduated top 25% of class	37
Graduated top 50% of class	62

FINANCIAL FACTS

Tuition	$12,260
Room & board	$4,640
Estimated book expense	$600
% frosh receiving aid	89
% undergrads receiving aid	75
% frosh w/ grant	88
Avg. grant	$6,587
% frosh w/ loan	65
Avg. loan	$2,985

SAINT JOSEPH'S COLLEGE (ME)

278 White's Bridge Road, Windham, ME 04062-1198 • Admissions: 207-892-6766 • Fax: 207-893-7861
• Financial Aid: 800-338-7057 • Web Site: www.sjcme.edu

Founded in 1912 by the Sisters of Mercy, Saint Joseph's College is located sixteen miles from Portland, and is the only Catholic college in Maine. Its 330-acre campus sits on the shores of Sebago Lake, complete with its own private beach. The college offers forty-one undergraduate majors within the areas of liberal arts and sciences, business, education, and nursing. Among the most popular majors are nursing, elementary education, and business administration. Academic programs at Saint Joseph's are bolstered by the college's participation in the Greater Portland Alliance, a consortium of six local colleges allowing cross-registration. Special facilities include television and radio studios. The college counts twenty-five registered clubs and organizations among its extracurricular offerings, which also includes athletic teams in five sports for men and six for women.

ADMISSIONS

The admissions committee considers (in descending order of importance): HS record, class rank, test scores, recommendations, essay. *Also considered (in descending order of importance):* extracurriculars, personality, special talents, alumni relationship, geographical distribution. Either the SAT or ACT is required; SAT is preferred. An interview is recommended. Admissions process is need-blind. *High school units required/ recommended:* 18 total units are required; 21 total units are recommended; 4 English required, 2 math required, 3 math recommended, 2 science required, 3 science recommended, 2 foreign language recommended, 2 social studies required, 2 history recommended. *Special Requirements:* Lab biology and chemistry required of nursing and science program applicants.

FINANCIAL AID

Students should submit: FAFSA, CSS Profile (due), a copy of parents' most recent income tax filing. The Princeton Review suggests that all financial aid forms be submitted as soon as possible after January 1. *The following grants/scholarships are offered:* Pell, SEOG, academic merit, the school's own scholarships, the school's own grants, state scholarships, state grants, private scholarships, private grants, ROTC, foreign aid. *Students borrow from the following loan programs:* Stafford, unsubsidized Stafford, Perkins, PLUS, state loans, federal nursing loans, private loans. College Work-Study Program is available. Institutional employment is available. The off-campus job outlook is good.

STUDENT BODY

Total undergrad enrollment	744
% male/female	36/64
% from out of state	43
% transfers	16
% from catholic high school	12
% live on campus	75
% African American	1
% Asian	1
% Caucasian	97
% Hispanic	1
# of countries represented	6

ACADEMICS

Calendar	semester
Student/teacher ratio	15:1
FT faculty	45
% faculty from religious order	15
% graduate in 4 yrs.	60

Most Popular Majors
nursing
elementary education
business administration

ADMISSIONS

Admissions Rating	74
# of applicants	852
% of applicants accepted	80
% of acceptees attending	37

Deadlines

Regular admission	rolling
Regular notification	rolling

FRESHMAN PROFILE

Average verbal SAT	540
Average math SAT	510
Minimum TOEFL	500
Average HS GPA or Avg	83.0

FINANCIAL FACTS

Tuition	$11,270
Room & board	$5,650
Estimated book expense	$600
% frosh receiving aid	88
% undergrads receiving aid	89
% frosh w/ grant	84
Avg. grant	$3,980
% frosh w/ loan	83
Avg. loan	$3,430

SAINT JOSEPH'S UNIVERSITY

5600 City Avenue, Philadelphia, PA 19131 • *Admissions: 610-660-1300* • *Fax: 610-660-1314*
• *Financial Aid: 610-660-1340* • *E-mail: adm@sju.edu* • *Web Site: www.sju.edu*

Saint Joseph's University was founded in 1851 by the Jesuits. The college is on a 60-acre campus in Philadelphia's downtown. Forty-five majors are available in a wide range of academic disciplines, the most popular of which are psychology, food marketing, and biology. Noteworthy facilities include a Brazilian institute, a faith and justice institute, and a food marketing academy. Sixty registered clubs and organizations are available, including a chapter of Amnesty International, and athletic teams are fielded in nine sports for men and seven for women. The men's basketball team won the Atlantic 10 Conference championship in 1997, and made it to the round of sixteen teams in the NCAA Division I tournament before ultimately losing to Kentucky.

ADMISSIONS

The admissions committee considers (in descending order of importance): HS record, class rank, test scores, recommendations, essay. *Also considered (in descending order of importance):* extracurriculars, alumni relationship, geographical distribution, personality, special talents. Either the SAT or ACT is required; SAT is preferred. An interview is recommended. *High school units required/recommended:* 15 total units are required; 4 English required, 3 math required, 2 science required, 3 foreign language required. Rank in top two-fifths of secondary school class. *Special Requirements:* TOEFL is required of all international students.

FINANCIAL AID

Students should submit: FAFSA (due March 1), the school's own financial aid form, state aid form, a copy of parents' most recent income tax filing. The Princeton Review suggests that all financial aid forms be submitted as soon as possible after January 1. *The following grants/scholarships are offered:* Pell, SEOG, academic merit, athletic, the school's own scholarships, the school's own grants, state scholarships, state grants, private scholarships, private grants, foreign aid. *Students borrow from the following loan programs:* Stafford, unsubsidized Stafford, Perkins, PLUS, the school's own loan fund, supplemental loans, private loans. Applicants will be notified of awards beginning March 15. College Work-Study Program is available. Institutional employment is available. The off-campus job outlook is good.

STUDENT BODY

Total undergrad enrollment	3,626
% male/female	47/53
% from out of state	46
% transfers	14
% live on campus	57
% African American	9
% Asian	3
% Caucasian	83
% Hispanic	2
% international	3
# of countries represented	70

ACADEMICS

Calendar	semester
Student/teacher ratio	18:1
FT faculty	371
% graduate in 4 yrs.	72

Most Popular Majors
psychology
food marketing
biology

ADMISSIONS

Admissions Rating	80
% of acceptees attending	33

Deadlines

Regular admission	rolling
Regular notification	rolling

FRESHMAN PROFILE

Minimum TOEFL	500
Graduated top 10% of class	34
Graduated top 25% of class	64
Graduated top 50% of class	95

FINANCIAL FACTS

Tuition	$14,500
Room & board	$6,500
Estimated book expense	$500
% frosh receiving aid	91
% undergrads receiving aid	80

SAINT LEO COLLEGE

P.O. Box 2008, Saint Leo, FL 33574 • Admissions: 904-588-8283 • Fax: 604-588-8349
• Financial Aid: 352-588-8270 • E-mail: admissns@saintleo.edu • Web Site: www.saintleo.edu

Founded in 1889 by the Benedictines as the first Catholic college in Florida, Saint Leo College became coed in 1960. The college is on a 170-acre campus twenty-five miles north of Tampa. Saint Leo offers twenty-five majors, mainly within the liberal arts and sciences, business, and education. Most popular among these offerings are business administration, criminology, and education. Thirty-one clubs and organizations are registered on campus, including musical ensembles, a variety of media, and service organizations (most interesting of which is the parachute club!). Athletic teams are fielded in four sports for men, three for women. Saint Leo's baseball team is nationally competitive, ranking among the top ten teams in NCAA Division II in recent years.

ADMISSIONS

The admissions committee considers (in descending order of importance): HS record, test scores, recommendations, essay, class rank. *Also considered (in descending order of importance):* personality, extracurriculars, alumni relationship, special talents. Either the SAT or ACT is required. An interview is recommended. Admissions process is need-blind. *High school units required/recommended:* 16 total units are required; 4 English required, 3 math required, 2 science required, 3 social studies required.

FINANCIAL AID

Students should submit: FAFSA (due March 1), the school's own financial aid form (due April 1), state aid form a copy of parents' most recent income tax filing. The Princeton Review suggests that all financial aid forms be submitted as soon as possible after January 1. *The following grants/scholarships are offered:* Pell, SEOG, academic merit, the school's own scholarships, the school's own grants, state scholarships, state grants, private scholarships, private grants. *Students borrow from the following loan programs:* Stafford, unsubsidized Stafford, PLUS, the school's own loan fund, supplemental loans, private loans. College Work-Study Program is available. Institutional employment is available. The off-campus job outlook is good.

STUDENT BODY

Total undergrad enrollment	902
% male/female	40/60
% from out of state	41
% transfers	25
% from catholic high school	10
% live on campus	61
% African American	3
% Asian	1
% Caucasian	84
% Hispanic	6
% Native American	1
% international	5
# of countries represented	21

ACADEMICS

Calendar	semester
Student/teacher ratio	12:1
FT faculty	76
% faculty from religious order	5

Most Popular Majors
business administration
criminology
education

ADMISSIONS

Admissions Rating	63
% of acceptees attending	29

Deadlines

Regular admission	8/1
Regular notification	rolling

FRESHMAN PROFILE

Range verbal SAT	370-450
Average verbal SAT	407
Range math SAT	400-500
Average math SAT	446
Range ACT	17-23
Average ACT	21
Minimum TOEFL	550

FINANCIAL FACTS

Tuition	$9,900
Room & board	$5,140
Estimated book expense	$1,200
% frosh receiving aid	49
% undergrads receiving aid	65
% frosh w/ grant	72
Avg. grant	$3,700
% frosh w/ loan	47
Avg. loan	$2,427

SAINT LOUIS UNIVERSITY

221 North Grand Boulevard, Saint Louis, MO 63103 • *Admissions: 314-977-2500* • *Fax: 314-977-3079*
• *Financial Aid: 314-977-2350* • *E-mail: admitme@sluvca.slu.edu* • *Web Site: www.slu.edu*

Saint Louis University was founded in 1818 by the Jesuits, and was the first university west of the Mississippi. The university's 200-acre campus is located in the heart of the city. Fifty-three majors are available from within the liberal arts and sciences, business, education, and health sciences. Most popular majors include nursing, finance, and psychology. Facilities of note include an art gallery, museum, an urban affairs center, and a center for entrepreneurial studies (the new hot business major these days). Ninety-eight registered clubs and organizations, and twelve honor societies are found on campus; activities range from political groups to musical ensembles, a radio station, and weekly newspaper. Athletic teams are fielded in eight sports each for men and women; none are more dominant than men's soccer, who are nine-time national champions.

ADMISSIONS

The admissions committee considers (in descending order of importance): HS record, test scores, class rank, recommendations, essay. *Also considered (in descending order of importance):* alumni relationship, extracurriculars, personality, special talents. Either the SAT or ACT is required; ACT is preferred. An interview is recommended. Admissions process is need-blind. *High school units required/recommended:* 16 total units are recommended; 4 English recommended, 3 math recommended, 2 science recommended, 2 foreign language recommended, 2 social studies recommended. *Special Requirements:* A portfolio is required for art program applicants. An audition is required for music program applicants. TOEFL is required of all international students. Personal statement required of physical and occupational therapy program applicants.

FINANCIAL AID

Students should submit: FAFSA (due March 1). The Princeton Review suggests that all financial aid forms be submitted as soon as possible after January 1. *The following grants/scholarships are offered:* state scholarships. *Students borrow from the following loan programs:* Stafford, PLUS. College Work-Study Program is available. Institutional employment is available. The off-campus job outlook is excellent.

STUDENT BODY

Total undergrad enrollment	9,476
% male/female	48/52
% from out of state	36
% transfers	11
% live on campus	35
% African American	8
% Asian	4
% Caucasian	72
% Hispanic	2
% Native American	1
# of countries represented	83

ACADEMICS

Calendar	semester
Student/teacher ratio	5:1
FT faculty	2553
% faculty from religious order	2
% graduate in 4 yrs.	58

Most Popular Majors
nursing
finance
psychology

ADMISSIONS

Admissions Rating	74
# of applicants	3,760

% of applicants accepted	76
% of acceptees attending	37

Deadlines

Early decision/action	12/1
Regular admission	8/1
Regular notification	rolling

FRESHMAN PROFILE

Range ACT	22-28
Average ACT	25
Minimum TOEFL	500
Average HS GPA or Avg	3.4
Graduated top 10% of class	33

Graduated top 25% of class	65
Graduated top 50% of class	91

FINANCIAL FACTS

Tuition	$13,900
Room & board	$5,110
Estimated book expense	$800
% frosh receiving aid	85
% undergrads receiving aid	80
% frosh w/ grant	70
Avg. grant	NR
% frosh w/ loan	85
Avg. loan	$4,557

SAINT MARTIN'S COLLEGE

5300 Pacific Avenue SE, Lacey, WA 98503 • Admissions: 360-438-4311 • Fax: 360-459-4124
• Financial Aid: 360-438-4397 • E-mail: admissions@stmartin.edu • Web Site: www.stmartin.edu

Saint Martin's College was founded in 1895 by the Benedictines, and became coed in 1967. The college is situated on a 380-acre campus four miles from the state capital of Olympia, and sixty mile from Seattle. Twenty-four majors are available at Saint Martin's, focused mainly within the liberal arts and sciences, business, education, and nursing. Among the most popular majors are education and psychology. Noteworthy facilities include a museum that houses collections of Native American artifacts and contemporary Northwest art. The college reports twenty-four registered clubs and organizations offering a fairly standard selection of activities, including student government, a newspaper, a magazine, and yearbook. Athletic teams are fielded in basketball and golf for both men and women.

ADMISSIONS

The admissions committee considers (in descending order of importance): HS record, test scores, essay, recommendations, class rank. *Also considered (in descending order of importance):* alumni relationship, extracurriculars, personality, special talents. Either the SAT or ACT is required. An interview is recommended. *High school units required/recommended:* 17 total units are required; 20 total units are recommended; 4 English required, 2 math required, 3 math recommended, 2 science required, 2 foreign language recommended, 1 social studies required, 1 history required. Minimum composite ACT score of 18 (combined SAT I score of 800) and minimum 2.5 GPA in academic courses required. *Special Requirements:* Special admissions requirements for nursing program applicants. Minimum 3.0 GPA required of education program applicants.

FINANCIAL AID

Students should submit: FAFSA (due March 1), the school's own financial aid form (due March 1). The Princeton Review suggests that all financial aid forms be submitted as soon as possible after January 1. *The following grants/scholarships are offered:* Pell, SEOG, academic merit, athletic, the school's own scholarships, the school's own grants, state scholarships, state grants, private scholarships, private grants, federal nursing scholarship, ROTC, foreign aid. *Students borrow from the following loan programs:* Stafford, unsubsidized Stafford, Perkins, PLUS, the school's own loan fund, supplemental loans, federal nursing loans, health professions loans, private loans. Applicants will be notified of awards beginning April 1. College Work-Study Program is available. Institutional employment is available. The off-campus job outlook is excellent.

STUDENT BODY		ACADEMICS		Deadlines		FINANCIAL FACTS	
Total undergrad enrollment	1,061	Calendar	semester	Regular admission	8/1	Tuition	$12,610
% male/female	42/58	Student/teacher ratio	18:1	Regular notification	rolling	Room & board	$4,590
% from out of state	20	FT faculty	80			Estimated book expense	$670
% transfers	70	% graduate in 4 yrs.	42	**FRESHMAN PROFILE**		% frosh receiving aid	38
% from catholic high school	30			Average verbal SAT	490	% undergrads receiving aid	55
% live on campus	20	**Most Popular Majors**		Average math SAT	490	% frosh w/ grant	73
% African American	5	education		Average ACT	23	Avg. grant	$4,417
% Asian	4	psychology		Minimum TOEFL	525	% frosh w/ loan	95
% Caucasian	84	**ADMISSIONS**		Average HS GPA or Avg	3.3	Avg. loan	NR
% Hispanic	1	Admissions Rating	68	Graduated top 10% of class	26		
% Native American	1	# of applicants	187	Graduated top 25% of class	52		
% international	5	% of applicants accepted	88	Graduated top 50% of class	86		
# of countries represented	7	% of acceptees attending	53				

SAINT MARY COLLEGE

4100 South 4th St. Trafficway, Leavenworth, KS 66048 • Admissions: 913-758-6118 • Fax: 913-758-6140
• Financial Aid: 800-752-7043

Saint Mary College was founded in 1923 by the Sisters of Charity. The college's 200-acre campus is located twenty-six miles from Kansas City. Twenty-seven majors are offered within the liberal arts and sciences, business, and education. Most popular academic options include elementary education, business, and psychology. There are twelve registered clubs and organizations on campus, and activities focus mainly on musical ensembles and other standard offerings such as a student newspaper. Athletic teams are fielded in three sports for men and five for women.

ADMISSIONS

The admissions committee considers (in descending order of importance): HS record, test scores, class rank, recommendations. *Also considered (in descending order of importance):* personality. Either the SAT or ACT is required; ACT is preferred. *High school units required/recommended:* 16 total units are required; 4 English recommended, 2 math recommended, 1 science recommended, 2 foreign language recommended, 2 social studies recommended. Minimum composite ACT score of 19, rank in top third of secondary school class, and minimum 2.5 GPA recommended.

FINANCIAL AID

Students should submit: FAFSA, state aid form. The Princeton Review suggests that all financial aid forms be submitted as soon as possible after January 1. *The following grants/scholarships are offered:* state scholarships. *Students borrow from the following loan programs:* Stafford, PLUS. College Work-Study Program is available. Institutional employment is available. The off-campus job outlook is fair.

STUDENT BODY

Total undergrad enrollment	839
% male/female	28/72
% from out of state	60
% transfers	35
% live on campus	20
% African American	16
% Asian	4
% Caucasian	69
% Hispanic	5
% Native American	2
% international	5
# of countries represented	11

ACADEMICS

Calendar	semester
Student/teacher ratio	8:1
FT faculty	108

Most Popular Majors
elementary education
business
psychology

ADMISSIONS

Admissions Rating	74
% of acceptees attending	36

Deadlines

Regular admission	rolling
Regular notification	rolling

FRESHMAN PROFILE

Average ACT	21
Minimum TOEFL	500
Graduated top 10% of class	25
Graduated top 25% of class	60
Graduated top 50% of class	95

FINANCIAL FACTS

Tuition	$9,750
Room & board	$4,950
Estimated book expense	$500
% frosh receiving aid	90
% undergrads receiving aid	85
% frosh w/ grant	82
Avg. grant	NR
% frosh w/ loan	29
Avg. loan	$2,211

SAINT MARY'S COLLEGE (CA)

1928 Saint Mary's Road, Moraga, CA 94575 • Admissions: 510-631-4000 • Fax: 510-376-2150
• Financial Aid: 510-631-4370 • E-mail: admissions@stmarys-ca.edu • Web Site: www.stmarys-ca.edu

Saint Mary's College was founded in 1863 by the Christian Brothers, and became coed in 1970. The college is located on a 450-acre campus twelve miles from Oakland and twenty miles from San Francisco. The college offers twenty-six majors within six schools: liberal arts, science, economics and business administration, the intercollegiate nursing program, education, and the school of extended education. Most popular academic disciplines are business administration, communications, and psychology. Special facilities include the Hearst Art Gallery. Extracurricular activities focus on student government, musical ensembles and other arts groups, a student newspaper and magazine, and film, television, and radio groups. Athletic teams are fielded in ten sports for men, eight for women.

ADMISSIONS

The admissions committee considers (in descending order of importance): HS record, test scores, recommendations, class rank, essay. *Also considered (in descending order of importance):* personality, special talents, alumni relationship, extracurriculars, geographical distribution. Either the SAT or ACT is required. An interview is recommended. Admissions process is need-blind. *High school units required/recommended:* 16 total units are recommended; 4 English recommended, 3 math recommended, 2 science recommended, 2 foreign language recommended, 2 social studies recommended, 1 history recommended. *Special Requirements:* Algebra I and II, plane geometry, trigonometry, physics, and chemistry recommended of applicants to School of Science.

FINANCIAL AID

Students should submit: FAFSA (due March 2), state aid form (due March 2). The Princeton Review suggests that all financial aid forms be submitted as soon as possible after January 1. *The following grants/scholarships are offered:* Pell, SEOG, academic merit, the school's own scholarships, the school's own grants, state grants, private scholarships, private grants, foreign aid. *Students borrow from the following loan programs:* Stafford, unsubsidized Stafford, Perkins, PLUS, the school's own loan fund, supplemental loans, private loans. Applicants will be notified of awards beginning April 15. College Work-Study Program is available. Institutional employment is available. The off-campus job outlook is excellent.

STUDENT BODY		ACADEMICS				
Total undergrad enrollment	2,153	Calendar	4-1-4	% of applicants accepted	83	Graduated top 10% of class 36
% male/female	46/54	Student/teacher ratio	14:1	% of acceptees attending	22	Graduated top 25% of class 80
% from out of state	16	FT faculty	383			Graduated top 50% of class 99
% transfers	22	% faculty from religious order	12	**Deadlines**		
% from catholic high school	43	% graduate in 4 yrs.	68	Early decision/action	11/30	**FINANCIAL FACTS**
% live on campus	63			Regular admission	2/1	Tuition $15,880
% African American	11	**Most Popular Majors**		Regular notification	rolling	Room & board $7,109
% Asian	67	business administration				Estimated book expense $648
% Caucasian	14	communications		**FRESHMAN PROFILE**		% frosh receiving aid 53
% Hispanic	14	psychology		Range verbal SAT	510-600	% undergrads receiving aid 53
% Native American	1			Average verbal SAT	562	% frosh w/ grant 41
% international	4	**ADMISSIONS**		Range math SAT	500-600	Avg. grant $8,923
# of countries represented	37	Admissions Rating	75	Average math SAT	557	% frosh w/ loan 67
		# of applicants	2,607	Average ACT	24	Avg. loan $2,747
				Minimum TOEFL	525	
				Average HS GPA or Avg	3.4	

SAINT MARY'S COLLEGE (IN)

Notre Dame, IN 46556 • Admissions: 219-284-4587 • Fax: 219-284-4716
• Financial Aid: 219-284-4557 • E-mail: admission@saintmarys.edu • Web Site: www.saintmarys.edu/

Saint Mary's College was founded in 1844 by the Sisters of the Holy Cross in response to the petitions of parents who desired a Christian education for their daughters. The college sprawls out on a 275-acre campus six miles from South Bend. Saint Mary's promotes a life of intellectual vigor, aesthetic appreciation, religious sensibility, and social responsibility. Thirty-eight majors are available within the liberal arts and sciences, business, and nursing. Among the most popular academic choices are business administration, elementary education, and communications. Noteworthy facilities include an art gallery, a nature trail, and a campus in Rome. The college counts fifty-one registered clubs and organizations among its extracurricular offerings. Saint Mary's campus ministry cultivates a Christian community of intellectual inquiry, liturgical prayer, and social action. A large percentage of students are active in the local community, and service groups venture as far as Latin America and Europe for summer volunteer work. Athletic teams are fielded in eight sports.

ADMISSIONS

The admissions committee considers (in descending order of importance): HS record, class rank, recommendations, test scores, essay. *Also considered (in descending order of importance):* alumni relationship, extracurriculars, geographical distribution, personality, special talents. Either the SAT or ACT is required. An interview is recommended. Admissions process is need-blind. *High school units required/recommended:* 16 total units are required; 4 English required, 3 math required, 1 science required, 2 foreign language required, 2 social studies required. *Special Requirements:* TOEFL is required of all international students. Additional math and science units recommended of mathematics, science, and nursing program applicants. Audition recommended of music program applicants. Portfolio recommended of art program applicants.

FINANCIAL AID

Students should submit: FAFSA, CSS Profile (due), state aid form. The Princeton Review suggests that all financial aid forms be submitted as soon as possible after January 1. *The following grants/scholarships are offered:* Pell, SEOG, academic merit, the school's own scholarships, the school's own grants, state scholarships, state grants, private scholarships, ROTC, foreign aid. *Students borrow from the following loan programs:* Stafford, unsubsidized Stafford, Perkins, PLUS, the school's own loan fund, private loans. College Work-Study Program is available. Institutional employment is available. The off-campus job outlook is good.

STUDENT BODY		ACADEMICS				FINANCIAL FACTS	
Total undergrad enrollment	1,527	Calendar	semester	% of applicants accepted	82	Tuition	$14,170
% male/female	0/100	Student/teacher ratio	11:1	% of acceptees attending	53	Room & board	$4,966
% from out of state	78	FT faculty	114	**Deadlines**		Estimated book expense	$500
% transfers	12	% faculty from religious order	3	Regular admission	8/1	% frosh receiving aid	70
% from catholic high school	48	% graduate in 4 yrs.	69	Regular notification	rolling	% undergrads receiving aid	67
% live on campus	89					% frosh w/ grant	68
% African American	1	**Most Popular Majors**		**FRESHMAN PROFILE**		Avg. grant	$6,000
% Asian	2	business administration		Average verbal SAT	560	% frosh w/ loan	60
% Caucasian	92	elementary education		Average math SAT	550	Avg. loan	$3,375
% Hispanic	3	communication		Average ACT	25		
% international	2			Average HS GPA or Avg	3.5		
# of countries represented	20	**ADMISSIONS**					
		Admissions Rating	78				
		# of applicants	793				

SAINT MARY'S UNIVERSITY OF MINNESOTA

700 Terrace Heights, Winona, MN 55987 • *Admissions: 507-457-1700* • *Fax: 507-457-1633*
• *Financial Aid: 507-457-1437* • *E-mail: admissions@smumn.edu* • *Web Site: 140.190.128.190/smc/homepage.html*

Saint Mary's University of Minnesota, founded in 1912, is administered by the Christian Brothers. The university's 400-acre campus, on the scenic bluffs of the Mississippi River Valley, is two hours southeast of Minneapolis-St. Paul. Saint Mary's offers fifty-six academic majors within the liberal arts and sciences, business, and education; the most popular programs include marketing, psychology, and education. Over the past few years an ambitious campus construction program has produced a state-of-the-art performing arts center, an indoor ice facility, chapel renovations, a science building addition, residence halls, renovated classrooms, and a library addition. A new indoor recreation/fitness center includes a pool, running track, multipurpose courts, a dance studio, and exercise room. Saint Mary's intercollegiate sports program faces some of the country's toughest Division III competition, with great success. The university is an ice hockey power, and the women's soccer program has won its conference title seven times in the past ten years, participating in the NCAA national championship tournament for six consecutive years.

ADMISSIONS

The admissions committee considers (in descending order of importance): HS record, test scores, class rank, essay, recommendations. *Also considered (in descending order of importance):* extracurriculars, personality, special talents, alumni relationship, geographical distribution. Either the SAT or ACT is required; ACT is preferred. An interview is recommended. Admissions process is need-blind. *High school units required/recommended:* 18 total units are recommended; 4 English recommended, 3 math recommended, 2 science recommended, 2 social studies recommended. Minimum composite ACT score of 18 and minimum C+, rank in top half of secondary school class recommended.

FINANCIAL AID

Students should submit: FAFSA (due March 15), the school's own financial aid form (due March 15). The Princeton Review suggests that all financial aid forms be submitted as soon as possible after January 1. *The following grants/scholarships are offered:* Pell, SEOG, academic merit, the school's own scholarships, the school's own grants, state scholarships, state grants, private scholarships, private grants, ROTC, foreign aid. *Students borrow from the following loan programs:* Stafford, unsubsidized Stafford, Perkins, PLUS, the school's own loan fund, supplemental loans, state loans, private loans. College Work-Study Program is available. Institutional employment is available. The off-campus job outlook is fair.

STUDENT BODY

Total undergrad enrollment	1,451
% male/female	48/52
% from out of state	49
% transfers	5
% from catholic high school	36
% live on campus	87
% African American	1
% Asian	3
% Caucasian	94
% Hispanic	1
% Native American	1
% international	5
# of countries represented	12

ACADEMICS

Calendar	semester
Student/teacher ratio	31:1
FT faculty	301
% faculty from religious order	30
% graduate in 4 yrs.	51

Most Popular Majors
marketing
psychology
education

ADMISSIONS

Admissions Rating	72
# of applicants	1,014
% of applicants accepted	88
% of acceptees attending	48

Deadlines

Regular admission	rolling
Regular notification	rolling

FRESHMAN PROFILE

Range ACT	19-24
Average ACT	22
Minimum TOEFL	500
Average HS GPA or Avg	3.1
Graduated top 10% of class	14
Graduated top 25% of class	35
Graduated top 50% of class	63

FINANCIAL FACTS

Tuition	$11,700
Room & board	$3,900
Estimated book expense	$400
% frosh receiving aid	91
% undergrads receiving aid	66
% frosh w/ grant	78
Avg. grant	$4,152
% frosh w/ loan	72
Avg. loan	$3,382

SAINT MARY'S UNIVERSITY

One Camino Santa Maria, San Antonio, TX 78228 • Admissions: 210-436-3126 • Fax: 210-431-2226
• Financial Aid: Call-Admissions • Web Site: stmarytx.edu

Saint Mary's University was founded in 1852 by the Marianists. The university is located on a 135-acre residential campus five miles from downtown San Antonio. Forty-three undergraduate majors are available within the liberal arts and sciences, business, education, engineering, and health sciences. Literally half of Saint Mary's students continue on to graduate or professional school upon graduation. Fifty student-run clubs and organizations are offered on campus, including a chapter of Amnesty International, a broad range of musical ensembles, and political and social-action groups. Athletic teams are fielded in five sports each for men and women.

ADMISSIONS

Special Requirements: TOEFL is required of all international students.

FINANCIAL AID

Students should submit: FAFSA (due April 1), a copy of parents' most recent income tax filing (due April 1). The Princeton Review suggests that all financial aid forms be submitted as soon as possible after January 1. *The following grants/scholarships are offered:* Pell, SEOG, academic merit, the school's own scholarships, the school's own grants, state grants, private scholarships, private grants, ROTC. *Students borrow from the following loan programs:* Stafford, unsubsidized Stafford, Perkins, PLUS, the school's own loan fund, supplemental loans, private loans. College Work-Study Program is available.

STUDENT BODY

% from out of state	5
% from catholic high school	30
% live on campus	44
% African American	3
% Asian	3
% Caucasian	28
% Hispanic	64
% international	3

ACADEMICS

Calendar	semester
Student/teacher ratio	14:1
FT faculty	302
% graduate in 4 yrs.	58

ADMISSIONS

Admissions Rating	76
# of applicants	1,223
% of applicants accepted	87
% of acceptees attending	48

Deadlines

Regular admission	8/15

FRESHMAN PROFILE

Average verbal SAT	530
Average math SAT	530
Average ACT	22
Minimum TOEFL	550
Average HS GPA or Avg	3.3
Graduated top 10% of class	36
Graduated top 25% of class	65
Graduated top 50% of class	85

FINANCIAL FACTS

Tuition	$9,934
Room & board	$3,773
Estimated book expense	$1,000
% frosh receiving aid	72
% undergrads receiving aid	72
% frosh w/ grant	74
Avg. grant	$4,200
% frosh w/ loan	81
Avg. loan	$5,860

COLLEGE OF SAINT MARY

1901 South 72nd Street, Omaha, NE 68124 • Admissions: 402-399-2405 • Fax: 402-399-2412
• Financial Aid: 402-399-2415

The Sisters of Mercy founded the College of Saint Mary in 1923 in order to assist women in becoming teachers. The college sits on a 25-acre campus. Twenty-eight majors are offered within the liberal arts and sciences, business, education, and nursing. Most popular academic programs include computer information management, business administration, and paralegal studies. Twelve registered clubs and organizations are available at the college. The pastoral council is an elected body of students who develop programs to meet the spiritual needs of the college community. A new fitness center opened in 1995, featuring a gymnasium, elevated walk track, and a six-lane, twenty-five-yard swimming pool. Athletic teams are fielded in five sports.

ADMISSIONS

The admissions committee considers (in descending order of importance): class rank, HS record, test scores. *Also considered (in descending order of importance):* extracurriculars, personality, special talents, alumni relationship. Either the SAT or ACT is required; ACT is preferred. An interview is recommended. *High school units required/recommended:* 16 total units are required; 4 English required, 2 math required, 2 science required, 2 social studies required. Two of the following are required: minimum composite ACT score of 19, rank in top half of secondary school class, and minimum 2.0 GPA. *Special Requirements:* Chemistry and biology required of nursing and occupational therapy program applicants; recommended of medical records administration and medical technology program applicants.

FINANCIAL AID

Students should submit: FAFSA, the school's own financial aid form, a copy of parents' most recent income tax filing. The Princeton Review suggests that all financial aid forms be submitted as soon as possible after January 1. *Students borrow from the following loan programs:* Stafford, PLUS. Institutional employment is available. The off-campus job outlook is good.

STUDENT BODY
Total undergrad enrollment	1,304
% male/female	1/99
% from out of state	7
% transfers	54
% from catholic high school	27
% live on campus	42
% African American	3
% Asian	1
% Caucasian	93
% Hispanic	1
% Native American	1

ACADEMICS
Calendar	semester
Student/teacher ratio	8:1
FT faculty	138
% graduate in 4 yrs.	55

Most Popular Majors
computer information management
business administration
paralegal studies

ADMISSIONS
Admissions Rating	66
# of applicants	384
% of applicants accepted	81
% of acceptees attending	47

Deadlines
Regular admission	rolling
Regular notification	rolling

FRESHMAN PROFILE
Average ACT	21
Minimum TOEFL	550
Average HS GPA or Avg	3.2
Graduated top 10% of class	20
Graduated top 25% of class	44
Graduated top 50% of class	80

FINANCIAL FACTS
Tuition	$10,996
Room & board	$4,080
Estimated book expense	$600
% frosh receiving aid	96
% undergrads receiving aid	87

SAINT MICHAEL'S COLLEGE

Winooski Park, Colchester, VT 05439 • Admissions: 802-654-2000 • Fax: 802-654-2591
• Financial Aid: 802-654-3243 • E-mail: admission@smcvt.edu • Web Site: www.smcvt.edu

Saint Michael's College was founded in 1904 by the Fathers of Saint Edmund. The college's campus sits on a 400-acre hilltop, three miles from Burlington. Twenty-six majors are offered in the liberal arts and sciences, business, education, and engineering. Most popular among academic options are business administration, psychology, and English literature. Noteworthy facilities include an observatory. Saint Michael's provides thirty-six clubs and organizations. A nationally recognized volunteer program has helped build homes in rural Alabama, tutored local children, and served as big brothers and sisters. Also available are music and arts ensembles, several publications, and last—but far from least—the Ski Connection, through which the college works with nearby ski resorts to get affordable deals on season ski passes. Free college transportation runs regularly to the slopes. Saint Michael's fields athletic teams in eleven sports each for men and women; men's hockey is one of the top teams in NCAA Division II.

ADMISSIONS
The admissions committee considers (in descending order of importance): HS record, class rank, test scores, recommendations, essay. *Also considered (in descending order of importance):* alumni relationship, extracurriculars, geographical distribution, personality, special talents. Either the SAT or ACT is required; SAT is preferred. An interview is recommended. Admissions process is need-blind. *High school units required/recommended:* 16 total units are required; 20 total units are recommended; 4 English required, 3 math required, 4 math recommended, 3 science required, 4 science recommended, 2 foreign language required, 4 foreign language recommended, 2 social studies required, 2 history required. Minimum combined SAT I score of 1000, rank in top third of secondary school class, and minimum 3.0 GPA recommended. *Special Requirements:* Physics recommended of science program applicants.

FINANCIAL AID
Students should submit: FAFSA (due March 15), the school's own financial aid form (due March 15), state aid form, a copy of parents' most recent income tax filing (due March 15). The Princeton Review suggests that all financial aid forms be submitted as soon as possible after January 1. *The following grants/scholarships are offered:* Pell, SEOG, academic merit, the school's own scholarships, the school's own grants, state scholarships, state grants, private scholarships, private grants. *Students borrow from the following loan programs:* Stafford, unsubsidized Stafford, Perkins, PLUS, the school's own loan fund, supplemental loans, private loans. College Work-Study Program is available. Institutional employment is available. The off-campus job outlook is good.

STUDENT BODY		ACADEMICS					
Total undergrad enrollment	1,989	Calendar	semester	% of applicants accepted	62	Graduated top 25% of class	54
% male/female	45/55	Student/teacher ratio	10:1	% of acceptees attending	34	Graduated top 50% of class	94
% from out of state	81	FT faculty	266	**Deadlines**		**FINANCIAL FACTS**	
% transfers	10	% faculty from religious order	4	Early decision/action	11/15	Tuition	$14,640
% from catholic high school	18	% graduate in 4 yrs.	78	Regular admission	2/1	Room & board	$6,375
% live on campus	85			Regular notification	4/1	Estimated book expense	$350
% African American	2	**Most Popular Majors**				% frosh receiving aid	67
% Asian	1	business administration		**FRESHMAN PROFILE**		% undergrads receiving aid	48
% Caucasian	92	psychology		Range verbal SAT	528-613	% frosh w/ grant	62
% international	4	English literature		Average verbal SAT	566	Avg. grant	$5,200
# of countries represented	25	**ADMISSIONS**		Range math SAT	510-597	% frosh w/ loan	64
		Admissions Rating	86	Average math SAT	552	Avg. loan	$4,600
		# of applicants	2,278	Minimum TOEFL	550		
				Graduated top 10% of class	21		

SAINT NORBERT COLLEGE

100 Grant Street, De Pere, WI 54115 • Admissions: 414-337-3005 • Fax: 414-337-4072
• Financial Aid: 414-403-3071 • E-mail: admit@sncac.snc.edu • Web Site: www.snc.edu

The Premonstratensians, or Norbertines, founded Saint Norbert College in 1898. Named after Norbert of Xanten, the college's 72-acre campus covers more than a half mile of the west bank of Wisconsin's scenic Fox River, five miles from Green Bay. Saint Norbert offers forty-eight majors within the areas of liberal arts and sciences, business, and education. Business administration, communication arts, and elementary education are among the most popular academic options. Facilities and equipment of note include an art gallery, a nursery school, a state-of-the-art multimedia theater, a nuclear magnetic resonator, and a scanning electron microscope. The college counts sixty-five clubs and organizations involved in extracurricular activities. Pursuits range from a variety of publications and performing arts groups to a chapter of Amnesty International and a leadership and service program that offers seminars, workshops, academic courses, internships, and volunteer activities. Saint Norbert fields intercollegiate athletic teams in nine sports each for men and women, and is a major force in Division III men's ice hockey. The college works hard to keep the education they offer affordable; each year more than 17 million dollars in financial aid is made available to students.

ADMISSIONS

The admissions committee considers (in descending order of importance): HS record, class rank, test scores, recommendations, essay. *Also considered (in descending order of importance):* alumni relationship, extracurriculars, special talents, personality. Either the SAT or ACT is required. An interview is recommended. Admissions process is need-blind. *High school units required/recommended:* 16 total units are recommended; 4 English recommended, 3 math recommended, 3 science recommended, 3 foreign language recommended, 2 social studies recommended, 1 history recommended. Minimum combined SAT I score of 900 (composite ACT score of 19), rank in top half of secondary school class, and minimum 2.5 GPA recommended.

FINANCIAL AID

Students should submit: FAFSA (due March 1), the school's own financial aid form (due March 1), state aid form, a copy of parents' most recent income tax filing (due March 1). The Princeton Review suggests that all financial aid forms be submitted as soon as possible after January 1. *The following grants/scholarships are offered:* Pell, SEOG, academic merit, the school's own scholarships, the school's own grants, state scholarships, state grants, private scholarships, private grants, ROTC, foreign aid. *Students borrow from the following loan programs:* Stafford, unsubsidized Stafford, Perkins, PLUS, the school's own loan fund, supplemental loans, private loans. College Work-Study Program is available. Institutional employment is available. The off-campus job outlook is excellent.

STUDENT BODY		ACADEMICS	
Total undergrad enrollment	2,011	Calendar	semester
% male/female	44/56	Student/teacher ratio	12:1
% from out of state	29	FT faculty	170
% transfers	11	% faculty from religious order	1
% from catholic high school	25	% graduate in 4 yrs.	72
% live on campus	84		
% African American	1	**Most Popular Majors**	
% Asian	2	business administration	
% Caucasian	94	communication arts	
% Native American	2	elementary education	
% international	1		
# of countries represented	11	**ADMISSIONS**	
		Admissions Rating	83
		# of applicants	1,409

		FINANCIAL FACTS	
% of applicants accepted	89	Tuition	$13,700
% of acceptees attending	42	Room & board	$4,845
Deadlines		Estimated book expense	$550
Regular admission	rolling	% frosh receiving aid	88
Regular notification	rolling	% undergrads receiving aid	85
FRESHMAN PROFILE		% frosh w/ grant	54
Range ACT	21-26	Avg. grant	$5,572
Average ACT	24	% frosh w/ loan	61
Minimum TOEFL	550	Avg. loan	$2,405
Average HS GPA or Avg	3.3		
Graduated top 10% of class	31		
Graduated top 25% of class	56		
Graduated top 50% of class	87		

SAINT PETER'S COLLEGE

2641 Kennedy Blvd., Jersey City, NJ 07306 • Admissions: 201-915-9000 • Fax: 201-432-5860
• Financial Aid: 201-915-9308 • E-mail: admissions@spcwva.spc.edu

Saint Peter's College is a Jesuit institution founded as a college for men in 1872; it began admitting women in 1966. Saint Peter's 10-acre campus, located across the Hudson River from lower Manhattan, serves its students with two schools—the college of arts and sciences and the school of business administration. The college offers thirty-four bachelor's degree programs, the most popular of which are business management, accounting, and elementary education. Noteworthy on campus are television production facilities, a center for government affairs, and new student housing. Saint Peter's counts fifty registered clubs and organizations providing a broad selection of activities ranging from student government and choral groups to multiethnic organizations and spiritual retreats. Saint Peter's offers a variety of sports across all seasons; men's and women's basketball teams are strong competitors in the Metro Atlantic Athletic Conference.

ADMISSIONS

The admissions committee considers (in descending order of importance): HS record, class rank, test scores, essay, recommendations. *Also considered (in descending order of importance):* personality, special talents, extracurriculars, alumni relationship. Either the SAT or ACT is required; SAT is preferred. An interview is recommended. Admissions process is need-blind. *High school units required/recommended:* 16 total units are required; 4 English required, 3 math required, 2 science required, 2 foreign language required, 2 history required. Minimum SAT I score of 400 in both verbal and math, rank in top two-fifths of secondary school class, and minimum 2.0 GPA recommended. *Special Requirements:* An R.N. is required for nursing program applicants.

FINANCIAL AID

Students should submit: FAFSA (due February 15). The Princeton Review suggests that all financial aid forms be submitted as soon as possible after January 1. *The following grants/scholarships are offered:* state scholarships. *Students borrow from the following loan programs:* Stafford, PLUS. Applicants will be notified of awards beginning March 4. College Work-Study Program is available. Institutional employment is available. The off-campus job outlook is excellent.

STUDENT BODY

Total undergrad enrollment	3,437
% male/female	47/53
% from out of state	14
% transfers	7
% from catholic high school	35
% live on campus	20
% African American	11
% Asian	10
% Caucasian	59
% Hispanic	20

ACADEMICS

Calendar	semester
Student/teacher ratio	11:1

FT faculty	355
% faculty from religious order	13
% graduate in 4 yrs.	47

Most Popular Majors

business management
accounting
elementary education

ADMISSIONS

Admissions Rating	64
# of applicants	1,947
% of applicants accepted	83
% of acceptees attending	40

Deadlines

Regular admission	rolling
Regular notification	rolling

FRESHMAN PROFILE

Range verbal SAT	390-520
Average verbal SAT	460
Range math SAT	390-520
Average math SAT	460
Minimum TOEFL	500
Average HS GPA or Avg	3.0
Graduated top 10% of class	16

FINANCIAL FACTS

Tuition	$11,228
Room & board	$5,530
Estimated book expense	$700
% frosh receiving aid	75
% undergrads receiving aid	75
% frosh w/ grant	69
Avg. grant	NR
% frosh w/ loan	33
Avg. loan	$2,301

THE COLLEGE OF SAINT ROSE

432 Western Avenue, Albany, NY 12203 • *Admissions: 518-454-5150* • *Fax: 518-454-2013*
• *Financial Aid: 518-454-5168* • *E-mail: admit@rosner.strose.edu* • *Web Site: www.strose.edu*

Founded in 1920 by the Sisters of Saint Joseph of Carondelet as a women's college, the College of Saint Rose became coed in 1970. The college is located on a 21-acre campus in New York State's capital. Saint Rose offers thirty-seven majors, mostly within the liberal arts and sciences, business, and education. The campus features an art gallery, music studio, observatory, communications studio, and a speech and hearing clinic. Twenty-five clubs and organizations are registered at Saint Rose, offering an opera company and numerous other musical groups, and many religious, multicultural, and community service organizations. The college offers eight intercollegiate sports for men, ten for women; both basketball programs enjoy top-ten rankings among NCAA Division II competition.

ADMISSIONS

The admissions committee considers (in descending order of importance): HS record, test scores, class rank, recommendations, essay. *Also considered (in descending order of importance):* alumni relationship, extracurriculars, geographical distribution, personality, special talents. Either the SAT or ACT is required; SAT is preferred. An interview is recommended. Admissions process is need-blind. *High school units required/recommended:* 16 total units are required; 4 English required, 3 math required, 2 science required, 4 history required. Minimum combined SAT I score of 800 and rank in top half of secondary school class required. *Special Requirements:* A portfolio is required for art program applicants. An audition is required for music program applicants.

FINANCIAL AID

Students should submit: FAFSA (due March 1), the school's own financial aid form (due March 1), state aid form (due March 1), a copy of parents' most recent income tax filing (due March 1). The Princeton Review suggests that all financial aid forms be submitted as soon as possible after January 1. *The following grants/scholarships are offered:* Pell, SEOG, academic merit, athletic, the school's own scholarships, the school's own grants, state scholarships, state grants, private scholarships, private grants, foreign aid. *Students borrow from the following loan programs:* Stafford, unsubsidized Stafford, Perkins, PLUS, the school's own loan fund, supplemental loans, private loans. College Work-Study Program is available. Institutional employment is available. The off-campus job outlook is excellent.

STUDENT BODY		ACADEMICS		Deadlines		FINANCIAL FACTS	
Total undergrad enrollment	3,519	Calendar	semester	Regular admission	rolling	Tuition	$11,024
% male/female	27/73	Student/teacher ratio	15:1	Regular notification	rolling	Room & board	$5,646
% from out of state	1	FT faculty	262			Estimated book expense	$800
% transfers	60	**Most Popular Majors**		**FRESHMAN PROFILE**		% frosh receiving aid	85
% live on campus	26	education		Average verbal SAT	524	% undergrads receiving aid	82
% African American	3	business administration		Average math SAT	513	% frosh w/ grant	53
% Asian	1	communication disorders		Average ACT	22	Avg. grant	$3,000
% Caucasian	94			Minimum TOEFL	500	% frosh w/ loan	61
% Hispanic	1	**ADMISSIONS**		Graduated top 25% of class	34	Avg. loan	$2,650
% international	1	Admissions Rating	74	Graduated top 50% of class	34		
# of countries represented	29	# of applicants	1,044				
		% of applicants accepted	75				
		% of acceptees attending	44				

COLLEGE OF SAINT SCHOLASTICA

1200 Kenwood Avenue, Duluth, MN 55811 • Admissions: 218-723-6046 • Fax: 218-723-6290
• Financial Aid: 218-723-6047 • E-mail: admissions@stfl.css.edu • Web Site: www.css.edu

The College of Saint Scholastica was founded in 1912 by a group of pioneering Benedictine Sisters who offered college courses to six young women. The college's 160-acre campus is set on a hill overlooking Lake Superior, two miles from downtown Duluth. Saint Scholastica offers twenty-eight majors within the liberal arts and sciences, business, education, and health sciences. Adjoining the campus are Saint Scholastica Priory, home of the Benedictine Sisters, and the Benedictine Health Center, which provides opportunities for practical experience for the college's health sciences students. Forty-one clubs and organizations provide extracurricular opportunities that are focused around a variety of performing arts organizations, religious groups, and community-service programs. Athletic teams (six sports each for men and women) represent Saint Scholastica in intercollegiate competition.

ADMISSIONS

The admissions committee considers (in descending order of importance): test scores, class rank, HS record, recommendations, essay. *Also considered (in descending order of importance):* alumni relationship, extracurriculars, geographical distribution, personality, special talents. Either the SAT or ACT is required; ACT is preferred. An interview is recommended. Admissions process is need-blind. *High school units required/recommended:* 4 English recommended, 3 math recommended, 3 science recommended, 3 foreign language recommended, 3 social studies recommended. *Special Requirements:* An audition is required for music program applicants. TOEFL is required of all international students.

FINANCIAL AID

Students should submit: FAFSA (due March 15), the school's own financial aid form (due March 15). The Princeton Review suggests that all financial aid forms be submitted as soon as possible after January 1. *The following grants/scholarships are offered:* state scholarships. *Students borrow from the following loan programs:* Stafford, PLUS. Applicants will be notified of awards beginning March 1. College Work-Study Program is available. Institutional employment is available. The off-campus job outlook is good.

STUDENT BODY
Total undergrad enrollment	1,588
% male/female	26/74
% from out of state	13
% transfers	27
% from catholic high school	10
% live on campus	38
% Asian	1
% Caucasian	96
% Native American	2
% international	1
# of countries represented	5

ACADEMICS
Calendar	quarter
Student/teacher ratio	11:1
FT faculty	167
% faculty from religious order	25
% graduate in 4 yrs.	49

Most Popular Majors
education
nursing
physical therapy

ADMISSIONS
Admissions Rating	71
% of acceptees attending	44

Deadlines
Regular admission	rolling
Regular notification	rolling

FRESHMAN PROFILE
Average verbal SAT	460
Average math SAT	503
Average ACT	23
Minimum TOEFL	550
Graduated top 10% of class	30
Graduated top 25% of class	63
Graduated top 50% of class	92

FINANCIAL FACTS
Tuition	$13,056
Room & board	$3,807
Estimated book expense	$501
% frosh receiving aid	90
% undergrads receiving aid	90
% frosh w/ grant	87
Avg. grant	NR
% frosh w/ loan	86
Avg. loan	$3,662

UNIVERSITY OF SAINT THOMAS (MN)

2115 Summit Avenue, St. Paul, MN 55105 • Admissions: 612-962-6150 • Fax: 612-962-6160
• Financial Aid: 612-962-6550 • E-mail: admissions@stthomas.edu • Web Site: www.stthomas.edu

The University of Saint Thomas, the largest private college in Minnesota, was founded in 1885 by the Diocese of Saint Paul; it became coed in 1977. The university's 78-acre campus is located five miles from downtown Saint Paul. Saint Thomas is largely a commuter college; less than a third of its students live on campus. A choice of fifty-five undergraduate majors, primarily within the liberal arts and sciences, business, and education, includes Chinese language, Catholic studies, systems engineering, and telecommunications. Among the most popular programs are business, journalism, and sociology. Seventy-two clubs and organizations are registered at Saint Thomas, offering an impressive range of extracurricular options, including a chapter of Amnesty International, Volunteers in Action, Peace, and Justice, a variety of performing arts groups, and several publications. Saint Thomas is dominant in almost every sport in which it competes. Women's basketball ranks among the top teams in Division III; the women's outdoor track team was the runner-up in national-championship competition in 1995. Men's ice hockey and cross-country teams are also perennial powerhouses.

ADMISSIONS
The admissions committee considers (in descending order of importance): HS record, test scores, class rank, essay, recommendations. *Also considered (in descending order of importance):* alumni relationship, extracurriculars, personality, special talents. Either the SAT or ACT is required; ACT is preferred. An interview is recommended. Admissions process is need-blind. *High school units required/recommended:* 3 total units are required; 15 total units are recommended; 4 English recommended, 3 math required, 4 math recommended, 2 science recommended, 3 foreign language recommended. Minimum composite ACT score of 20 and rank in top two-fifths of secondary school class required. *Special Requirements:* TOEFL is required of all international students.

FINANCIAL AID
Students should submit: FAFSA. The Princeton Review suggests that all financial aid forms be submitted as soon as possible after January 1. *The following grants/scholarships are offered:* Pell, SEOG, academic merit, the school's own scholarships, the school's own grants, state scholarships, state grants, private scholarships, private grants, ROTC, foreign aid. *Students borrow from the following loan programs:* Stafford, unsubsidized Stafford, Perkins, PLUS, the school's own loan fund, state loans. College Work-Study Program is available. Institutional employment is available. The off-campus job outlook is excellent.

STUDENT BODY		ACADEMICS		Deadlines		FINANCIAL FACTS	
Total undergrad enrollment	3,983	Calendar	4-1-4	Regular admission	rolling	Tuition	$13,728
% male/female	47/53	Student/teacher ratio	17:1	Regular notification	rolling	Room & board	$4,559
% from out of state	17	FT faculty	231			Estimated book expense	$500
% transfers	32	% graduate in 4 yrs.	47	**FRESHMAN PROFILE**		% frosh receiving aid	77
% live on campus	29			Average verbal SAT	553	% undergrads receiving aid	73
% African American	3	**Most Popular Majors**		Average math SAT	558	% frosh w/ grant	74
% Asian	4	business		Average ACT	23	Avg. grant	$6,405
% Caucasian	90	journalism		Minimum TOEFL	550	% frosh w/ loan	57
% Hispanic	2	sociology		Average HS GPA or Avg	3.3	Avg. loan	$5,822
% international	1	**ADMISSIONS**					
# of countries represented	26	Admissions Rating	73				
		# of applicants	1,950				
		% of applicants accepted	90				
		% of acceptees attending	49				

UNIVERSITY OF SAINT THOMAS (TX)

3800 Montrose Boulevard, Houston, TX 77006 • Admissions: 713-525-3500 • Fax: 713-525-3558
• Financial Aid: 713-525-2170 • E-mail: admissions@basil.stthom.edu • Web Site: basil.stthom.edu/home

The University of Saint Thomas was founded by the Basilians in 1887. Saint Thomas is situated on a 20-acre campus three miles from downtown Houston. Though largely a commuter campus, housing is available. The university offers twenty-five majors, focused on the liberal arts and sciences, and business. Among the most popular academic choices are business administration, psychology, and accounting. Saint Thomas counts thirty clubs and organizations on campus, including numerous musical groups, Aquinas leadership and service honors association, and several publications. Campus facilities include an institute for storm research. Athletics are offered at the club and intramural levels only.

ADMISSIONS

The admissions committee considers (in descending order of importance): HS record, class rank, test scores, recommendations, essay. *Also considered (in descending order of importance):* personality, special talents, extracurriculars. Either the SAT or ACT is required. An interview is recommended. *High school units required/recommended:* 16 total units are required; 4 English required, 3 math required, 2 science required, 2 foreign language required, 1 social studies required, 1 history required. Minimum combined SAT I score of 900 (composite ACT score of 21) and rank in top half of secondary school class recommended. *Special Requirements:* An audition is required for music program applicants.

FINANCIAL AID

Students should submit: FAFSA (due March 1), the school's own financial aid form (due March 1), a copy of parents' most recent income tax filing (due May 1). The Princeton Review suggests that all financial aid forms be submitted as soon as possible after January 1. *The following grants/scholarships are offered:* Pell, SEOG, academic merit, athletic, the school's own scholarships, the school's own grants, state scholarships, state grants, private scholarships, private grants, ROTC. *Students borrow from the following loan programs:* Stafford, unsubsidized Stafford, Perkins, PLUS, the school's own loan fund, supplemental loans, private loans. College Work-Study Program is available. Institutional employment is available. The off-campus job outlook is good.

STUDENT BODY

Total undergrad enrollment	1,403
% male/female	34/66
% from out of state	10
% transfers	49
% live on campus	14
% African American	6
% Asian	7
% Caucasian	62
% Hispanic	24
% Native American	1
% international	7
# of countries represented	15

ACADEMICS

Calendar	semester
Student/teacher ratio	13:1
FT faculty	173

Most Popular Majors
business administration
psychology
accounting

ADMISSIONS

Admissions Rating	89
% of acceptees attending	59

Deadlines

Regular admission	rolling
Regular notification	rolling

FRESHMAN PROFILE

Average ACT	26
Minimum TOEFL	550
Graduated top 10% of class	45
Graduated top 25% of class	77
Graduated top 50% of class	96

FINANCIAL FACTS

Tuition	$9,840
Room & board	$4,180
Estimated book expense	$512
% frosh receiving aid	45
% undergrads receiving aid	60
% frosh w/ grant	41
Avg. grant	$4,720
% frosh w/ loan	41
Avg. loan	$2,265

SAINT THOMAS AQUINAS COLLEGE

125 Route 340, Sparkill, NY 10976 • Admissions: 914-398-4000 • Fax: 914-398-4224
• Financial Aid: 914-398-4100 • E-mail: joestacenroll@rockland.net • Web Site: www.stac.edu

Saint Thomas Aquinas College was founded in 1952 by the Dominicans; it became coed in 1967. The college's 43-acre campus is located fifteen miles from New York City. Thirty-two majors are offered, primarily within the liberal arts and sciences, business, and education. Among the most popular programs are business administration, education, and communications. Forty-one registered clubs and organizations are active at Saint Thomas; options include radio, student government, drama, television, and community service organizations. The college fields intercollegiate athletic teams in three sports for men, five for women. Men's basketball has ranked among the top twenty-five teams in the NAIA for nine of the past fourteen years.

ADMISSIONS

The admissions committee considers (in descending order of importance): HS record, class rank, test scores, recommendations, essay. *Also considered (in descending order of importance):* alumni relationship, extracurriculars, personality, special talents. ; SAT is preferred. An interview is recommended. *High school units required/recommended:* 17 total units are required; 4 English required, 2 math required, 2 science required, 1 foreign language required, 1 history required. Minimum SAT I scores of 400 in both verbal and math, rank in top half of secondary school class.

FINANCIAL AID

Students should submit: FAFSA, the school's own financial aid form, a copy of parents' most recent income tax filing. The Princeton Review suggests that all financial aid forms be submitted as soon as possible after January 1. *The following grants/scholarships are offered:* Pell, SEOG, the school's own scholarships, the school's own grants, private scholarships, private grants, foreign aid. *Students borrow from the following loan programs:* Stafford, unsubsidized Stafford, Perkins, PLUS, the school's own loan fund, supplemental loans, private loans. College Work-Study Program is available. Institutional employment is available. The off-campus job outlook is good.

STUDENT BODY		ACADEMICS		Deadlines		FINANCIAL FACTS	
Total undergrad enrollment	2,101	Calendar	4-1-4	Regular admission	rolling	Tuition	$9,900
% male/female	39/61	Student/teacher ratio	17:1	Regular notification	rolling	Room & board	$6,450
% from out of state	40	FT faculty	125			Estimated book expense	$500
% transfers	36			**FRESHMAN PROFILE**		% frosh receiving aid	66
% live on campus	10	**Most Popular Majors**		Average verbal SAT	510	% undergrads receiving aid	75
% African American	7	business administration		Average math SAT	490		
% Asian	2	education		Minimum TOEFL	500		
% Caucasian	86	communication arts		Average HS GPA or Avg	2.8		
% Hispanic	5			Graduated top 10% of class	15		
% international	5	**ADMISSIONS**		Graduated top 25% of class	48		
# of countries represented	9	Admissions Rating	71	Graduated top 50% of class	88		
		# of applicants	873				
		% of applicants accepted	77				
		% of acceptees attending	40				

SAINT THOMAS UNIVERSITY

16400 N.W. 32nd Avenue, Miami, FL 33054 • *Admissions: 305-628-6546* • *Fax: 305-628-6510*
• *Financial Aid: 305-628-6547* • *E-mail: dperry@stu.edu* • *Web Site: www.stthomasu.ca*

The Augustinians founded Saint Thomas University in 1961; it became coed in 1975. The university is currently sponsored by the Archdiocese of Miami. Saint Thomas's 140-acre campus is located ten miles from downtown Miami. Thirty-five undergraduate majors are offered at the university, centered within the liberal arts and sciences, business, and education. Popular majors include business management, education, and psychology. Opportunities outside the classroom include twenty-nine registered clubs and organizations, and activities run the gamut from arts and media to volunteer programs and social-action groups, among them Students for Global Preservation. Athletic teams compete at the intercollegiate level in five sports for men, four for women. The women's basketball program at Saint Thomas is highly ranked in the Southern Region of NCAA Division III.

ADMISSIONS

The admissions committee considers (in descending order of importance): HS record, class rank, test scores, recommendations, essay. *Also considered (in descending order of importance):* alumni relationship, extracurriculars, geographical distribution, personality, special talents. Either the SAT or ACT is required. An interview is recommended. *High school units required/recommended:* 16 total units are required; 4 English required, 3 math required, 2 science required, 1 foreign language required, 3 social studies required. Rank in top three-fifths of secondary school class and minimum 2.0 GPA required. *Special Requirements:* TOEFL is required of all international students.

FINANCIAL AID

Students should submit: FAFSA (due April 1), the school's own financial aid form (due April 1), state aid form (due April 1). The Princeton Review suggests that all financial aid forms be submitted as soon as possible after January 1. *The following grants/scholarships are offered:* Pell, SEOG, academic merit, athletic, the school's own scholarships, the school's own grants, state scholarships, state grants, private scholarships, private grants. *Students borrow from the following loan programs:* Stafford, unsubsidized Stafford, Perkins, PLUS, the school's own loan fund, supplemental loans, private loans. Applicants will be notified of awards beginning April 1. College Work-Study Program is available. Institutional employment is available. The off-campus job outlook is good.

STUDENT BODY

Total undergrad enrollment	1,607
% male/female	43/57
% from out of state	17
% transfers	48
% from catholic high school	25
% live on campus	30
% African American	18
% Asian	1
% Caucasian	23
% Hispanic	40
% Native American	1
# of countries represented	45

ACADEMICS

Calendar	semester
Student/teacher ratio	21:1
FT faculty	137
% faculty from religious order	10

Most Popular Majors
business/management
education
psychology

ADMISSIONS

Admissions Rating	62
% of acceptees attending	63

Deadlines

Regular admission	rolling
Regular notification	rolling

FRESHMAN PROFILE

Minimum TOEFL	500
Graduated top 10% of class	10
Graduated top 25% of class	30
Graduated top 50% of class	70

FINANCIAL FACTS

Tuition	$10,800
Room & board	$4,000
Estimated book expense	$500
% frosh receiving aid	85
% undergrads receiving aid	82
% frosh w/ grant	34
Avg. grant	$5,000
% frosh w/ loan	53
Avg. loan	NR

SAINT VINCENT COLLEGE

300 Fraser Purchase Road, Latrobe, PA 15650 • Admissions: 412-539-9761 • Fax: 412-537-4554
• Financial Aid: 412-537-4540 • E-mail: tpratt@stvincent.edu • Web Site: www.stvincent.edu

Saint Vincent College was founded in 1846 by the Benedictines. The college's 100-acre campus is located in Pennsylvania's Laurel Highlands recreational region, thirty-five miles from Pittsburgh. Saint Vincent describes itself as an "educational community rooted in the tradition of the Catholic faith, the heritage of Benedictine monasticism, and the love of values inherent in the liberal approach to life and learning." Noteworthy facilities include a planetarium, an art gallery, an observatory, a radio telescope, and a life sciences research center. The college offers forty-three majors, mostly within the liberal arts and sciences, and business. The most popular programs are psychology, business administration, and biology. There are twenty-six registered clubs and organizations at Saint Vincent. Among activities offered are student government, radio and television, a variety of performing arts groups, several publications, and a pro-life club. Intercollegiate athletic teams compete for Saint Vincent in six sports for men and five sports for women.

ADMISSIONS

The admissions committee considers (in descending order of importance): HS record, class rank, recommendations, test scores, essay. *Also considered (in descending order of importance):* alumni relationship, extracurriculars, personality, special talents. Either the SAT or ACT is required; SAT is preferred. An interview is recommended. Admissions process is need-blind. *High school units required/recommended:* 15 total units are required; 4 English required, 2 math required, 1 science required, 2 foreign language required, 3 social studies required. *Special Requirements:* A portfolio is required for art program applicants. An audition is required for music program applicants. TOEFL is required of all international students. 1 unit each of plane geometry, algebra, and physics and 1/2 unit of trigonometry required of engineering program applicants.

FINANCIAL AID

Students should submit: FAFSA (due May 1). The Princeton Review suggests that all financial aid forms be submitted as soon as possible after January 1. *The following grants/scholarships are offered:* Pell, SEOG, academic merit, athletic, the school's own scholarships, the school's own grants, state scholarships, state grants, private scholarships, private grants, ROTC. *Students borrow from the following loan programs:* Stafford, unsubsidized Stafford, Perkins, PLUS, the school's own loan fund, supplemental loans, private loans. College Work-Study Program is available. Institutional employment is available. The off-campus job outlook is good.

STUDENT BODY

Total undergrad enrollment	1,215
% male/female	50/50
% from out of state	12
% transfers	14
% from catholic high school	35
% live on campus	75
% African American	1
% Asian	1
% Caucasian	95
% Hispanic	1
% Native American	1
% international	1
# of countries represented	10

ACADEMICS

Calendar	semester
Student/teacher ratio	11:1
FT faculty	106
% faculty from religious order	25
% graduate in 4 yrs.	68

Most Popular Majors
psychology
business administration
biology

ADMISSIONS

Admissions Rating	72
# of applicants	652

% of applicants accepted	85
% of acceptees attending	49

Deadlines

Regular admission	rolling
Regular notification	rolling

FRESHMAN PROFILE

Range verbal SAT	470-590
Range math SAT	480-590
Minimum TOEFL	525
Average HS GPA or Avg	3.2
Graduated top 10% of class	27
Graduated top 25% of class	54
Graduated top 50% of class	84

FINANCIAL FACTS

Tuition	$12,400
Room & board	$4,410
Estimated book expense	$350
% frosh receiving aid	84
% undergrads receiving aid	80
% frosh w/ grant	75
Avg. grant	$1,400
% frosh w/ loan	69
Avg. loan	$3,000

SAINT XAVIER UNIVERSITY

3700 W. 103rd Street, Chicago, IL 60655 • Admissions: 312-298-3050 • Fax: 312-298-3076
• Financial Aid: 312-298-3070 • E-mail: morrison@sxu.edu • Web Site: www.xu.edu

Founded in 1847 by the Sisters of Mercy as a university for women, Saint Xavier University became coed in 1969. Fifteen miles from Chicago's Loop, the university's 47-acre campus is located in a residential neighborhood on the southwest side of the city. Saint Xavier offers thirty-eight majors within four schools: arts and sciences, the Graham School of Management, education, and nursing. Popular programs include business administration, nursing, and education. Notable facilities include an art gallery, a music performance studio, a theater, and reading and speech clinics. There are thirty-one registered clubs and organizations at the university. Activities include film and radio, several publications, multicultural and international organizations, and numerous musical ensembles. Athletic teams are fielded in baseball, basketball, football, and soccer for men, and cross-country, softball, and volleyball for women.

ADMISSIONS

The admissions committee considers (in descending order of importance): HS record, class rank, recommendations, test scores. *Also considered (in descending order of importance):* extracurriculars, personality, special talents, alumni relationship. Either the SAT or ACT is required; ACT is preferred. An interview is recommended. Admissions process is need-blind. *High school units required/recommended:* 16 total units are recommended; 4 English recommended, 3 math recommended, 2 foreign language recommended, 4 social studies recommended. Remaining units may be selected from any subjects accepted by secondary school for graduation. *Special Requirements:* TOEFL is required of all international students. 1 unit of chemistry required of nursing program applicants.

FINANCIAL AID

Students should submit: FAFSA (due May 1). The Princeton Review suggests that all financial aid forms be submitted as soon as possible after January 1. *The following grants/scholarships are offered:* Pell, SEOG, academic merit, the school's own scholarships, the school's own grants, state scholarships, state grants, private scholarships, private grants. *Students borrow from the following loan programs:* Stafford, unsubsidized Stafford, Perkins, PLUS, the school's own loan fund, supplemental loans, private loans. Applicants will be notified of awards beginning February. College Work-Study Program is available. Institutional employment is available. The off-campus job outlook is good.

STUDENT BODY

Total undergrad enrollment	3,353
% male/female	29/71
% from out of state	5
% transfers	67
% from catholic high school	37
% live on campus	10
% African American	12
% Asian	1
% Caucasian	79
% Hispanic	6
% Native American	1
% international	1
# of countries represented	19

ACADEMICS

Calendar	4-1-4
Student/teacher ratio	17:1
FT faculty	265
% faculty from religious order	4

Most Popular Majors
business administration/manage
nursing
education

ADMISSIONS

Admissions Rating	65
% of acceptees attending	44

Deadlines

Regular admission	rolling
Regular notification	rolling

FRESHMAN PROFILE

Minimum TOEFL	550
Graduated top 10% of class	10
Graduated top 25% of class	80
Graduated top 50% of class	100

FINANCIAL FACTS

Tuition	$11,970
Room & board	$4,985
% frosh receiving aid	65
% undergrads receiving aid	80
% frosh w/ grant	88
Avg. grant	$5,600
% frosh w/ loan	69
Avg. loan	$2,541

SALVE REGINA UNIVERSITY

100 Ochre Point Avenue, Newport, RI 02840 • Admissions: 401-847-6650 • Fax: 401-847-1384
• Financial Aid: 401-847-6650-ext.-2901 • E-mail: sruadmis@salve3.salve.edu • Web Site: www.salve.edu

The Religious Sisters of Mercy founded Salve Regina University in 1934. The university is situated on a 120-acre campus on Rhode Island Sound, forty miles from Providence and seventy miles from Boston. Salve Regina awards degrees in thirty-two majors, mostly in the liberal arts and sciences, business, education, and health sciences. Nursing, criminal justice, and elementary education are among the most popular academic programs. Campus facilities of note include an art gallery and a theater. The university offers thirty-four clubs and organizations, and nine honor societies. Activities worth particular mention include an artists guild, a chamber orchestra, jazz band, and the Administration of Justice Club. Salve Regina fields athletic teams in nine sports each for men and women.

ADMISSIONS

The admissions committee considers (in descending order of importance): HS record, class rank, recommendations, test scores, essay. *Also considered (in descending order of importance):* extracurriculars, personality, special talents, alumni relationship. Either the SAT or ACT is required. An interview is recommended. Admissions process is need-blind. *High school units required/recommended:* 16 total units are recommended; 4 English recommended, 3 math recommended, 2 science recommended, 2 foreign language recommended, 1 history recommended. *Special Requirements:* TOEFL is required of all international students. Chemistry required of nursing program applicants.

FINANCIAL AID

Students should submit: FAFSA (due March 1), CSS Profile (due March 1), the school's own financial aid form (due March 1), state aid form (due March 1), a copy of parents' most recent income tax filing (due March 1). The Princeton Review suggests that all financial aid forms be submitted as soon as possible after January 1. *The following grants/scholarships are offered:* Pell, SEOG, academic merit, the school's own scholarships, the school's own grants, state scholarships, state grants, private scholarships, private grants. *Students borrow from the following loan programs:* Stafford, unsubsidized Stafford, Perkins, PLUS, the school's own loan fund, supplemental loans, health professions loans, private loans. Applicants will be notified of awards beginning March. College Work-Study Program is available. Institutional employment is available. The off-campus job outlook is good.

STUDENT BODY		ACADEMICS		ADMISSIONS			
Total undergrad enrollment	1,463	Calendar	semester	Admissions Rating	65	Graduated top 10% of class	7
% male/female	33/67	Student/teacher ratio	10:1	# of applicants	1,628	Graduated top 25% of class	21
% from out of state	73	FT faculty	212	% of applicants accepted	86	Graduated top 50% of class	52
% transfers	15	% faculty from religious order	18	% of acceptees attending	28	**FINANCIAL FACTS**	
% live on campus	52	% graduate in 4 yrs.	64			Tuition	$14,990
% African American	1			**Deadlines**		Room & board	$6,900
% Asian	2	**Most Popular Majors**		Regular admission	8/1	Estimated book expense	$400
% Caucasian	94	nursing		Regular notification	rolling	% frosh receiving aid	45
% Hispanic	2	administration of justice				% undergrads receiving aid	61
% Native American	1	elementary education		**FRESHMAN PROFILE**		% frosh w/ grant	68
% international	2			Range verbal SAT	430-540	Avg. grant	$5,800
# of countries represented	21			Average verbal SAT	486	% frosh w/ loan	63
				Range math SAT	420-520	Avg. loan	$4,971
				Average math SAT	467		
				Minimum TOEFL	550		

UNIVERSITY OF SAN DIEGO

*5998 Alcala Park, San Diego, CA 92110 • Admissions: 619-260-4506 • Fax: 619-260-2210
• Financial Aid: 619-260-4514 • E-mail: cronin@acusd.edu • Web Site: www.acusd.edu*

Founded in 1949 by the Society of the Sacred Heart, the University of San Diego is located on a 180-acre campus five miles from the city's downtown. The university offers thirty-nine majors in the liberal arts and sciences, business, education, engineering, and nursing. Most popular academic programs include business administration, communications, and psychology. Facilities of note are an art gallery and a child development center; Sea World's Hubb Institute research facilities are available to marine studies students. Sixty-five clubs and organizations are registered at San Diego, offering an impressive range of extracurricular options including a broad spectrum of multicultural and ethnic organizations. A broad selection of intercollegiate, intramural, and club athletics can be found at the university, including eight intercollegiate teams each for men and women. The men's soccer team is considered to be one of the best in the NCAA.

ADMISSIONS

The admissions committee considers (in descending order of importance): HS record, test scores, recommendations, essay. *Also considered (in descending order of importance):* extracurriculars, alumni relationship, personality, special talents. Either the SAT or ACT is required; SAT is preferred. Admissions process is needblind. *High school units required/recommended:* 20 total units are recommended; 4 English recommended, 4 math recommended, 3 science recommended, 4 foreign language recommended, 2 social studies recommended, 2 history recommended. Minimum combined SAT I score of 1050 and minimum 3.2 GPA recommended. *Special Requirements:* An RN is required for nursing program applicants. TOEFL is required of all international students. Audition required of Choral Scholar Program applicants.

FINANCIAL AID

Students should submit: FAFSA (due February 20), the school's own financial aid form, state aid form (due March 2). The Princeton Review suggests that all financial aid forms be submitted as soon as possible after January 1. *The following grants/scholarships are offered:* Pell, SEOG, academic merit, the school's own scholarships, the school's own grants, state grants, private scholarships, private grants, ROTC, foreign aid. *Students borrow from the following loan programs:* Stafford, unsubsidized Stafford, Perkins, PLUS, the school's own loan fund, supplemental loans, private loans. College Work-Study Program is available. Institutional employment is available. The off-campus job outlook is good.

STUDENT BODY		ACADEMICS				FINANCIAL FACTS	
Total undergrad enrollment	3,915	Calendar	trimester	% of applicants accepted	81	Tuition	$14,860
% male/female	45/55	Student/teacher ratio	13:1	% of acceptees attending	30	Room & board	$6,500
% from out of state	40	FT faculty	514	**Deadlines**		Estimated book expense	$650
% transfers	26	% faculty from religious order	6	Regular admission	1/15	% frosh receiving aid	55
% from catholic high school	22	% graduate in 4 yrs.	68	Regular notification	4/15	% undergrads receiving aid	50
% live on campus	50					% frosh w/ grant	48
% African American	2	**Most Popular Majors**		**FRESHMAN PROFILE**		Avg. grant	$8,250
% Asian	10	business administration		Minimum TOEFL	550	% frosh w/ loan	48
% Caucasian	69	communications studies		Graduated top 10% of class	40	Avg. loan	$3,300
% Hispanic	14	psychology		Graduated top 25% of class	70		
% Native American	1			Graduated top 50% of class	90		
% international	4	**ADMISSIONS**					
# of countries represented	55	Admissions Rating	74				
		# of applicants	4,331				

UNIVERSITY OF SAN FRANCISCO

2130 Fulton Street, San Francisco, CA 94117 • *Admissions: 415-422-6563* • *Fax: 415-422-2217*
• *Financial Aid: 415-422-6303* • *Web Site: www.usfca.edu*

The University of San Francisco was founded in 1855 by the Jesuits, and became coed in 1964. San Francisco's largest private university, USF's 54-acre campus is near Golden Gate Park, three miles from the city's downtown. Undergraduates from forty-five states and sixty foreign countries are represented in the student body. Thirty majors are available at San Francisco, mostly within the liberal arts and sciences, business, and nursing. Popular academic disciplines include nursing and communications. Among facilities worthy of note are an institute for Chinese-Western cultural history. The university reports thirty-seven registered clubs and organizations on campus, providing a broad range of activities; among them are thirteen ethnic clubs. USF's intercollegiate athletic teams, the Dons, compete in seven sports each for men and women. Men's soccer is nationally competitive.

ADMISSIONS

The admissions committee considers (in descending order of importance): HS record, recommendations, class rank, test scores, essay. *Also considered (in descending order of importance):* extracurriculars, alumni relationship, personality, special talents. Either the SAT or ACT is required; SAT is preferred. An interview is recommended. Admissions process is need-blind. *High school units required/recommended:* 20 total units are recommended; 4 English recommended, 3 math recommended, 2 science recommended, 2 foreign language recommended, 3 social studies recommended. Rank in top quarter of secondary school class and minimum 3.0 GPA recommended. *Special Requirements:* TOEFL is required of all international students.

FINANCIAL AID

Students should submit: FAFSA (due March 2), state aid form (due March 2), a copy of parents' most recent income tax filing. The Princeton Review suggests that all financial aid forms be submitted as soon as possible after January 1. *The following grants/scholarships are offered:* Pell, SEOG, academic merit, athletic, the school's own scholarships, the school's own grants, state scholarships, state grants, private scholarships, private grants, ROTC. *Students borrow from the following loan programs:* Stafford, unsubsidized Stafford, Perkins, PLUS, the school's own loan fund, supplemental loans, private loans. Applicants will be notified of awards beginning April 1. College Work-Study Program is available. Institutional employment is available. The off-campus job outlook is good.

STUDENT BODY		ACADEMICS		Deadlines		FINANCIAL FACTS	
Total undergrad enrollment	4,570	Calendar	semester	Regular admission	2/15	Tuition	$14,920
% male/female	38/62	Student/teacher ratio	11:1	Regular notification	rolling	Room & board	$6,934
% from out of state	22	FT faculty	742			Estimated book expense	$750
% transfers	48	% faculty from religious order	10	**FRESHMAN PROFILE**		% frosh receiving aid	43
% from catholic high school	32	% graduate in 4 yrs.	61	Range verbal SAT	480-600	% undergrads receiving aid	38
% live on campus	32			Range math SAT	480-600	% frosh w/ grant	55
% African American	5	**Most Popular Majors**		Range ACT	21-26	Avg. grant	$3,380
% Asian	18	nursing		Minimum TOEFL	550	% frosh w/ loan	51
% Caucasian	48	communications		Average HS GPA or Avg	3.3	Avg. loan	$2,603
% Hispanic	8			Graduated top 10% of class	25		
% Native American	1	**ADMISSIONS**		Graduated top 25% of class	55		
# of countries represented	70	Admissions Rating	77	Graduated top 50% of class	88		
		# of applicants	2,574				
		% of applicants accepted	77				
		% of acceptees attending	31				

Santa Clara University

500 El Camino Real, Santa Clara, CA 95053 • Admissions: 408-554-4000 • Fax: 408-554-5255
• Financial Aid: 408-554-4505 • E-mail: ugadmissions@scu.edu • Web Site: www.scu.edu

Founded by the Jesuits in 1851, Santa Clara University is the oldest institution of higher learning in California. The university's 104-acre campus is one mile from San Jose and forty-five miles from San Francisco. The university's three divisions—arts and sciences, business, and engineering—offer thirty-six majors. Among the most popular are finance, political science, and English. An historic mission church, an art gallery, a theater, a media lab, a retail management institute, a computer design center, and engineering labs are among facilities of note on campus. Over 100 clubs and organizations are available at the university; among these are many social-action and multicultural groups. Sports are available at the intercollegiate, intramural, and club levels; men's and women's teams compete in eight NCAA sports each in the West Coast Conference. Men's basketball and soccer have long histories of success; the soccer team won the national championship in 1989.

ADMISSIONS

The admissions committee considers (in descending order of importance): HS record, test scores, recommendations, class rank, essay. *Also considered (in descending order of importance):* extracurriculars, alumni relationship, geographical distribution, personality, special talents. Either the SAT or ACT is required; SAT is preferred. An interview is recommended. Admissions process is need-blind. *High school units required/recommended:* 16 total units are recommended; 4 English recommended, 3 math recommended, 1 science recommended, 3 foreign language recommended, 1 history recommended. Electives should be chosen from advanced courses in foreign language, math, lab science, or history. *Special Requirements:* An audition is required for music program applicants. TOEFL is required of all international students.

FINANCIAL AID

Students should submit: FAFSA (due February 1), CSS Profile (due February 1), a copy of parents' most recent income tax filing (due May 1). The Princeton Review suggests that all financial aid forms be submitted as soon as possible after January 1. *The following grants/scholarships are offered:* Pell, SEOG, athletic, the school's own scholarships, the school's own grants, state scholarships, state grants, private scholarships, private grants, federal nursing scholarship, ROTC. *Students borrow from the following loan programs:* Stafford, unsubsidized Stafford, Perkins, PLUS, the school's own loan fund, supplemental loans, federal nursing loans, private loans. College Work-Study Program is available. Institutional employment is available. The off-campus job outlook is good.

STUDENT BODY

Total undergrad enrollment	4,230
% male/female	47/53
% from out of state	34
% transfers	15
% from catholic high school	35
% live on campus	43
% African American	3
% Asian	19
% Caucasian	60
% Hispanic	13
% Native American	1
% international	9
# of countries represented	29

ACADEMICS

Calendar	quarter
Student/teacher ratio	14:1
FT faculty	554
% faculty from religious order	15

Most Popular Majors
finance
political science
English

ADMISSIONS

Admissions Rating	78
# of applicants	4,940
% of applicants accepted	76
% of acceptees attending	29

Deadlines

Regular admission	1/15
Regular notification	rolling

FRESHMAN PROFILE

Range verbal SAT	530-620
Range math SAT	540-640
Minimum TOEFL	550
Average HS GPA or Avg	3.5
Graduated top 10% of class	38
Graduated top 25% of class	70
Graduated top 50% of class	92

FINANCIAL FACTS

Tuition	$16,455
Room & board	$7,026
Estimated book expense	$630
% frosh receiving aid	72
% undergrads receiving aid	68
% frosh w/ grant	72
Avg. grant	$8,732
% frosh w/ loan	57
Avg. loan	$2,654

COLLEGE OF SANTA FE

1600 St. Michael's Dr., Santa Fe, NM 87505 • Admissions: 505-473-6131 • Fax: 505-473-6127
• Financial Aid: 505-473-6454 • E-mail: admission@fogelson.csf.edu • Web Site: www.state.nm.us/csf

The College of Santa Fe, New Mexico's largest private college, was founded 1947 by the Christian Brothers. The college's 98-acre residential campus is located about three miles from the plaza in downtown Santa Fe. Thirty-seven majors are offered primarily in the liberal arts and sciences, business, and education. Special academic facilities include the Garson Communications Center and Studios (the production facility for the films City Slickers and Wyatt Earp) and the Greer Garson Theater. A new visual arts center is planned for 1998. The college offers twelve registered clubs and organizations, with a variety of arts, media, social, and cultural groups. Santa Fe does not offer intercollegiate athletic teams; a variety of intramural sports are available, including skiing.

ADMISSIONS

The admissions committee considers (in descending order of importance): HS record, test scores, essay, recommendations, class rank. *Also considered (in descending order of importance):* personality, extracurriculars, special talents, alumni relationship, geographical distribution. Either the SAT or ACT is required. An interview is recommended. Admissions process is need-blind. *High school units required/recommended:* 16 total units are required; 3 English required, 4 English recommended, 2 math required, 4 math recommended, 2 science required, 4 science recommended, 2 foreign language recommended, 2 social studies required, 1 history recommended. Minimum composite ACT score of 19 (combined SAT I score of 900) and minimum 2.5 GPA required. *Special Requirements:* An audition is required for music program applicants. TOEFL is required of all international students. Audition required of performing arts program applicants.

FINANCIAL AID

Students should submit: FAFSA (due March 1), the school's own financial aid form (due March 1), state aid form. The Princeton Review suggests that all financial aid forms be submitted as soon as possible after January 1. *The following grants/scholarships are offered:* state scholarships. *Students borrow from the following loan programs:* Stafford, PLUS. College Work-Study Program is available. Institutional employment is available. The off-campus job outlook is good.

STUDENT BODY

Total undergrad enrollment	1,556
% male/female	43/57
% from out of state	60
% transfers	28
% from catholic high school	12
% live on campus	52
% African American	3
% Asian	3
% Caucasian	76
% Hispanic	15
% Native American	2
% international	1
# of countries represented	7

ACADEMICS

Calendar	semester
Student/teacher ratio	9:1
FT faculty	170
% faculty from religious order	1
% graduate in 4 yrs.	38

Most Popular Majors
moving image arts
performing arts
art

ADMISSIONS

Admissions Rating	71
# of applicants	536
% of applicants accepted	79
% of acceptees attending	35

Deadlines

Regular admission	3/15
Regular notification	rolling

FRESHMAN PROFILE

Range verbal SAT	372-588
Average verbal SAT	556
Range math SAT	490-540
Average math SAT	523
Range ACT	16-27
Average ACT	24
Minimum TOEFL	500
Average HS GPA or Avg	3.1

Graduated top 10% of class	17
Graduated top 25% of class	44
Graduated top 50% of class	75

FINANCIAL FACTS

Tuition	$11,796
Room & board	$4,400
Estimated book expense	$600
% undergrads receiving aid	90
% frosh w/ grant	56
Avg. grant	NR
% frosh w/ loan	80
Avg. loan	$2,500

UNIVERSITY OF SCRANTON

800 Linden St., Scranton, PA 18510 • Admissions: 717-941-7400 • Fax: 717-941-4370
• Financial Aid: 717-941-7700 • E-mail: admissions@uofs.edu • Web Site: www.uofs.edu

The Jesuits founded the University of Scranton in 1888. Located on a 50-acre campus, the university is two hours from both New York City and Philadelphia. Fifty-three majors within the liberal arts and sciences, business, education, engineering, and health sciences are available at Scranton. Most popular of these academic offerings are biology, accounting, and communications. Noteworthy campus facilities are a fine arts center and a horticulture conservatory. A broad selection of eighty clubs and organizations and twenty-five honor societies are registered on campus, among them political and social groups, collegiate volunteers, religious organizations, and a variety of musical ensembles. Athletic teams are fielded in ten sports for men and eight for women; also available are club and intramural sports. In the course of the past twenty-four years, Scranton has produced more than sixty Fulbright Scholars.

ADMISSIONS

The admissions committee considers (in descending order of importance): HS record, class rank, test scores, recommendations, essay. *Also considered (in descending order of importance):* alumni relationship, extracurriculars, personality. Either the SAT or ACT is required; SAT is preferred. An interview is recommended. Admissions process is need-blind. *High school units required/recommended:* 18 total units are required; 20 total units are recommended; 4 English required, 3 math required, 4 math recommended, 3 science required, 4 science recommended, 2 foreign language required, 2 social studies required, 2 history required. Rank in top two-fifths of secondary school class and minimum 3.0 GPA recommended. *Special Requirements:* Clinical observation required of occupational therapy and physical therapy program applicants.

FINANCIAL AID

Students should submit: FAFSA (due February 15), the school's own financial aid form (due February 15). The Princeton Review suggests that all financial aid forms be submitted as soon as possible after January 1. *The following grants/scholarships are offered:* Pell, SEOG, athletic, state scholarships, state grants, private scholarships, private grants. *Students borrow from the following loan programs:* Stafford, unsubsidized Stafford, Perkins, PLUS, supplemental loans, private loans. Applicants will be notified of awards beginning March 15. College Work-Study Program is available. Institutional employment is available. The off-campus job outlook is good.

STUDENT BODY
Total undergrad enrollment	3,173
% male/female	45/55
% from out of state	53
% transfers	7
% from catholic high school	50
% live on campus	75
% African American	1
% Asian	2
% Caucasian	84
% Hispanic	1
% international	2
# of countries represented	19

ACADEMICS
Calendar	4-1-4
Student/teacher ratio	13:1
FT faculty	387
% faculty from religious order	10
% graduate in 4 yrs.	81

Most Popular Majors
biology
accounting
communication

ADMISSIONS
Admissions Rating	84
# of applicants	4,790
% of applicants accepted	68
% of acceptees attending	30

Deadlines
Regular admission	3/1
Regular notification	rolling

FRESHMAN PROFILE
Range verbal SAT	510-610
Average verbal SAT	578
Range math SAT	480-600
Average math SAT	563
Minimum TOEFL	525
Average HS GPA or Avg	3.1
Graduated top 10% of class	23
Graduated top 25% of class	50
Graduated top 50% of class	76

FINANCIAL FACTS
Tuition	$14,800
Room & board	$6,074
Estimated book expense	$650
% frosh receiving aid	72
% undergrads receiving aid	82
% frosh w/ grant	58
Avg. grant	$4,400
% frosh w/ loan	61
Avg. loan	$3,500

SEATTLE UNIVERSITY

Broadway and Madison, Seattle, WA 98122 • Admissions: 206-296-6000 • Fax: 206-296-5656
• Financial Aid: 206-296-5840 • E-mail: admission@seattleu.edu • Web Site: www.seattleu.edu/home.html

Seattle University was founded in 1891 by the Jesuits; it became coed in 1933. The university is situated on a 46-acre campus in the city's downtown. Forty-four degree programs are available in the liberal arts and sciences, business, engineering, and nursing. Noteworthy facilities include the university design center (one of only two facilities of its kind in the U.S.), an art gallery, a theater, and an island campus used for seminars. Eighty clubs and organizations offering a wide range of activities are available; most notable are the university's broad selection of musical ensembles and performing arts groups. Athletic competition at the intercollegiate level is offered in five sports each for men and women; an extensive selection of intramural and club sports are available.

ADMISSIONS

The admissions committee considers (in descending order of importance): HS record, class rank, test scores, recommendations, essay. *Also considered (in descending order of importance):* alumni relationship, extracurriculars, geographical distribution, personality, special talents. Either the SAT or ACT is required. An interview is recommended. Admissions process is need-blind. *High school units required/recommended:* 16 total units are required; 4 English required, 2 math required, 1 science required, 2 foreign language required, 1 social studies required, 1 history required. Additional secondary school units recommended in each subject. Minimum combined recentered SAT I score of 950, rank in top half of secondary school class, and minimum 2.5 GPA required; minimum combined SAT I score of 1100 and 3.0 GPA recommended. *Special Requirements:* TOEFL is required of all international students. Minimum of 3 units of math (trigonometry recommended), and 2 units of lab science required of most applicants to School of Science and Engineering.

FINANCIAL AID

Students should submit: FAFSA (due February 15), the school's own financial aid form (due February 15), state aid form, a copy of parents' most recent income tax filing (due April 14). The Princeton Review suggests that all financial aid forms be submitted as soon as possible after January 1. *The following grants/scholarships are offered:* Pell, SEOG, academic merit, athletic, the school's own scholarships, the school's own grants, state scholarships, state grants, private scholarships, private grants, ROTC, foreign aid. *Students borrow from the following loan programs:* Stafford, unsubsidized Stafford, Perkins, PLUS, the school's own loan fund, supplemental loans, state loans, federal nursing loans, private loans. Applicants will be notified of awards beginning March 15. College Work-Study Program is available. Institutional employment is available. The off-campus job outlook is excellent.

STUDENT BODY

Total undergrad enrollment	3,272
% male/female	42/58
% from out of state	43
% transfers	48
% live on campus	27
% African American	3
% Asian	16
% Caucasian	72
% Hispanic	2
% Native American	1
# of countries represented	63

ACADEMICS

Calendar	quarter
Student/teacher ratio	15:1
FT faculty	397
% faculty from religious order	8
% graduate in 4 yrs.	57

Most Popular Majors
nursing
psychology
accounting

ADMISSIONS

Admissions Rating	80
% of acceptees attending	29

Deadlines

Regular admission	6/1
Regular notification	rolling

FRESHMAN PROFILE

Range verbal SAT	480-600
Average verbal SAT	539
Range math SAT	470-600
Average math SAT	541
Minimum TOEFL	520
Graduated top 10% of class	29
Graduated top 25% of class	54
Graduated top 50% of class	82

FINANCIAL FACTS

Tuition	$14,265
Room & board	$5,283
Estimated book expense	$600
% frosh receiving aid	76
% undergrads receiving aid	71
% frosh w/ grant	66
Avg. grant	$5,276
% frosh w/ loan	69
Avg. loan	$4,958

SETON HALL UNIVERSITY

400 South Orange Avenue, South Orange, NJ 07079 • Admissions: 201-761-9332 • Fax: 201-761-9452
• Financial Aid: 201-761-9350 • E-mail: shu@shu.edu • Web Site: www.shu.edu

Founded in 1856, Seton Hall University was the first Diocesan university in the United States. The university's 200-acre campus is located fourteen miles from New York City. Five colleges at Seton Hall—arts and sciences, business, education, nursing, and continuing education and community services—offer forty-one majors. Facilities of note include three museums—art, Native American, and natural history, a theater-in-the-round, an archaeological research center, an educational media center, computer graphics and communications labs, a center for entrepreneurial studies, and a television studio. One hundred and nine registered clubs and organizations and seventeen honor societies are found on campus. The university's activities range from performing arts ensembles, a radio station, and newspaper to a chapter of Amnesty International, and a Puerto Rican Institute. Athletic teams compete in the Big East Conference in ten sports for men and nine for women. Men's basketball at Seton Hall is nationally competitive.

ADMISSIONS

The admissions committee considers (in descending order of importance): HS record, class rank, test scores, essay, recommendations. *Also considered (in descending order of importance):* alumni relationship, extracurriculars, geographical distribution, personality, special talents. Either the SAT or ACT is required. An interview is recommended. Admissions process is need-blind. *High school units required/recommended:* 16 total units are required; 4 English required, 3 math required, 1 science required, 2 foreign language required, 2 social studies required. Minimum combined SAT I score of 900, rank in top two-fifths of secondary school class, and minimum 2.5 GPA recommended. *Special Requirements:* 2 units of lab science required of nursing program applicants. *The admissions office says:* "The personal attention given each application is what makes the admissions process at Seton Hall different. Every prospective student's file is read by two counselors, a committee review is held weekly, and folders are not assigned numeric averages."

FINANCIAL AID

Students should submit: FAFSA. The Princeton Review suggests that all financial aid forms be submitted as soon as possible after January 1. *The following grants/scholarships are offered:* Pell, SEOG, academic merit, athletic, the school's own scholarships, the school's own grants, state scholarships, state grants, private scholarships, private grants, foreign aid. *Students borrow from the following loan programs:* Stafford, unsubsidized Stafford, Perkins, PLUS, the school's own loan fund, supplemental loans, state loans, private loans. College Work-Study Program is available. Institutional employment is available. The off-campus job outlook is excellent. Freshmen are discouraged from working.

STUDENT BODY		ACADEMICS		Deadlines		FINANCIAL FACTS	
Total undergrad enrollment	4,096	Calendar	semester	Regular admission	3/1	Tuition	$13,050
% male/female	48/52	Student/teacher ratio	14:1	Regular notification	rolling after 1/1	Room & board	$7,020
% from out of state	16	FT faculty	781			Estimated book expense	$700
% transfers	30	% graduate in 4 yrs.	65	**FRESHMAN PROFILE**		% frosh receiving aid	70
% from catholic high school	40			Range verbal SAT	460-560	% undergrads receiving aid	80
% live on campus	50	**Most Popular Majors**		Average verbal SAT	513	% frosh w/ grant	70
% African American	11	business		Range math SAT	450-560	Avg. grant	$7,400
% Asian	4	communication		Average math SAT	510	% frosh w/ loan	60
% Caucasian	65	criminal justice		Range ACT	21-22	Avg. loan	$2,500
% Hispanic	8			Minimum TOEFL	550		
% international	2	**ADMISSIONS**		Average HS GPA or Avg	3.0		
# of countries represented	43	Admissions Rating	70	Graduated top 10% of class	13		
		# of applicants	4,915	Graduated top 25% of class	32		
		% of applicants accepted	80	Graduated top 50% of class	67		
		% of acceptees attending	25				

Seton Hill College

Seton Hill Drive, Greensburg, PA 15601 • Admissions: 412-834-2200 • Fax: 412-830-4611
• Financial Aid: 412-838-4293 • E-mail: admit@setonhill.edu

Seton Hill College was founded in 1883 by the Sisters of Charity as a women's college; its School of Visual and Performing Arts also admits men. The college is situated on a 200-acre campus thirty miles from Pittsburgh. Forty majors are available at Seton Hill, focused mainly within the liberal arts and sciences, business, education, and nursing. Among the most popular majors are visual and performing arts, psychology, and management. Noteworthy facilities include an on-campus nursery and kindergarten, an art gallery, a theater and concert hall, the National Catholic Center for Holocaust Education, the National Education Center for Women in Business, and a folklife documentation center. The college reports twenty-five registered clubs and organizations offering a selection of activities including student government, a newspaper, a magazine, film and television, and numerous performing arts organizations. Intercollegiate athletic teams are fielded in seven sports; among them is an equestrian team.

ADMISSIONS

The admissions committee considers (in descending order of importance): HS record, recommendations, test scores, class rank, essay. *Also considered (in descending order of importance):* personality, special talents, alumni relationship, extracurriculars, geographical distribution. Either the SAT or ACT is required. An interview is recommended. *High school units required/recommended:* 15 total units are required; 4 English required, 2 math required, 1 science required, 2 foreign language required, 2 social studies required. *Special Requirements:* A portfolio is required for art program applicants. An audition is required for music program applicants. Audition required of theatre program applicants.

FINANCIAL AID

Students should submit: FAFSA (due March 15), the school's own financial aid form (due Janaury 15), state aid form (due March 15), a copy of parents' most recent income tax filing (due June 1). The Princeton Review suggests that all financial aid forms be submitted as soon as possible after January 1. *The following grants/scholarships are offered:* Pell, SEOG, academic merit, athletic, the school's own scholarships, the school's own grants, state scholarships, state grants, private scholarships, private grants, foreign aid. *Students borrow from the following loan programs:* Stafford, unsubsidized Stafford, Perkins, PLUS, the school's own loan fund, supplemental loans, private loans. College Work-Study Program is available. Institutional employment is available. The off-campus job outlook is good.

STUDENT BODY

Total undergrad enrollment	899
% male/female	6/94
% from out of state	19
% transfers	18
% live on campus	65
% African American	6
% Asian	3
% Caucasian	85
% Hispanic	5
% international	2
# of countries represented	7

ACADEMICS

Calendar	semester
Student/teacher ratio	10:1
FT faculty	93
% faculty from religious order	15
% graduate in 4 yrs.	52

Most Popular Majors
psychology
management

ADMISSIONS

Admissions Rating	68
# of applicants	318
% of applicants accepted	92
% of acceptees attending	40

Deadlines

Regular admission	8/1
Regular notification	rolling

FRESHMAN PROFILE

Range verbal SAT	470-590
Range math SAT	430-550
Minimum TOEFL	550
Graduated top 10% of class	28
Graduated top 25% of class	57
Graduated top 50% of class	80

FINANCIAL FACTS

Tuition	$12,210
Room & board	$4,570
Estimated book expense	$600
% frosh receiving aid	83
% undergrads receiving aid	69
% frosh w/ grant	84
Avg. grant	$8,000
% frosh w/ loan	80
Avg. loan	$2,500

SIENA COLLEGE

515 Loudon Road, Loudonville, NY 12211 • Admissions: 518-783-2423 • Fax: 518-783-2436
• Financial Aid: 518-783-2427 • Web Site: www.siena.edu

Founded in 1937 by the Franciscans, Siena College sits on a 155-acre residential campus two miles from Albany, New York's capital. Siena offers twenty-four majors within three divisions: liberal arts, science, and business. Most popular disciplines include accounting, marketing and management, and biology. Noteworthy campus features include a residential townhouse complex; Friars live in all traditional housing units on campus. The college has over seventy registered clubs and organizations, offering a variety of performing arts groups, publications, film and radio, religious organizations, multicultural unions, and volunteer-community service opportunities. A broad selection of intercollegiate, intramural, and club sports are offered by the college; four-fifths of the student body participate. In what seems to be a Catholic tradition, men's basketball is, of course, Siena's most nationally competitive team. The college competes in the Metro Atlantic Athletic Conference, whose membership is comprised entirely of Catholic institutions.

ADMISSIONS

The admissions committee considers (in descending order of importance): HS record, class rank, recommendations, test scores, essay. *Also considered (in descending order of importance):* personality, alumni relationship, extracurriculars, special talents. Either the SAT or ACT is required. An interview is recommended. Admissions process is need-blind. *High school units required/recommended:* 19 total units are required; 23 total units are recommended; 4 English required, 3 math required, 4 math recommended, 3 science required, 4 science recommended, 2 foreign language required, 3 foreign language recommended, 4 social studies required, 3 history required, 4 history recommended. Additional units of math and science recommended.

FINANCIAL AID

Students should submit: FAFSA (due February 1), the school's own financial aid form (due February 1), state aid form (due February 1), a copy of parents' most recent income tax filing (due April 15). The Princeton Review suggests that all financial aid forms be submitted as soon as possible after January 1. *The following grants/scholarships are offered:* Pell, SEOG, academic merit, athletic, the school's own scholarships, the school's own grants, state scholarships, state grants, private scholarships, private grants, ROTC. *Students borrow from the following loan programs:* Stafford, unsubsidized Stafford, Perkins, PLUS, the school's own loan fund, supplemental loans, private loans. Applicants will be notified of awards beginning April 1. College Work-Study Program is available. Institutional employment is available. The off-campus job outlook is good.

STUDENT BODY		ACADEMICS		Deadlines		FINANCIAL FACTS	
Total undergrad enrollment	3,285	Calendar	semester	Regular admission	3/1	Tuition	$11,840
% male/female	46/54	Student/teacher ratio	13:1	Regular notification	3/15	Room & board	$5,435
% from out of state	15	FT faculty	255			Estimated book expense	$600
% transfers	5	% faculty from religious order	7	**FRESHMAN PROFILE**		% frosh receiving aid	79
% live on campus	64			Range ACT	22-26	% undergrads receiving aid	72
% African American	2	**Most Popular Majors**		Average ACT	24	% frosh w/ grant	66
% Asian	2	accounting		Minimum TOEFL	550	Avg. grant	$3,989
% Caucasian	94	marketing/management		Graduated top 10% of class	22	% frosh w/ loan	60
% Hispanic	2	biology		Graduated top 25% of class	59	Avg. loan	$2,556
% international	1	**ADMISSIONS**		Graduated top 50% of class	91		
# of countries represented	3	Admissions Rating	72				
		% of acceptees attending	32				

SIENA HEIGHTS COLLEGE

1247 E. Siena Hts. Drive, Adrian, MI 49221 • Admissions: 517-263-0731 • Fax: 517-264-7704
• Financial Aid: 517-264-7130 • Web Site: www.sienahts.edu

Siena Heights College was founded in 1919 by the Dominicans; it became coed in the late 1960s. The college's 440-acre campus is located thirty miles from Toledo and sixty miles from Detroit. Thirty-one majors are offered within the liberal arts and sciences, business, and education. Most popular academic options include human services, business administration, and English. Campus features worth noting include a Montessori school and an art gallery. There are thirty registered clubs and organizations on campus; activities are focused mainly on music and arts ensembles, publications, multicultural organizations, volunteer and social-action groups, and academic honor societies. Athletic teams at Siena Heights are dominant in intercollegiate competition. In 1994 the college won conference championships in every sport in which its teams competed. Men's baseball and basketball, and women's softball teams are all nationally ranked in the NAIA.

ADMISSIONS

The admissions committee considers (in descending order of importance): HS record, test scores, recommendations, class rank. *Also considered (in descending order of importance):* personality, alumni relationship, extracurriculars, special talents. Either the SAT or ACT is required; ACT is preferred. An interview is recommended. Admissions process is need-blind. *High school units required/recommended:* 4 English recommended, 2 math recommended, 1 science recommended, 2 foreign language recommended, 2 social studies recommended, 2 history recommended. Minimum composite ACT score of 17 and minimum 2.3 GPA required. *Special Requirements:* An audition is required for music program applicants.

FINANCIAL AID

Students should submit: FAFSA. The Princeton Review suggests that all financial aid forms be submitted as soon as possible after January 1. *The following grants/scholarships are offered:* Pell, SEOG, academic merit, athletic, the school's own scholarships, the school's own grants, state scholarships, state grants, private scholarships, private grants. *Students borrow from the following loan programs:* Stafford, unsubsidized Stafford, Perkins, PLUS, the school's own loan fund, supplemental loans, state loans, private loans. Applicants will be notified of awards beginning March 1. College Work-Study Program is available. Institutional employment is available. The off-campus job outlook is good.

STUDENT BODY		ACADEMICS		Deadlines		FINANCIAL FACTS	
Total undergrad enrollment	993	Calendar	semester	Regular admission	8/15	Tuition	$9,970
% male/female	45/55	Student/teacher ratio	8:1	Regular notification	rolling	Room & board	$4,220
% from out of state	16	FT faculty	140			Estimated book expense	$400
% from catholic high school	17	% faculty from religious order	1	**FRESHMAN PROFILE**		% frosh receiving aid	95
% live on campus	40			Average ACT	21	% undergrads receiving aid	86
% African American	4	**Most Popular Majors**		Minimum TOEFL	500		
% Asian	1	human services					
% Caucasian	88	business administration					
% Hispanic	7	English					
% international	2	**ADMISSIONS**					
# of countries represented	6	Admissions Rating	73				
		% of acceptees attending	52				

SPALDING UNIVERSITY

851 South Fourth Avenue, Louisville, KY 40203 • *Admissions: 502-585-7111* • *Fax: 502-585-7158*
• Financial Aid: Call-Admissions • *E-mail: admission@spalding28.win.net* • *Web Site: win.net/-spaldingu.*

Spalding University was founded in 1814 by the Sisters of Charity, and became coed in 1968. The university is located on a small campus in the heart of downtown Louisville. Spalding is primarily a commuter school, but maintains one coed residence hall. Twenty-nine majors are offered within five schools: arts and sciences, business, education, nursing and health sciences, and professional psychology and social work. Most popular academic disciplines are in the health sciences and education. Special facilities include an art gallery. Extracurricular activities focus on student government, performing arts groups, a student newspaper, and numerous student professional organizations. We can't help but mention the annual "Running of the Rodents," a race run with student-trained rats. Athletic teams are fielded in three sports each for men and women; Spalding competes in the Kentucky Intercollegiate Athletic Association of the NAIA.

ADMISSIONS

Special Requirements: TOEFL is required of all international students.

FINANCIAL AID

Students should submit: FAFSA (due March 1), the school's own financial aid form (due March 1), a copy of parents' most recent income tax filing (due March 1). The Princeton Review suggests that all financial aid forms be submitted as soon as possible after January 1. *Students borrow from the following loan programs:* Stafford, PLUS. College Work-Study Program is available.

STUDENT BODY		ACADEMICS		FRESHMAN PROFILE		FINANCIAL FACTS	
% from out of state	13	Calendar	semester	Average ACT	20	Tuition	$9,000
% live on campus	10	Student/teacher ratio	12:1	Minimum TOEFL	550	Room & board	$2,650
% African American	9	FT faculty	98	Graduated top 10% of class	10	Estimated book expense	$700
% Asian	1			Graduated top 25% of class	45	% frosh receiving aid	91
% Caucasian	90	**ADMISSIONS**		Graduated top 50% of class	85	% undergrads receiving aid	90
% international	1	Admissions Rating	66			% frosh w/ grant	66
		% of acceptees attending	48			Avg. grant	NR
						% frosh w/ loan	64
		Deadlines				Avg. loan	$3,152
		Regular admission	8/15				

SPRING HILL COLLEGE

4000 Dauphin Street, Mobile, AL 36608 • Admissions: 334-380-4000 • Fax: 334-460-2186
• Financial Aid: 334-380-3460 • E-mail: admit@sch.edu • Web Site: www.shc.edu

The first institution of higher learning in Alabama, Spring Hill College was founded in 1830 by the bishop of Mobile, and is now administered by the Jesuits. The college also enjoys a prominent position in Catholic higher education; it is the fifth oldest Catholic college in the U.S., and was the first Catholic college in the Southeast. The college's historic 500-acre campus is located in a seaport metropolitan area on the Gulf Coast, sixty miles from Pensacola, Florida. The college offers forty-two majors in the liberal arts and sciences, business, education, and nursing. Most popular academic programs include business management, communications, and biology. Facilities of note are an eighteen-hole golf course, a human relations center, and a public broadcasting station. Sixty-eight clubs and organizations are registered at Spring Hill, offering an impressive range of extracurricular options including numerous publications, the Spring Hill Ocean Research and Exploration Society, and a variety of performing arts groups. The college fields intercollegiate athletic teams in seven sports for men, six for women; noteworthy among sports offered is sailing.

ADMISSIONS

The admissions committee considers (in descending order of importance): HS record, test scores, class rank, recommendations, essay, *Also considered (in descending order of importance):* personality, alumni relationship, extracurriculars, geographical distribution, special talents. Either the SAT or ACT is required. An interview is recommended. Admissions process is need-blind. *High school units required/recommended:* 16 total units are required; 4 English required, 2 math required, 2 science required, 2 foreign language recommended, 2 social studies required, 2 history required. Additional units in math, science, and history recommended. Minimum combined SAT I score of 850 (composite ACT score of 20), rank in top half of secondary school class, and minimum 2.5 GPA required. *Special Requirements:* TOEFL is required of all international students.

FINANCIAL AID

Students should submit: FAFSA (due March 1), the school's own financial aid form (due March 1). The Princeton Review suggests that all financial aid forms be submitted as soon as possible after January 1. *The following grants/scholarships are offered:* Pell, SEOG, academic merit, athletic, the school's own scholarships, the school's own grants, state grants, private scholarships, private grants, ROTC, foreign aid. *Students borrow from the following loan programs:* Stafford, unsubsidized Stafford, Perkins, PLUS, the school's own loan fund, supplemental loans, private loans. Applicants will be notified of awards beginning March 1. College Work-Study Program is available. Institutional employment is available. The off-campus job outlook is good.

STUDENT BODY		ACADEMICS		% of applicants accepted	90	Graduated top 10% of class	25
Total undergrad enrollment	1,161	Calendar	semester	% of acceptees attending	36	Graduated top 25% of class	47
% male/female	44/56	Student/teacher ratio	13:1			Graduated top 50% of class	73
% from out of state	48	FT faculty	109	**Deadlines**			
% transfers	19	% faculty from religious order	33	Regular admission	rolling	**FINANCIAL FACTS**	
% from catholic high school	48	% graduate in 4 yrs.	63	Regular notification	rolling	Tuition	$12,420
% live on campus	68					Room & board	$4,960
% African American	7	**Most Popular Majors**		**FRESHMAN PROFILE**		Estimated book expense	$600
% Asian	1	business management		Range verbal SAT	510-600	% frosh receiving aid	70
% Caucasian	86	communication arts		Average verbal SAT	529	% undergrads receiving aid	68
% Hispanic	4	biology		Range math SAT	500-590	% frosh w/ grant	50
% international	2			Average math SAT	506	Avg. grant	$6,215
# of countries represented	5	**ADMISSIONS**		Range ACT	22-26	% frosh w/ loan	49
		Admissions Rating	70	Average ACT	23	Avg. loan	$3,434
		# of applicants	630	Minimum TOEFL	500		
				Average HS GPA or Avg	3.0		

STONEHILL COLLEGE

320 Washington Street, North Easton, MA 02357 • Admissions: 508-230-1373 • Fax: 508-230-3732
• Financial Aid: 508-565-1088 • Web Site: www.stonehill.edu

Stonehill College was founded in 1948 by the Congregation of the Holy Cross. The college is located on a 375-acre residential campus twenty miles from Boston. Thirty-one majors are available, most within the liberal arts and sciences, business, and education. Most popular disciplines are psychology, biology, and accounting. Facilities worth noting on campus include an institute of law and society, and an observatory. Forty-seven student-run clubs and organizations are offered on campus, including a chapter of Amnesty International, Habitat for Humanity, several publications and media groups, performing arts ensembles, and political and social-action groups. Athletic teams are fielded in ten sports each for men and women; noteworthy are equestrian and sailing teams, and a nationally ranked women's basketball team.

ADMISSIONS

The admissions committee considers (in descending order of importance): HS record, class rank, test scores, recommendations, essay. *Also considered (in descending order of importance):* alumni relationship, extracurriculars, geographical distribution, personality, special talents. Either the SAT or ACT is required. Admissions process is need-blind. *High school units required/recommended:* 16 total units are required; 4 English required, 2 math required, 1 science required, 2 foreign language required, 1 history required. Minimum combined SAT I score of 1000 and rank in top quarter of secondary school class recommended. *Special Requirements:* TOEFL is required of all international students. Additional units in science and math recommended of science program applicants.

FINANCIAL AID

Students should submit: FAFSA (due February 15), CSS Profile (due), state aid form, a copy of parents' most recent income tax filing (due March 15). The Princeton Review suggests that all financial aid forms be submitted as soon as possible after January 1. *The following grants/scholarships are offered:* Pell, SEOG, athletic, the school's own scholarships, the school's own grants, state scholarships, state grants, private scholarships, private grants. *Students borrow from the following loan programs:* Stafford, unsubsidized Stafford, Perkins, PLUS, the school's own loan fund, supplemental loans, private loans. Applicants will be notified of awards beginning April 1. College Work-Study Program is available. Institutional employment is available. The off-campus job outlook is good.

STUDENT BODY		ACADEMICS		Deadlines		FINANCIAL FACTS	
Total undergrad enrollment	2,833	Calendar	semester	Regular admission	2/1	Tuition	$13,720
% male/female	42/58	Student/teacher ratio	11:1	Regular notification	3/15 - 4/1	Room & board	$6,660
% from out of state	32	FT faculty	268			Estimated book expense	$522
% transfers	12	% faculty from religious order	8	**FRESHMAN PROFILE**		% frosh receiving aid	68
% live on campus	80	% graduate in 4 yrs.	79	Range verbal SAT	440-530	% undergrads receiving aid	67
% African American	1			Average verbal SAT	480	% frosh w/ grant	63
% Asian	1	**Most Popular Majors**		Range math SAT	490-590	Avg. grant	$4,793
% Caucasian	97	psychology		Average math SAT	530	% frosh w/ loan	82
% Hispanic	1	biology		Minimum TOEFL	550	Avg. loan	$3,165
% international	1	accounting		Graduated top 10% of class	23		
# of countries represented	17			Graduated top 25% of class	65		
		ADMISSIONS		Graduated top 50% of class	95		
		Admissions Rating	72				
		% of acceptees attending	23				

THOMAS MORE COLLEGE

Thomas More Parkway, Crestview Hills, KY 41017 • *Admissions: 606-344-3332* • *Fax: 606-344-3345*
• *Financial Aid: 606-344-3331* • *E-mail: corrigan@thomasmore.edu* • *Web Site: www.thomasmore.edu*

Thomas More College was founded in 1921 through a joint venture of the Sisters of Notre Dame, the Congregation of Divine Providence, and the Benedictine Sisters; it is now sponsored by the Diocese of Covington. It became coed in 1941. The college's 320-acre campus is located eight miles from Cincinnati, Ohio. Over twenty majors are offered at Thomas More, centered within the liberal arts and sciences, business, and health sciences. Popular majors include business administration, biology, and accounting. Campus facilities of note include an art gallery. Opportunities outside the classroom include thirty-six registered clubs and organizations. Activities include student government, a campus newspaper, performing arts organizations, social-action groups, and volunteer programs. Thomas More fields six intercollegiate athletic teams for men, five for women.

ADMISSIONS

The admissions committee considers (in descending order of importance): HS record, test scores, class rank, recommendations. *Also considered (in descending order of importance):* extracurriculars, personality, special talents, alumni relationship. Either the SAT or ACT is required. An interview is recommended. *High school units required/recommended:* 16 total units are required; 4 English recommended, 2 math recommended, 2 science recommended, 2 foreign language recommended, 2 social studies recommended. Minimum composite ACT score of 20 (combined SAT I score of 900), rank in top half of secondary school class, and minimum B average required.

FINANCIAL AID

Students should submit: FAFSA (due March 1), the school's own financial aid form (due March 1), state aid form. The Princeton Review suggests that all financial aid forms be submitted as soon as possible after January 1. *Students borrow from the following loan programs:* Stafford, PLUS. College Work-Study Program is available. Institutional employment is available. The off-campus job outlook is excellent.

STUDENT BODY

Total undergrad enrollment	1,258
% male/female	48/52
% from out of state	39
% live on campus	30
% African American	5
% Asian	1
% Caucasian	88
% Hispanic	1
% Native American	1
% international	2
# of countries represented	6

ACADEMICS

Calendar	semester
Student/teacher ratio	10:1
FT faculty	130
% faculty from religious order	10

Most Popular Majors
business administration
biology
accountancy

ADMISSIONS

Admissions Rating	70
% of acceptees attending	37

Deadlines

Regular admission	8/15
Regular notification	rolling

FRESHMAN PROFILE

Average verbal SAT	452
Average math SAT	512
Average ACT	23
Minimum TOEFL	515
Graduated top 10% of class	19
Graduated top 25% of class	43
Graduated top 50% of class	71

FINANCIAL FACTS

Tuition	$10,450
Room & board	$4,286
Estimated book expense	$500
% frosh receiving aid	68
% undergrads receiving aid	70
% frosh w/ grant	39
Avg. grant	NR
% frosh w/ loan	68
Avg. loan	$1,860

TRINITY COLLEGE (D.C.)

125 Michigan Avenue, NE, Washington, D.C. 200171094 • *Admissions: 202-884-9400* • *Fax: 202-939-5134*
• *Financial Aid: 202-884-9530*

The Sisters of Notre Dame de Namur founded Trinity College in 1897. The college admits women only, and is on a 26-acre campus in Washington's northeast section. Trinity offers twenty-one majors, primarily within the liberal arts and sciences, business, and education. Popular majors include business administration, political science, and psychology. The college adheres to an honor code. Facilities of note include an art gallery. There are thirty-five registered clubs and organizations at the College; among the activities offered are a range performing arts groups, political organizations, and publications. Intercollegiate athletic teams are fielded in seven sports. Trinity offers opportunities for study abroad in twenty-three foreign countries.

ADMISSIONS

The admissions committee considers (in descending order of importance): HS record, test scores, recommendations, essay, class rank. *Also considered (in descending order of importance):* extracurriculars, geographical distribution, personality, special talents, alumni relationship. Either the SAT or ACT is required. An interview is required. Admissions process is need-blind. *High school units required/recommended:* 17 total units are required; 4 English required, 3 math required, 2 science required, 3 foreign language required, 3 social studies required. Minimum combined SAT I score of 900, rank in top half of secondary school class, and minimum B average. *Special Requirements:* TOEFL is required of all international students.

FINANCIAL AID

Students should submit: FAFSA, state aid form, a copy of parents' most recent income tax filing (due June 15). The Princeton Review suggests that all financial aid forms be submitted as soon as possible after January 1. *The following grants/scholarships are offered:* Pell, SEOG, academic merit, the school's own scholarships, the school's own grants, state grants, private scholarships, private grants. *Students borrow from the following loan programs:* Stafford, Perkins, PLUS, private loans. College Work-Study Program is available. Institutional employment is available. The off-campus job outlook is excellent.

STUDENT BODY		ACADEMICS		Deadlines		FINANCIAL FACTS	
Total undergrad enrollment	309	Calendar	semester	Regular admission	3/1	Tuition	$11,750
% male/female	0/100	Student/teacher ratio	8:1	Regular notification	rolling	Room & board	$6,430
% from out of state	89	FT faculty	48			Estimated book expense	$1,000
% transfers	19	% graduate in 4 yrs.	75	**FRESHMAN PROFILE**		% frosh receiving aid	81
% live on campus	95			Average verbal SAT	560	% undergrads receiving aid	76
% African American	28	**Most Popular Majors**		Average math SAT	520	% frosh w/ grant	50
% Asian	4	business administration		Average ACT	24	Avg. grant	$6,000
% Caucasian	55	political science		Minimum TOEFL	500	% frosh w/ loan	69
% Hispanic	9	psychology		Average HS GPA or Avg	3.1	Avg. loan	$2,500
# of countries represented	7	**ADMISSIONS**					
		Admissions Rating	75				
		# of applicants	256				
		% of applicants accepted	85				
		% of acceptees attending	47				

TRINITY COLLEGE OF VERMONT

Colchester Avenue, Burlington, VT 05401 • Admissions: 802-658-0337 • Fax: 802-658-5446
• Financial Aid: 802-658-0337,-ext.-529 • E-mail: plaferri@charity.trinityvt.edu

Trinity College was founded as a women's college in 1925 by the Sisters of Mercy; men are admitted into the college's nontraditional program only. The college is situated on a 19-acre residential campus ten minutes from downtown Burlington, ninety miles from Montreal. Trinity awards degrees in twenty-four majors, most within the liberal arts and sciences, business, education, and health sciences. Business adminstration, psychology, and elementary education are the most popular academic programs. Campus facilities of note include a museum. The college's fourteen clubs and organizations offer a range of options for activities outside the classroom, among which are several community service organizations, performing arts ensembles, a peace and justice club, academic interest groups, and the U.S.-Canadian Multicultural Club. Trinity fields intercollegiate athletic teams in basketball and soccer.

ADMISSIONS

The admissions committee considers (in descending order of importance): HS record, test scores, class rank, recommendations, essay. *Also considered (in descending order of importance):* extracurriculars, personality, special talents, alumni relationship, geographical distribution. Either the SAT or ACT is required. An interview is recommended. Admissions process is need-blind. *High school units required/recommended:* 14 total units are recommended; 4 English recommended, 2 math recommended, 2 science recommended, 2 foreign language recommended, 2 social studies recommended, 2 history recommended. Minimum 2.0 GPA required.

FINANCIAL AID

Students should submit: FAFSA (due March 1), the school's own financial aid form (due March 1), state aid form (due March 1), Divorced Parents form, a copy of parents' most recent income tax filing (due March 1). The Princeton Review suggests that all financial aid forms be submitted as soon as possible after January 1. *Students borrow from the following loan programs:* Stafford, PLUS. Applicants will be notified of awards beginning April 1. College Work-Study Program is available. Institutional employment is available. The off-campus job outlook is good.

STUDENT BODY		ACADEMICS		ADMISSIONS		Graduated top 50% of class	73
Total undergrad enrollment	889	Calendar	semester	Admissions Rating	64	**FINANCIAL FACTS**	
% male/female	6/94	Student/teacher ratio	10:1	# of applicants	217	Tuition	$12,120
% from out of state	34	FT faculty	106	% of applicants accepted	94	Room & board	$6,012
% from catholic high school	8	% faculty from religious order	4	% of acceptees attending	50	Estimated book expense	$550
% live on campus	68	% graduate in 4 yrs.	57			% frosh receiving aid	76
% Caucasian	98			**Deadlines**		% undergrads receiving aid	76
% Native American	1	**Most Popular Majors**		Regular admission	rolling	% frosh w/ grant	94
% international	1	business administration		Regular notification	rolling	Avg. grant	NR
# of countries represented	6	psychology		**FRESHMAN PROFILE**		% frosh w/ loan	92
		elementary education		Average verbal SAT	420	Avg. loan	$2,949
				Average math SAT	430		
				Minimum TOEFL	550		
				Graduated top 10% of class	11		
				Graduated top 25% of class	36		

VILLANOVA UNIVERSITY

800 Lancaster Avenue, Villanova, PA 19085 • *Admissions: 610-519-4000* • *Fax: 610-519-6450*
• *Financial Aid: 610-519-4010* • *E-mail: gotovu@ucis.vill.edu* • *Web Site: www.vill.edu*

The Augustinians founded Villanova University in 1842. The university's impressive 222-acre campus is twelve miles from Philadelphia. Students may choose from fifty-five majors in four colleges: liberal arts and sciences, commerce and finance, engineering, and nursing. Among facilities and equipment worth noting are astronomy and astrophysics observatories, an art gallery, an electron microscope, and an arboretum. Villanova offers 130 clubs and organizations on campus, among them many musical ensembles, political groups, ethnic cultural organizations, numerous religious, social-action and volunteer groups, and twenty-eight honor societies. The university offers a wide variety of men's and women's intercollegiate athletic teams; intramural sports are also abundant. In what many consider to be the greatest upset in college basketball history, the Wildcats defeated Georgetown for the national championship in 1985. Women's cross-country won six consecutive national championships from 1989 to 1994. Villanova has produced over forty Olympic track-and-field athletes.

ADMISSIONS

The admissions committee considers (in descending order of importance): HS record, class rank, test scores, recommendations, essay. *Also considered (in descending order of importance):* alumni relationship, extracurriculars, geographical distribution, personality, special talents. Either the SAT or ACT is required; SAT is preferred. An interview is required. Admissions process is need-blind. *High school units required/recommended:* 16 total units are required; 4 English required, 3 math required, 4 math recommended, 2 science required, 3 science recommended, 2 foreign language required, 1 social studies required, 2 history required. *Special Requirements:* TOEFL is required of all international students. Interview required of pre-dental, pre-optometry, allied health, and accelerated medical school program applicants.

FINANCIAL AID

Students should submit: FAFSA (due February 15), the school's own financial aid form (due March 15), a copy of parents' most recent income tax filing (due March 15). The Princeton Review suggests that all financial aid forms be submitted as soon as possible after January 1. *The following grants/scholarships are offered:* Pell, SEOG, academic merit, the school's own scholarships, the school's own grants, state scholarships, state grants, private scholarships, private grants, foreign aid. *Students borrow from the following loan programs:* Stafford, unsubsidized Stafford, Perkins, PLUS, the school's own loan fund, supplemental loans, state loans, private loans. Applicants will be notified of awards beginning April 1. College Work-Study Program is available. Institutional employment is available. The off-campus job outlook is excellent.

STUDENT BODY		ACADEMICS		Deadlines		Room & board	$7,000
Total undergrad enrollment	6,000	Calendar	semester	Early decision/action	12/1	Estimated book expense	$800
% male/female	50/50	Student/teacher ratio	14:1	Regular admission	1/15	% frosh receiving aid	53
% from out of state	65	FT faculty	867	Regular notification	4/1	% undergrads receiving aid	53
% transfers	7	% faculty from religious order	10			% frosh w/ grant	50
% from catholic high school	45			**FRESHMAN PROFILE**		Avg. grant	$6,200
% live on campus	95	**Most Popular Majors**		Range verbal SAT	550-650	% frosh w/ loan	55
% African American	3	accountancy		Range math SAT	580-690	Avg. loan	$1,929
% Asian	4	nursing		Minimum TOEFL	550		
% Caucasian	90	finance		Average HS GPA or Avg	3.5		
% Hispanic	3	**ADMISSIONS**		Graduated top 10% of class	36		
% international	2	Admissions Rating	82	Graduated top 25% of class	63		
# of countries represented	51	# of applicants	9,247	Graduated top 50% of class	93		
		% of applicants accepted	65	**FINANCIAL FACTS**			
		% of acceptees attending	26	Tuition	$18,600		

VITERBO COLLEGE

815 South 9th Street, La Crosse, WI 54601 • Admissions: 608-791-0419 • Fax: 608-791-0433
• Financial Aid: 608-791-0487

Viterbo College was founded in 1890 by the Franciscan Sisters of Perpetual Adoration, Third Order Regular. The college is situated on a 6-acre campus. Fifty-four majors are offered through five schools at Viterbo: business, education, fine arts, letters and sciences, and nursing. Most popular of these offerings are nursing, business, and fine arts. Facilities of note include a fine arts center and a music museum. Forty clubs and organizations include student government, a variety of publications, musical ensembles, drama, dance, fellowship organization, and social groups. Viterbo fields intercollegiate athletic teams in baseball, basketball, and soccer for men; basketball, soccer, softball, and volleyball for women.

ADMISSIONS

The admissions committee considers (in descending order of importance): test scores, class rank, HS record, recommendations, essay. *Also considered (in descending order of importance):* special talents, extracurriculars, alumni relationship, personality. Either the SAT or ACT is required; ACT is preferred. An interview is required. *High school units required/recommended:* 16 total units are required; 4 English required, 2 math required, 2 science required, 2 social studies required. Minimum composite ACT score of 20, rank in top half of secondary school class, and minimum 2.5 GPA recommended. *Special Requirements:* A portfolio is required for art program applicants. An audition is required for music program applicants. TOEFL is required of all international students. Chemistry required of dietetics, medical technology, and nursing program applicants.

FINANCIAL AID

Students should submit: FAFSA, the school's own financial aid form. The Princeton Review suggests that all financial aid forms be submitted as soon as possible after January 1. *The following grants/scholarships are offered:* Pell, SEOG, the school's own scholarships, the school's own grants, state scholarships, state grants, private scholarships, private grants, foreign aid. *Students borrow from the following loan programs:* Stafford, unsubsidized Stafford, Perkins, PLUS, the school's own loan fund, supplemental loans, state loans, private loans. College Work-Study Program is available. Institutional employment is available. The off-campus job outlook is excellent.

STUDENT BODY

Total undergrad enrollment	1,042
% male/female	25/75
% from out of state	23
% transfers	27
% from catholic high school	30
% live on campus	60
% African American	1
% Asian	1
% Caucasian	95
% Hispanic	1
% international	1
# of countries represented	8

ACADEMICS

Calendar	semester
Student/teacher ratio	11:1
FT faculty	105
% faculty from religious order	2

Most Popular Majors
nursing
business
fine arts

ADMISSIONS

Admissions Rating	65
% of acceptees attending	52

Deadlines

Early decision/action	12/15
Regular admission	8/1
Regular notification	rolling

FRESHMAN PROFILE

Average verbal SAT	450
Average math SAT	400
Minimum TOEFL	550
Graduated top 10% of class	18
Graduated top 25% of class	52
Graduated top 50% of class	70

FINANCIAL FACTS

Tuition	$9,780

Room & board	$3,750
Estimated book expense	$600
% frosh receiving aid	95
% undergrads receiving aid	97

WALSH UNIVERSITY

2020 Easton Street NW, North Canton, OH 44720 • Admissions: 330-490-7172 • Fax: 330-490-7165
• Financial Aid: 800-362-9846 • E-mail: admissions@walsh.edu • Web Site: www.walsh.edu

Founded in 1958 by the Christian Brothers, Walsh University was named for Bishop Emmet M. Walsh of the Diocese of Youngstown. The university is on a 58-acre campus twenty miles from Akron, sixty miles from Cleveland. More than a third of the university's student body are nontraditional students, older than typical college age. Walsh offers fifty-one majors, primarily within the liberal arts and sciences, business, education, and nursing. The most popular majors are business, nursing, and education. Facilities of note on campus include a new residence hall with apartment-style suites and newly donated land that will nearly doubled the size of the campus. Clubs and organizations at Walsh are numerous. Among the activities offered are a range of performing arts groups, publications, campus ministry, and volunteer groups, including Habitat for Humanity. Intercollegiate athletic teams are fielded in eight sports each for men and women. During the 1995–96 school year, the Walsh Cavaliers won championships in men's basketball, and men's and women's tennis.

ADMISSIONS

The admissions committee considers (in descending order of importance): HS record, test scores, essay, class rank, recommendations. *Also considered (in descending order of importance):* alumni relationship, extracurriculars, personality, special talents. Either the SAT or ACT is required; ACT is preferred. An interview is recommended. Admissions process is need-blind. *High school units required/recommended:* 16 total units are required; 4 English required, 3 math required, 3 science required, 2 foreign language required, 3 social studies required. Minimum composite ACT score of 18 and minimum 2.5 GPA recommended. *Special Requirements:* TOEFL is required of all international students.

FINANCIAL AID

Students should submit: FAFSA, the school's own financial aid form. The Princeton Review suggests that all financial aid forms be submitted as soon as possible after January 1. *The following grants/scholarships are offered:* state scholarships. *Students borrow from the following loan programs:* Stafford, PLUS. College Work-Study Program is available. Institutional employment is available. The off-campus job outlook is good.

STUDENT BODY		ACADEMICS		ADMISSIONS		FINANCIAL FACTS	
Total undergrad enrollment	1,261	Calendar	semester	Admissions Rating	70	Tuition	$9,900
% male/female	46/54	Student/teacher ratio	12:1	% of acceptees attending	176	Room & board	$4,760
% from out of state	15	FT faculty	125			Estimated book expense	$500
% transfers	29	% faculty from religious order	5	**Deadlines**		% frosh receiving aid	85
% live on campus	30	% graduate in 4 yrs.	53	Regular admission	rolling	% undergrads receiving aid	85
% African American	6			Regular notification	rolling	% frosh w/ grant	38
% Asian	3	**Most Popular Majors**				Avg. grant	NR
% Caucasian	91	business		**FRESHMAN PROFILE**		% frosh w/ loan	60
% international	3	nursing		Average ACT	21	Avg. loan	$2,862
# of countries represented	11	education		Minimum TOEFL	550		

WHEELING JESUIT UNIVERSITY

316 Washington Avenue, Wheeling, WV 26003 • Admissions: 304-243-2359 • Fax: 304-234-2243
• Financial Aid: 304-243-2304 • E-mail: admissions@wic.edu • Web Site: www.wju.edu

Wheeling Jesuit University was founded in 1954 as a coed university; it is the only Jesuit school to admit women from its inception. The university lies on a 70-acre campus sixty miles from Pittsburgh. Wheeling offers thirty-eight majors in the liberal arts and sciences, business, and health sciences. Most popular academic programs include psychology, nursing, and biology. A variety of clubs and organizations are registered at the University, offering a range of extracurricular options; among them are music and arts activities, cultural groups, volunteer and community service groups, and a student-run bar. Wheeling competes in intercollegiate athletics in six sports for men, seven for women. NASA's National Technology Transfer Center, the Classroom of the Future, and Center for Educational Technologies Laboratories are all located on the Wheeling Jesuit campus.

ADMISSIONS

The admissions committee considers (in descending order of importance): HS record, class rank, test scores, recommendations. *Also considered (in descending order of importance):* extracurriculars, personality, alumni relationship, special talents. Either the SAT or ACT is required. An interview is recommended. Admissions process is need-blind. *High school units required/recommended:* 17 total units are required; 4 English required, 2 math required, 3 math recommended, 1 science required, 2 science recommended, 2 foreign language recommended, 2 social studies required. Minimum combined SAT I score of 850 (composite ACT score of 20), rank in top half of secondary school class, and minimum 2.0 GPA required.

FINANCIAL AID

Students should submit: FAFSA (due March 1), state aid form. The Princeton Review suggests that all financial aid forms be submitted as soon as possible after January 1. *The following grants/scholarships are offered:* Pell, SEOG, academic merit, athletic, the school's own scholarships, the school's own grants, state scholarships, state grants, private scholarships, private grants, federal nursing scholarship, foreign aid. *Students borrow from the following loan programs:* Stafford, unsubsidized Stafford, Perkins, PLUS, the school's own loan fund, supplemental loans, federal nursing loans, private loans. College Work-Study Program is available. Institutional employment is available. The off-campus job outlook is fair.

STUDENT BODY

Total undergrad enrollment	1,296
% male/female	41/59
% from out of state	60
% transfers	17
% live on campus	65
% African American	1
% Asian	1
% Caucasian	93
% Hispanic	2
% international	5
# of countries represented	19

ACADEMICS

Calendar	semester
Student/teacher ratio	16:1
FT faculty	90
% faculty from religious order	9
% graduate in 4 yrs.	64

Most Popular Majors
psychology
nursing
biology

ADMISSIONS

Admissions Rating	70
% of acceptees attending	40

Deadlines

Regular admission	rolling
Regular notification	rolling

FRESHMAN PROFILE

Average verbal SAT	441
Average math SAT	493
Minimum TOEFL	550
Graduated top 10% of class	21
Graduated top 25% of class	41
Graduated top 50% of class	83

FINANCIAL FACTS

Tuition	$13,000
Room & board	$4,870
Estimated book expense	$600
% frosh receiving aid	80
% undergrads receiving aid	78
% frosh w/ grant	78
Avg. grant	$5,461
% frosh w/ loan	78
Avg. loan	$3,193

XAVIER UNIVERSITY (OH)

3800 Victory Parkway, Cincinnati, OH 45207 • *Admissions: 513-745-3301* • *Fax: 513-745-2969*
• *Financial Aid: 513-745-3142* • *E-mail: xuadmit@admin.xu.edu* • *Web Site: www.xavier.xu.edu*

The Jesuits founded Xavier University in 1831. The university is located on a 100-acre campus, five miles from Cincinnati's downtown. Fifty majors within the liberal arts and sciences, business, education, health sciences, and a variety of career-oriented disciplines are available at Xavier. Most popular of these academic offerings are liberal arts, marketing, and communications. A very high percentage of students at Xavier go on to graduate school. Noteworthy campus facilities include a student-run professional art gallery, an observatory, and a Montessori laboratory school. A bountiful variety of one hundred clubs and organizations are registered on campus, among them numerous performing arts organizations, several publications, radio and film, student volunteer services, campus ministry, and ethnic cultural groups. Athletic teams are fielded in eight sports each for men and women in the Atlantic Ten Conference; men's basketball is nationally competitive.

ADMISSIONS

The admissions committee considers (in descending order of importance): HS record, test scores, recommendations, class rank. *Also considered (in descending order of importance):* extracurriculars, alumni relationship, personality, special talents. Either the SAT or ACT is required. An interview is recommended. Admissions process is need-blind. *High school units required/recommended:* 15 total units are required; 4 English required, 2 math required, 2 science required, 2 foreign language required, 3 social studies required. Minimum composite ACT score of 20 (combined SAT I score of 800) and minimum 2.4 GPA recommmended.

FINANCIAL AID

Students should submit: FAFSA (due February 15), state aid form (due February 15). The Princeton Review suggests that all financial aid forms be submitted as soon as possible after January 1. *The following grants/ scholarships are offered:* state scholarships. *Students borrow from the following loan programs:* Stafford, PLUS. Applicants will be notified of awards beginning March 1. College Work-Study Program is available. Institutional employment is available. The off-campus job outlook is excellent.

STUDENT BODY		ACADEMICS		Deadlines		FINANCIAL FACTS	
Total undergrad enrollment	3,956	Calendar	semester	Regular admission	8/1	Tuition	$12,950
% male/female	46/54	Student/teacher ratio	14:1	Regular notification	rolling	Room & board	$5,480
% from out of state	30	FT faculty	442	**FRESHMAN PROFILE**		Estimated book expense	$650
% transfers	17	% faculty from religious order	13	Range verbal SAT	420-540	% frosh receiving aid	86
% live on campus	50			Average verbal SAT	475	% undergrads receiving aid	83
% African American	6	**Most Popular Majors**		Range math SAT	450-600	% frosh w/ grant	27
% Asian	2	liberal arts		Average math SAT	521	Avg. grant	NR
% Caucasian	70	marketing		Range ACT	21-27	% frosh w/ loan	31
% Hispanic	2	communications		Minimum TOEFL	525	Avg. loan	$1,914
% Native American	1	**ADMISSIONS**		Graduated top 10% of class	28		
% international	2	Admissions Rating	74	Graduated top 25% of class	52		
# of countries represented	50	% of acceptees attending	39	Graduated top 50% of class	75		

XAVIER UNIVERSITY OF LOUISIANA

7325 Palmetto Street, New Orleans, LA 70125 • Admissions: 504-483-7411 • Fax: 504-482-2740
• Financial Aid: 504-483-3517 • E-mail: apply@xula.edu • Web Site: www.xu.edu

Xavier University of Louisiana was founded in 1925 by the Sisters of the Blessed Sacrament; it is the only predominantly black Catholic university in the Western Hemisphere. The university's 29-acre commuter campus is located minutes from downtown New Orleans. Xavier offers forty-one majors within two undergraduate colleges: arts and sciences, and pharmacy. Among the most popular majors are biology, psychology, and chemistry. That should come as no surprise; Xavier ranks first in the nation in the number of African American students earning degrees in the physical sciences, and first nationally in the placement of African American graduates into both pharmacy and medical schools. The university has educated nearly twenty-five percent of all African American pharmacists in the country. Students needing a break from the rigors of academe can take advantage of the university's fifty-nine clubs and organizations. Intercollegiate athletics are offered in basketball, cross-country, and tennis for both men and women; intramural and club sports can also be found on campus.

ADMISSIONS

The admissions committee considers (in descending order of importance): HS record, test scores, class rank, recommendations, essay. *Also considered (in descending order of importance):* personality, extracurriculars, special talents. Either the SAT or ACT is required. Admissions process is need-blind. *High school units required/recommended:* 16 total units are required; 4 English required, 2 math required, 1 science required, 1 social studies required. Additional units of math, social studies, and foreign language recommended. Minimum composite ACT score of 16 and minimum 2.0 GPA required. *Special Requirements:* A portfolio is required for art program applicants. An audition is required for music program applicants.

FINANCIAL AID

Students should submit: FAFSA (due April 1), the school's own financial aid form. The Princeton Review suggests that all financial aid forms be submitted as soon as possible after January 1. *The following grants/scholarships are offered:* Pell, SEOG, academic merit, athletic, the school's own scholarships, the school's own grants, state scholarships, state grants, private scholarships, private grants, federal nursing scholarship, ROTC, United Negro College Fund. *Students borrow from the following loan programs:* Stafford, unsubsidized Stafford, Perkins, PLUS, the school's own loan fund, supplemental loans, state loans, private loans. Applicants will be notified of awards beginning June 15. College Work-Study Program is available. Institutional employment is available. The off-campus job outlook is good.

STUDENT BODY

Total undergrad enrollment	2,956
% male/female	29/71
% from out of state	43
% transfers	3
% live on campus	33
% African American	97
% Asian	1
% Caucasian	1
% Hispanic	1
% international	1

ACADEMICS

Calendar	semester
Student/teacher ratio	14:1

FT faculty	258
% faculty from religious order	6
% graduate in 4 yrs.	66

Most Popular Majors

biology/pre-med
psychology
chemistry/pre-med

ADMISSIONS

Admissions Rating	71
# of applicants	3,072
% of applicants accepted	81
% of acceptees attending	32

Deadlines

Regular admission	3/1
Regular notification	4/1

FRESHMAN PROFILE

Range verbal SAT	460-580
Average verbal SAT	517
Range math SAT	440-560
Average math SAT	501
Range ACT	18-24
Average ACT	20
Minimum TOEFL	550
Average HS GPA or Avg	3.0

FINANCIAL FACTS

Tuition	$7,700
Room & board	$4,700
Estimated book expense	$650
% frosh receiving aid	80
% undergrads receiving aid	85
% frosh w/ grant	49
Avg. grant	$1,700
% frosh w/ loan	62
Avg. loan	$2,791

ALBERTUS MAGNUS COLLEGE

700 Prospect Street, New Haven, CT 06511 • Admissions: 203-773-8501 • Fax: 203-785-8652
• Financial Aid: Call-Admissions • E-mail: admissions@albertus.edu • Web Site: albertus.edu

Albertus Magnus is located on a 40-acre campus, ninety miles from New York City. Originally a women's college, it was founded in 1925 by the Dominican Sisters, and became coed in 1986. The college offers over twenty-five majors, and its advantageous location affords many opportunities for internships. Albertus Magnus athletic teams compete in NCAA Division III, and enjoy the use of impressive facilities for a school of this size. A unique "tri-session plan" gives students the option of graduating in three years by enrolling in three academic terms each year instead of two. Not that everyone's in a hurry to leave—on-campus housing consists of estate homes that have been converted to student residences.

STUDENT BODY

% from out of state	27
% from catholic high school	40
% live on campus	60
% African American	10
% Asian	1
% Caucasian	83
% Hispanic	3
% Native American	1

ACADEMICS

Calendar	trimester
Student/teacher ratio	27:1
FT faculty	44
% faculty from religious order	2

ADMISSIONS

Admissions Rating	79
# of applicants	583
% of applicants accepted	47
% of acceptees attending	46

Deadlines

Regular admission	rolling

FRESHMAN PROFILE

Range verbal SAT	570-440
Average verbal SAT	525
Range math SAT	550-430
Average math SAT	510
Average ACT	23
Minimum TOEFL	500
Average HS GPA or Avg	2.7
Graduated top 10% of class	19
Graduated top 25% of class	52
Graduated top 50% of class	93

FINANCIAL FACTS

Tuition	$13,000
Room & board	$5,836
Estimated book expense	$600
% frosh receiving aid	80
% undergrads receiving aid	63
% frosh w/ grant	80
Avg. grant	NR
% frosh w/ loan	80
Avg. loan	$2,533

AVILA COLLEGE

11901 Wornall Road, Kansas City, MO 64145 • Admissions: 816-942-8400 • Fax: 816-942-3362
• Financial Aid: Call-Admissions • E-mail: admissions@mail.avila.edu • Web Site: avila.edu

Founded in 1916 by the Sisters of Saint Joseph of Carondelet, Avila College is situated on a 50-acre campus in a residential neighborhood ten miles from downtown. The first private women's college in Kansas City, it became coed in 1969. Avila is proud of its dedication to providing both a classic liberal arts experience and practical career training. The college offers forty undergraduate degree programs in a broad range of both liberal arts and career-oriented disciplines, including such majors as business administration and management, clinical laboratory science, and medical radiologic technology. Noteworthy campus facilities include a theater and art gallery, but the college also makes available to its students a radiological laboratory and media production facilities—rare at a college of this size. The campus ministry is active both on and off-campus; students travel to places such as Mexico to provide services and messages of hope to others. All students are encouraged to volunteer their time and talents to area nonprofit agencies.

STUDENT BODY

% from out of state	26
% from catholic high school	23
% live on campus	13
% African American	9
% Asian	1
% Caucasian	87
% Hispanic	2
% Native American	1
% international	4

ACADEMICS

Calendar	semester
Student/teacher ratio	9:1
FT faculty	142
% faculty from religious order	50
% graduate in 4 yrs.	47

ADMISSIONS

Admissions Rating	70
# of applicants	308
% of applicants accepted	91
% of acceptees attending	33

Deadlines

Regular admission	rolling

FRESHMAN PROFILE

Range ACT	19-25
Average ACT	22
Minimum TOEFL	550
Average HS GPA or Avg	3.2
Graduated top 10% of class	13
Graduated top 25% of class	51
Graduated top 50% of class	78

FINANCIAL FACTS

Tuition	$10,100
Room & board	$4,150
Estimated book expense	$600
% frosh receiving aid	95
% undergrads receiving aid	85
% frosh w/ grant	76
Avg. grant	$4,095
% frosh w/ loan	72
Avg. loan	$3,200

BAYAMON CENTRAL UNIVERSITY

PO Box 1725, Bayamon, PR 00960 • Admissions: 809-786-3030 • Fax: 809-740-2200
• Financial Aid: Call-Admissions

Founded in 1970 and affiliated with the Dominican Fathers, Bayamon Central University began as a satellite campus for the Catholic University of Puerto Rico. The university's 54-acre campus is on a hill overlooking the city of Bayamon, one of Puerto Rico's largest cities, just a few miles from San Juan. Bayamon Central offers over twenty-eight majors in disciplines ranging from the liberal arts and sciences to business and education. The university seeks to preserve and develop the riches of the Spanish language and culture, thus all classroom instruction is in Spanish and the core curriculum includes Spanish language courses. (Fluency in Spanish is a requirement for admission; nearly all students here are from Spanish-speaking families.) Most students come from the Bayamon area. There is no on-campus housing, but the university does provide assistance in finding local lodging for students who come from a distance. Facilities at Bayamon Central include a library of the Dominican Order.

BRESCIA COLLEGE

717 Frederica Street, Owensboro, KY 42301 • Admissions: 502-686-4241 • Fax: 502-686-4266
• Financial Aid: Call-Admissions • E-mail: admissions@brescia.edu • Web Site: brescia.edu

Brescia College was founded in 1950 by the Ursuline Sisters of Mount Saint Joseph (originally from Brescia, Italy). The college's small campus is located in western Kentucky, between Evansville, Indiana and Louisville, about two hours north of Nashville, Tennessee. Over two dozen majors are offered at the college in disciplines that include the liberal arts and sciences, business, and education. Popular programs include business, education, and psychology. All freshmen participate in assessment that enables them to identify possible career options. Brescia guarantees that students who complete its career development program will attain a job or gain acceptance to graduate school within twelve months of graduation. If unsuccessful in this regard, graduates can return to the college to pursue additional coursework on a tuition-free basis. Residential life here is also noteworthy; housing consists of a series of large homes on the edge of the campus, each of which accommodates a small group of students.

STUDENT BODY

% from out of state	14
% from catholic high school	20
% live on campus	16
% African American	2
% Asian	1
% Caucasian	94
% Hispanic	1
% Native American	1
% international	1

ACADEMICS

Calendar	semester
Student/teacher ratio	11:1
FT faculty	59
% faculty from religious order	10
% graduate in 4 yrs.	50

ADMISSIONS

Admissions Rating	72
# of applicants	221
% of applicants accepted	84
% of acceptees attending	45

Deadlines

Regular admission	rolling

FRESHMAN PROFILE

Range ACT	18-25
Average ACT	22
Minimum TOEFL	500
Average HS GPA or Avg	3.3
Graduated top 10% of class	18
Graduated top 25% of class	55
Graduated top 50% of class	86

FINANCIAL FACTS

Tuition	$8,400
Room & board	$3,456
Estimated book expense	$700
% frosh receiving aid	39
% undergrads receiving aid	59

BRIAR CLIFF COLLEGE

3303 Rebecca Street Box 2100, Sioux City, IA 51104 • Admissions: 712-279-5200 • Fax: 712-279-5410
• Financial Aid: Call-Admissions • E-mail: dieger@briar cliff.edu • Web Site: briar.cliff.edu

Briar Cliff College was founded in 1930, and became coed in 1966. Minutes from downtown Sioux City, the college is located on a 70-acre campus near the point where the states of Iowa, Nebraska, and South Dakota converge. Briar Cliff was founded by the Franciscans, with the assistance of members of the Sioux City business community who committed themselves to raising funds to support the college. In the Franciscan tradition of service—caring and openness to all—Briar Cliff emphasizes combining a broad intellectual background with career development. The college offers twenty-eight academic programs; among the most popular disciplines are business, nursing, and education. Extracurricular opportunities are of a wide variety, including a campus magazine, film, radio, television groups, music ensembles, a volunteer bureau, and organizations devoted to politics, religion, and ethnic relations. Community service is given particular emphasis through the BCCares program.

STUDENT BODY		ACADEMICS					
% from out of state	28	Calendar	quarter	% of applicants accepted	85	Graduated top 10% of class	8
% live on campus	69	Student/teacher ratio	14:1	% of acceptees attending	48	Graduated top 25% of class	33
% African American	2	FT faculty	80			Graduated top 50% of class	65
% Asian	1	% faculty from religious order	7	**Deadlines**			
% Caucasian	92	% graduate in 4 yrs.	46	Regular admission	9/1	**FINANCIAL FACTS**	
% Hispanic	2					Tuition	$11,280
% Native American	1	**ADMISSIONS**		**FRESHMAN PROFILE**		Room & board	$3,912
% international	8	Admissions Rating	72	Average ACT	22	Estimated book expense	$600
		# of applicants	453	Minimum TOEFL	500	% frosh receiving aid	95
				Average HS GPA or Avg	3.1	% undergrads receiving aid	95

CHRISTENDOM COLLEGE

134 Christendom Drive, Front Royal, VA 22630 • Admissions: 540-636-2900 • Fax: 540-636-1655
• Financial Aid: Call-Admissions • E-mail: cc-adm@shentel.ent • Web Site: www.crnet.org/christdm/christdm.htm

Christendom College is unique among U.S. Catholic institutions of higher learning. The college was founded in 1977 by lay Catholics, and is under the authority of the Bishop of Arlington. Located in northern Virginia, about an hour from Washington, Christendom's 100-acre campus sits on the banks of the Shenendoah River. Prayer and worship are a normal part of everyday life at Christendom; before every class there is prayer and before every meal there is grace. Mass is offered twice a day, along with daily exposition of the Blessed Sacrament and a Rosary; on first Fridays there is all-night adoration. Students follow a dress code. The college offers seven majors: classics, English, French, history, philosophy, political science and government, and theological studies. Christendom's small size limits the scope of extracurricular offerings, but those activities that are available provide a worthwhile range of options.

EDGEWOOD COLLEGE

855 Woodrow Street, Madison, WI 53711 • Admissions: 608-257-4861 • Fax: 608-257-1455
• Financial Aid: Call-Admissions

Edgewood College was founded in 1881 by the Dominican Sisters of Sinsinawa as a school for girls. It became a junior college in 1927, expanded into a four-year college in 1941, and went coed in 1970. The college is located on a 55-acre campus eighty-two miles from Milwaukee. Forty-nine majors are offered, mainly within the areas of liberal arts and sciences, business, education, and nursing. The most popular academic areas are the latter three—business, education, and nursing. Noteworthy facilities include a biological research station and an art gallery. The college's many extracurricular activities include several social-action groups, among them Amnesty International and Habitat for Humanity, and a variety of musical offerings.

STUDENT BODY

% from out of state	10
% live on campus	33
% African American	2
% Asian	3
% Caucasian	72
% Hispanic	1
% international	5

ACADEMICS

Calendar	4-1-4
Student/teacher ratio	13:1
FT faculty	144
% faculty from religious order	4
% graduate in 4 yrs.	36

ADMISSIONS

Deadlines

Regular admission	8/1

FRESHMAN PROFILE

Range ACT	17-25
Minimum TOEFL	550
Graduated top 10% of class	24
Graduated top 25% of class	63
Graduated top 50% of class	94

FINANCIAL FACTS

Tuition	$9,000
Room & board	$3,800
Estimated book expense	$600
% frosh receiving aid	80
% undergrads receiving aid	80

KANSAS NEWMAN COLLEGE

3100 McCormick Ave., Wichita, KS 67213 • Admissions: 316-942-4291 • Fax: 316-942-4483
• Financial Aid: Call-Admissions • E-mail: harrisd@ksnewman.edu • Web Site: ksnewman.edu

Kansas Newman College was founded in 1933 by the Sisters Adoresses of the Blood of Christ. The college is located on a 51-acre campus ten minutes from downtown Wichita. Kansas Newman offers twenty-six majors, mainly within the liberal arts and sciences, business, education, and health sciences. Most popular among these offerings are health sciences, business, and education. Facilities of note are a planetarium and a photography lab. Clubs and organizations on campus include musical ensembles, theater and dance, and a variety of media. Athletic teams are fielded in three sports for men, four for women.

STUDENT BODY

% from out of state	9
% from catholic high school	10
% live on campus	10
% African American	5
% Asian	1
% Caucasian	88
% Hispanic	4
% Native American	2
% international	1

ACADEMICS

Calendar	semester
Student/teacher ratio	7:1
FT faculty	262

ADMISSIONS

Deadlines

Regular admission	rolling

FRESHMAN PROFILE

Average verbal SAT	414
Average math SAT	466
Average ACT	22
Minimum TOEFL	530
Graduated top 10% of class	20
Graduated top 25% of class	52
Graduated top 50% of class	80

FINANCIAL FACTS

Tuition	$8,500
Room & board	$3,770
Estimated book expense	$780
% frosh receiving aid	97
% undergrads receiving aid	70

MARYLHURST COLLEGE

P.O. Box 261, Marylhurst, OR 97036 • Admissions: 503-636-8141 • Fax: 503-636-9526
• Financial Aid: Call-Admissions

Marylhurst College was founded in 1893 by the Sisters of the Holy Names of Jesus and Mary, and was the first liberal arts college for women in the Pacific Northwest. It became coed in 1974. On the banks of the Willamette River, this commuter campus is located ten miles from Portland. The majority of undergraduate students are transfers. Students may choose from fourteen majors within the liberal arts and sciences, and business. The most noteworthy academic options are art therapy and communications. Extracurricular activities center around music, career-oriented groups, and the campus ministry. The college does not compete in intercollegiate sports, and offers no intramural or club sports.

STUDENT BODY		ACADEMICS		ADMISSIONS		FRESHMAN PROFILE	
% from out of state	3	Calendar	quarter	**Deadlines**		**FINANCIAL FACTS**	
% African American	1	Student/teacher ratio	6:1	Regular admission	rolling	Tuition	$8,955
% Asian	1	FT faculty	234			Estimated book expense	$600
% Caucasian	94					% frosh receiving aid	65
% Hispanic	1					% undergrads receiving aid	65
% Native American	1						
% international	1						

MOUNT ALOYSIUS COLLEGE

7373 Admiral Peary Highway, Cresson, PA 16630 • Admissions: 814-886-4131 • Fax: 814-886-2978
• Financial Aid: Call-Admissions

The Sisters of Mercy founded Mount Aloysius College in 1939. The 125-acre campus is twelve miles from Altoona and thirty miles from Johnstown. While housing is available, the majority of the college's students are commuters. Mount Aloysius offers twenty-four majors, most of which are two-year programs in health sciences; bachelor's degrees are offered in the liberal arts and sciences, and nursing. The health sciences and business majors are the most popular programs. A new health and science facility is among noteworthy campus features; a new library was opened in 1995. Fifteen clubs and organizations at the college include numerous music groups, several career-oriented academic clubs, and a children's advocacy group. Mount Aloysius competes in the National Junior College Athletic Association (NJCAA) in men's basketball. Intramural baseball, tennis, basketball, and women's club volleyball are also available.

MOUNT MARY COLLEGE

2900 N. Menomonee River Pkwy, Milwaukee, WI 53222 • Admissions: 414-258-4810 • Fax: 414-256-1224
• Financial Aid: Call-Admissions • E-mail: reilly@mtmary.edu • Web Site: mtmary.edu

Mount Mary College was founded in 1913 by the Sisters of Notre Dame; it's Wisconsin's oldest liberal arts college for women. The college's 80-acre campus, located in a residential area of Milwaukee, is seven miles from downtown. Thirty degree programs are offered, mainly within the liberal arts and sciences, business, and education. Of note are majors in interior design, hotel and restaurant management, and fashion design and illustration. Extracurriculars include student government, several publications, music groups, and cultural organizations. The Living Water Campus Ministry offers students the opportunity for community outreach. Intercollegiate athletic teams compete for Mount Mary in five sports—fencing, soccer, softball, tennis, and volleyball.

STUDENT BODY

% from out of state	11
% from catholic high school	18
% live on campus	15
% African American	6
% Asian	2
% Caucasian	88
% Hispanic	2
% international	1

ACADEMICS

Calendar	semester
Student/teacher ratio	8:1
FT faculty	152
% faculty from religious order	31
% graduate in 4 yrs.	4

ADMISSIONS

Admissions Rating	74
# of applicants	193
% of applicants accepted	85
% of acceptees attending	53

Deadlines

Regular admission	8/15

FRESHMAN PROFILE

Average ACT	23
Minimum TOEFL	500
Average HS GPA or Avg	3.0
Graduated top 10% of class	16
Graduated top 25% of class	32
Graduated top 50% of class	65

FINANCIAL FACTS

Tuition	$10,230
Room & board	$3,490
Estimated book expense	$500
% frosh receiving aid	93
% undergrads receiving aid	69
% frosh w/ grant	75
Avg. grant	$3,300
% frosh w/ loan	64
Avg. loan	$2,235

PONTIFICAL CATHOLIC UNIVERSITY

2250 Las Americas Avenue, Suite 584, Ponce, PR 00731 • Admissions: 809-841-2000 • Fax: 809-840-4295
• Financial Aid: Call-Admissions

Pontifical Catholic University of Puerto Rico was founded in 1948 by the Diocese of San Juan, and is the largest Catholic university in the Caribbean. The bilingual university's 79-acre commuter campus is sixty miles south of San Juan. Pontifical Catholic University is regarded by many as the center of Catholic thought on the island; the university's Encarnación Valdés Library houses a Puerto Rican collection containing a vast selection of documents and publications relating to the Commonwealth. PCU offers forty-six majors within the areas of liberal arts and sciences, business, education, and nursing; most popular areas of study include business, education, and social science. A variety of clubs and organizations offer the standard complement of college activities, including student government, music and arts groups, television, radio, and a number of academic honor societies and religious organizations. Intercollegiate athletic offerings include thirteen sports for men and eleven for women—among them are table tennis and men's water polo.

PRESENTATION COLLEGE

1500 North Main Street, Aberdeen, SD 57401 • Admissions: 605-225-0420 • Fax: 605-229-8489
• Financial Aid: Call-Admissions

Presentation College was founded in 1951 by the Sisters of the Presentation of the Blessed Virgin Mary, and became coed in 1968. The college is located on a 100-acre commuter campus. Presentation also has a campus on the Lakota reservation offering coursework in several areas and an associate's degree in nursing. Five bachelor's degree programs and a variety of two-year associate's degrees are offered, primarily within the health sciences, business, and education. The most popular majors are overwhelmingly those offered within the health sciences. Activities include a student newspaper, student government, yearbook, music and arts groups, and a Native American club. Men's and women's basketball are the only intercollegiate athletic teams; intramurals are offered in basketball, table tennis, and volleyball.

UNIVERSITY OF THE SACRED HEART

P.O. Box 12383, Loiza Station, Santurce, PR 00914 • Admissions: 809-728-1602
• Financial Aid: Call-Admissions

The University of the Sacred Heart in Puerto Rico was founded in 1935. Its campus in Santurce, part of greater San Juan, is an historical and educational landmark. A special feature is the Museo de Arte Contemporaneo (Museum of Contemporary Art). The university offers two dozen majors, focusing primarily on the liberal arts and sciences, business, and a variety of career-oriented programs of a technological nature. The most popular areas of study by far are business and marketing and communications. Virtually all of Sacred Heart's students are from Puerto Rico. Though the university is mainly a commuter campus, there is a small amount of housing available to women. A limited range of extracurriculars offer opportunities for involvement in student government, the arts, and a variety of media, including a magazine, newspaper, radio, and television. Seven intercollegiate sports are offered for men, five for women. An annual athletic highlight is the Thanksgiving marathon.

COLLEGE OF SAINT JOSEPH IN VERMONT

Clement Road, Rutland, VT 05701 • Admissions: 802-773-5905 • Fax: 802-773-5900
• Financial Aid: Call-Admissions

The College of Saint Joseph in Vermont, originally referred to as the College of Saint Joseph the Provider, was founded in 1950 by the Sisters of Saint Joseph. Its 90-acre campus is seventy miles from Burlington. The college offers eighteen majors in four divisions: Arts and Sciences, Business, Psychology and Human Services, and Education. Student activities at Saint Joseph range from choral and drama groups to academic honor societies and outdoor recreational pursuits, such as skiing, hiking, camping, and canoeing. The college's Fighting Saints compete in men's soccer and basketball and women's soccer, basketball, and softball in the Mayflower Conference of the NAIA. Students who are members of a parish in the Diocese of Vermont may be recommended by their pastors for a $2,000 ($500 per year) parish scholarship.

STUDENT BODY
% from out of state	25
% live on campus	25
% African American	3
% Asian	4
% Caucasian	90
% Hispanic	1
% Native American	1
% international	4

ACADEMICS
Calendar	semester
Student/teacher ratio	8:1
FT faculty	53

ADMISSIONS

Deadlines
Regular admission	rolling

FRESHMAN PROFILE
Minimum TOEFL	500
Graduated top 10% of class	12
Graduated top 25% of class	21
Graduated top 50% of class	36

FINANCIAL FACTS
Tuition	$8,300
Room & board	$4,850
Estimated book expense	$450
% frosh receiving aid	66
% undergrads receiving aid	75

SAINT MARY'S COLLEGE (MI)

3535 Indian Trail, Orchard Lake, MI 48033 • Admissions: 810-683-0523 • Fax: 810-683-0402
• Financial Aid: Call-Admissions

Saint Mary's College was founded in 1885 for the purpose of educating Polish immigrants. The college's commuter campus is located twenty-five miles from downtown Detroit. Religious observance is required of all students. Fourteen majors are offered, predominantly within the liberal arts and sciences and business. Most popular academic disciplines are business, social sciences, and philosophy. Facilities of note include a Polish studies center and Polish-American sports hall of fame. Activities include musical ensembles, radio, a student newspaper, and yearbook. Athletic offerings are intramural only.

ADMISSIONS

Deadlines
Regular admission	8/15

FINANCIAL FACTS
Tuition	$6,300
Room & board	$4,500
Estimated book expense	$500

SAINT MARY-OF-THE-WOODS COLLEGE

St. Mary-of-the-Wood, IN 47876 • Admissions: 812-535-5106 • Fax: 812-535-4613
• Financial Aid: Call-Admissions • E-mail: smwcadms@woods.smwc.edu • Web Site: woods.smwc.edu

Founded in 1840 by the Sisters of Providence, Saint Mary-of-the-Woods College is the oldest Catholic women's college in the United States. The college sits on a 200-acre campus four miles from Terra Haute and seventy miles from Indianapolis. Saint Mary offers thirty-five majors within the liberal arts and sciences, business, and education. Of particular interest is the Mari Hulman George School of Equine Studies, complete with an indoor and outdoor arena. Most popular disciplines include the social sciences, business and marketing, and education. A special program for single mothers enables them to live on campus with their children ages three to eight. The college has twenty-six registered clubs and organizations, and fields basketball, softball, and equestrian athletic teams.

STUDENT BODY

% from out of state	30
% live on campus	25
% African American	2
% Asian	3
% Caucasian	92
% Hispanic	2
% international	6

ACADEMICS

Calendar	semester
Student/teacher ratio	22:1
FT faculty	55
% graduate in 4 yrs.	62

ADMISSIONS

Deadlines

Regular admission	rolling

FRESHMAN PROFILE

Average verbal SAT	428
Average math SAT	466
Average ACT	21
Minimum TOEFL	500
Graduated top 10% of class	20
Graduated top 25% of class	40
Graduated top 50% of class	76

FINANCIAL FACTS

Tuition	$11,940
Room & board	$4,570
Estimated book expense	$1,000
% frosh receiving aid	80
% undergrads receiving aid	84

SILVER LAKE COLLEGE

2406 South Alverno Road, Manitowoc, WI 54220 • Admissions: 414-684-5955 • Fax: 414-684-7082
• Financial Aid: Call-Admissions • E-mail: admslc@sl.edu • Web Site: sl.edu/slc.html

The Franciscan Sisters founded Silver Lake College in 1935. The college is situated on a 30-acre campus adjacent to Silver Lake, thirty miles from Green Bay in northeastern Wisconsin. All students commute. Twenty-eight majors are offered within two divisions: arts and sciences, and professional studies, which offers programs in business, manufacturing systems engineering technology, and education—the latter three are among the most popular academic disciplines at the college. Facilities of note include a nature preserve, media production center, and a fine arts studio. Clubs and organizations offer a small selection of activities; among them are a multicultural exchange club, several academic interest groups, and a theater company. Athletic teams compete in the National Small College Athletic Association in women's basketball, softball, and volleyball; no intercollegiate sports are available for men. The college sponsors recreational teams in the local Manitowoc Recreation Department leagues.

STUDENT BODY

% from out of state	2
% from catholic high school	6
% live on campus	10
% African American	1
% Asian	1
% Caucasian	95
% Hispanic	1
% Native American	1
% international	1

ACADEMICS

Calendar	semester
Student/teacher ratio	11:1
FT faculty	107
% faculty from religious order	55
% graduate in 4 yrs.	23

ADMISSIONS

Admissions Rating	66
# of applicants	62
% of applicants accepted	92
% of acceptees attending	60

Deadlines

Regular admission	rolling

FRESHMAN PROFILE

Minimum TOEFL	550
Average HS GPA or Avg	2.8
Graduated top 10% of class	3
Graduated top 25% of class	13
Graduated top 50% of class	45

FINANCIAL FACTS

Tuition	$9,400
Room & board	$4,054
Estimated book expense	$530
% frosh receiving aid	95
% undergrads receiving aid	90

URSULINE COLLEGE

2550 Lander Road, Pepper Pike, OH 44124 • Admissions: 216-449-4203 • Fax: 216-449-3180
• Financial Aid: Call-Admissions • E-mail: dgiaco@en.com • Web Site: home.earthlink.net/~ursuline

The Ursuline Sisters founded Ursuline College in 1871; it admits women only. The college's small-town campus is located ten miles from Cleveland. Ursuline offers twenty-five academic majors, primarily within the liberal arts and sciences, business, education, and nursing. Popular programs include nursing, business administration, fashion design and merchandising, and interior design. Joint academic ventures include junior-year programs in fashion merchandising and design at Fashion Institute of Technology in New York City. Noteworthy campus features include an art gallery. A variety of standard activities—student government, a literary magazine, ethnic organizations, and several campus and spiritual life committees—are available; no athletic programs are offered.

STUDENT BODY

% from out of state	1
% live on campus	6
% African American	16
% Asian	1
% Caucasian	81
% Hispanic	1
% Native American	1
% international	1

ACADEMICS

Calendar	semester
Student/teacher ratio	11:1
FT faculty	141
% faculty from religious order	23

ADMISSIONS

Admissions Rating	60

Deadlines

Regular admission	rolling

FRESHMAN PROFILE

Average verbal SAT	404
Average math SAT	434
Average ACT	21
Minimum TOEFL	500
Graduated top 10% of class	12
Graduated top 25% of class	41
Graduated top 50% of class	77

FINANCIAL FACTS

Tuition	$10,710
Room & board	$4,330
Estimated book expense	$500

CHAPTER 8
TABLE OF CATHOLIC ELEMENTS

STATE INDEX

Alabama

California

Colorado

Connecticut

District of Columbia

Florida

Illinois

Indiana

Iowa

SIZE

Large

Moderate

Medium

ENVIRONMENT

Urban

THE AUTHORS

Edward Custard has about twenty years of experience in college admissions and counseling. A former admissions director at two highly selective colleges, he has worked at five colleges, two of which were Roman Catholic. (One, a Sacred Heart college, no longer is Catholic; the other, a Franciscan college, no longer *is*.) Ed was the first regularly-scheduled on-line admissions expert in cyberspace, and is co-author of The Princeton Review's *Best 311 Colleges* guide and editor of *The Complete Book of Colleges*. In addition to his work for The Princeton Review, Ed runs an educational consulting firm, Carpe Diem ETC, in Sugar Loaf, NY. Ed is a graduate of Manhattanville College in Purchase, NY.

Dan Saraceno also has about twenty years of experience in college admissions and related service areas. A former director of admissions, he has worked at five colleges, three of which are Roman Catholic. Dan's work has been with institutions affiliated with the Franciscans, Dominicans, and Jesuits–the "Holy Trinity" of college-running Catholic Orders. He has also served as Acting Director of Admissions for Tufts University School of Veterinary Medicine, Vice President at Maguire Associates (a leading enrollment management consulting firm), and Vice President of Harp Marketing Group (a direct marketing firm specializing in college admissions). He was a member of the Capuchin Franciscans as a minor seminarian in the early 1970s. Dan is a graduate of Mount Saint Mary College in Newburgh, NY.

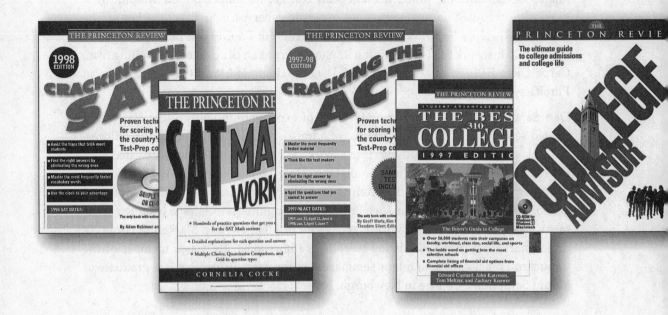

CRACKING THE AP BIOLOGY EXAM 1997-98 EDITION
0-679-76927-7 $16.00

CRACKING THE AP CALCULUS EXAM AB & BC 1997-98 EDITION
0-679-76926-9 $16.00

CRACKING THE AP CHEMISTRY EXAM 1997-98 EDITION
0-679-76928-5 $16.00

CRACKING THE AP ENGLISH LITERATURE EXAM 1997-98 EDITION
0-679-76924-2 $16.00

CRACKING THE AP U.S. HISTORY EXAM 1997-98 EDITION
0-679-76925-0 $16.00

CRACKING THE CLEP 1998 EDITION
0-679-77867-5 $20.00

CRACKING THE SAT II: BIOLOGY SUBJECT TEST 1998 EDITION
0-679-77863-2 $17.00

CRACKING THE SAT II: CHEMISTRY SUBJECT TEST 1998 EDITION
0-679-77860-8 $17.00

CRACKING THE SAT II: ENGLISH SUBJECT TEST 1998 EDITION
0-679-77858-6 $17.00

CRACKING THE SAT II: FRENCH SUBJECT TEST 1998 EDITION
0-679-77865-9 $17.00

CRACKING THE SAT II: HISTORY SUBJECT TEST 1998 EDITION
0-679-77861-6 $17.00

CRACKING THE SAT II: MATH SUBJECT TEST 1998 EDITION
0-679-77864-0 $17.00

CRACKING THE SAT II: PHYSICS SUBJECT TEST 1998 EDITION
0-679-77859-4 $17.00

CRACKING THE SAT II: SPANISH SUBJECT TEST 1998 EDITION
0-679-77862-4 $17.00

www.review.com

Expert Advice

Counselor-O-Matic

Pop Surveys

www.review.com

Paying for It

www.review.com

Getting In

THE PRINCETON REVIEW

Word du Jour

www.review.com

College Talk

Find-O-Rama College Search

www.review.com

www.review.com

Click HERE for MSN
The Microsoft Network

Best Schools

SAT Survival

www.review.com